ARMY OF SHADOWS

The publisher gratefully acknowledges the generous
contribution to this book provided by the Literature in
Translation Endowment Fund of the University of
California Press Foundation, which is supported
by a major gift from Joan Palevsky.

ARMY OF SHADOWS

PALESTINIAN COLLABORATION
WITH ZIONISM, 1917–1948

Hillel Cohen

Translated by Haim Watzman

UNIVERSITY OF CALIFORNIA PRESS

BERKELEY   LOS ANGELES   LONDON

University of California Press, one of the most distinguished university presses in the United States, enriches lives around the world by advancing scholarship in the humanities, social sciences, and natural sciences. Its activities are supported by the UC Press Foundation and by philanthropic contributions from individuals and institutions. For more information, visit www.ucpress.edu.

University of California Press
Berkeley and Los Angeles, California

University of California Press, Ltd.
London, England

Library of Congress Cataloging-in-Publication Data

Cohen, Hillel.
  [Tseva ha-tselalim. English]
  Army of shadows : Palestinian collaboration with Zionism, 1917–1948 / Hillel Cohen ; translated by Haim Watzman.
      p.   cm.
  Includes bibliographical references and index.
  ISBN: 978-0-520-25221-9 (cloth : alk. paper)
  1. Jewish-Arab relations—History—1917–1948.
  2. Collaborationists.   3. Palestinian Arabs—Politics and government—20th century.   4. Zionism—History—20th century.   5. Jews—Palestine—Politics and government—20th century.   I. Title.
  DS119.7.C632513   2008
  956.94'04—dc22   2007011571

Manufactured in the United States of America

15   14   13   12   11   10   09   08   07
10   9   8   7   6   5   4   3   2   1

This book is printed on Natures Book, which contains 50% postconsumer waste and meets the minimum requirements of ANSI/NISO Z39.48-1992 (R 1997) (*Permanence of Paper*).

Contents

Acknowledgments

First, I wish to thank Abu-'Atiyyah and his friends for inviting me, as a boy, to listen to their conversations, and the many Palestinian nationalists, "collaborators," and Islamists who shared their views and experiences with me. Though this research is based on documents, I do believe that the long, long days I have spent among Palestinians since childhood helped me understand what lies beyond the written word.

I am grateful to Moshe Maoz, who advised me in this research; to Salim Tamari, who inspired my view of early Palestinian nationalism; to Avraham Sela for sharing his vast knowledge with me; to Alon Kadish; to Saleh 'Abd al-Jawwad for his invaluable comments; to Neve Gordon, whose friend I have been lucky enough to be; and to Dror Yinon, whose questions helped me understand what I sought. None of them is responsible for the content of this book and, in fact, most of them do not entirely agree with my analysis of the collaborators' motives. But I owe a debt of gratitude to them, and to many other colleagues and friends with whom I discussed the subject for long hours.

I am grateful to the Oral History division of the Avraham Harman Institute of Contemporary Jewry, which allowed me to use testimonies of land purchasers from the Mandate period that had been sealed until now, and to the following institutions, which provided me with grants to pursue this project: the Harry S. Truman Institute for the Advancement of Peace; the Cherrick Center for the Study of Zionism, the Yishuv, and the State of Israel; and the Yad Ora Memorial Fund—all of the Hebrew University of Jerusalem; the Chaim Herzog Center for Middle East Studies and Diplomacy of Ben-Gurion University of the Negev; and Yad Ben-Zvi in Jerusalem. A grant from the Yitzhak Rabin Center for Israel Studies in 2001 enabled me to commence the research, and the British Council gave me a Chevening Scholarship for 2003 that enabled me, as a visiting fellow at the Department of War Studies, King's College, London, to complete the first draft of this book.

Last but not least, I thank the generous support of the Emory University Institute for the Study of Modern Israel and its director, Professor Kenneth W. Stein, for providing the subvention for translating the manuscript. Neither the Institute nor Dr. Stein is responsible for the content of this work.

INTRODUCTION

The large pine tree in Abu-'Atiyyah's vineyard, not far from 'Ayn Yalu in southern Jerusalem, was in the mid-1970s a meeting place for Palestinian fellahin from the surrounding area. Some of them, like Abu-'Atiyyah, were refugees from the former village of al-Maliha. The tree also attracted roaming boys, like me, from nearby Jerusalem neighborhoods and passersby on their way to or from one of the local springs or the Palestinian villages of Beit Safafa, Walaja, and Battir. There was always a jerry can of drinking water waiting in the shade, embers were always glowing and ready for brewing a pot of tea, and the visitors conducted lively conversations about any and every subject. But the fellahin were especially fixated on telling stories from the period of the British Mandate. They analyzed the Arab defeat by Israel in 1948 and how they were uprooted from al-Maliha. Time after time, they spoke of Sheikh 'Abd al-Fattah Darwish.

In the 1940s, Darwish was the chief of a *nahiya,* a cluster of villages southwest of Jerusalem. In the stories told by the men under the tree, he appeared as a hugely powerful man who lorded over the region's villages and became a prominent figure in Jerusalem as well. They told of his American automobile, the first car in al-Maliha, and pointed out his home-cum-castle, which still stood, occupied by Jewish families. From time to time they retold the story of how Arab rebels besieged the house in 1938, and how the sheikh repelled the attackers. They also told of his son Mustafa, an officer in the British Mandate's police force, who was

1

executed by the rebels that same year, and about the revenge taken much later on the murderers.

The stories testified to their tellers' mixed feelings about the Darwish family. For villagers who were active in the Arab rebellion of 1936–39, 'Abd al-Fattah was a traitor. But for others he was their leader. I also learned that, after 1948, Darwish was elected to the Jordanian parliament. By then he was a refugee in the West Bank town of Beit Jala, an hour's walk from al-Maliha but separated from it by the Green Line, the border that divided Israel and Jordan. But he remained a man of great influence. When he died, his son Hasan took his parliamentary seat.

The hottest arguments under the tree were, naturally enough, about the evacuation in 1948. Darwish, so the men related, had good connections with the Zionists and tried to use them to keep the fighting away from the village. They didn't say much about the nature of these connections but discreetly pointed out plots of land, some nearby and some more distant, that, they said, Darwish had sold to Jews. Yet the war of 1948 proved stronger than Darwish and his connections. He managed for several months to prevent Arab militias from using al-Maliha as a base from which to send sorties against Jews, but in the spring of that year a Sudanese unit deployed in the village. They were under the command of the Egyptian expeditionary force that attacked Jewish Jerusalem from the south. The Jewish forces—Etzel and the Haganah—launched preemptive attacks, forcing the Sudanese soldiers to abandon the village. All al-Maliha's inhabitants left as well. Like many other Palestinian Arabs, they thought they would be gone for no more than a few weeks. But not long thereafter, Jewish immigrants were settled in their homes. The villagers found refuge in Beit Jala and in the adjacent al-'A'idah refugee camp.

When the refugees from al-Maliha discussed the events of that year, under the pine tree and at family gatherings, they voiced different opinions about Darwish's position in the war. It was clear to all that he had acted contrary to the Palestinian national leadership, personified by the grand mufti, Hajj Amin al-Husseini. The central point of debate was whether it would have been better to heed Hajj Amin's call to fight or to take Darwish's view that the best policy was to reach an agreement with the Jews. Some said Darwish was no more than a collaborator. Others insisted that he had been a gifted statesman who understood the forces at play better than did the national leadership.

From my in-depth study of the 1948 war, conducted some twenty-five years after these conversations, I have learned that Darwish was just one of many regional leaders throughout Palestine who established ties with the Yishuv, the Jewish community in Palestine, during the period of the British Mandate and the war of 1948. Their view of the world was entirely different from that of the official Arab national institutions. They saw no fundamental problem in selling land to Jews, they opposed the Arab rebellion in the 1930s, they rejected the leadership of Hajj Amin, and they did not take part in the attempt to prevent the establishment of a Jewish state in 1948. It is hard to gauge the extent to which the Arab masses accepted their position, but these regional leaders had considerable influence. It partly explains, for example, the very low participation of Palestinian Arabs in the armed struggle against the Jews in 1948. It is an often-forgotten fact that only a few thousand Palestinians out of a population of 1.3 million volunteered for the Arab Liberation Army led by Fawzi al-Qawuqji or the local militias that went by the name of Holy Jihad.[1] It also helps explain the nonaggression pacts that were reached between Jewish and Arab villages throughout the country, in violation of the Arab national leadership's orders.

The scholarly literature on the Mandatory period and 1948 war barely addresses these local leaders. They had influence and status, yet they have been expunged from Palestinian history—primarily because they acted on the local rather than the national stage. Men like Darwish in southern Jerusalem, 'Abd al-Rahman al-'Azzi in and around Beit Jibrin, Sayf al-Din Zu'bi in the Nazareth area, and Rabbah 'Awad in the Western Galilee each acted within his own region. Early historical writing, which focused on political history and national institutions, attributed little importance to local leaders. Palestinian historiography ignored them for another reason. Most Palestinian historians were influenced by the Palestinian national movement and analyzed events solely according to the national paradigm. Thus they did not give any significant attention to approaches and people outside the hegemonic national current—a familiar phenomenon when nations write their histories.

Oddly enough, early Israeli historiography ignored them as well. Perhaps this was because the actions of the local leaders called into question the Zionist claim that the Palestinians had fought with all their might to prevent the establishment of a Jewish state in part of Palestine after the UN resolution of 29 November 1947. This claim had political rather than historiographic significance, since it served to justify Israel's refusal to allow Palestinian war refugees to return to their homes. (Nowadays the principal Israeli argument against their return is the need to preserve the Jewish character of the Israeli state, but that is another issue.)

This book comes to fill that gap, to retell the stories of Darwish and other local leaders, and thus of the entire Mandate. In addressing local events and putting them in their broader context, it seeks to incorporate into the historical narrative the point of view of the Palestinian Arab "collaborators" with the Jews. My guiding principle is that the history of a nation is not restricted to the chronicles of its national institutions, certainly not during a period when national ideas are not commonly held. This is all the more true in the Palestinian case, in which the public was not entirely united behind its leadership and the leadership was not always attentive to the public's needs.

Comments I have received from readers of the Hebrew edition of this book have taught me that this point should be clarified and stressed. I believe that shedding light on the opponents of the national movement in general, and on collaborators in particular, may contribute not only to the understanding of the phenomenon of Palestinian collaboration but also to the understanding of Palestinian society as a whole. This is not to argue that collaboration among Palestinians was more widespread than nationalism. The fact that only 7 percent of the land of Palestine was acquired by Jews before 1948, most of it from non-Palestinians, is only one testimony to the existence of national feelings among Palestinians. Furthermore, barely any Palestinians were Zionist enthusiasts. But ideology was not the only determinant of how individual Palestinians acted in their daily affairs. In fact, they took a range of practical attitudes toward the Zionists, from active resistance through passivity to accommodation and collaboration. And, indeed, thousands of Palestinians did sell land to Jews, and people from the very heart of the national movement contacted Zionist activists and assisted them. To ignore this is to disregard an essential feature of the history of the Palestinian people and of Jewish-Arab relations in Mandatory Palestine, one that had a tremendous effect on the lives of the inhabitants there. This book therefore aims to depict the diversity of attitudes and practices toward Zionism as well as differing attitudes toward what it meant to be a Palestinian nationalist. To do this, I pose the question "Who is a traitor?" and present the different ways the question was answered.

WHO IS A TRAITOR?

Accusations of treason against public figures and popular debates about who is a traitor are recurrent in a wide range of societies, particularly during periods of political tension and national struggle. The very existence of the debate shows that there is no unequivocal definition of treason, no universal test to distinguish between patriots and traitors. Treason is ultimately a social construct. Definitions vary with circumstances. It depends on who does the defining, how they analyze the political situation, and, of course, what their values are. The evasiveness of the concept of treason and its socially constructed value is amply demonstrated by a long list of political biographies with the phrase "traitor or patriot?" in their titles.[2] Such a debate is by no means restricted to historians, and opposing claims are often made by the actors themselves, as I show throughout this book.

A further inquiry into these rival claims reveals that, although they disagree about which acts constitute treason, all agree on one principle: the determining factor is whether the actions taken were for or against the national interest. The argument between the two sides is, in fact, over the nature of the national interest at a given point in time. Quite often the argument stems from fundamental divisions between sociopolitical forces about the nature of the national ethos or national objectives. In addition, the ideological battle over treason between different currents is often part of a leadership struggle. When different groups demand the authority to define treason, they are, in fact, demanding the legitimacy to shape the national ethos and to use violence against traitors. In other words, they claim the authority of a state (or future state).

A current example is the former chief of the Palestinian Preventive Security force in the West Bank, Jibril Rajoub. When he held that post in the 1990s, he was responsible for security coordination with Israel. As a result, Hamas denounced him as a traitor. Yet, at the time, the Palestinian Authority officially supported Rajoub's work with the Israelis and saw it as furthering Palestinian interests. Similar disputes took place during the Mandate, reflecting contradictory views current in Palestinian society at the time.

As an Israeli Jew, I have no standing to determine who is a traitor to the Palestinian cause. As a researcher, however, I can study the Palestinian discourse on treason and collaboration to find out which acts were defined as treason and by whom. I can inquire into the extent these definitions were accepted, examine how the definitions changed over time, take note of alternative definitions, explore the social backgrounds of those labeled collaborators, and show how collaboration (and accusations of collaboration) affected the lives of these people and of the Palestinians as a whole. Furthermore, I can relate how Palestinians actively aided the Zionist enterprise and what their motives were for doing so. In this way I can trace the development of Palestinian nationalist thinking and practice in all its diversity and the effect of the "war on collaboration" on Palestinian society during the Mandate.

In Palestinian society, to call someone a collaborator is to call him a traitor. But in this book the term is not judgmental. When I refer to someone as a "traitor" or a "collaborator," I do so only because his contemporaries labeled him as such. I examine so-called collaborators of all types—informers, weapons dealers, pro-Zionist propagandists, political collaborators, and others—but leave the moral and political judgment to my readers. This neutral stance is a direct consequence of my methodology, but it also fits my own attitude toward collaboration, be it by Palestinians or others. Personally, I do not see so-called treason as wrong by definition. Sometimes an act defined by one's compatriots as treason is the right thing to do. It depends, among other things, on whom one betrays and the consequences of the betrayal. I have elaborated this claim elsewhere with Ron Dudai.[3]

STUDYING EARLY PALESTINIAN NATIONALISMS

The lack of a clear, unified system of national values among Palestinians during the Mandate should not surprise us, since diversity and conflicts characterize all human societies. The fact that the idea of nationalism was fairly new among Palestinians in the period under discussion only amplified this diversity. The picture of a united Palestinian nation that struggled against the Zionist invasion should be modified to include consideration of the variety of contemporary Palestinian attitudes regarding the correct response to Zionism. Furthermore, both elites and the masses had diverse approaches toward Palestinian nationalism itself.

A true understanding of early Palestinian nationalism requires us, as Zachary Lockman has written, "to avoid operating from within nationalism's conception of itself," and surely to avoid imposing concepts developed in later years. Rather, in Lockman's words,

> We need . . . to acquire more complex, nuanced, and historically grounded understanding of why particular people thought and acted as they did, however we ultimately judge their actions in moral or political terms. This, in turn, requires a more subtle and flexible conception of national identity, one that treats it as a complex of ideas, symbols, sentiments, and practices which people from various sociopolitical groups appropriate and deploy selectively and contingently, rather than some essence which is derivable from the writings and speeches of nationalist thinkers, leaders or activists.[4]

Therefore, instead of looking at events only from the perspective of the national institutions, I seek to view them also through the eyes of those whom the national movement considered traitors or those who chose to be passive and not to take part in the national struggle. As I show, these Palestinians also used nationalist symbols and had nationalist sentiments. Like the villagers interviewed by Ted Swedenburg who participated in the rebellion and portrayed themselves as the real nationalists and the nationalist urban elites as traitors,[5] some of the "collaborators" also maintained that they were acting in the true national interest. The national leadership, they charged, was merely looking after its own welfare. In other words, the "traitors" viewed themselves as loyal Palestinian Arabs, more loyal than the national leaders.

Broadly speaking, two camps or schools of thought were prevalent among the Arabs of Palestine at this period. They differed over many issues, and their rivalry was rooted in social and political structures whose origins lay deep in the Ottoman period. But the dispute over the central national question—the attitude toward Zionism—can be formulated easily, even if its unambiguous dichotomous form is simplistic. The mainstream national movement, led by al-Husseini, maintained that the Zionist movement had to be fought to the bitter end. The Zionists could never be a negotiating partner. The other camp, whose voice was less prominent, in part because it included many members of the silent Palestinian public who preferred not to speak out, believed that the Zionists could not be defeated and that the common good of Palestinian Arabs demanded coexistence with Jews. This was the case before the war of 1948, and it was the case during the war. Beyond the question of who turned out to be right, it is clear that this was a dispute between two camps, both of which were committed to doing (among other things) what was best for the Palestinian Arab public.

Obviously the picture is more complicated. There were other factors, beyond ideology and the analysis of the balance of power, that motivated the opponents of the national movement to cooperate with the Zionists. In this they were no different from the fiercest national leaders, who also on occasion acted on the basis of their personal and family interests. Among the rivals of the national movement were some for whom nationality was simply not a focal point of their identities. There were also those who acted on the basis of the calculus of internal politics. The fissures that cut through Palestinian society—between villagers, city dwellers, and Bedouin, between the rival families of the urban elite, between classes, between ethnic and religious groups, between different regions, and between families in the rural elite—often impelled people to compete with a rival family or rival ideology without taking into account the consequences in the national arena. These internal conflicts sometimes provided the crucial reasons that local and other leaders, from the 1920s onward, were willing to make alliances with Zionist institutions.

Likewise, the execution of "traitors" by nationalist activists, sometimes at the behest of the Husseini leadership, was not motivated solely by national interests. Sometimes such executions furthered partisan and personal agendas. Such acts pushed opposition even further into the arms of the Zionist movement. The persistence of ties between the Palestinian opposition and the Zionists through the end of the Mandate testifies to the role the national leadership played in fragmenting its own society.

The problematic nature of Hajj Amin's leadership and the internal fissures in Palestinian society have been well analyzed by Issa Khalaf in his *Politics in Palestine*.[6] However, insufficient scholarly attention has been given to the connections Hajj Amin's opponents and other Palestinian public figures had with Zionist institutions and to the belief system they developed as a result of these connections. The premise that the Zionists could not be defeated, together with hostility toward Hajj Amin, certainly led many to take a passive stance, to support Emir 'Abdallah of Transjordan, and in many cases to help the Zionists. The Arabists of the Jewish Agency and the Haganah, who maintained contact over many years with Hajj Amin's opponents, reinforced this tendency.

Another focus of this study is the Zionists' success in penetrating deep into Palestinian Arab society during the Mandate in pursuit of intelligence and influence. In certain ways this was an exceptional achievement. Although the Zionist movement was more organized than the Palestinian Arab national movement and enjoyed British support during the Mandate's first two decades, it was neither an occupying force nor a colonial power. Yet it was able to exploit social splits to recruit collaborators. Hajj Amin's political intransigence and his view that anyone who opposed his leadership was a traitor to the Palestinian Arab nation helped the Zionists enlist Palestinian support. It created common interests for them and Hajj Amin's Arab opponents; both wanted to weaken the mufti and undermine the legitimacy of the national leadership.

THE STRUCTURE OF THE BOOK

Collaboration took different forms during these years, depending mostly on the way Zionist decision makers analyzed the state of the conflict. This brings us to a unique feature of the Palestinian national movement.

A national movement generally faces the difficulty of disseminating its ideology among an internally divided public. But the Palestinian Arabs faced an additional problem; they had to confront the intensive penetration of their ranks by a rival national movement. I therefore devote chapter 1 to the Zionist ideology and praxis in this regard.

The Palestinian national movement was hardly blind to what the Zionists were doing. It put a great deal of energy into battling "traitors" and "collaborators." But first it had to define treason in accordance with the new circumstances it faced—that is, in light of a new world order in which nationalism had become a major source of identity. Thus it had to uproot norms and attitudes of the prenational era, in which the Jews were considered a protected minority rather than an enemy, and instill new norms. The national movement's initial definitions of collaboration and the means, educational and violent, with which it attempted to disseminate and inculcate these definitions in the public are analyzed in chapter 2. In chapter 3 I consider the collaborators of the period preceding the Arab rebellion of 1936–39 and the way they viewed Palestinian nationalism. I also describe the methods used by Zionist institutions to enlist collaborators as well as the means, some of them morally and legally ambiguous, collaborators used to help the Zionists. These first three chapters make up part I of the book, which covers the years 1917–35. Part II focuses on the rebellion and the way treason was defined from 1936 onward. Here I also address how collaborators were pursued during the rebellion years and how they responded to this increased pressure. This period is one in which the mufti's opponents reached a final determination that their personal and political interests, as well as the Palestinian national interest, required a compromise with the Zionist movement. The Mandate's last decade and the war of 1948 are my subjects in part III. This period shows, perhaps better than the others, the importance of social and economic ties between Jews and Arabs in decisions made by Palestinian Arabs not to obey the Arab national movement's orders to boycott and wage war against the Jews.

My understanding is that Hajj Amin's opponents did not act solely on the basis of their individual interests or craving for money but, rather, analyzed the situation in Palestine differently than did the national leadership. If that is the case, then, in today's terms, Hajj Amin's struggle took place in a discourse of justice, and his demand was for absolute justice in which all of the land of Palestine would remain in the hands of its Arab inhabitants. His opponents' discourse, in contrast, was one of the possible. They did not stress the question of who was right or the nature of absolute justice. Instead, they addressed the balance of power in the field and the interests and capabilities of both sides.

It is neither possible nor necessary to judge this historic dispute. On the one hand, there can be little doubt that the mufti's inflexible position and refusal to accept any partition proposal were the major reasons for the outbreak of war in 1948. On the other hand, the Arab leadership did not believe that cooperation and compromise would lead the Zionists to recognize Palestinian Arab national rights. As Khalaf wrote, "Even if the Palestinian national movement had accepted the idea of a Jewish state, it is highly improbable that this state would have welcomed those Palestinians who would have come under its jurisdiction or been contained by the neighboring Palestinian state."[7]

Despite all differences, one may see in the approach of the mufti's opponents the roots of the concept of *summud,* developed in the Occupied Territories in the early 1970s—the ethic of holding fast to the land even at the price of a limited amount of cooperation with Israel. *Summud* grew out of the conviction that one could be a nationalist Palestinian, without taking up the armed struggle against Israel, by holding on stubbornly to the land and to Arab culture. Actually this attitude, if not the term itself, was widespread among Palestinian citizens of Israel from 1948 onward. Initially condemned by Palestinian Arab nationalists, it received wide legitimacy when the Palestinians in the Occupied Territories chose a parallel path. In a certain sense, this was also the rationale of Hajj Amin's opponents during the 1920s and 1930s as they realized that his actions and opposition to any compromise would eventually lead to the destruction of Palestinian Arab society and the ejection of Palestinian Arabs from their land. One of the purposes of those who opposed the mufti was to prevent this and to hold fast to their land. Under the social and political circumstances of that time, the only way open to them was to detach themselves from the central current of the national movement, adopt "local nationalism," and collaborate with the Zionists. A main argument against these collaborators is that they were a critical source of Zionist power, and that without their aid (in land sales, in security matters, and in politics) the Jews might have been defeated. But, again, I leave such judgments to the readers.

A NOTE ON SOURCES

Although the original motivation for this work was stories I heard from Palestinians in the West Bank and the Galilee, I make little use of oral testimony. The exception is testimonies housed at the Hebrew University of Zionist activists who bought land from Arabs during the Mandate. Rather, my research is based almost entirely on Zionist, Arab, and, to a lesser extent, British archival sources. The Arab sources include documents of the Higher Arab Committee and the Supreme Muslim Council, the Arab press (which provides information on the discourse about treason), and diaries and memoirs from the period. The Zionist sources are more numerous. The most important of these are the reports and correspondence of Zionist intelligence agencies and figures, kept in the Central Zionist Archives and the Haganah Archives. The memoirs of intelligence operatives and land purchasers are another important source.

PART I

TWO NATIONALISMS MEET, 1917–1935

CHAPTER 1

UTOPIA AND ITS COLLAPSE

IN SEARCH OF POLITICAL COOPERATION

In July 1921 a formal delegation representing Palestinian Arab national institutions set out for London in a desperate, last-minute attempt to persuade Britain to back away from the Balfour Declaration and its commitment to allow Jewish immigration into Palestine. Hasan Shukri, mayor of Haifa and president of the Muslim National Associations, sent the following telegram to the British government:

> We strongly protest against the attitude of the said delegation concerning the Zionist question. We do not consider the Jewish people as an enemy whose wish is to crush us. On the contrary. We consider the Jews as a brotherly people sharing our joys and troubles and helping us in the construction of our common country. We are certain that without Jewish immigration and financial assistance there will be no future development of our country as may be judged from the fact that the towns inhabited in part by Jews such as Jerusalem, Jaffa, Haifa, and Tiberias are making steady progress while Nablus, Acre, and Nazareth where no Jews reside are steadily declining.[1]

This was one of many telegrams sent to the British high commissioner in Palestine and the British government by the Muslim National Associations and other Arab pro-Zionist organizations. Its purpose was twofold: to portray the national institutions of Palestinian Arabs as unrepresentative and illegitimate, and to promote the ratification of the Mandate. Shukri and his associates, from cities and villages throughout Palestine, did not send these messages of their own volition. The motivating force behind them was the Zionist Executive, which also financed the activities of these organizations.

Seeking support among Palestine's Arabs was an innovation for the Zionist movement. In its early days, when Palestine was part of the Ottoman Empire, the movement put its major effort into world diplomacy, and the fruit of these labors was the Balfour Declaration. The question of future relations with the Arab inhabitants of the country was set aside. Only after the British conquest in 1917 did the Zionist movement's leaders begin to confront this challenge. The result was an ambitious program to obtain wide-ranging Palestinian Arab cooperation with the Zionist enterprise. When, in 1919, Chaim Weizmann signed an agreement about Palestine with Emir Faysal, one of the leaders of the Arab national movement, it reinforced the sense that the Arabs would consent to a Zionist homeland in their midst.*

But at the same time, Palestinian Arab nationalists, some of whom had been opposing Zionism at the end of the Ottoman period, began to reorganize. Their new position was much improved, for the principle of self-determination for the region's peoples had been accepted by the international community. Furthermore, the Balfour Declaration and the Zionist aspiration to establish a Jewish state magnified the fears of the wider Arab public. Both of these intensified nationalist sentiments. Opposition to Zionism spread and found expression in the establishment, beginning in 1918, of the Muslim-Christian Associations. This was followed by anti-British and anti-Zionist demonstrations and attacks on Jews in April 1920 and May 1921.

The Zionist movement developed the strategy as a response to this process, with the objective of undermining the evolution of a Palestinian nationality from within. The means were Arab political figures and collaborators. Zionist activists on all levels were involved. The moving force was the Zionist Executive's Arabist, Chaim Margaliot Kalvarisky, a veteran land purchaser for the Jewish Colonization Association who was well connected among the Arabs. Above him in the hierarchy stood Col. Frederick Kisch, a retired British intelligence officer and head of the Zionist Executive's political department in Palestine. The president of the

---

*Faysal, the son of Sharif Hussein the Hashemite, served as his father's liaison with the British and led the great Arab revolt against the Ottomans during World War I. Despite Faysal's senior position in the Arab national movement, it quickly became clear that the agreement had no practical significance whatsoever. Faysal himself had reservations about it, and the Palestinian Arabs utterly opposed it.

Zionist movement, Dr. Chaim Weizmann, was also involved in the contacts. The three of them claimed, at least for external consumption, that Jewish immigration would do only good for the country's Arab residents. They believed that they could buy local Arab leaders. Most important, they refused to recognize the authenticity of Arab nationalism in Palestine. The telegrams sent to the British government by Arab oppositionists were part of that strategy.

During his visit to Palestine in spring 1920, Weizmann held a series of meetings with various Palestinians. Apparently the encounters gave reason for optimism. He drank coffee with Bedouin sheikhs in the Beit She'an/Beisan Valley and was received ceremonially in Abu-Ghosh, near Jerusalem. In Nablus the former mayor, Haidar Tuqan, promised to disseminate Zionism throughout the Samarian highlands.

Weizmann's meetings were arranged by members of the intelligence office of the Elected Assembly, the body responsible for intelligence and political activities within the Arab population. At the conclusion of his visit, Weizmann asked the office to draw up a comprehensive plan for countering Arab opposition to Zionism. Its proposal was as follows:

1. Cultivation of the agreement with Haidar Tuqan. Tuqan, who had served as mayor of Nablus at the end of the Ottoman period and represented the city in the Ottoman parliament after 1912, received £1,000 from the Zionist leader. In exchange, he promised to organize a pro-Zionist petition in the Nablus region and to open a pro-Zionist cultural and political club in the city.

2. Creation of an alliance with the influential emirs on the eastern side of the Jordan, based on the assumption that they would be reluctant to support a national movement led by urban elites, and thus be natural allies of the Zionists.

3. Establishment of an alliance with Bedouin sheikhs in southern Palestine, in order to sever the connections that already existed between them and nationalist activists.

4. Purchase of newspapers hostile to Zionism in order to ensure a pro-Zionist editorial policy. This tactic was based on faith in the power of the written word and on the assumption that presentation of the Zionist case could prevent the spread of Palestinian nationalism to the broader public.

5. Organization and promotion of friendly relations with Arabs, and the opening of cooperation clubs.

6. Provocation of dissension between Christians and Muslims.[2]

This is a key document. In 1920, Jews were just a bit more than a tenth of the country's population, but the principles the document sets out have remained a basis for the relationship between the two peoples to this day. It advocated three strategies. The first was support of opposition forces within the Arab public with the object of creating an alternative leadership. The second was to deepen fissures within Palestinian society by separating the Bedouin from the rest of the population and fomenting conflict between Christians and Muslims (and Druze). The final strategy was developing a propaganda machine of newspapers and writers who would trumpet the advantages that would accrue to Palestine's Arabs if they did not oppose Zionism.

The plan was based on the presumption that there was no authentic Arab national movement in Palestine. This was true to a certain extent, but those who promoted it ignored the process taking place before their eyes. So, for example, Dr. Nissim Maloul, secretary for Arab affairs of the National Council, the governing body of the Jewish community in Palestine, termed a furious demonstration he witnessed in Jaffa in February 1920 a "counterfeit nationalist demonstration." He noted that most of the participants were fellahin, poor Arab farmers, "whose costume and countenances indicate that they do not know for what reason and why they are standing there." At the Zionist Congress a year later labor leader Berl Katznelson used similar phrases.[3] Such people chose to believe that opposition would lapse with the economic growth accompanying Jewish settlement. Such faith was reinforced when they found collaborators, whose very existence and enlistment served as proof that their perception was correct.

Kalvarisky organized the collaborators in nationwide political frameworks. The Muslim National Associations were set up first, then the farmers' parties. Members of the associations were not necessarily nationalists, and members of the farmers' parties were not necessarily farmers.

THE MUSLIM NATIONAL ASSOCIATIONS

Kalvarisky, who was appointed to head the Zionist Executive's Arab department when it was established, set Zionist policy toward the Palestinians for some fifteen years. Aiming to change Zionist as well as Arab attitudes, he sincerely believed in the possibility of cooperation on the part of Palestine's Arabs:

> If we justify practically our claim that the establishment of a Jewish national home will bring benefit to its non-Jewish residents as well, we will find among most of the Muslim effendis, including most of their leaders, an element that will oppose the path of violence and hostility and will

resign from the Muslim-Christian Associations. It will not be difficult to break the Muslim-Christian alliance, but it cannot be done by direct and open action in that direction. A frontal attack will only strengthen that unity. The only way is to win the hearts of the Muslim members one by one, by granting a part of the economic benefits they expect from the establishment of a Jewish national home. After purchasing the effendis, most of the population of Palestine, which will in the future as in the past continue to be led by this caste, will also come over to our side.[4]

Though some challenged Kalvariski's intriguing analysis, for a variety of sometimes contradictory reasons, his plan was approved.[5] Thus commenced systematic Zionist intervention in Palestinian Arab politics.

The organizations Kalvarisky established with his Arab partners were meant to serve as a counterweight to the Muslim-Christian Associations, which were the hard kernel of the Palestinian Arab national movement. He dubbed his groups the Muslim National Associations. The name was designed to enable their members to feel "nationalist," as the times demanded, while sharpening the distinction between Christians and Muslims, a division rooted deeply in the local heritage the Arab national movement sought to diminish.

These associations' public activity was limited to public assemblies and petitions to the British authorities. In the petitions, which accompanied each stage of the political struggle of the 1920s, the Muslim National Associations attacked the Palestinian national movement and expressed explicit or indirect support for Zionist immigration to Palestine, for the British Mandate, and for the Balfour Declaration.

After the ratification of the Mandate in July 1922, the associations' members continued to help the Zionist movement, but in a new guise. The British were organizing elections for a legislative council that was to contain both Arabs and Jews. The Fifth Palestinian Congress, at which most of the Arab political organizations in the country were represented, decided to boycott the elections on the grounds that they were being conducted under the terms of the Mandate, which the Congress considered invalid. The Zionist Executive, for its part, viewed the council as a tool for advancing its interests, so it supported the elections.[6] While the Arab Executive Committee was holding public assemblies all over the country and emissaries of the mufti of Jerusalem, the spiritual and political leader of Palestinian Muslims, were preaching against the elections in the mosques, the Zionist Executive used the Muslim National Associations to encourage broad Arab participation in the elections.

On the coastal plain the pro-Zionist campaign was organized by Ibrahim 'Abdin of al-Ramla, whose family had a long history of ties with the Zionist movement. In Gaza the head of the local association, Kamel al-Mubashir, conveyed to Dr. Maloul optimistic reports on the chances of success. In Hebron pro-Zionist activity was directed by Murshid Shahin, a former police officer, who reported that there was intense resistance to elections in his city.[7]

Shahin's evaluation was closer to reality. Except for some isolated areas (including Acre, a focal point of opposition activity, and al-Ramla thanks to 'Abdin's work), Arab voter turnout was thin. As a result, the legislative council was not established. The failure did not, however, bring about a profound change in the Zionist institutions' approach or tactics. The contrary was true.[8]

THE FARMERS' PARTIES:
FIRST ROUND, 1924–1926

In 1924 a new component of Arab pro-Zionist activity made its appearance—the farmers' parties, a loose network of political parties set up in different parts of the country at the initiative of the Zionist movement or as a joint initiative. From the Zionist point of view, these parties would maintain and deepen the divide between Arab villagers and urban Arabs and weaken the Arab national movement. Colonel Kisch, who oversaw the establishment of the local parties, recommended that these branches be led by men he had met during his travels—Fares al-Mas'oud of Burqa, a village in the highlands near Nablus; 'Afif 'Abd al-Hadi of Jenin; 'Abdallah Hussein of the village of Qumey in the Jezreel Valley; and Sa'id al-Fahoum of Nazareth.[9] These men belonged, for the most part, to leading regional families or families with land in the village, and not to the fellah class.

Even though many of the members of the farmers' parties were already connected with the Zionist movement through the Muslim National Associations, the new organizational structure and the parties' wide distribution gave them new energy. Influential heads of families from the Mt. Hebron region (such as Musa Hadeib of Duwaimah) and the Jerusalem highlands (such as 'Abd al-Hamid Abu-Ghosh) became more active. In Nablus, Haidar Tuqan renewed his activity and led the new party. He reported to Kalvarisky in winter 1924 that he had already succeeded in organizing 200 villages under the banner of the party.[10] This was an exaggeration, growing perhaps out of a desire to get the

Zionist Executive to increase its financial support. But in the atmosphere of political stagnation that prevailed in the mid-1920s, even the plan offered by the parties' activists to compete in the elections to the Supreme Muslim Council and oust Hajj Amin al-Husseini was not perceived as completely implausible.[11]

The Palestinian opposition reached the pinnacle of its power in the mid-1920s, in parallel with the waning of the Arab national institutions.[12] But the Zionist movement was not able to exploit this opportunity. In 1926–27 the Yishuv was, like the Zionist movement overseas, deep in a financial crisis. The financial crisis in Eastern Europe had halted the flow of capital to Jews in Palestine, the construction sector had collapsed, and businesses had gone bankrupt. Jewish emigration from Palestine increased, and the movement's shrunken funds were directed to coping with economic problems. In the absence of funding, the farmers' parties ceased to function almost completely—until after the events of August 1929.

THE RIOTS OF 1929 AND THEIR AFTERMATH

The bloody riots of 1929, in which some 130 Jews were murdered in communities and settlements throughout the country, forced the Zionist movement and British administration to rethink their strategies. On September 13 of that year the British Colonial Office appointed the Shaw Commission "to enquire into the immediate causes which led to the recent outbreak in Palestine and to make recommendations as to the steps necessary to avoid a recurrence." In the wake of the commission's conclusions, which questioned Britain's commitment to a Jewish national home in Palestine, the British government appointed Sir John Hope-Simpson to examine the question of Jewish immigration, settlement, and development of the country. He commenced his work in May 1930.[13]

In reaction to the commissions, the Zionist movement again needed the good services of collaborators, who, at the behest of the Zionists, persuaded dozens of Arabs to sign petitions formulated by the United Bureau (the body established after the riots to coordinate activities of the Zionist Executive and Jewish National Council). According to the United Bureau, the petitions were intended to prove that

> the masses of the fellahin oppose the incitement and bloodshed of the Supreme Muslim Council, and that they wish for peaceful relations with the Jews and do not see the Council as their proxy. In this way we intend

to dilute the impression the world has received that the [Muslim] Council expresses the desires of the broad masses of the people and that it speaks and acts in the name of all the Arabs in the country.[14]

The goals were very similar to those of the petitions of the previous decade—to challenge the legitimacy of the Supreme Muslim Council and to highlight the benefits accruing to Arabs from Jewish settlement.[15] Some took an additional step. As'ad al-Fahoum of Nazareth, Fares al-Mas'oud of the Nablus highlands, Muhammad Hajj Dahoud of Jerusalem, and others established an association in opposition to the mufti and reported to the Zionist Executive—again with hyperbole— that 345 villages had joined them with the goal "of saving the country from the tyranny of Hajj Amin Husseini and his cousin (Jamal Husseini)." They even demanded of the high commissioner and the Colonial Office that they dismiss the mufti from all his positions.[16] They made the same charge against the head of the Palestinian national movement that he and his supporters made against them and other collaborators, claiming that his actions were dictated by personal interests.

In addition to submitting petitions, the Zionist Executive needed Arab witnesses to testify before the commission of inquiry about the chain of events. Many of those with ties to the Zionist movement refused to testify out of fear that they would be exposed. In the end, only a handful appeared. One of them was the *mukhtar* (village elder) of Battir (southwest of Jerusalem), whose alias was "Na'aman." His operative, Aharon Haim Cohen, recalled twenty years later that he was "a good man and loyal friend [with whom] the foundation was laid for the Shai [the Haganah's intelligence service]."[17] "Na'aman" collected information from the villages in his vicinity about the Arab attack on the Jewish village of Har-Tuv and conveyed his findings to both the police (who arrested the suspects) and the commission. He reported, among other things, that the planner and executor of the attack was Sami al-Husseini, the son of the chairman of the Arab Executive Committee, Musa Kazem al-Husseini. The mukhtar of Battir brought with him two sheikhs from the nearby village of al-Khader, who reported that emissaries from the Supreme Muslim Council had spread false rumors in their village to the effect that Jews had destroyed the mosque of Omar and killed 500 Muslims.[18]

Another witness before the commission was Muhammad Tawil, who was also active in the area of pro-Zionist propaganda. He gave testimony on the massacre of the Jews of Safed ("My heart pained me at these events, because it was clear to me that the Arabs fell upon innocent Jews for no reason"),[19] but his testimony failed to impel the commission to lay the responsibility for the riots on any Arab organization or leader.[20]

THE COLLAPSE OF THE PRO-ZIONIST PARTIES

The pro-Zionist petitions organized after the 1929 riots were the signal for the farmers' parties to resume their activity (the Muslim National Associations had slowly disbanded in the mid-1920s). This revival owed much to the local change of atmosphere after the riots, but also to the world Zionist movement's resurgence, which shored up the shaky finances of the Zionist administration in Palestine.

Most of the effort was made in the villages of the Jerusalem region. Attorney Isma'il al-Khatib of 'Ayn Karem and the sheikhs of the Darwish family of al-Maliha, who headed the villages of the Bani-Hasan subdistrict *(nahiya)*, worked to organize these villages independently of the Arab national institutions. Their purpose, however, was to protect their interests against those of the urban elite. Unlike with the Muslim National Associations, collaboration with the Zionists was not a part of their public agenda. But the United Bureau followed their activities closely and tried to channel them for the benefit of the Zionist cause. It made use of A. H. Cohen's connections with senior members of the Darwish family and of the connections members of the bureau in Tel Aviv had with the mayor of Jaffa, 'Omar al-Baytar, an opposition figure who was involved in the initiative of al-Khatib and the Darwishes. (Al-Baytar sold the Zionists the land on which the town of Bnai Berak had been founded in 1924.)[21]

The high point of the endeavor was a village convention in 'Ajjur. The members of the 'Azzi family, the dominant one in the Beit Jibrin area, took part in convening it. The Zionist Executive allocated 50 Palestinian pounds for the delegates' travel and provisions—on condition that they pass resolutions against the Arab delegation's trip to London and announce the establishment of an Arab executive committee separate from that of the urban Arabs. About 500 people convened in 'Ajjur on 27 March 1930, many of them heads of families and villages from the Jerusalem hills, Mt. Hebron, and the coastal plain in the environs of Gaza. The convention was meant to issue a call to split away from the Arab Executive Committee to protect the interests of the fellahin. The United Bureau waited for encouraging reports from their people on-site, but members of the Arab Executive Committee ruined the scheme. They showed up at 'Ajjur, spoke against dividing the nation, and intimated that the Zionists were behind the whole move. The assembly broke up in the midst of harsh recriminations, which brought an end to this attempt to establish alternative leadership.[22]

The 'Ajjur convention was not fundamentally a pro-Zionist enterprise. It was an internal Palestinian initiative that its leaders hoped to further through their clandestine ties with the Zionists. The Zionists, for their part, hoped to exploit it to cripple the Arab national leadership. At the same time, parties in direct contact with the Zionist movement burgeoned. Fares al-Mas'oud of Nablus revived his party and wrote to Kalvarisky that, after a tour of the Jenin district, Nazareth, Tiberias, and Haifa, he was convinced that the Arabs in these areas were "prepared to work for peace and mutual understanding." He proposed to reorganize the quiescent farmers' parties in order to convene a national convention. Muhammad Tawil announced the establishment of the Northern Farmers' Party.[23] Hajj Saleh al-Sabbah founded a village organization with Kalvarisky's help. He claimed that eighteen villages east of Nablus and another nineteen north of the city had joined it. Two of the fifteen articles in its charter provided that the organization would refrain from politics and detach itself from the Arab Executive Committee.[24] Aid to a party with these principles indicated the beginning of a change in the Zionist conception: financial support was no longer conditional on active pro-Zionism. Disassociation from the opponents of Zionism was sufficient.

Kalvarisky was buoyant about the revival. Even the collapse of the 'Ajjur convention did not change his view: "There is a great deal of agitation among the fellahin to link up with the Jews and to work shoulder to shoulder for the advancement of agriculture. Not a day goes by that I do not receive delegations from all parts of the country on this matter. They all demand unity with the Jews," he wrote in a memorandum. He believed with all his heart in the importance of this activity: "Neither [British foreign secretary] MacDonald nor [Prime Minister] Lloyd George will come to our aid in bad times. The sympathy of the Arab nation is what will redeem us. In order to purchase that sympathy, contact between the two elements and common labor are vital."[25]

Others were more doubtful. Shabtai Levi, later mayor of Haifa and a member of the special committee established to encourage support for Zionism among the rural population, argued at a meeting in May 1930 that "there is no reason to hope for truly friendly relations between the Jewish fellah and the Arab fellah." Nevertheless, his practical conclusion was identical: the Arab fellahin would join forces with the Jews not out of love of Zionism but rather to protect their own interests.[26]

Activity reached a new peak in March 1931, before Chaim Weizmann's visit to Palestine. Representatives of all the fellahin organizations and other friends of the Zionist movement made contact with the movement's offices and asked to be allowed to meet Weizmann, in opposition to the explicit position of the Supreme Muslim Council.[27]

Cooperation with the Zionists was not limited to the farmers' parties. In Nablus and Jerusalem there were active associations for Jewish-Arab friendship (the Semitic Union), and Hebron's top leaders sought to meet Weizmann and discuss with him the return of Jews to their city. A workers' party was founded in Jaffa by two Nablusites who were close to Kalvarisky, Akram Tuqan and 'Aref al-'Asali. Its platform stated that "the party has no political affiliation." Jews who in subsequent years became central activists in Jewish-Arab relations attended the first meeting of the Jerusalem Semitic Union. Among them were Re'uven Zaslani (Shiloah), later a member of the foreign service and the Mossad, Israel's intelligence agency, and Eliahu Sasson, later a member of the Jewish Agency's political division and the Israeli foreign service.[28]

The Zionist movement and the farmers' parties hoped that the parties would fill the vacuum created by the decline of both the Husseinis (the Majlissiyyun) and their opponents the Nashashibis (the Mu'aradah), brought on by the two families' long-running feud. Fahoum of Nazareth even reported to Moshe Shertok (Sharret), then an official in the Jewish Agency's political department, that both groups were courting him, but that he was waiting to hear what the Zionists had to offer.[29] Another person waiting was 'Abd al-Qader Shibl, an attorney from Acre who had organized a fellahin congress some two months before the 1929 riots. He became the great hope of the Zionist movement's Arabists at the end of 1931. At the beginning of 1932, Shibl began organizing a second fellahin congress. Before it convened he met several times with Kalvarisky and Shertok.[30]

At these meetings the Jewish representatives took an interest in resolutions the convention might pass about the sale of land to Jews. Shibl could promise only that the gathering would not make decisions that were negative from the Zionist point of view. In exchange he asked that Jews buy 16,000 dunams (4 dunams = 1 acre) near Shefa'amr from his father (Shertok promised to pass the request on to the authorized institutions). He also asked for 30 Palestinian pounds for expenses.[31]

The Arab bureau decided to give Shibl the money, and the next day A. H. Cohen went to Jaffa to participate in the convention as a correspondent for the newspaper *Palestine Bulletin*. But this convention was even more of a failure than the one at 'Ajjur. Shibl had expected 400 delegates, but only a few dozen showed up at the Abu-Shakkush cinema. He refused to leave his hotel room for the convention site until the rest of the invited delegates appeared. Hours went by, and the delegates who had arrived dispersed. Shibl made excuses about giving back the money, and this last attempt to organize the fellahin also evaporated.[32]

THE POLITICAL CHANNEL: THE NAKED TRUTH

After more than a decade of effort, the Zionist movement abandoned its strategy of establishing or encouraging organizations and parties to constitute an alternative leadership for Palestine's Arabs. There were many reasons, but in retrospect it seems that the principal one was that the policy was futile. It was based on false assumptions. The Zionists had believed that the Arabs of Palestine had no real national sentiments. They also had assumed that conflicting interests between urban and rural Arabs and between Christians and Muslims would tilt the latter of each of those pairs toward the Zionist cause. But the Zionists realized, later than they might have, that there were national sentiments in both cities and villages, and among both Christians and Muslims. They realized that many Arab villagers preferred to follow the new national leadership, or to avoid any political activity, rather than to follow the traditional landowning leaders. This is not to say that all the population supported the militant path chosen by Hajj Amin; it is to say that the fear of takeover by the Zionists rendered overt political alliance with them unacceptable for the majority of the Palestinian population.

Another factor that forced a change of strategy was economic. Despite its omnipotent image in the Arab public, the Zionist Executive suffered a chronic fiscal deficit that limited its ability to help its Arab allies. This financial difficulty was exacerbated by embezzlement perpetrated by some of the paid collaborators and by their failure to fulfill their commitments.[33]

Internal processes within the Zionist movement also contributed to changing policy. Mapai, the labor Zionist party led by David Ben-Gurion, had gained strength. As a result there were personnel changes in the management of the Jewish Agency, the institution that now constituted the autonomous self-governing body of Jews in Palestine. Among the changes were new heads of the agency's political department and Arab bureau. In August 1931, Chaim Arlorsoroff was elected head of the political department. One of his decisions was to neutralize Kalvarisky and the native

Oriental Jews while reinforcing Moshe Shertok. Arlorsoroff wrote in his diary that work in the Arab field should be pursued by professionals, "no longer on a diplomacy of bribery on the one hand and Sephardic acquaintance on the other."[34] Ben-Gurion similarly rejected negotiations based on bribery.[35]

Shertok himself wrote an in-depth analysis of the attempts to establish dependent organizations and the reasons they failed. "The Arab resistance places Zionism in a horrible spiritual plight . . . and it is only natural that if a person is in spiritual distress and seeks for a way out of his tribulations, and this proves not to be easy, it is natural that he falls into illusions." The basic illusion was that it was possible to achieve general political cooperation by granting financial inducements while ignoring Palestinian-Arab nationalism:

> The foundation of this theory—as odd as it may seem—is principally materialist. Zionism, which by its very nature is at its sources an idealistic movement, while being a political-national movement in its forms of organization and action, tried to resolve for itself the Arab problem in terms of a purely materialist-sociological explanation, without taking into account the factors of politics, the factors of national consciousness, the factors of ethnic instinct that are at work here.
>
> This theory said: we are bringing a blessing on the Arabs of the country, and a blessing means a material blessing. We are enriching the land, we are enriching them, we are raising their standard of living; indeed, we are bringing them not only material blessings but also a blessing in a more sublime sense. We are making possible wider public services, and by doing that we are making possible a rise in the level of education, making possible better education for the Arab child, a fairer status for the woman and the family, we are bringing light to the land. In general the Arab masses benefit from this blessing that we are bringing to the land, and therefore there are no contradictions between our fundamental interests and their fundamental interests, but rather a great correspondence, even if there are some discrepancies. . . .
>
> The unrealism of this conception was evident in the fact that in our attitude to the Arab we tried to strip him of the entire realistic framework that he lived in and to depict him not as an Arab but as merely a human being.[36]

Following this evocative analysis, Shertok maintained that Arab nationalism in Palestine was an established fact, and that there was no way to reach an agreement that was acceptable to both competing national movements. His conclusion was that the Zionists had to put their principal effort into building Zionism's strength and into propaganda that would advertise that strength, in the hope that recognition of that power would impel the Arabs to compromise.[37] The contacts with Arab opposition political figures such as Hasan Sidqi al-Dajani and Ragheb Nashashibi (and more rarely with members of the mainstream) did not end, but their success was no longer perceived as a necessary condition for the continuation of Zionist activity.

PRESS AND PROPAGANDA

Recognition of the need to spread the Zionist message among the Arabs of Palestine was not new. The older generation, headed by Kalvarisky, sought to construct an information campaign directed over the heads of the Arab leadership and press. Kalvarisky wrote to the Zionist Executive:

> In my opinion, nothing has done us more damage and ruined relations between Jews and Arabs than the Arab press. From the day it was born in the Land of Israel (al-Karmil—immediately after the revolution of the Turks) to the present it has not ceased to denounce us and malign our name. This virulent activity has instilled deep hatred of us in the hearts of the Arabs and has poisoned the atmosphere not only in this land but also in the Arab countries (Transjordan, Syria, Egypt, and others). To clear the air and turn the Arab heart toward us again, it is vital that we gain influence over the Arab press, directly and indirectly.[38]

The first steps toward influencing the Arabic press were made as early as 1911, and in the early 1920s two newspapers received support from the Zionists: the Jaffa paper al-Akhbar (under Christian ownership and editorship of Jewish Zionist Nissim Maloul) and the Jerusalem newspaper Lisan al-'Arab, edited by Ibrahim Najjar. Both were supposed to publish pro-Zionist articles but did not always live up to this commitment. In April 1923, Kalvarisky had to admit that, despite the flow of funds to him, Najjar had not kept his end of the bargain. In general, Najjar takes neutral positions, Kalvarisky reported to the Zionist Executive, but "at times he abandons his neutral position and assails us and criticizes our actions." Kalvarisky found himself in the classic trap of those who manage collaborators: He presumed that if he ended his support of Najjar, whom he described as "devious as a snake and a man of talent," his newspaper would begin to print fierce anti-Zionist propaganda and might even publicize Kalvarisky's tactics. On the other hand, he could not be sure that increasing the sums given to Najjar would lead to greater obedience. In the end Kalvarisky chose to continue funding Najjar despite his disappointment. He hoped to make Lisan al-'Arab the mouthpiece of the Muslim National Associations, if not of the Zionist movement itself.[39]

In addition to buying newspapers and their editors secretly, the Zionists continued to seek out writers to publish articles praising Zionism and Jewish-Arab brotherhood under their own bylines or pseudonyms. One of those enlisted in this campaign was Sheikh As'ad al-Shuqayri of Acre (the father of Ahmad, later founder of the PLO and its chairman in 1964–68). Sheikh al-Shuqayri had been a senior cleric in the Turkish army, had taken part in various oppositionist initiatives, and did not conceal his ties with the Zionists. In 1925 he wrote to Kalvarisky that he was prepared to write "longer articles and in that way you will gain both materially and ideologically." His assistant, Sa'id Abu-Hamad, did the same.[40]

These commissioned articles appeared in the Arabic press only as long as there was funding for them. During the recession of 1926–27 the flow of money ceased, and the propaganda effort resumed only after the riots of 1929 with the flowering of the Arabic press. Many newspapers appeared and disappeared, and the United Bureau established after the riots tried to obtain influence over some of them. Buying the hearts, or at least the pens, of Arab journalists was discussed several times in the bureau. A summary of one of the discussions casts light on the Yishuv leadership's perception of the role this propaganda campaign was to play:

> The United Bureau and the press department should help Arab newspapers who are influenced by us fight the attacks of those who hate us and neutralize their accusations and admonish them about the unjust and baseless attitude they have toward the acts of Jews in Palestine, noting the damage and loss caused to Arabs by their opposition to reach agreement and understanding with Jews.
>
> Emphasize the Arabs' inability to build Palestine with their own powers alone without the help of Jews, and the impossibility of development and progress if the two peoples do not work shoulder to shoulder. . . .
>
> Stress the difficulty and the disturbances and the backsliding caused to all branches of life by the riots and insecurity in the country, from which both peoples suffer. . . .
>
> Produce informational material on Jews' good intentions regarding Arabs, in keeping with the leaders' declarations and the Zionist Congresses, etc.[41]

Despite the 1929 riots, some Zionist officials continued to ignore the national character of Arab opposition to Zionism—in no little part because there were Arabs who also ignored it and cooperated in the propaganda effort. The most productive of these propagandists was apparently Muhammad Tawil, a clerk and writer of court pleas in northern Palestine.[42] Tawil was also active in the farmers' parties and, as we have seen, testified before the Shaw Commission against the mufti. Author of a wide variety of journalistic pieces that fit well with the Zionist line, he had no compunctions about attacking Christians and what he saw as the unnatural bond the nationalist movement had created between them and Muslims. He argued that Jews and Muslims had more in common, and that Christians had joined the national movement only to advance their own narrow interests.[43] He also issued proclamations, pamphlets, and books denouncing the mufti and the Supreme Muslim Council. In his 1930 book *Tariq al-Hayah* (Way of Life) he fiercely attacked Hajj Amin al-Husseini. The mufti had failed as a leader, he argued; his policies were leading to the loss of Palestine, and the money he collected for national purposes had disappeared. In an open letter to the head of the Arab Executive Committee, Musa Kazem al-Husseini, Tawil wrote: "Your negative methods have harmed the country and brought devastation on the lives of its people. . . . Muslims want to live with Jews in Palestine . . . work to improve the internal state of the country as the Zionists are doing. . . . history will demand an accounting from you."[44]

At the beginning of the 1930s, more Arab writers made themselves available to the Zionist movement. One of the most prominent of them, Zahed Shahin of Nablus, who was in touch with Kalvarisky and Yitzhak Ben-Zvi, chairman of the National Council, offered articles for publication in the Hebrew press. Ben-Zvi said that he preferred that his attacks on Arab leaders appear in Arab newspapers.[45] Additional propaganda publications were written by leaders of the Nablus farmers' party and founders of the party in Jaffa, such as Akram Tuqan and 'Aref al-'Asali. Tuqan published pamphlets under the title *al-Haqa'iq al-Majhoula* (Hidden Truths), in which he laid out proposals for Jewish-Arab cooperation based on his own experience as a party organizer. 'Asali issued a booklet, *The Arabs and the Jews in History*, in which he argued that the two peoples were closely related and stated that "the artificial alienation and separation between them are largely the result of politics."[46]

Three tactics were notable in the work of Arab mercenary writers: they portrayed Zionism's positive features and an idealized model of Jewish-Arab relations; they cast the Palestinian Arab leadership in a negative light; and they tried to widen the religious fissure in Arab society.

These tactics were consistent with the program drafted at the beginning of the 1920s, but as the illusion dissipated and the Zionist leadership abandoned its hope for general Arab acquiescence in the establishment of a Jewish national home in Palestine, the use of Arab newspapers focused primarily on deepening the fissures in Palestinian Arab society and presenting the strength of the Zionist movement—just as Shertok had proposed.

SELLERS ONLY: LAND BROKERS

Zionism's efforts to "redeem the land" were a part of Jewish immigration to Palestine from its very beginnings. Without Jewish-owned real estate, the Zionists could not immigrate in increasing numbers, establish settlements, or build a new Jewish society based on the return to the land. Palestinian cooperation was a necessary condition for realization of this Zionist vision.

Despite restrictions imposed by the Ottoman government and the opposition that began to make itself heard in the Arab public, by 1917 the Zionist movement had managed to purchase more than 420,000 dunams, most of it in five blocks: the eastern parts of the Upper and the Lower Galilee; the Hadera–Zikhron Ya'akov block, on the coastal plain south of Haifa; the Petah Tikva–Kfar Saba block, northeast of Jaffa; and the Judean colonies southeast of Jaffa. Generally speaking, the sellers were owners of large swathes of land; most of them were Arabs from neighboring countries (absent landlords), and the rest were Palestinian Arabs and some Europeans.[47]

Land purchases continued after World War I, and the political border drawn between the British Mandate in Palestine and the French Mandate in Syria and Lebanon accelerated the sale of large estates whose owners lived in Beirut (e.g., a branch of the Sursuq family) or Damascus (e.g., the family of Algerian emir 'Abd al-Qader). With the beginning of British rule, Yehoshua Hankin renewed his efforts to buy land in the Jezreel Valley in the north from the Sursuq family. In 1920 he signed a contract for the purchase of 70,000 dunams.[48] In 1924 the Zionist movement bought an additional 15,500 dunams from Linda and Nicholas Sursuq and 25,000 dunams from Alexander Sursuq. A year later 28,000 dunams more of the valley were purchased from the Sursuqs and another Beirut family, the Tuweinis, in addition to land in the Zevulun Valley, along Haifa Bay. In 1927 the Zionists bought lands in the Heffer Valley (Wadi al-Hawareth), south of Haifa—some 30,000 dunams that were auctioned off after a legal dispute among the owners, the Tayyan family of Lebanon and their creditors.[49] The heirs of 'Abd al-Qader, who owned thousands of dunams in eastern Galilee, continued to sell.

These huge land purchases were accomplished by two Zionist organizations set up for this purpose, the Jewish National Fund (known as KKL, Keren Kayemet le-Yisra'el) and the PLDC (Palestine Land Development Company, known as Hachsharat ha-Yishuv in Hebrew). As Jewish immigration increased and the demand for land amplified, the willingness of Palestinian Arabs to sell to Jews grew apace. As a result, by 1930 the Jewish population owned 1,200,000 dunams, of which about 450,000 had been purchased from foreign landowners, approximately 680,000 from local owners of large estates, and the remaining 75,000 from fellahin smallholders.[50]

The deals made with the large estate owners had the most significant effect on the map of Jewish settlement. In 1921 Nasrallah Khuri of Haifa sold Hankin the land on which the Jewish settlement of Yagur was established; in 1924 the Shanti family of Qalqiliya sold the land on which Magdiel was established; the sheikh of the Abu-Kishek tribe sold, in 1925, the lands on which Ramat ha-Sharon, Ramatayim, Bnei Berak, and other settlements were built (this after he offered the land to several Jewish buyers in order to bid up the price). Another piece of Bnei Berak was bought from the mayor of Jaffa, 'Omar al-Baytar, and his brother, 'Abd al-Ra'ouf. The sheikh of the village Umm Khaled, Saleh Hamdan, sold his village's land in 1928, and the city of Netanya was built there. In 1932 the Hanun family of Tulkarem sold about 10,000 dunams, on which Even-Yehuda was established. That same year Mustafa Bushnaq sold, with the assistance of the Shanti family, land on the Sharon plain on which Kfar Yona was built; in 1933 Isma'il Natour of Qalansawa sold the lands on which Qadima was built. The Shukri brothers and 'Abd al-Rahman al-Taji al-Farouqi sold 2,000 dunams from the land of the Arab village of Zarnuqa, on which the Jewish kibbutzim Givat Brener, Na'an, and Gibton were built. Sheikh As'ad al-Shuqayri sold 700 dunams that became the neighborhood of Neve Sha'anan in Haifa. And this is but a partial list.[51]

Yet, although most of this land was sold by large landowners, it is important to remember that numerically there were many times more fellahin who sold land to the Zionists. In the two years between June 1934 and August 1936, Jews bought more than 53,000 dunams in 2,339 land sales. Of these, 41 sales involved more than 500 dunams and 164 involved 100 to 500 dunams. The vast majority—2,134 sales—were of plots of less than 100 dunams.[52] This means that thousands of Arabs of all walks of life—poor and rich, Christian and Muslim, members of the political mainstream and oppositionists, city dwellers, Bedouin, and villagers—acted contrary to the norms laid down by their national movement.

This assistance to the Zionists went beyond land sales to other forms of cooperation. Zionist land buyers needed information about land available for sale, and they received this first and foremost from their informants. KKL and other purchasers used agents to find potential sellers. Moshe Goldenberg, a KKL official, explained how the system worked in the Beit She'an (Beisan) area:

> Sheikh Rashid Hasan was a fine and well-known figure. He was the mukhtar of the town of Beisan and, of course, there were many people in the town who were interested in selling. . . . He would find the people in Beisan who had to sell for economic reasons, for all sorts of reasons, and he'd send them to me, and I would take them to Haifa and they would sell their land. Not a single plot in Beisan was sold without his knowledge.[53]

Concluding a deal was relatively simple when the voluntary seller applied via such a collaborator to KKL, knew the boundaries of his plot, and possessed ownership documents. But the ownership of many plots Zionist agencies wanted to buy was not clear, and they needed to obtain information about the owners or locate documents. Arab collaborators helped in these tasks as well. For example, difficulties arose during the purchase of land at the village of Taybe-Zu'biyya in the eastern Lower Galilee in the early 1930s. The purchase was handled by Aharon Danin, who related:

> One of the village elders, an uncle of Sayf al-Din Zu'bi [later vice-speaker of the Israeli Knesset], Ibrahim 'Abd al-Rahman Zu'bi . . . was then the village mukhtar, and I went to him. This gentile, really, a gentile with a physique, puts his hand on his eyes and says, ya bnayya [my son], take a pen and start writing. A phenomenal memory. He began by telling me immediately who were the owners of 72 and a half parcels, and began one by one . . . how the ownership was split, whom they sold it to. I found the registration according to the instructions he gave me. Some in Jenin, some in Nablus, and some in Tyre in Lebanon [because the region had been transferred from one district to another].[54]

After the owners were located, they had to be convinced to sell their land. Here professional land brokers or influential figures entered the picture and helped persuade the hesitant. Such was the case in the aforementioned sale of Zu'bi lands: "The head of the tribe was Muhammad Sa'id

Zu'bi, the father of [future] Member of the Knesset Sayf [al-Din] Zu'bi. It would be hard to say that he was an intermediary. It wasn't mediation. It was more relationships, I won't say family, but he brought about the sale of lands that in his opinion were dispensable for the owner."[55]

That was the case when the "persuader" was a local leader. Sometimes the task was handled by a professional land broker. As Danin described it, "We had agents among them who could, by the strange approaches that our cousins have, bring certain people to sell."[56] His brother, Ezra Danin, recounted the way one of these brokers worked: "[Sharif] Shanti had a clear conception that he had to buy *musha'* [land belonging in common to the villagers]. When he needed to buy something from the village, he'd use his tricks to cause horrible arguments and dissent in the villages, which could force them to need a lot of money, for lawsuits and self-defense or attack. In situations like these he would buy lands and we bought from him."[57]

Purchase was sometimes not sufficient. The next stage was removal of the tenant farmers who lived on the land, or clearing away trespassers who had squatted on it so that they could receive compensation. Collaborators assisted in these areas as well. Hankin enlisted thugs from Nazareth to take possession of lands he bought in Ma'lul (near the Jewish settlement Nahalal): "Hankin used one of the hooligans of Nazareth who had both land and property in Ma'lul. His name was Sa'id Khuri. This Sa'id was later murdered by his brother over money matters," Aharon Danin related. The Jaffa newspaper *al-Hayat* reported that Hankin paid agents to persuade the tenant farmers in Wadi al-Hawareth (the Heffer Valley) to sign (in exchange for payment) release documents for their lands.[58]

Collaborators had a function in the following stages as well, such as marking the land and guarding it against squatters (in cases where establishment of a Jewish settlement was not organized immediately). The third Danin brother, Hiram, recalled that the son of the former mayor of Beersheva, Mahmoud Abu-Dalal, worked as a tractor operator for PLDC and marked out lands the company purchased in the Negev. This achieved two goals: it actively took possession of the land, and it provided a steady job for the mayor's son, therefore ensuring that the mayor could not oppose the land deals.[59] Marking land was sometimes a risky matter. In one case, a boy from the village of 'Attil who was helping buyers stake out lands in Wadi Qabani was shot at by a posse of Arabs who sought to prevent the land transfer.[60]

This help was not restricted to the practical level. As the British, responding to Arab pressure, took steps to limit Jewish land purchases, the Zionists enlisted Arabs to join them in opposing this initiative. When Hope-Simpson arrived in Palestine in summer 1930, several Arabs appeared before him and claimed that Jewish immigration and land sale to Jews would actually help the Arab population—claims that matched those of the Zionist institutions. One of these Arabs was Fayyad al-Khadraa (al-Jarrar), who said:

> I have about 5,000 dunams that are no use at all, and I owe money to creditors. If the gates of immigration were open I could hope that in a year or two companies of immigrants would come to buy 4,000 dunams of land from me, which will rescue me from my debts and allow me to cultivate what is left of my land and in that way I could live happily, me and my descendants after me.

Hafez Hamdallah of 'Anabta, west of Nablus, spoke in the same vein. Hamdallah, whose ties with the Haganah's intelligence service (the Shai) are noted later, testified to the benefits derived from the sale of 2,000 dunams in the Heffer Valley to Yehoshua Hankin. Three more men made similar statements in their testimony before the commission.[61]

Despite the ongoing campaign against land sales, many Palestinian Arabs continued to sell land to Jews throughout the period of the Mandate. It seems that Palestinian Arabs as a group accepted the nationalist ideas formulated by the national institutions, but that individually many of them put their personal interests before their political ideas.

KNOWLEDGE IS POWER: INFORMERS AND SPIES

As opposition to Zionism grew, so did the Zionists' need to gather intelligence—political and military—about the general trends and operational plans of the Palestinian national movement and its radical activists. The first initiatives to establish an intelligence service that would recruit Arab agents and informers were made immediately after the British conquest. Members of early Zionist defense organizations ha-Shomer and Nili competed to receive responsibility for this task. In spring 1918, members of ha-Shomer submitted a proposal to the Elected Assembly laying out the subjects worth collecting information on. They offered themselves for the job. The subjects were the location of land for sale, the influence of Christians on the population at large, events among the Bedouin, and "study of the Arab attitude toward us"—in other words, political intelligence.[62] Members of Nili submitted a parallel proposal, and in the end the job was assigned to them. This established the Elected Assembly's information office.[63] Its staff managed collaborators within Arab organizations in Palestine and adjacent countries and gave special weight to early-warning intelligence. The office's staff, made up of residents of the established *moshavot*, the Zionist farming villages established under Ottoman rule, already had a comprehensive network of acquaintances among Arabs that allowed them to obtain considerable information. The office's hundreds of intelligence reports, preserved in the Zionist archives, contain minute details that testify to deep intelligence penetration of Palestinian Arab society.[64]

In addition, Jews who did not work for the intelligence office but had their own connections with Arabs also obtained information from their contacts. So, for example, in 1920, during a concentrated effort to gather intelligence on an organization called al-Jam'iyyah al-Fida'iyyah (the Association of Self-Sacrificers) operating in Damascus, Jaffa, and Jerusalem, an Arab from Jaffa approached Yosef Rivlin, who was living in Damascus and working as a teacher. The informant, named Husni, provided information about the organization's plans ("to commit terrorist acts in Jerusalem and assassinate [British high commissioner] Herbert Samuel"). He also gave the names of the organization's leaders ('Aref al-'Aref, Muhammad al-Imam, 'Abd al-Qader al-Muzaffar, and others) and even volunteered to assist in activities against it by joining the assassins and traveling with them to Jerusalem, so that he could "hand them over at the right moment."[65]

At this same time, a network of Palestinian Arab spies was also active in Syria. They were sent by the Elected Assembly via brothers Yisrael and Yonatan Blumenfeld. The cell was headed by Murshid Shahin of Hebron, who was enlisted by Ibrahim 'Abdin of Ramla. Shahin recruited five men, who gave him information on events throughout the country. He was later sent to Syria and Transjordan on short intelligence assignments, along with four of his colleagues. Their mission was, apparently, tracking Palestinian nationalist activists who were staying in these countries.[66]

The riots of April 1920 began with the Nebi Musa celebrations and ended with the attack on Jerusalem's Jews, in which five were killed, 211 wounded, and many homes and businesses looted. During the following summer the information office received considerable intelligence on plans to attack British and Zionist officials. Yet, even though the office's staff gave full attention to every scrap of information, the riots of 1921 caught the Yishuv insufficiently prepared. In the wake of these events, the Yishuv's intelligence activities were again augmented. Most of those involved were members of the old *moshavot*, some of them veterans of the information office, who tracked assailants independently of the Haganah, the Yishuv's defense organization established in 1920.[67] Here began the familiar and natural pattern of collecting increased intelligence *after* terrorist attacks. After a short period there was again a lull in intelligence activities for a few years, although information gathering never ceased entirely.[68] Nevertheless, except for a short period, during this time there was no real organized intelligence activity or operation of informants in any regular, ongoing way. A significant leap came after the riots of 1929, when Zionist institutions reevaluated the entire subject of Jewish-Arab relations in Palestine.

• • •

Two weeks before the riots broke out in 1929, the Haganah mustered its members in Jerusalem on a field in the Beit ha-Kerem neighborhood. The commander announced an alert and asked who was prepared to serve as a spy in Arab territory. A. H. Cohen, then a 17-year-old print worker, recalled that he stepped forward—and saw that he was alone. He was summoned to a meeting with Yitzhak Ben-Zvi, who instructed him to leave his job and begin gathering intelligence.[69] Within a short time, Cohen became one of the lynchpins of Zionist intelligence activity—which shows just how lacking in intelligence infrastructure the Zionist institutions were.

Cohen specialized in two methods. One was undercover spying in Arab guise, the other overseeing agents. He received his instructions from the United Bureau, which had since its establishment in 1929 been responsible for gathering information on the Arab camp. The principal agent Cohen operated was the mukhtar of the village of Battir, who was known as "Na'aman" (mentioned above as having testified against the mufti's men in 1929). On Cohen's testimony, "Na'aman" enlisted the mukhtars of the villages of Beit Safafa, Walaja, Wadi Fukin, and others to assist him.

A good example of the type of work Cohen engaged in is the finding of weapons caches in Gaza. He and two of his helpers went to Gaza equipped with false papers that identified them as representatives of the Arab Executive Committee sent to examine the state of the weapons in the city. After examining the weapons, the three returned to Jerusalem, and Cohen reported to Ben-Zvi on the locations of weapons. "The next day the British took two wagons loaded with rifles from those places."[70]

Kalvarisky continued to be in charge of political intelligence. His most important informant was Abed Rashid Qawwas (al-Mutanabbi), whose alias was "Ovadiah." "Ovadiah" provided a continuous stream of information, and his reports arrived once every week or two. He reported on a plan to renew the boycott of Jewish merchandise, on internal discussions in the Arab Executive Committee concerning leaks to the Jews, and on the mufti's efforts to broaden his influence in the country.[71] After a brief period, his operators grew suspicious that "Ovadiah" took his information from the Arabic press, fleshing it out with his imagination. In contrast, the information provided by "Na'aman" was confirmed when it was cross-checked with additional sources, such as material from secret recordings and photographed copies of documents from the Muslim Council and the Executive Committee obtained by the Bureau.[72]

Jerusalem, the hub of the Palestinian Arab national movement, was also at the center of Zionist intelligence activity, but the intelligence web was also spread throughout the rest of the country. The men who represented Tiberias (Zaki Alhadif) and Haifa (Shabtai Levi) in the United Bureau also operated informants in their cities and in the north in general, and Arab activists in the Palestine Labor League (an Arab affiliate of the Histadrut, the Zionist labor federation) more than once passed on information to Ben-Zvi and their acquaintances in the Histadrut's local workers' councils.[73] There were also local networks set up by guards, mukhtars of Jewish settlements, and others that depended largely on Arab neighbors and friends who shared information—whether in the form of warnings or otherwise—about what was happening around them.[74] During that same period the Haganah began to institutionalize its intelligence work and share information its agents gathered with the Arab bureau of the Jewish Agency's political department.[75]

In summer 1933, David Ben-Gurion joined the Zionist Executive and added impetus to its intelligence activity. The Arab bureau added new informants and defined areas of information gathering with the purpose of arriving at a clearer picture of activities in Arab society.[76] The intelligence network was not limited to Palestine's borders. Members of the Jewish Agency's political department also operated in Syria, Lebanon, and Iraq, and even more so in Transjordan, where their ties with Emir 'Abdallah grew stronger. This work was in part political and in part alarmist intelligence. In the mid-1930s the focus in Palestine was on the latter and on the attempt to find Sheikh Izz al-Din al-Qassam and his band and other underground groups.[77]

On the eve of the rebellion of 1936, a great deal of information flowed in from various regions, both to the Arab bureau of the Jewish Agency and to the Haganah's intelligence division, on the growing tensions within the Arab public and the organization of armed groups and mounting expressions of extremism in internal forums (especially among the young).[78] This did not prevent the rebellion from catching the Yishuv by surprise, but the failure to prepare for it was not due just to the immaturity of the information-gathering system. There were two additional factors: lack of information about the precise time when violence would erupt (information that did not exist), and failure to analyze the existing information properly. In any case, Arab informers proved the usefulness of a well-developed system of collaborators. The ongoing rebellion increased Jews' dependence on intelligence-gathering collaborators, and the collaborators also became a central issue for the Palestinian Arabs, who saw the fight against them as an essential part of the rebellion, as we see in part II.

MONEY HAS NO ODOR: ECONOMIC COOPERATION

Zionists also aspired to cooperate with Arabs in the economic field. Zionist interest in such cooperation had two components, practical and public relations. On the practical side, the Arabs of Palestine were a natural market for consumer goods produced in the Jewish sector and had buying power that was important for Jewish businesses. They thus supported the Yishuv's economy. In addition, it was important for the Zionists to avoid giving the rest of the world the impression that they were creating a separate economy at the expense of the country's natives. After all, the Balfour Declaration, the basis of Zionist argument in international politics, stipulated that Jewish immigration was not to prejudice the rights of Palestine's non-Jews. It is in this context that Meir Dizengoff's statement in 1920 should be read: "The main thing is to make them parties in our business activities; [otherwise] people overseas will come to conduct an investigation of the situation and find that we have really entered into our own cocoon and have no regard for the great Arab masses who live in the country."[79]

The Palestinian national movement, for its part, tried from time to time to impose a boycott on Jewish products for these same reasons. It sought to harm the Jewish economy and to prevent the Zionists from depicting the relations between Jews and Arabs as mutually beneficial. This, for example, was the basis of Arab opposition to connecting Arab villages and towns to the electrical grid set up by Zionist entrepreneur Pinhas Rutenberg. Agreeing to such linkage would, they felt, not only be seen as consent to the grant of the sole franchise for the production of electricity (and use of water) to a Zionist Jew but also make them permanently dependent on the Zionists. Rutenberg used a tactic like that of Kalvarisky (and with much more success): when he sought to connect Jaffa to the grid, he gave a bribe of 1,000 Palestinian pounds to one of the most influential Arabs in the city, and he achieved his goal.[80]

After the 1929 riots, the Arab Executive Committee declared an economic boycott, an idea that had been suggested several times before. It called on the Arab public not to buy in Jewish stores and to purchase only Arab products. The United Bureau set out to fight the boycott. Its members tracked the Muslim Council's enforcement squads and handed its members over to the police if they violated the law. The Bureau also tried to use collaborators to break the boycott.

Ya'akov Mizrahi, a Haifa merchant, reported to the Bureau in January 1930 on an assembly of dignitaries and businessmen in Nablus who discussed the boycott. Mizrahi apparently heard about it from one of his friends. Ahmad al-Shak'a, a well-known merchant (who apparently also dealt in land sales), spoke there heatedly in favor of sanctions against Jewish goods, but sheikhs from the surrounding villages were opposed. They claimed that the city merchants supported the boycott in order to force farmers to take loans from them at exorbitant interest rates, and so to preserve the city's dominance over the villages.[81] The United Bureau encouraged such thinking at that time, with the aim of deepening the fissure between cities and villages.

The Bureau tracked the boycott in Hebron as well. According to A. H. Cohen's report in spring 1931, a delegation from the Arab Executive Committee did not succeed in persuading Hebron's merchants to join the sanctions. Their reason was economic—they received 80 percent of their merchandise from Jewish businessmen, on credit terms no Arab would give them. This group was headed by merchants and dignitaries who even expressed a desire to meet Chaim Weizmann during his visit. They told Cohen that they ardently wanted Jews, who had fled Hebron after the massacre, to return to live in the City of the Patriarchs.[82]

In some cases the violators of the boycott were linked to political parties supported by the Zionist movement. The Bureau's intention was to impel Jewish businessmen to develop commercial relations with the violators and to strengthen them economically. It also pursued an information campaign, publicizing the damage done to the Arab population at large by the boycott and the profits being raked in by businessmen with connections to the national movement. The propagandist Muhammad Tawil took an active part in this campaign.[83]

In fact, the boycott did not hold up for long, because Arab merchants needed Jewish merchandise and gradually but increasingly began violating the ban. The dissipation of the boycott accelerated when many Arab merchants saw their competitors buying Jewish merchandise, openly or under the table, whether because of Zionist encouragement or for economic reasons. Here too it turned out that, in the absence of unity, nationalist sentiment was often no match for personal interest.

In addition to cooperation between businessmen and merchants, socialist Zionist bodies initiated cooperation on a class basis. This included the establishment of Arab workers' organizations as well as the Palestine Labor League, the Arab branch of the Histadrut. The conventional scholarly wisdom is that the purpose of organizing Arab workers and raising their wages was to keep them from competing with Jewish workers whose wages were higher. In other words, the purpose was to improve the lot of the Jewish, rather than the Arab, workers.[84] In this sense the Arab workers' organizations were part of the Zionist project. However, the Arab national institutions' opposition to Arabs joining Jewish-Arab labor unions did not necessarily derive from this economic analysis. Principally, they opposed any link at all to Zionist institutions. An example of such opposition came during the Haifa carpenters and garment workers' strike in 1925. The strike was organized by Avraham Khalfon and his pro-Zionist assistant, Phillip Hasson. The Arabic newspaper al-Karmil expressed support for the strike in principle but warned Arab workers against the trap the Zionists were setting for them. "They want to enrich themselves at the expense of the workers' sweat."[85]

It was no coincidence that the northern port city was a focal point of labor organization. The city had large factories that employed Jews and Arabs and a powerful workers' council. Even on the eve of the great Arab rebellion, when Haifa was a center of religious-nationalist activity inspired by Sheikh Izz al-Din al-Qassam, some activist Arab workers who had ties to the Histadrut's workers' council continued to maintain good relations with Zionist activists. At that time the contacts broadened into actual intelligence activity, which further confirmed Arab nationalist fears about cooperation of any sort with Jews.

• • •

The switch in emphasis from recruiting political collaborators to security-intelligence work testifies to a changed perception of reality by the Yishuv's leadership. No longer naïvely believing that Arabs would accept

Jewish immigration as a blessing, they now recognized that armed conflict was inevitable. No longer were the Arabs a mixed multitude without a political agenda. The Zionists recognized (though not fully) that the Palestinian Arabs had gained a national consciousness. From the moment the Zionists had this insight, the Arab population was seen, first and foremost, as an enemy. As an enemy, they were an intelligence target, and those whose opposition to Zionism was less virulent, or whose personal interests were more powerful than their national affiliation, became potential informers.

The cause of this conceptual transformation by Yishuv leaders lay first and foremost in the changes in the Palestinian public's political awareness. One of the principal expressions of this was the ever-increasing intensity of the nationalists' battle against collaborators. The message conveyed by this struggle was not directed at Jews, nor at the collaborators alone. It was directed at the Arab public as a whole. The nationalist leaders sought to use it to instill national norms—what was permitted and what forbidden, what behavior was acceptable and what was treasonable. At the same time, the struggle was also intended to make clear to the masses who decided what was permitted and what forbidden, who determined what actions were fitting and what despicable. It was meant, in other words, to show who was in charge.

CHAPTER 2

WHO IS A TRAITOR?

The collapse of the Ottoman Empire and the British conquest of Palestine not only brought about a change in Zionist policy; it also brought Palestine and the rest of the Middle East into the age of nationalism. That required, and led to, a profound change in the self-perception of the Palestinian population. Previously, core identities and the most important social divisions had been based on religion: Muslims, Christians, and Jews. After World War I the national divide—Jewish/Arab—came to the fore. Behavioral norms changed as a result. Actions that had been perceived as legitimate by most Arabs until late in the Ottoman period, such as selling land and having other economic relations with Jews, became deplorable under the new norms. Naturally enough, the new self-perception was a slow process with opposition and setbacks. It could not have been achieved without the national institutions and social agents who took it upon themselves to promote it.

The first political-nationalist clubs were established by members of the urban elite, led by the Husseini and Nashashibi families of Jerusalem: al-Nadi al-'Arabi (the Arab Club) and al-Muntada al-Adabi (the Literary Club), respectively. The two families were also involved in the Muslim-Christian Associations, which had chapters throughout the country and became the first Palestinian national representative body. A few members of the rising national movement had been involved in the clandestine Arab national movement under the Ottomans, and ideas of nation were not new to them. Others had been part of the Ottoman administration and joined the national movement as a result of the new world order.

The initial instinct of some prominent members of the Arab national movement in Palestine was to view the country as part of a future united Arab kingdom, to be headed by Faysal, the Hashemite leader of the Arab rebellion who established his capital in Damascus. But Faysal's regime collapsed in summer 1920 soon after its establishment. Furthermore, Palestine faced problems not shared by the rest of the Arab world—Jewish immigration and settlement. As a result, Palestine's Arabs ceased to view Palestine as "southern Syria" and began to nurture a distinct Palestinian identity with its own political, national, and territorial parameters.[1]

The advocates of this new nationalism had to develop Palestinian national institutions, instill Palestinian Arab national awareness in the populace, and formulate political norms. In the face of the Zionist project of creating a Jewish homeland, Palestinian Arab nationalists expressed their national ethos and rules of behavior mainly in negative form: it was prohibited to sell land to Jews, it was forbidden to cooperate with them politically, and no useful information should be conveyed to them. Arab nationalist newspapers devoted a great deal of space to reviling those who violated these prohibitions, and this verbal censure was supplemented by social sanctions and physical violence.

In fact, Jewish immigration and settlement in Palestine had aroused opposition in some circles since the 1880s. But the opposition did not encompass all parts of the public.[2] Many Arabs put family and economic interests before national sentiments. Now, in the 1920s, what had previously been a vague sense of antagonism to Zionism took on a new conceptual framework: nationalism. In the space of just a few years, Palestinian Arab consciousness underwent a striking metamorphosis. New discourse was developed and terms that had not existed in the past, or that previously had entirely different meanings—such as "treason" and "collaboration"—were recast and became common currency.[3] They were used to delegitimize opponents, not only in the framework of the national struggle but also in internal conflicts over leadership.[4] In the decades to come, this had severe consequences for Palestinian society and its ability to confront Zionism.

TREASON: NEW NATIONALISM, NEW NORMS

The Great Betrayal: The Sale of Land

The national leadership's first task was to raise public consciousness about the idea of nation in general and the danger posed by Zionism in particular. Even before World War I, the Arabic press had enlisted in this mission, including Haifa's *al-Karmil,* edited by Najib Nassar and founded in 1908; the 'Isa brothers' *Filastin,* published in Jaffa and founded in 1911; and the Jerusalem newspaper *al-Munadi.*[5] In addition to the many theoretical articles about Zionism and the steps needed to counter it, these newspapers published articles decrying cooperation with the Zionists. Land sales were the principal form of cooperation the newspapers condemned, since both nations realized that territory was a necessary condition for realizing their national idea. An article published in July 1911 by Mustafa Effendi Tamr, a teacher of mathematics at a Jerusalem school, is a good example. After describing Zionism as the greatest danger facing the natives of Palestine, he launched a frontal attack on sellers of land:

> You are selling the property of your fathers and grandfathers for a pittance to people who will have no pity on you, to those who will act to expel you and expunge your memory from your habitations and disperse you among the nations. This is a crime that will be recorded in your names in history, a black stain and disgrace that your descendants will bear, which will not be expunged even after years and eras have gone by.[6]

A few weeks later *Filastin* published an article stating that "all land belongs to God, but the land on which we live belongs to the homeland [*watan*], at the command of God." Another article in the same issue described the home of a villager in Anatolia being razed after he sold land to Germans. The newspaper called the land sale "treason."[7] To local readers, the message was clear.

Such was the spirit of the local press in the final years of Ottoman rule. The national Arab newspapers sought to advance four central ideas: that Arab nationalism was both necessary and relevant, that it was a religious duty (for both Muslims and Christians), that Zionism was a major threat to the Arab nation, and that abetting the rival nationalism was tantamount to betrayal of the Arab nation.

Opposition to land sales was one of the principal focal points around which the Arab national idea in Palestine coalesced. It was the place where the national idea adopted by the urban elite intersected with villagers' fears that the Jews would buy up more land and dispossess them. This fear intensified as precedents were set in which tenant farmers were removed from land purchased by the Zionists.[8] After the British conquest, attachment to the land became a central component of national identity and its sale the archetypical act of treason. In an article of September 1921 in *Filastin,* a writer who called himself "Raqib" (observer) appealed to his readers:

Keep your blessed land. Reinforce its buildings so that they do not fall and its trees so that they do not die, lest your land and the land of your brothers be given to foreigners. The soil is the homeland, and a people that has no soil also has no homeland. Do not sell the land you inherited; it is your pride and the foundation of your glory. Do not cast away that which was entrusted into your hands so that you can improve it during your life and pass it on to its owners at your death. It is their [the heirs'] right and do not deny it to them, because that is a betrayal [khiyana] for which there is no absolution.[9]

"Raqib" noted the importance of land to the individual and to the family, but this was not its greatest significance. Land was of supreme importance to the nation. A people without its own soil could not have a homeland, so the sale of land was a heinous crime. His article is an early example of how the traitor is portrayed in Palestinian national writing. The traitor is the polar opposite of those who follow the straight path of Palestinian Arab nationalism. He is corrupt and avaricious. The nationalist, in contrast, is a *sharif*, a man of honor (the term still serves today as the opposite of "collaborator"). He is also *'afif* (modest, restrained), *shahm* (chivalrous), *abi* (forceful), *miqdam* (courageous), and *munsif* (just). This is a most important stage in the process of stigmatization: after a given act is defined as negative, its perpetrators are tagged as being the opposite of all that is noble and worthy.[10]

During the first half of the 1920s, as the extent of land sales came to public notice, the condemnations of collaborators grew more severe. The land sellers were "the true enemies of the homeland" and "human devils."[11] After a dozen years of struggle, the faction that rejected land sales had become strong enough that it did not hesitate to attack the sellers by name, even when they were influential and prominent.[12] Yet Arabs continued to sell land, and not always in secret. Clearly, a part of the public openly disregarded the orders of the national institutions.

In 1925 a Muslim religious authority issued, for the first time, a *fatwa* (Muslim legal ruling) forbidding land sales to Jews. This, the ruling declared, was an act of sacrilege. Written by the mufti of Gaza, Hajj Muhammad Sa'id al-Husseini, it appeared in the Haifa newspaper *al-Yarmuk*, edited by Rashid Hajj Ibrahim. Al-Husseini's most important legal statement was that Jews had ceased to be a protected minority *(ahl al-dhimma)* whose rights were to be respected by Muslims. Their status had changed, he wrote, because they were seeking to take control of the country. Therefore, Christians who aided Jews were to be deported from the country, and Muslims who helped Jews were to be considered heretics and *murtaddun*, Muslims who had abandoned their faith; their wives were to be withheld from them, they were not to be buried in Muslim cemeteries, and other Muslims were forbidden to pray for them.[13]

The fatwa did not receive much attention, perhaps because it arrived from the periphery and perhaps because of the temporary lull in land sales brought on by the economic downturn of the late 1920s.[14] But in 1929, when the Zionist movement again received funds to purchase land on a massive scale, the direct attacks on sellers resumed.[15]

The disparity between public declarations and the actions of individual Arabs was impossible to ignore. Akram Zu'itar, a journalist, educator, and prominent national activist, wrote in his diary:

> Oof, oof, what can we do? The subject of brokers who sell Arab land to Jews is becoming more and more severe. . . . The son of the mayor of Tulkarem, Salameh 'Abd al-Rahman, is deeply involved in land specula- tion, and there is no one who will cast stones at him, much less open fire on him. A member of the Supreme Muslim Council sells land to the Jews and remains a respected personage, Tulkarem is full of land brokers, and Haifa's city elders make deals with Jews, and the same is true in Gaza and Beersheva. How many senior government officials who speak in the name of Arab nationalism and help make land deals easier, and so far not a sin- gle land broker [simsar] was boycotted, even though they ought to get the death penalty. . . . God will not bless the land brokers, nor the nation that does not strike at them.[16]

In many cases newspapers refrained from publishing the names of land sellers for inappropriate reasons, such as their family or political connections. They made do with allusions and warnings.[17] Arab nation- alism had gained a foothold yet clearly was still not the principal deter- minant of conduct in Palestinian Arab society. But the term simsar (pl. samasirah) nevertheless became an insult. The national public, with the support of the press, quickly began to view the use of violence against land sellers as legitimate.[18]

In the 1930s land sales became a central issue in Palestinian political discourse. Izzat Darwaza, a writer, educator, and leader of the Istiqlal Party, wrote a novella about a simsar who tried to entice a landowner to sell his holdings. He described the way the Zionist institutions worked and the moral deterioration of the samasirah.[19] The poet Ibrahim Tuqan of Nablus wrote poems condemning the samasirah.[20] Most important, Hajj Amin al-Husseini exercised his religious authority for the first time to issue the fatwa forbidding the sale of land to Jews. This ruling was the beginning of a religious national awakening campaign that encompassed the entire country. The fatwa was disseminated by clerics and representatives of the Supreme Muslim Council and read aloud in city and village mosques. Throughout Palestine—in Jerusalem and its environs, in the villages of the Hebron district, in Beisan, in the Negev, in the Judean foothills, Samaria, and the Galilee—public assemblies were held at which the ruling was proclaimed. The assembled audience swore that they would not sell and would not abet the sale of land to Jews.[21]

The press and religious establishment worked hand in hand. When the newspaper *al-Jami'ah al-'Arabiyyah* learned of the sale of tens of thousands of dunams in the Negev to Jews, it published a call to the heads of the Bedouin tribes there "to eliminate the phenomenon of land dealings, to ostracize and humiliate the *samasirah* and to use *all other means* [emphasis added] against them."[22] Later the mufti and his staff conducted a series of visits to the sheikhs of the Negev tribes, read the fatwa before them, and had them take oaths on the Qur'an not to sell any of their land or provide aid to land sellers. The sheikhs were also enjoined to sign a petition stating that "the members of a tribe are to shun and scorn any person who is proved to have betrayed the homeland by selling lands or speculating in them or expressing loyalty to the Zionists. They will not shake his hand and will not eat with him." The editor of *al-Jami'ah al-'Arabiyyah,* who was present at this ceremony, reported that some of the sheikhs wept when they signed the petition. He presumed that these were tears of remorse for having been involved in previous land deals.[23]

In January 1935 the first assembly of Muslim religious scholars (*'ulama*) in Palestine convened. Land sales were at the center of its discussions. At the convention's conclusion the 'ulama issued an additional religious legal ruling, written by unanimous consent (*ijma'*). The text of this fatwa (with only minor deletions) follows. It is a seminal text in the religious approach to the land issue.

> After study and discussion of the entire matter and support for what was said in these venerable fatawa, we have reached agreement that the seller and speculator and agent in [the sale of] the land of Palestine to Jews and he who abets them
>
>> First: acts for and causes the removal of the Muslims from their lands.
>> Second: prevents the mention of Allah's name in mosques and works to destroy them.*
>> Third: accepts the Jews as rulers, since he abets their victory over the Muslims.

*This is a reference to a Qur'anic verse (*surat al-baqara* [2] verse 114) stating that there is no act more serious than preventing prayer in mosques. It is noteworthy that early commentators understood this verse as a condemnation of the Romans and Persians, who

Fourth: offends Allah and his messenger and the faithful.

Fifth: betrays [kha'in] Allah and his messenger and believers.

From a study of the irrefutable proofs of rulings in cases such as these that are in the verses of Allah's book, as the supreme one said: "O believers, do not betray Allah and the prophet. . . ."

And from all the above-said, which includes the reasons, the results, the utterances, and the fatwa, it transpires that one who sells land to Jews in Palestine, whether he did so directly or through an intermediary, as well as the speculator or agent in this sale and those who knowingly facilitate and help them in any way, one may not pray for them [at their deaths] or bury them in Muslim graves and one should abandon them and ban them and despise them and not become friendly with them or get close to them, even if they are parents or children or brothers or spouses.[24]

This fatwa was more significant than its predecessors because it was widely disseminated and represented a consensus of Muslim legal authorities rather than an individual opinion. The first signatory was the mufti of Jerusalem, Hajj Amin, and he was followed by Muhammad Amin al-'Uri, a member of the Shar'i court of appeals in Jerusalem. Other signatories were the muftis of Jenin and Beersheva, the Shafi'i mufti of Jerusalem, the muftis of Nablus, Safed, and Tiberias, and the qadis (judges in Muslim courts) of other cities.

The fatwa combines nationalist and religious arguments. In Islam, after all, there is no separation between religion and state. Fatwa applies the traditional concept of khiyana—betrayal—to traitors against the national cause. The ruling stresses Jerusalem's importance to Islam, and the holy city's sanctity is expanded to encompass all of Palestine. No less important is the severity of the social sanctions to be applied to land sellers and the ruling that even members of traitors' immediate families are required to sever their contacts with them.

A short time later, Christian clerics seconded the opinion of their Muslim colleagues. A congress of Christian Arab clergymen issued a declaration forbidding the sale of land to Jews. Its wording was notably similar to that of the ruling of the 'ulama. The sanctity of the land was not restricted to Christianity's holy sites but applied to the entire country: "Whoever sells or speculates in the sale of any portion of the homeland is considered the same as one who sells the place of Jesus' birth or his

---

forbade the Children of Israel to pray in Jerusalem; see, for example, Tafsir Muqatil bin Suliman (died 768) (Cairo, 1979–89), 1:132–133. It is thus an interesting example of Qur'an interpretation changing in response to political developments.

tomb and as such will be considered a heretic against the principles of Christianity and all believers are required to ban and interdict him."[25]

In some cases, the public campaign succeeded in compelling Palestinians to call off land sales. 'Abd al-Fattah Darwish, from the leading family of the Bani-Hasan *nahiya,* bought hundreds of dunams in the village of Suba, west of Jerusalem, with the intention of selling them to Jews (the original sellers claimed that they were unaware of his intentions). The Supreme Muslim Council learned of the purchase and sent Sheikh Rashid al-'Alami to impress on the villagers the serious nature of their actions and to inform them of Darwish's plans. In his speech to the villagers, al-'Alami called Darwish *kha'in al-umma wa-al-watan* (a traitor to the nation and the homeland). Declaring that God would take revenge on Darwish by magnifying his suffering, he called on the people of Suba to cancel the transaction, and they swiftly obeyed.[26]

Over time, the press, mufti and religious establishment (which joined the struggle only in the early 1930s), and national poets and intellectuals succeeded in establishing a norm that land sale to a Jew was an unpardonable religious and national sin. Land sales were located at the intersection of "the spirit of the nation," the very real fears of those who were liable to find themselves dispossessed of their property as a result of such real estate deals, religious ruling, and more abstract nationalist ideas. Together these created a complete rejection of land sales to Jews, and the sellers were indelibly branded as sinners.

But this proved insufficient. Sales did not end, and in November 1934 a man selling land in the village of Lifta, just west of Jerusalem, was attacked by Arab nationalists.[27] This was a demonstration that, on the one hand, not everyone accepted the authority of the national institutions, and, on the other hand, nationalists were prepared to escalate their response to such deviators.

The Flow of Information

Providing information to the Zionist movement's intelligence organs was another area of collaboration, but at this time it received far less attention than land sales in the press. The reason was, first and foremost, that the phenomenon was relatively limited during the Mandate's early years. Furthermore, intelligence gathering is characteristically covert.

As tensions rose between Jews and Arabs, Arab nationalists grew more aware that there were informers among their people. It is no coincidence that as early as 1932 the British Criminal Investigations Department received information about sermons given by sheikhs Izz al-Din al-Qassam and Bader al-Khatib, who said that the only fit punishment for informers and spies was death. The newspaper *al-Jami'ah al-Islamiyyah* denounced a police informer who reported on the Friday sermon given in his city. Not coincidentally, the preacher who was the subject of the report was also a writer for the newspaper. A report from Tulkarem told of the establishment of a secret society pledged to fight informers.[28] These reports came in as the Arab national struggle grew more extreme. And as the British and Zionists intensified their intelligence efforts in response, militant Arab groups became increasingly aware of this activity and began to legitimize the execution of informers.

Until the Arab revolt, however, the Palestinian public was generally unconcerned with the issue, which was addressed largely in closed forums and only occasionally found expression in the press. When Sheikh 'Aref al-Ahmad of the village of Rummana was arrested on suspicion of membership in the Qassam gang, the newspaper *al-Liwaa* expressed no more than regret that an informer had made the arrest possible.[29] An open, comprehensive, and vigorous struggle against purveyors of information began only after the rebellion broke out.

The Personal Is Political

In politics, unlike in land sales and informing, the definition of treason was ambiguous, elusive, and a matter of dispute. Sometimes it is difficult to recognize when a person was reviled as a traitor only by a specific political group, and it is not always possible to distinguish between national interests and personal, political, and family interests when the label was applied.

From the beginning of his political career, Hajj Amin al-Husseini made efficient use of his power to brand people as traitors in his struggle for the leadership of the Palestinian movement. In his first two contests, for the position of mufti of Jerusalem and for the head of the Supreme Muslim Council, he had opponents who said he was not fit for the job. Al-Husseini charged that his rival for the position of mufti, Hussam al-Din Jarallah, had been bought by the Jews. The qadi of Jerusalem, Sa'id al-'Uri, maintained that Hajj Amin was not worthy of heading the Supreme Muslim Council and said that it would be better for the British to continue to manage Muslim affairs. Al-Husseini and his followers accused al-'Uri of being a traitor to Islam and forced him to resign his position.[30]

The contemporary Palestinian national press hardly held back its criticism of those who collaborated with the Zionists in the framework of the Muslim National Associations. *Filastin* called them the "Destructive Associations" and described them as having been born of the personal ambitions of their founders for the purpose of "opposing the nationalists and disseminating the spirit of schism and antagonism, while being supported by an invisible hand"—that is, the Zionists. It attacked those of the associations' members who signed pro-Zionist petitions, terming them "accursed traitors," and stated that they carried no weight with the Palestinian public.[31]

The Muslim National Associations met with opposition throughout the country. The secretary of the Jenin branch of the Muslim-Christian Associations, Nafe' al-'Abbushi, reported on the pro-Zionist activity of "a few lowlifes who have sold their consciences" and on the fight he and his colleagues were waging against them.[32] *Filastin* published an article by 'Aref al-'Azzouni of Jaffa in which he warned the residents of his city against joining the Muslim National Associations: "We wish to warn our brothers, the Muslim people of Jaffa, about these dangerous clubs. They are headed by people with influence over the masses, who beg at the doors of the Jewish associations and coordinate their activity with them."[33] It is hardly surprising, then, that British and Zionist intelligence agents reached the conclusion that the members of the associations were "met with contempt and belligerence by all levels of the public."[34]

Nevertheless, the nationalists had to explain how it was that representatives of dozens of villages signed pro-Zionist petitions time and again. A long article published in *Filastin* immediately after the approval of the Mandate argued that the villagers were misled by "people who serve as tools in the hands of the Zionists for material gain, which they received as the price of their treason."[35]

The farmers' parties of the 1920s were given similar treatment. Immediately after they were formed, the editors of the Arab newspapers (with the exception of the editor of *Lisan al-'Arab*, which was funded by the Zionist Executive) decided to wage a public campaign against them. The press wrote frequently about the Zionist institutions' involvement in these parties and about how their membership was made up of Arabs who had sold land to Jews and of people who had been active in the Muslim National Associations.[36] These repeated attacks made it difficult for the leaders of these parties to gain public legitimacy and expand their membership. As a result, their disintegration was just a matter of time.

Al-Husseinis versus Nashashibis

The traitor label was not attached just to land dealers and parties supported by the Zionists. The opposition faction led by the Nashashibi family, which had been on the side of the attackers of the Muslim National Associations, quickly found itself under attack in its rivalry with the Husseini faction. This rivalry was between two camps that both called themselves nationalist—their members had taken part in the national movement from its inception. Nevertheless, labeling the Nashashibis and their allies traitors was a central tactic in the Husseini propaganda campaign for leadership.

The roots of the rivalry lay in the competition between the two families for prestige, status, and jobs—a contest that began at the end of the Ottoman period. It turned into open hostility when Ragheb Nashashibi consented to accept the post of Jerusalem's mayor after the British deposed Musa Kazem al-Husseini in 1920.[37] The competition became manifestly political because of the Husseini faction's opposition to the establishment of autonomous governing institutions in Palestine, which the Nashashibis favored. But in their public attitude toward Zionism the Nashashibis moved between utter opposition and moderate opposition. They had no compunctions about accusing the Arab Executive of taking too moderate a line with the Zionists. In fact, over the years the Nashashibis did have contact with Zionist leaders, but it was always fruitless.[38]

The Husseinis began calling the Nashashibis traitors in the early 1920s.[39] During the first municipal election campaign, in 1927, the process accelerated. The anti-Nashashibi campaign was led by the newspaper *al-Jami'ah al-'Arabiyyah,* which commenced publication at the beginning of that year under the editorship of Munif al-Husseini. The newspaper regularly attacked the Husseinis' rivals while giving favorable coverage to supporters of the Supreme Muslim Council and Hajj Amin. The elections, set for April, were a major subject in the newspaper from the day it was founded. In its second issue the editor called the existing municipal councils and their heads—most of whom were from the Nashashibi camp—an "unvirtuous" opposition (*ghayr sharifa,* a term used for traitors) fighting the national movement and aiding the British government and the Zionists.[40]

Two months later the newspaper again accused the municipal councils, especially the one in Jerusalem headed by Ragheb Nashashibi, of acting against the national movement in Palestine "and against the will and the interests of the inhabitants." The article was published on the front page under the headline "The Battle at the Gate" and concluded: "The nation cannot be fooled. Its word is the word of Allah, and the word of Allah is that which decides."[41]

In short, the same tactics used against land sellers and members of Kalvarisky's associations were used against the Nashashibis. The writer gave nationalism (as he perceived it) religious force and equated not being nationalist with duplicity and dishonor. Furthermore, he blamed the mayors for the country's woes, with the aim of depriving the Nashashibis of public legitimacy.

As the election campaign became more vituperative, especially in Jerusalem, so did the tone of the Husseini camp, to the point that they explicitly accused the Nashashibis of treason. A proclamation al-Husseini's supporters in the Greek Orthodox community published in *al-Jami'ah al-'Arabiyyah* put it this way:

> It would be an embarrassment and a disgrace to bring about a victory of the [incumbent, Nashashibi-headed] city council. It has been ascertained that these candidates rely on the Jews, and the Jews, as everyone knows, do this for their own purposes, since they reached an agreement with them, and the agreement is treason [*khiyana*]. Are we to stain our name and give up our honored position? Will we betray our homeland? Because voting for the city council's candidates constitutes treason against the homeland.[42]

The Husseinis did not call the Nashashibis traitors only within the Palestinian community. They directed these accusations at the Jewish voting public as well. In a manifesto published *in Hebrew* aimed at undermining the understanding between the Nashashibis and the city's Jewish leadership, they wrote: "Jewish voter, your vote will no longer decide the election, your vote can only affect the friendly neighborly relations with the Arab nation. Vote for the Arab Nation Executive Slate [the Husseini list]. Do not give the haters of Israel a platform to incite that all the Jews are as one with the traitors, the Nashashibis, who hate the Arab nation."[43]

Despite their belligerent tone, the Husseinis themselves negotiated with the Zionist Executive in the period before the election, with the goal of gaining Jewish votes.[44] They did so as they accused the Nashashibis of pursuing the same tactic. After all, in the dynamic of accusations of treason it is not just actions that make a difference. It is also, perhaps principally, the ability to maneuver public opinion.

The Nashashibis won the Jewish vote in the 1927 elections, and

Ragheb Nashashibi succeeded in holding on to the mayor's office. From that point onward the slander against him and his faction rose to a new level. This was the first manifestation of a process that would be of decisive importance. The Husseinis now branded all their opponents traitors, even if they were established and well-known nationalists. So, for example, the label was applied to the newspaper *Filastin* and its editor 'Isa al-'Isa, who had borne the flag of Arab nationalism as early as the twilight years of the Ottoman Empire. The Husseinis called on the public to boycott that newspaper.[45]

The struggle against the Nashashibis continued at varying levels of intensity during the years that followed. On the eve of the great Arab rebellion, the two camps were locked in an intractable dispute. The Husseini faction, which dominated the Palestinian national institutions, defined all who did not support Hajj Amin as a traitor. Pretty soon the accusations against the Nashashibis became a self-fulfilling prophecy. The attacks on the Nashashibis beginning in summer 1936 compelled them to cooperate with the Zionists and British to suppress the rebellion. But first we should look at how the lives of those who were branded traitors were affected during the years preceding the revolt.

THE TRAITOR'S FATE: FROM PROSCRIPTION TO DEATH

Bans, Threats, and Beatings

Explicit calls to use violence against collaborators were first heard in the internal deliberations of the Arab national institutions in the early 1920s. In June 1920 the Muslim-Christian Association of Jerusalem decided to set up a network of agents in every village in the country. These people would be charged with identifying who was planning to sell land to Jews. The prospective sellers would be warned, and if they did not heed the warnings they would be executed. Hasan Tutanji and Ishaq Darwish, two men close to Hajj Amin al-Husseini, were charged with implementation. Journalists who published stories favoring Zionism were to expect the same treatment.[46] The threatened violence was not actually carried out, but nationalist activists in the cities summoned mukhtars from the villages in their area and cautioned them not to sell land to Jews: "Islam does not forgive traitors," they were told.[47]

The beginning of the organized public campaign against collaborators can be dated to the elections to the legislative council in 1923. When the elections were announced, Palestinian Arab nationalists declared that they would boycott them and began to harass all those who planned to participate. The first sanction was social ostracism. A pro-Zionist activist from Hebron, Murshid Shahin, reported to Dr. Nissim Maloul, who coordinated the Zionist Executive's election campaign in the Arab sector, that "they—the opponents—have declared that all those who participate in the elections will not bury their dead in Muslim cemeteries, and that they will not be allowed to pray in the patriarch's tomb."[48] Even death would not free traitors from the ban.

Such threats became common. Yosef Davidesko, the liaison for the pro-Zionist associations in the north of the country (and later a member of the Shai), reported to Maloul: "The threats are simple: that every candidate in the elections cannot be sure he will live."[49] Ibrahim 'Abdin, a prominent member of the pro-Zionist associations, was one of those who received threats, as was reported later to the National Council. One day in September 1922 as he sat in a café in Ramla, his hometown, three men approached him and said: "The national home [of the Jews] has already been canceled. Soon the Turks will come back, and then we will slaughter you." They left the café after cursing 'Abdin and the British government and its supporters.[50]

The threats and ostracism swayed some, but loyal pro-Zionist activists like Shahin were not deterred. With them, the nationalists resorted to indirect violence. Shahin describes this, and the general atmosphere in Hebron, in another letter:

> I entered the government palace to receive forms for the elections, and since the governor was not there, I approached the secretary Anton Effendi and I asked him for fifteen forms. He told me that the time of the elections was over . . . and finally he gave me seven forms instead of the fifteen I asked for. When I took the papers into my hand I warned him not to announce the fact in the city, etc. That same night hooligans from the Muslim-Christian society dug up cauliflower I had sown at the cost of 15 Egyptian pounds. That was done to intimidate those who participate in the elections.[51]

These were sporadic incidents, but in one area—religion—the nationalist circles had almost complete control. They took advantage of their power to dismiss "the Jews' friends" from the religious positions they held. There is no shortage of examples. Sheikh Sa'id al-'Uri, the Shar'i qadi of Jerusalem, was known as a leading opponent of Hajj Amin and a friend of the Jews. He was fired. Sheikh Muhammad Adib Ramadan, the preacher of the Great Mosque in Ramla and principal of the Arab school there, gave sermons on interreligious brotherhood and against violence of all kinds. His local opponents reported this to the Supreme Muslim Council and added that he received money from the Jews. He was dismissed and forced to leave the city.[52] The qadi of Beisan, Sheikh Muhammad Nabhani, was relieved of his duties after being accused of corruption, a charge he denied. He was known for his good relations with Jews and his support for the Mandate. He asked Colonel Kisch to help him get his position back.[53]

False accusations were a common tactic. Amin Khawajah of Ni'lin, who collected signatures for pro-Zionist petitions before the ratification of the Mandate, was arrested late at night by the British police after an informer told the authorities that he had married two people against their will two years earlier. Sheikh Yusuf 'Arsan of the Bani-Saqer tribe of the Beit She'an Valley and a member of that town's Muslim National Association was incarcerated for twenty days after his nationalist enemies accused him of stealing cattle, a charge that was never proved.[54]

The Zionist Executive claimed that the ongoing harassment of its collaborators was the work of nationalist Christians who held positions in the British administration. They maintained that Nicola Saba, advisor to the governor of Nazareth and later a district officer, had instigated the arrest of 'Arsan. In the same period, Christian officials also brought about the dismissal of Haifa's mayor, Hasan Shukri, who served as president of the Muslim National Associations in Haifa and in Palestine as a whole.[55]

By mid-1923 nationalist circles could already point to a series of successes. They had elected Hajj Amin mufti of Jerusalem and head of the Supreme Muslim Council while branding his rivals traitors. They had stymied the legislative council elections, which had been supported by the Zionists and their allies. They had purged pro-Zionist and even neutral clergymen from positions of influence. The statement that the preacher and nationalist 'Abd al-Qader al-Muzaffar made after the legislative council elections proved to be accurate: "If [the collaborators] do not repent their deeds and return to the bosom of nationalism, the nation will ostracize them, just as traitors are ostracized. They will have no forgiveness and they will not be treated as a brother treats a brother, so that they will serve as an example to others."[56] The irony of fate is that al-Muzaffar himself was accused of treason two decades later. He was attacked with a Molotov cocktail after criticizing the mufti for his alliance with the Nazi regime.

The threat of social ostracism proved to be an effective deterrent.

British sources reported in December 1921 that the pro-Zionist associations were losing members, and the trend continued in the months that followed. Sometimes the resigning members placed notices in newspapers so that the public would know that they had returned to "the nation's bosom." One person who did this was Fa'iq al-Dajani, a member of the Jerusalem Muslim National Association. He declared explicitly that he was resigning from the association, which was funded by Kalvarisky, in obedience to public opinion.[57]

The nationalists' successes in creating an anti-Zionist atmosphere, disrupting the elections, and harassing members of the Muslim National Associations had their effect. The pool of potential Zionist supporters among Palestine's Arabs, which had never been large to begin with, shrank even further. The nationalists proved that the pro-Zionist organizations and political parties were not a significant factor in Palestinian Arab society.

But the years 1924–28 were a nadir for the Palestinian national movement. The Arab Executive nearly disappeared, and what remained of it was "no more than an office run by Jamal al-Husseini," as Yehoshua Porath put it. There was little popular or political activity: "It would have seemed that even the Palestinians' resistance to Zionism had totally disappeared. Even the traditional strikes on Balfour Declaration Day were forgotten," Porath wrote.[58] It is no wonder, then, that the issue of treason no longer appeared on the Arab public agenda. The result was that even a man like Fares al-Mas'oud, who headed the farmers' party of the Nablus mountains and received orders directly from Kalvarisky, took part in negotiations between the Husseinis and their opponents in 1925 in preparation for the Seventh Palestinian Congress.[59]

In summer 1928 all that changed. The Palestinian Arab Executive began to function again, and the Supreme Muslim Council commenced a propaganda campaign against Jewish attempts to take control of the Western Wall, the Jewish holy site at the foot of the Temple Mount/ al-Haram al-Sharif. The propaganda intensified in summer 1929 and reached a climax in the riots of August of that year. Arabs attacked isolated Jewish settlements and Jewish communities in the cities of Palestine, among them Jerusalem, Safed, and Hebron. Some 130 Jews were killed.

The renewed activity of the Palestinian national institutions and mounting tension led not only to a surge in attacks on Jews but also to aggression against so-called collaborators. Actual physical attacks were only a matter of time. In autumn 1929, for the first time, a Palestinian public figure was murdered for collaborating with the Zionists—Sheikh

Musa Hadeib from the village of Duwaimah, head of the farmers' party of Mt. Hebron.

The First Political Murder

Musa Hadeib was murdered in Jerusalem's Old City, near the Jaffa Gate, on 13 October 1929. It was the day before Yom Kippur, a tense time for Jews and Arabs in Jerusalem. The Supreme Muslim Council succeeded that year in persuading the British administration to forbid Jews to blow the shofar, the ram's horn whose trumpet blast was sounded at the conclusion of the fast, near the Western Wall. The Council also announced a strike the next day. The commission of inquiry into the bloody events of August 1929 that arrived in Palestine that week also raised tensions, especially in Jerusalem and Hebron. No one knows why Hadeib came to Jerusalem that day, and his murderers were never apprehended. But both his family and the Zionist Executive claimed that the Husseinis and their minions were responsible.

According to an anonymous tip received by the Hadeib family, the murderers were members of the Maraqa clan, a nationalist Hebron family whose patriarch, Sheikh Taleb Maraqa, was then on trial for his involvement in the Hebron massacre. The three murderers disguised themselves as women, so the information said, and were sent on their mission by the mufti. Arab policemen witnessed the murder, recorded the license plate number of the car the assailants used, and even identified the murderers, but they ignored the information on orders from Hajj Amin.[60]

The mufti and his men had good reason to murder Hadeib. He belonged to one of the most influential families in the Mt. Hebron area and founded the local branch of the Muslim National Associations. In summer 1921 he commenced contacts with Kalvarisky and expressed his willingness to sell land to Jews.[61] When popular opposition to the Muslim National Associations intensified in winter 1921, Hadeib was not deterred and did not resign. On the contrary. According to a British intelligence report, Hadeib planned to collect weapons in order to repel attacks on him and his supporters by the Muslim-Christian Associations.[62] Like other village leaders who tried to prevent power from concentrating in the hands of the urban elite, Hadeib also joined the network of farmers' parties and headed one of them in the Mt. Hebron area from its establishment onward. However, unlike his colleagues, who avoided addressing controversial political issues in public whenever possible, Hadeib included in his party's platform an explicit statement of support for the British Mandate.[63] He also did not hesitate to host High Commissioner Herbert Samuel in his village and even invited Colonel Kisch to take part in the visit as well. According to the Arab press, Hadeib was in regular contact with Kisch and provided him with intelligence. Kisch denied the charges, and in a letter to the chief of police in Jerusalem, Maj. Alan Saunders, he stressed that his relations with Hadeib were limited. Kisch added that the murdered man had not served as a spy in any shape or form, and that the crime he was murdered for was his friendly relations with Jews.[64]

The degree to which Hadeib was an informer was apparently of little interest to those sent to murder him. Hadeib was simply well placed to serve as an example of the fate that awaited anyone who cooperated with the Zionists. He had been willing to sell land, had been involved in the establishment of pro-Zionist organizations, and was a village leader who had offered an alternative to the hegemony of the Jerusalem elite.

Hadeib's murder was one of the manifestations of growing radicalism in the Palestinian Arab national movement from 1928 onward. Several radical elements ceased to recognize the Arab Executive as a legitimate leadership. One reason was the moderate stance taken by its chairman, Musa Kazem al-Husseini. Another was the participation of land sellers and other "traitors" in its ranks. Militant and jihadist cells began to appear and collect weapons in different parts of the country, and one of them, headed by Izz al-Din al-Qassam, began to attack Jews and British personnel in northern Palestine.[65] The jihadists intensified their death threats against collaborators. At the same time, the revival of the farmers' parties and the publication of the pro-Zionist testimony given by Arabs before the British commission of inquiry into the 1929 disturbances increased antagonism toward collaborators.

One such militant group, which called itself the Black Hand, was criticized even by the Palestinian Arab press. It sent threats to prominent figures, among them Ragheb Nashashibi. According to one Arab informer the organization warned Nashashibi against traveling to London with the Arab Executive delegation because it was certain that he would betray Palestinian interests. Another letter sent to members of the Supreme Muslim Council claimed that Nashashibi had received a large sum of money from Jews via his wife, in exchange for which he had promised to act in the Jews' interest in London.[66] The same informer also reported that a group of young men organized in Acre had come to Jerusalem and prepared a blacklist of five Arabs from their city who were suspected of treason in favor of the Jews and that "they contemplate killing them."[67]

About two months later an informer conveyed to his operators the Arab Executive's secret decisions: "Anyone who attaches himself to the Jews will be beaten and his property robbed, and everyone who sends a telegram against the delegation will be killed secretly." Likewise, he reported, special people were appointed to track who was negotiating with the Jews and to beat them, "and it was decided that if any newspaper . . . criticizes the delegation, the writer will be killed by gunshot."[68]

In the wake of these decisions (and the prevailing public atmosphere), collaborators were attacked in Nablus. One of the victims was 65-year-old Muhammad al-Titi, a member of the city's farmers' party. A few days after he met with Kalvarisky, when he was at home with his baby grandson, "the old man was awakened by an ax blow to his head as he slept. He raised his head after the blow to rise and resist his attacker but immediately received a second ax blow on his head and a club blow on his hand. He suffered two serious life-threatening wounds on his head, and the assailants disappeared immediately." So reported an intelligence source to the United Bureau, which added: "The inhabitants of Nablus are convinced that the assault was prepared and arranged by members of the Arab Executive and that the assailants are paid thugs who wanted to murder Muhammad al-Titi just as they murdered Musa Hadeib."[69]

Al-Titi was attacked again that same month, and the opposition newspaper *Mirat al-Sharq* reported on the attack with favor, as it did the attacks on Hasan al-Shak'a and other members of the farmers' party. The reporter explained that the reason for the attacks was that the victims had collected "signatures harmful to the homeland" at the behest of the Jews. *Mirat al-Sharq* also published an open call to the government and the police, stating that it was the victims who were the guilty parties, since their only occupation had been sabotaging public order and causing trouble.[70]

Threats against collaborators and groups organized to attack them were countrywide phenomena. Zahed Shahin of Nablus had to take refuge in Jerusalem. The mukhtar of Battir was beaten because he testified about the involvement of Sami al-Husseini (Musa Kazem's son) in an attack on the Jewish settlement of Har-Tuv. Muhammad Tawil of Tiberias, who testified before the commission of inquiry against the mufti, was pursued and forced to leave the country and find refuge in Turkey. The sheikh of Meroun, who helped Jews there, was accused of treason and attacked. Adversaries of Arab villagers of Hittin, who had helped Jews, made false accusations against them to the police.[71]

The definition of treason in some circles was broadened during this period to include Arabs who saved Jews during the riots of 1929 and those who violated the economic boycott of Jewish products. The Arab Executive's enforcement squads patrolled marketplaces and tried to prevent Arabs from buying Jewish goods. These inspectors had no compunctions about using force against consumers, relieving them of goods they had purchased and beating them bloody. Taking part in joint Arab-Jewish labor strikes was also declared treason, as was holding joint events of any kind.[72]

On the political level, threats were not directed only at members of the farmers' parties. They were made against anyone with political contact with Zionists. Musa Kazem al-Husseini participated in this campaign of intimidation even though he was perceived at the time to be close to the Nashashibis. Prior to Chaim Weizmann's visit to Palestine he sent thirty warning letters to notables in the Hebron area who wanted to bring Jews back into the city. The letters stated explicitly: "Any person who dares negotiate with Weizmann on any question will meet a bitter end." Hajj Amin sent his own letter with a more veiled threat to all the country's muftis: "Within the Arab movement there are here and there people who are prepared to sell their homeland for a smile from Weizmann and for a single loaf of bread. But the entire nation has the obligation to follow the actions of these people diligently."[73]

The threats were backed up with the apparatus to carry them out. In September 1930 an informer reported that Hajj Amim, during a visit to the village of Nebi Samwil, met an Arab from the village of Jimzu who had escaped from prison after being sentenced to fifteen years' hard labor. The mufti ordered him to form a band whose mission would be to liquidate Arab traitors.[74] Similar decisions were made in Jaffa and Tulkarem.[75] In March 1933 an informer reported that the mufti of Safed heard about an Arab from Ja'uni who was passing information to the Jews and responded: "*Halal qatluhu*" (It is permitted to kill him). Two days later the man was attacked and injured.[76] In fact, there were no reported murders of collaborators (including land speculators) until 1934. Apparently the violence against them was generally limited to that which was accepted in physical altercations in Palestinian society (*tuwash;* sing. *toshe*), involving controlled violence in which an effort is made to avoid killing.[77]

A change began in winter 1934. In November of that year the land speculator Saleh 'Isa Hamdan of Lifta village west of Jerusalem was murdered (*al-Jami'ah al-'Arabiyyah* reported that the bullets were meant for a prominent *simsar* who was walking next to him). United Bureau intelligence agent A. H. Cohen attributed the attack to a local group that sought to halt the flood of land sales to Jews in Lifta, which had started the previous summer. Police sources pointed in a similar direction, saying that the assailants were members "of a terrorist organization among whose members are people extremely close to Hajj Amin."[78] The battle against traitors seems to have received momentum and inspiration from the highest levels in the Husseini camp. After the strike and rebellion broke out in spring 1936, all remaining barriers were swept away.

• • •

By the end of this period, the nationalist discourse had clearly become deeply rooted in the Palestinian Arab public. The most obvious indication was the great preoccupation with the issue of treason and the switch in the struggle against "traitors" to physical attacks and even murder. Nevertheless, it is important to note that use of the ultimate sanction—murder—remained extremely rare even after the events of 1929. The greater part of the struggle was directed against Jews and was conducted by and large on the political field. This is in contrast to the period after 1935, in which the battle—against the British, against Jews, against collaborators, and against the opposition—moved into the military arena.

The wide-scale use of nationalist concepts did not, however, mean that the emergent Palestinian national sensibility had become what every national movement seeks to become: the principal component in the basket of identities of each individual and the one for which he is willing to kill and be killed.[79] The leading figures of the movement tried to turn Palestinian identity into just this (even if they themselves sometimes gave precedence to their personal and factional-family interests). They used three tools to pursue this goal: norms, coercion, and reward. Employing these, they first and foremost sought to prevent cooperation with the Zionist movement.[80]

The establishment of norms had two faces. Positively, it preached the new nationalist norms. Negatively, it labeled those who strayed from the norms as traitors. The press, the religious system (both Muslim and Christian), and the educational system served as central tools, both positive and negative. The coercion was a disciplinary system that supplemented the attachment of the traitor label to those who strayed from nationalist norms. The punishment for these deviants was meant to deter the public as a whole and to bring everyone within the boundaries of the norms. I have documented three major types of punishment: social ostracism, dismissal from employment, and physical attacks. In at least some cases there can be no doubt that these punishments served the Husseinis' attempt to establish a monopoly on the use of force. The decision by Nimer Hadeib, the son of Musa, to conduct a reconciliation ceremony *(sulha)* with Hajj Amin after his father's murder is an example of the coercive mechanism's success. Nimer promised to stop working with Jews and to pass on to the Supreme Muslim Council information about developments in the Zionist camp.[81]

The reward mechanism is best seen in the way Hajj Amin drew people to his side through his control of the religious establishment. So, for example, he was able to bring about a change in the positions of Arabs who had been friendly with Jews by bringing them into his circle and providing jobs. One instance of this was Sheikh 'Abd al-Hayy al-Khatib of Hebron. Al-Khatib had good contacts with the Zionists in the 1920s and supported the Muslim National Associations. By the end of the decade, however, after his appointment to the post of mufti of Hebron, he became the Jerusalem mufti's local auxiliary.

To what extent did the national leadership succeed, through these mechanisms, in bringing the public under its control? How effective was the central nationalist faction's fight against collaborators? To what degree was collaboration with the Zionists indeed perceived as a social deviation? One of the Husseini camp's unquestioned successes was that pro-Zionist organizations lost all legitimacy among Palestinian Arabs. On the other hand, the Husseini attempt to label the Nashashibis traitors was not entirely successful. In the 1934 municipal elections the Nashashibi faction still received considerable support. (Of course, this support derived in part from the fact that suffrage was restricted to people of high income, and the Nashashibis' public statements against Zionism were sufficient to gain them the support of many who opposed Zionism.)[82] But throughout this period Arabs nevertheless continued to provide aid to the Zionist movement in the form of economic cooperation, land sales, and intelligence.

The weakness of the national movement was caused in part by its own conduct. Sometimes its attempt to broaden the definition of treason to include all those who opposed the hegemonic nationalist al-Husseini faction acted to its detriment. With such a broad definition, the label became less effective. So, for example, when the Husseini faction declared that the editor of *Filastin*, who had for years been one of the important spokesmen for the national movement, was a traitor, small-time land sellers became less fearful of being given the same label. This also demonstrated the lack of consensus within the nation on the issue of treason, the lack of a unifying national ethos. Opposition figures noted this as early as 1927: "Were we to enumerate the number of traitors in the country in accordance with some of the newspapers, more than half of the country's inhabitants would be traitors. Is it logical that half the nation is betraying its homeland?" asked *Mirat al-Sharq*.[83]

The lively discourse in which the Husseinis were central participants did more than cheapen the concept of "traitor." It also undermined confidence in the leadership and its motives. Accusing the opposition of treason because of its ties to the Zionists at a time when the Husseini municipal slate acted in exactly the same way dealt a blow to the Husseinis' reputation, as did the Husseinis' silence when people in their camp sold land to the Jews, as was reported in the opposition press. This also damaged the campaign against land sales, despite the broad support this received. Newspaper readers had no way of knowing whether the condemnation of a given person derived from real national motives or from narrow political ones.[84] In addition, some people continued to collaborate with the Zionists in response to the leadership's attempts to suppress them.[85] As a result, even as the rejection of cooperation with the Zionists spread and became hegemonic, many continued to do just this, in different ways and for a variety of reasons.[86]

CHAPTER 3

WE, THE COLLABORATORS

In 1923 the Bedouin sheikhs of the Beit She'an Valley, members of the Muslim National Associations, invited British high commissioner Herbert Samuel to visit their camps. In their letter they told Samuel a little bit about themselves:

> We don't meddle in politics, don't attend rallies, and don't send delegations. We are simple people who live in tents and deal with our own affairs only. We agree with everything the government does. . . . We have seen no evil from the Jews. We have sold the American Jewish Agency some of our lands, and with the help of the money we received we are developing and cultivating the large tracts that still remain ours. We are pleased with these Jews, and we are convinced that we will work together to improve our region and to pursue our common interests.[1]

This is how ideal collaborators describe themselves. They agree with everything the government says; they sell land to Jews; they claim that Arabs also benefit from Jewish immigration; they are satisfied with things as they are. Zionists could endorse the letter, and it is indeed possible that Kalvarisky and his associates had a hand in drafting it. Nationalist Arabs would also happily agree with some details: these abettors of the Zionist project are naïve, don't understand politics, and are easily seduced. That is how the nationalists explained why some Arabs became collaborators.[2]

But the sheikhs who signed the letter were not as naïve as all that, and so-called collaborators could be found at all levels: in villages, Bedouin tribes, and cities, among leaders and among the common people. The assumption that money was the only motive that drew all these collaborators into the Zionists' arms is not accurate. It was undoubtedly important, but it was not the only reason.

Why did Arabs choose (or agree) to cooperate with the Zionist movement even before it reached the peak of its power? One major reason was the way they saw the three-way relationship among the British, Arabs, and Zionists. Many Arabs perceived the Zionists as part of the British administration. Beyond the Balfour Declaration and the official British support for Zionism, Jews who arrived with the Mandate were mostly European foreigners. They had close relations with the British establishment and were relatively powerful both politically and economically. This is the only explanation for the many requests leading Arabs made to their Zionist acquaintances for intercession with the British regime. Leaders of the Muslim National Associations asked the Zionist Elected Assembly for jobs in the police force and judicial system; Musa Hadeib asked the Zionist Executive to help get his son a position as a police officer. Haidar Tuqan requested Zionist assistance in winning back the mayor's chair in Nablus.[3] All these men viewed the Zionists as an arm of the British regime. In exchange for assistance, they were prepared to assist.

Beyond this elementary motive, however, Arabs who cooperated with the Zionists fell into four categories. The first were those who did so for personal gain, such as the *samasirah* and others who helped the Zionists in exchange for jobs or money. The second were those who acted in the name of communal interest, such as Bedouin tribal chiefs and village leaders. They saw their ties with the Jews as a way of helping not only themselves but also the group they identified with. The third category consisted of those who had (or claimed to have) nationalist motivations. They offered an alternative to the ideology and tactics of the Palestinian national movement on the grounds that in so doing they were acting in the interests of their nation. A fourth group was made up of collaborators whose motives were ethical and humanist. They had Jews as friends and neighbors and were disgusted by the violence of the Palestinian national movement.

These categories are not exclusive; some people acted out of more than one motive. Tribal leaders sought what was best for their tribes but also wanted to maintain their own status and earn money. "Moral" collaborators at times asked for compensation in exchange for their services. Land agents sometimes justified their actions with nationalist terminology; perhaps they even believed that they had chosen the right path. All in all, many did not act at this early stage with the intent to harm the national movement. They simply gave their own interests and principles priority over what was described by the national leadership as the nation's will.

THE OPPORTUNISTS

The Land Brokers

Thousands of Palestinians sold land to Jews during the Mandate's first two decades. Some did so because they were in debt or so that they could build a house for a son who was about to marry. Others wanted to move up the economic ladder, to buy a tractor or a truck. Some decided to cash in assets when land prices rose as a result of Zionist immigration. For all these, the sale of land was a one-time act, generally accompanied by serious misgivings. There was, however, a group of several dozen people who made land sales a vocation and their major source of livelihood. These were the *samasirah*.

The family of Tulkarem's mayor, 'Abd al-Rahman al-Hajj Ibrahim, and the Shanti family of Qalqilya were typical. Some members of these families worked alongside Zionist land purchasers from the Mandate's first days through the establishment of the state of Israel, sometimes at great personal risk. KKL, the major Zionist land purchasing organization, was eternally grateful. Nationalist Arabs held them in contempt and sometimes attacked them physically.

Yehoshua Hankin established a relationship with al-Hajj Ibrahim at the beginning of the 1920s, aimed at expanding the Jewish foothold in the country. As mayor, he was able to achieve a lot—sell his own land and persuade others to sell theirs. In short order his two sons, Salim and Salameh, entered the business, as did his son-in-law 'Ali al-Qasem. They had quite distinct personalities: "'Ali al-Qasem was a very brave, proud, but also clever gentile," recalled Aharon Danin, Hankin's assistant. Dr. Yosef Shadmon, who registered the purchased land, added that al-Qasem "stood out in his audacity, courage, valor, and desire to get rich."[4]

Al-Qasem worked alternately with and against the Zionists, depending on his evaluation of the costs and benefits. So, for example, he vandalized Jewish citrus groves on the Sharon plain in order to get the farmers to pay him to guard the groves. On the other hand, when a Jewish couple was murdered in summer 1931, he helped find the murderers—and in exchange received money from the Jews and a pistol license from the British.[5] He was also involved in land deals in different areas. Before and during the war of 1948, al-Qasem conveyed information to the Haganah and to Lehi (for the British, "Stern gang"), a small radical underground group—but also to the Arab forces. That was, at least, the opinion of Israel Defense Forces intelligence chief Issar Be'eri, who ordered al-Qasem liquidated. That operation led to Be'eri's ouster.*

Salim, the elder brother, also played both sides. He was one of the first members of the national movement and a member of the Arab Club (al-Nadi al-'Arabi) in Damascus in 1919, and he served as a member of the fourth and sixth Arab Executives. In the 1920s and early 1930s he worked with his father as a land agent for Hankin, with the full knowledge of his colleagues in the national movement.[6] When he realized that land dealing and nationalist activity could not mix, he decided to abandon the business. Aharon Danin described this transformation:

> Salim came to Hankin and said to him: "My father, I was earlier involved in Arab nationalism and today I want to go back to it, so I am ending my work with you and will commence operating against you." Hankin said: "I think you are making a mistake, but if that is your wish, do it." And the fact was that Salameh continued to work with us throughout that period and Salim began working against us, but our personal relations were quite sound.[7]

That conversation took place at the beginning of the 1930s, when the public campaign against land sales began. Just after Salim enlisted in the campaign alongside his former colleagues in the nationalist movement, the press reported on the involvement of competing clans—principally the Jayyusi and Hanun families—in land sales in the Tulkarem area. They in turn provided the anti-Husseini press with information on the involvement of Salim and his family in dubious dealings. They accused him of treason, espionage, and fomenting dissension. His nationalist activity was intended, they said, to raise his status in Jewish eyes and so enable him to raise his sales commissions. They pointed out that Yehoshua Hankin continued to visit Salim's house and wondered how

---

*In December 1948, al-Qasem's body was discovered in the Carmel forest. An investigation found that Issar Be'eri had ordered his execution because of suspicions that he intended to convey information to the enemy. Be'eri was brought up for court-martial, after some initial doubts, on charges of manslaughter and acting beyond his authority. In his defense, he claimed that he acted within his powers as commander of the intelligence service, and that standard law could not apply to covert actions. The court ordered him relieved of his command but did not reduce his rank. Later he was discovered to have been involved in other problematic incidents, such as the execution of Meir Tubiansky and an attempt to frame Abba Hushi. See Issar Harel, *Bitahon ve-Demokratya* [Defense and Democracy] (Tel Aviv, 1989), 114–115 (in Hebrew).

such a man could be considered a nationalist.[8] The dispute was not over principle; many of the accusers had themselves sold land.

Unlike Salim and 'Ali al-Qasem, Salim's brother, Salameh, continued to work openly and steadily as a land broker until and even after Israel was founded. In 1932, when the lands of the Sharon plain gradually filled with Jewish settlements, Akram Zu'itar lamented in his diary that there was no one in the entire nation who would rise up and murder Salameh.[9] Salameh was a hunchback, and that was his nickname among his Jewish associates. Yosef Shadmon wrote: "That hunchback was the king of land brokers in the Sharon. . . . Thanks to his work we bought most of the property there." And Aharon Danin added: "He was a very intelligent and clever gentile. He was a smart man. Knew how to lead things."[10] Salameh dealt only with land. Al-Qasem had a hand in everything.

The Shanti family was also prominent among the *samasirah*. As a result, in 1925 the heads of Qalqilya's families agreed not to sell land to foreigners or to the Jaffa branch of the Shanti family.[11] Yosef Weitz, who oversaw land purchases for KKL, thought that Kamel Shanti ought to get the credit for Jewish settlement in the Sharon region: "You could say that Shanti had a hand in purchasing the land for most of the settlements founded from 1930 onward." Shanti's principal motive was easy profit, but Weitz identified another motive as well: "He was close to the Jews, and especially the Jews of Petah Tikva . . . from his youth, and afterward because his wife was Jewish."[12] His rivals, some of them within his family, viewed him as an unabashed con man. In a lawsuit they filed against him in 1930, they argued that he registered land belonging to his underage relatives in his own name and then sold it to Hankin.[13]

Aharon Danin had this to say about another member of the family, Sharif Shanti:

> There was no other character like him. Sharp, cunning, a wrangler par excellence. It's rare to find a man who knows how to run things like that. He was a man who could not go straight. Even if he'd wanted to he couldn't do it. By his nature he couldn't. But he had an ability to work and an ability to invent that are beyond description. I kept my distance from him but I respected him a great deal. . . . He knew how to whip up a fight among Arabs, to lead them on.[14]

Ezra Danin explained what his brother meant by "run things": Sharif Shanti "would use his tricks to cause horrible fights and conflicts in the villages, which compelled them to need lots of money for lawsuits, self-defense, or offense. In such a situation he would buy land and we would buy from him."[15]

Thanks to these people, KKL was able not only to purchase land but also to preserve its self-image as a decent organization. It was the collaborators who picked the fights, cheated, and forged documents. It was they who took landowners to bars and prostitutes. KKL's hands remained clean. The *samasirah* were cast in the traditional role reserved for collaborators: they worked in the gray area between legal and illegal, on the margins of the manifestly immoral, and so allowed the Zionist institutions to maintain an appearance of integrity.

Testimony about the *samasirah* corroborates two elements of their public image: they were dishonest and deceitful, and they had abandoned a traditional lifestyle. The most extreme manifestations of the latter were residing in a Jewish settlement and marrying a Jewish woman, as was the case with Kamel and Sharif Shanti. Milder forms were participating in the nightlife of Jewish cities while casting off Islam's restrictions, and moving to one of the big cities. Sharif Shanti did this openly. In Ramadan in 1935 he broke the fast by eating in public and was brought to trial as a result.[16]

Such a lifestyle was also criticized by nationalist forces. When the Zionist Congress held in Zurich in July 1929 decided to allocate £1 million to buy land in Palestine, the newspaper *Filastin* retorted sarcastically: "This is both sad and joyful news. Sad, because with this money 400,000 dunams will be transferred into Jewish hands and thousands of fellahin will join the ranks of the dispossessed. But about twenty people—a portion of the nation that should not be discounted—will have all their worries dispelled and life will smile on them, because the bars and dance clubs will now be wide open for the *samasirah* and their friends."[17] The newspaper *al-Jami'ah al-'Arabiyyah* reported from the field during the heyday of the brokers: "The city of Tel Aviv, its streets and its cafés, buzz each day with large groups of fellahin and *samasirah* who humiliate themselves and sell the fertile lands of the foothills."[18] The land sellers were similarly presented in a play staged in Palestinian cities at the beginning of the 1930s, which portrayed them carousing with Jewish women.[19]

The *samasirah* who moved to Jewish cities seem to have done so not only because they were attracted by the more permissive lifestyle but also to get away from the hostility they encountered in their hometowns. This was one of their ways of defending themselves. Another was through family ties. As in al-Hajj Ibrahim's family, of which one son was a senior figure in the nationalist movement yet defended his *simsar* brother, so the Shanti family also had its senior nationalist. Ibrahim Shanti was a member of the pan-Arab al-Istiqlal Party and an editor of its newspaper, *al-Difa'*, the most popular paper of the 1930s.

The Careerists

Murshid Shahin of Hebron had been a police officer under Ottoman rule. A short time after the British conquest, he was relieved of his command because of accusations of unbecoming behavior. He decided to cast his lot with the Zionists. Through them, he presumed, he could get his job back. Unlike other Palestinians who worked with the Zionists, he did not simply express sympathy or sign a petition favoring Zionism. He set out for Syria and Transjordan as an emissary of the Elected Assembly and collected intelligence on Palestinian Arab nationalist activity. When he returned he helped found the Muslim National Association in Hebron, which was supported by the Zionist movement.

Hebron's city rabbi, Ya'akov Yosef Slonim, said of Shahin that "he leans to our side on all our issues, from the first moment and with all the warmth in his heart." The rabbi also speculated about his motives: Shahin hated the members of the Muslim-Christian Associations, which had been involved in his dismissal, and sought to return to the police force.[20] He reported that Shahin was not the only person interested in making contact with the Zionists in order to counter Hebron's Muslim-Christian Association: "Among many of the most prominent and influential of the Arabs there prevails a movement of awakening, to establish here a Muslim National Association out of hostility toward the tricks of the Muslim-Christian Association."[21] In other words, accepting help from and helping the Zionists derived, in his view, in part from competition over jobs in the British administration and political and social leadership in the new political order.

This was a common phenomenon in the 1920s. Many of those involved in the Muslim National Associations sought help in obtaining jobs. The chairman of the Elected Assembly, David Eder, met with them and listened to their requests. Musa Hadeib, who was later murdered, hoped to be appointed chief of police of the Hebron district. Khalil al-Rasas sought the position of Jerusalem's police chief, and Fa'iq al-Dajani wanted to be a judge and have two of his relatives appointed to administrative positions in the court system.[22]

Sheikh Taher al-Husseini, nephew of Hajj Amin, had similar aims. He wanted to be mufti in place of his uncle and was convinced that he was qualified for the job. He also thought the Zionists ought to be interested in supporting him. In spring 1930 he met several times with Jewish figures, among them Kalvarisky and Ben-Zvi, with the aim of obtaining their help in removing his uncle and getting himself appointed to the position. As a bonus, he offered a most important propaganda coup: he claimed to have in his possession a Turkish deed *(firman)* that authenticated the Jews' rights to the Western Wall. He also promised testimonies that would prove that Hajj Amin had been involved in the riots of 1929.[23] His promises remained on paper and Hajj Amin remained mufti. Taher's son, Zein al-Din, assisted the Zionists in another way. In the mid-1930s he began selling land to Jews and even completed a deal at the height of the Arab rebellion.[24]

Arabs who helped promote the Zionist political agenda and served as informants also asked for compensation. Money was indeed an important motive for collaborators, but some had broader considerations, on the local or national level. The fact that they also received money, and were sometimes blinded by bribes, does not mean the other motives were not real.

LOCAL LEADERS

The Bedouin

Bedouin tribal leaders have a history of cooperating with external powers. Bedouin often perceive their tribe, rather than their national or ethnic affiliation, as their principal focus of identity. This was certainly true of some of the tribes in northern and southern Palestine. During the national movement's formative years, the Bedouin did not view themselves as an integral component of the emerging Palestinian identity.[25] On the contrary, they saw the national movement as a threat, and some of them cooperated with the Zionists for this reason. They ignored the norm that forbade the sale of land and publicly opposed the decisions of the early Palestinian national congresses.[26] When the national movement put down roots, there were tribal leaders who became close to it, while others remained neutral. A few, like the leaders of the Ghazawiyya and Bani-Saqer tribes of the Beisan (Beit She'an) Valley, maintained open contact with Zionist institutions. Collaboration severely affected their lives and the lives of their tribes.*[27]

The Ghazawiyya tribe arrived in the Beisan Valley at the beginning of

---

*These tribes also took in Jews who wanted to become acquainted with their way of life close up. Pesach Bar-Adon (later a Haganah intelligence operative and archeologist) attached himself to the Ghazawiyya for a considerable time, and others lived with the Bani 'Arsan; see Bar-Adon's book, *Be-Ohaley Midbar* [In Desert Tents] (Jerusalem, 1981, in the eighteenth century and captured large territories on both sides of the Jordan. It was led by the Zeinati family. Muhammad, the oldest of the eight brothers who were born to the tribe's sheikh from his five wives, headed the family from the early 1920s. The Bani-Saqer tribe, which also controlled large parts of the Beisan Valley, was headed by the 'Arsan family. When the British took over the country, these tribes tried to rebel against the British garrison stationed in the region. The battle was fierce, but when the tribes were subdued they accepted the yoke of the new regime.[28]

Just as they at first refused to accept British rule, these sheikhs did not view the Palestinian national institutions as their representatives. They explicitly rejected the movement's values, as they expressed in their invitation to the British high commissioner in October 1923.[29]

This attitude, in which the tribe is the principal unit of identity and Arab national aspirations are disregarded (and perhaps rejected), enabled Zionist officials to purchase land from Bedouin and to use them for other missions as well. In retrospect, one could argue that these sheikhs did not assimilate the spirit of the times and the geopolitical and political changes taking place around them. From their point of view, however, they were simply attempting to preserve their positions and the independence of their tribes. This is how Yosef Weitz of KKL, who knew Zeinati, put it: "He served us with real intelligence and devotion. I couldn't say that he saw that as a goal, but he acted steadfastly. His steadfastness grew out of his robust spirit no less than it did from the power of money."[30]

Zionist activists had no compunctions about placing temptations before the sheikhs. According to a British report from 1923, Yisrael Blumenfeld and his partner, named Tannenbaum, invited the brothers Yusuf and Mutlaq al-'Arsan to Tel Aviv. The two land buyers spent a large sum of money to take the Bedouin brothers out on the town, and as a result Yusuf came down with a venereal disease. During the night out the Zionists offered a high price for the tribe's lands in the Beisan Valley.[31] The brothers agreed and also joined the pro-Zionist Muslim National Associations. At that very same time the leader of the neighboring tribe, Emir Muhammad Zeinati, began to work with the PLDC,

---

Hebrew) and Rechavam Ze'evi's introduction there. Yigal Ben-Natan wrote a novel, *Talja Arsan* (Tel Aviv, 1981, in Hebrew), inspired by Jewish shepherds who lived with the 'Arsan family. It tells of the love between one of the shepherds and the sheikh's daughter.

an executive arm of the Zionist movement. Emir Zeinati received a regular salary in exchange for his assistance in land purchases.

During the 1920s the ties between the sheikhs and the Zionist movement grew stronger. When Lord Balfour visited Palestine in April 1925, the Palestinian national leadership declared a day of mourning and a strike. The Beisan Valley sheikhs, for their part, invited Lord Balfour and his party of Zionist officials to visit their camps. "We drank two cups of coffee in order to observe the precept of hospitality and afterward we drove to rest in Nazareth," Kisch related.[32]

This demonstrative act served both sides. The Zionists could advertise that there were Arabs who supported Jewish settlement, and the tribal leaders displayed their independence. But they did not leave it at that. After the bloody events of 1929, the sheikhs began providing security assistance to the Zionists. They signed an agreement with KKL official Yosef Nahmani, who represented the Jewish settlements in the Galilee and Jezreel Valley. Bedouin leaders declared their willingness "to help Jews in their search for people who will harm Jewish lives and property." In addition, they issued general declarations of their desire to preserve friendly relations with Jews and promised to act to counter the economic boycott.[33]

The Beisan Valley sheikhs continued to cooperate with the Zionists during the early 1930s. The leadership families of both tribes, and each sheikh individually, competed over who could become closer to the Zionists and who could sell them more land. They each dealt in different ways with the negative label attached to them. The 'Arsans, one of whom (Nimer) was active in Palestinian national institutions, participated in a public assembly against land sales while continuing to sell their lands to KKL.[34] Muhammad Zeinati made no changes: "[He] was a very clever Arab, very smart, very strong. He didn't have to give explanations to anyone. He ruled the area without constraints. He had people who went with him," explained Moshe Goldenberg, who purchased land in the area for KKL. There was, however, an economic factor that impelled him to sell all his tribe's lands and move his people to Transjordan. "He simply got rich. . . . He reached the conclusion that the Bedouin couldn't live off agriculture. That they couldn't survive. And shepherds, they could be anywhere. It was a good deal with KKL. They received a lot of money and they could buy livestock. So it was with an entirely clear conscience. He undertook the sale of the land of his entire tribe."[35]

The aspiration for political independence thus went hand in hand with the desire to get rich. Goldenberg was a member of Kibbutz Beit

Alfa, at the juncture of the Jezreel and Beisan valleys. The kibbutz belonged to the ha-Shomer ha-Tza'ir movement, whose Marxist ideology saw the liberation of the Arab proletariat and peasantry as one of its goals. Goldenberg thus felt that he had to address the moral implications of land sales for the tribe. His conclusion was that it was "a good deal." It indeed was in the short run, and from the point of view of the tribe's leaders. But it was not necessarily a good one in the middle and long range and for the rest of the tribe's members. Jews established themselves in the Beisan (Beit She'an) Valley on the purchased lands, whereas the tribe's condition deteriorated and the leadership families degenerated.

After selling part of their land, the 'Arsan brothers were no longer the kind of Bedouin leaders they had been at the beginning of the century. Yusuf became "a drinker who had a *nargileh* permanently between his lips." His brother Nimer, who headed the family in the late 1920s through the 1930s, was much the same. This behavior could hardly escape Goldenberg's notice: "A handsome man, but got into bad company. Lived in the city in a two-story house, and didn't pay much attention to farming. All he was interested in was getting payment for his land and he gave us the land without asking questions."[36] Yosef Litvak and Yehoshua Barouchi of the Beit She'an Valley's first religious kibbutz, Tirat Tzvi, had a similar impression from their contacts with the 'Arsan brothers: "Nimer is something of a spendthrift. Spends a lot of time in the city, and for that reason is short on money. . . . He loves lucre like his brother." The only brother who was not like this was Fadel: "A smart Arab, very rich. . . . He opposed us vigorously," Goldenberg related. Barouchi and Litvak wrote that he also received money from PLDC but "always evaded helping us in any real way. There was also evidence that he interfered with the implementation of purchases," that is, he tried to prevent them.[37]

The Zeinatis also liked having a good time in the big city—and by city they did not mean Beisan. Muhammad Zeinati bought the used car of the British district governor, and the rest of the brothers began traveling all over the country in search of fun. "The large amounts of money the Zeinatis and their men had brought them into a kind of life entirely different from that of the Bedouin, who is known for his special customs and traditions. Endless trips to Haifa and other big cities, fancy hotels, Haifa's Carmel district, cafés, replacing horses with automobiles, installing a radio in their tents all caused a huge revolution in their lives and, necessarily, their religion," recalled a member of Kibbutz Maoz Hayyim who was in contact with them.[38]

The sheikhs quickly found themselves in a vicious financial circle. Their ostentatious lifestyle was expensive, and this led to fierce competition among the brothers. They fought over who would serve as agent for land deals involving members of their tribes, deals that were the source of sizable income. They sold more and more of their land and continued to mediate the sale of other people's land, but they could not keep up, as their Jewish contacts recalled:

> Although the brothers sold much land and made much money from that or from salaries or from serving as agents, they couldn't keep hold of the money and quickly wasted it, to the point that they needed afterward to ask for loans from the company. There were also serious quarrels over the payment of compensation. They had to pay the tenant farmers [in exchange for their displacement] and each of the brothers wanted to exploit and deceive his tenants and make money at their expense. It can thus be said with certainty that the tribe deteriorated over time. The endless conflicts forced no small number of families to leave Muhammad or one of the brothers and to move or to flee to Transjordan.[39]

Ironically, though the Zionists and sheikhs had hoped that their dealings would strengthen the tribes as institutions, they actually ended up causing their decline. The sheikhs no longer looked after the well-being of their people and instead squandered the money they received from the Zionists. Whoever could get away from them did so. Some sheikhs continued to cooperate with the Zionists, but they no longer held the positions of power they had once enjoyed. They ended badly. The leader of the Ghazawiyya tribe, Emir Muhammad Zeinati, was murdered in 1946 as he came out of a barbershop in Haifa. After his death, his heirs completed a deal that he had promoted in which they sold all their property to KKL and moved to land they bought in Transjordan. The Bani-Saqer tribe, led by the 'Arsan family, dispersed out of the region during the 1948 war.

Village Sheikhs

Palestine's villages, especially in the central highlands, have from ancient times been united in groups of some ten villages each. At the head of each of these groups, which were called *nawahi* (sing. *nahiya*), stood a family recognized as the regional leader. One member of this family served as the sheikh of the *nahiya*. These sheikhs had political and social strength and sometimes their own armed force. Some of them were recognized as leaders by the Ottomans or received administrative or economic positions.[40]

But the British administration did not recognize the *nawahi*. The crystallization of a national leadership headed by the urban elite also diminished the status of village sheikhs.* They had three options: try to fight the urban elite on their own; support the national urban leadership and derive power from whatever legitimacy the leadership would grant them; or unite forces with the major enemy of the national elite—the Zionists. The choice was not easy, and there were village leaders, like the *nahiya* sheikhs in the Jerusalem area, who shifted back and forth.

The Bani-Malek *nahiya* consisted of villages west of Jerusalem and was headed by the Abu-Ghosh clan. In the Ottoman period this family controlled the road from Jaffa to Jerusalem and collected tolls from travelers. In 1834, during the period of Egyptian rule, one of the family's heads had been appointed governor of Jerusalem. The family's rise was halted when the Ottomans regained control of Palestine.[41]

The connections between the Abu-Ghosh family and Zionist institutions began no later than the early twentieth century. In 1912 the family sold thousands of dunams around its village to Arthur Ruppin, who represented the Zionist movement. At the same time they cultivated ties with the French consulate in Jerusalem, through the mediation of the Franciscan monastery in the village.[42] They also tried the nationalist option: after the British conquest, a representative of the family, Sheikh 'Abd al-Hamid, joined the Muslim-Christian Association in Jerusalem and took part in the first national congress in 1919. Nevertheless, he did not sign the anti-Zionist memorandum drafted by the congress.[43] The disagreement between him and the majority camp, which was centered on the elite urban families, grew sharper the following year when 'Abd al-Hamid opposed concentrating authority in the hands of the Husseini family, and later in the year he resigned from the Muslim-Christian Associations. He and his men severed their connections with the national institutions and began taking independent stands. They did not take part in the disturbances of 1920 and even saw to it that Kiryat Anavim, the kibbutz next to the village, was not attacked. At the same time they prepared and circulated a pro-Zionist petition.[44] From this point forward, some of Abu-Ghosh's leaders worked alongside the Zionists.[45]

When 'Abd al-Hamid Abu-Ghosh left the Muslim-Christian Associations,

---

*Actually, these sheikhs began to lose their power in the late nineteenth century, during the Ottoman reforms, when urban personalities replaced them as tax collectors. This was a main source of the rivalry between them and the urban elite. After British occupation their status continued to deteriorate, since the *nawahi* were no longer recognized as administrative units.

tensions rose between his family and that organization. News of the Abu-Ghosh pro-Zionist petition campaign amplified the hostility of the national movement's leaders.[46] In response, the Muslim-Christian Associations encouraged the leaders of the Bani-Hasan *nahiya* southwest of Jerusalem, who were traditional rivals of the Abu-Ghosh family, to represent the village sector in the national institutions. Sheikh Sa'id Musa Darwish and later his cousin 'Abd al-Fattah Darwish, both from the village of al-Maliha, became confidants of Hajj Amin al-Husseini and his delegates in the villages.

But this alliance, too, did not last long. After the 1929 disturbances, the Supreme Muslim Council established an aid fund for the families of Arabs who had been wounded, killed, or arrested. The Darwishes assumed that one of them would be a member of the fund's board, but the mufti did not appoint any of them. When rumors began to spread that the greater part of the fund's money was ending up in private pockets, the Darwishes made their displeasure plain. The mufti stopped inviting them to meetings of his close advisors. In response, the Bani-Hasan leaders also decided to resign from the national institutions. In March 1930, on the Muslim holiday of 'Id al-Fitr, the mukhtars and sheikhs from the entire *nahiya* gathered at the home of Sheikh Sa'id Darwish in al-Maliha to convey holiday greetings. Darwish took advantage of the opportunity to rouse them against al-Husseini leadership: "You've groveled before the effendis long enough," he told them.

> Enough of flattering them and serving them forever. Don't believe their chatter. Rise up and look at your situation in the rooms of the nation's house. Rise up and search for a single fellah official on the Arab Executive and see if you can find one even in broad daylight. For a moment leave politics to the politicians, to those who have great fortunes and whose idleness drives them mad. We want nothing of either the Zionists or the Arab Executive. We have to come together ourselves. We must present our demands to the government. Why isn't there a trace of a fellah among the government's officials? Why don't we have governors and district officers of our own? Were we not created in the image of God? Do we lack men of wisdom and knowledge who can fill responsible positions in the service of the nation? After all, our people sit here and cite the names of the *'ulama* of their villages whose religious knowledge and wondrous sanctity is greater than that of Hajj Amin al-Husseini.[47]

This bitterness was the result of the disdain the urban leadership held for the villagers. The latter, especially their leaders, sensed that the leadership saw them not as equal partners but rather as tools to be used in the achievement of their goals. The practical expression of the rupture was the attempt to set up a rural party in cooperation with the 'Azzi family of Beit Jibrin, with the covert support of the Zionists.[48] As already noted, that effort ("the 'Ajjur conference") failed, but Darwish had already split with the Husseini leadership. He helped the Zionists buy land (at, among other places, Ramat Rachel just south of Jerusalem, in the area of the Valley of the Cross at what was then west of the city, and at the adjacent Givat Ram, where the Knesset building and Hebrew University were later erected). He later took part in additional organizations set up to oppose the national leadership.[49] The mufti's attempts to win back Darwish's allegiance did not succeed. At the beginning of 1932 he sent a letter to Darwish proposing that they speak in person. Al-Husseini argued that Darwish's actions were causing dissension within the Palestinian nation and helping its enemies. Darwish refused to meet the mufti. Three years later he agreed to see him, at which time the mufti tried to dissuade him from a land sale. The two did not reach an agreement, but Darwish took the opportunity to sell the mufti land he had intended to sell to Jews.[50]

The Darwishes and Abu-Ghoshes were not the only village leaders who collaborated with the Zionist movement. Sheikh Musa Hadeib of Duwaimah, the first Palestinian political leader to be assassinated, was another. Members of the 'Azzi clan, an influential family of Beit Jibrin, remained hostile to al-Husseini leadership (although relations fluctuated over the years), sold a portion of their land to Jews, and served as agents in the sale of other land. The members of the Khawajah family of Ni'lin, north of Lydda, first established ties with the Zionist movement before the British conquest. The head of the family, Sheikh Amin Khawajah, was the acknowledged leader of Ni'lin and the surrounding villages. In 1922 some members of his family solicited signatures on a petition supporting the Balfour Declaration and the Mandate. The Arab press vilified them.[51] A short time later, Sheikh Amin was put on trial for marrying a couple illegally. His Zionist contacts claimed that he was being harassed because of his ties with them and submitted a complaint to the Mandatory government's chief counsel, Wyndham Deedes. Deedes looked into Sheikh Amin's and similar cases involving friends of Jews who had suffered harassment. His intelligence operatives provided him with a less than flattering portrayal of the man: "He is involved in every village intrigue and has so gained influence over the fellahs of the lowest class. . . . considered politically dangerous because of his influence over the ignorant fellahs. Unreliable and unscrupulous."[52] When Sheikh Amin passed away in the 1920s, he was succeeded by his son Sakeb as repre-

sentative of the surrounding villages. Sakeb participated in the Seventh
Palestinian Congress of 1928, in which the village parties also took part.

In August 1929, during the riots, Sakeb Khawajah heard of a plan to
attack the Jewish settlement of Ben-Shemen. He went to the Jewish village's
gate and defended it with his rifle. A few months later he contacted Ben-
Shemen and asked for help reestablishing his family's ties with Zionist officials after a hiatus caused by the recession. He expressed a willingness to
sell land and joined an initiative to establish an organization of Arab villages that would separate itself completely from the Arab Executive. In this
framework he represented his district at the village congress in 'Ajjur.[53]
At the same time, Khawajah served as the villages' representative in the
Muslim-Christian Association of the Lydda region[54]—an attempt to
maneuver between opposing political forces in a situation of uncertainty.

Another village leader who helped and was helped by the Zionist
movement was 'Abd al-Latif Abu-Hantash of Qaqun in the Sharon area.
Like Khawajah, Abu-Ghosh, and Darwish, he was not consistent. Members of the Abu-Hantash family took part in the attack on the Jewish
moshava of Hadera in 1921[55] but quickly changed sides and established
ties with Zionist activists. 'Abd al-Latif was a member of his region's
farmers' party and was involved in land sales. Confident enough to
attack publicly leaders of the national movement who called on him not
to engage in land sales, he claimed that wealthy city Arabs who made
interest-bearing loans to the fellahin were the main cause of land sales.[56]

But make no mistake. Despite their declarations of acting in the interests of the fellahin and against exploitation by urban effendis, the sheikhs
did not always make the welfare of the villages their top priority. The
British viewed them as swindlers who were trying to take advantage of
both Jews and fellahin. In at least some cases Jews involved with them
had the same impression. British intelligence described Abu-Hantash
himself as a fraud and Jew hater and portrayed the Abu-Ghosh family's
informers in a highly negative light.[57] In many ways these village sheikhs
behaved just like the Bedouin sheikhs mentioned earlier: "He was the
king of Qaqun village," Aharon Danin said of Abu-Hantash. "Everyone
who needed to sell came to him. He would take the lion's share, and the
owner would get the tailings."[58] According to one Zionist source, 'Abd
al-Fattah Darwish of al-Maliha worked in a similar way: "[He] was one
of the toughs of the region's villages and used all sorts of acceptable and
unacceptable means to force landowners who owned land in common
with him to sell him their shares. He sold the land he concentrated in his
hands in this way to the Jews."[59] 'Abd al-Rahman al-'Azzi of Beit Jibrin,

sheikh of the *nahiya* of Qaysiyya al-Tahta, worked the same way. Though at first he treated the villagers fairly, when land purchases increased in his area and he needed money, he began to exert pressure. Said Yehoshua Palmon: "I have no doubt that he did everything he could to bring together 3,000 dunams. Conned widows, conned orphans, lent money, and then precisely when it was hard for the man he gave the loan to, he said: bring the money—or hand over the land." Palmon was one of the first members of the Haganah's intelligence service and the man who helped expand Jewish settlements in the Judean foothills.[60] He later served as David Ben-Gurion's advisor on Arab affairs.

This cooperation between Zionists and sheikhs was initially political, based on mutual opposition to al-Husseini leadership. But both the Zionists and the sheikhs quickly realized that the traditional, local leadership could not compete with the new nationalist leadership. As a result, the Zionists focused more and more on purchasing land from the sheikhs (and gathering intelligence with their backing), while the sheikhs focused on their personal financial gain.

The description of Sakeb Khawajah of Ni'lin by United Bureau intelligence activist A. H. Cohen reflects the dual character of these relations: "The impression Sakeb made on me was of a man who had knowledge and an understanding of the country's current diplomatic and political issues. On the other hand, he is also a man who will not do anything without being paid in advance. He can be loyal and devoted to his work but on condition that he is sure that doing so will bring profit to his own pockets."[61]

Nevertheless, it would be wrong to assume that these people's opposition to Hajj Amin and his policies derived only from the economic benefits they gained from the Zionists. The fact that many of them continued to cooperate with the Zionists—even during the Arab rebellion and war of 1948 and despite the harassment of the national movement and its attempts to attract them to the "nation's bosom"—demonstrates that there were other motives, more profound, behind their alliance with the Jews. These motives developed gradually, as shown in later chapters.

THE PATRIOTS

After Israel's establishment, Haifa's Jewish city council replaced the Arabic names of most of the city's streets with Jewish ones. There was one notable exception—the street named after Haifa's venerable mayor, Hasan Shukri. It is no coincidence that an important Haifa street bears his name to this day. Jews saw Shukri as a symbol of coexistence, an Arab who was willing to live with Jews. To Arab nationalists, however, Shukri was a collaborator and traitor.

Shukri was mayor at the time of the British conquest. When, on 11 September 1920, Herbert Samuel arrived in Palestine to serve as the first British high commissioner, Shukri sent him a telegram of congratulations. In doing so, he acted counter to the official Arab position; other Arab leaders boycotted the celebrations surrounding Samuel's investiture because they opposed the Mandate's charter and Samuel's Zionist sympathies. As a result, the members of Haifa's national committees pressured the British administration to dismiss Shukri. The British complied.[62] This was an opportunity to get rid of a man who had displayed pro-Zionist leanings as early as the end of the Ottoman period. Shukri had ties with Jewish land purchasers, among them Shabtai Levi of the Jewish Colonization Association, who would later himself be elected mayor of Haifa. For the Zionists, Shukri's dismissal demonstrated the influence of anti-Zionist Arab officialdom, mainly Christians, on the British. They awaited an opportunity to return Shukri to the mayor's seat. In the meantime, they enlisted him to head the Muslim National Association.

In this capacity, Shukri sent communications to the British government in which he expressed support for Jewish immigration and pointed to Haifa's development as an example of the advantages accruing to the Arabs from the influx of Jews. He was paid for this activity, but he also believed in it. When the members of Haifa's Muslim-Christian Association proposed that he switch allegiance to their group and with their support regain the mayoralty, he rejected the idea out of hand. In a letter to Moshe Shertok nearly two decades later, when the disciples of Sheikh Izz al-Din al-Qassam tried to assassinate him, Shukri wrote:

> If the intention of the assassin and those who sent him was to frighten me and shake my conviction in the justice of my cause, I can declare to you, my dear friend, that they have simply acted in vain. Even more than previously, I stand firm in spirit and imbued with awareness of the need to continue with the same line I have taken up until now in my public work. I hope that my old age will not shame my youth. If this despicable attack, which fortunately failed, will somehow help matters in this country, and especially the matter of public security, I will be thankful to that anonymous and cowardly attacker.[63]

This letter, written in Hebrew, was sent in 1937. Shukri was mayor again. His slate won the municipal elections of 1927 with the support of the city's Jews, who constituted about a third of the population. David

Hacohen, a Haganah official and Shukri's deputy on the city council, viewed him as "a unique phenomenon." In his memoirs he wrote, "The man passed all the cruelest tests in the most severe conditions. . . . [H]is hands are clean. . . . [N]ot a [public] penny went into his pockets."[64]

Shukri belonged to a small group of politicians who rejected the values of the Palestinian Arab national movement. Haidar Tuqan, who worked in coordination with Chaim Weizmann in the Nablus area, and As'ad al-Shuqayri, the respected 'alim (Muslim scholar) of Acre, followed this same tendency. Al-Shuqayri was widely known for his opposition to the national movement and his involvement in land sales. He met routinely with Zionist officials and had a part in every pro-Zionist Arab organization from the beginning of the British Mandate. Rejecting Hajj Amin's use of Islam to assail Zionism, he, like others, did not see the Jerusalem mufti as a serious religious figure.[65] (Ironically, his son, Ahmad, would later found the Palestine Liberation Organization.)

Although one may attribute these men's pro-Zionist activity to personal rivalries and financial gain, this is only partly true—just like the claim that the Husseinis and their supporters acted only out of personal interest. There were two different ideologies. One stressed the danger Zionism represented and concluded that it should be battled. The other argued that uncompromising war with Zionism would cause serious hardship to Palestine's Arabs and that it would thus be best to find ways to live with the Jews in peace. The mayor of Jerusalem, Dr. Mustafa al-Khalidi, stated the diagnosis that brought others (but not himself) to collaborate with the Zionists: "We must recognize the facts. The Jews have entered the country, become citizens, have become Palestinians, and they cannot be thrown into the sea. Likewise, they have bought land and received deeds in exchange for money and we must recognize them. There is no point is closing our eyes about such clear things," he said to his deputy, Daniel Oster, in mid-1935.[66]

Al-Khalidi himself maintained that Jewish immigration and settlement had to be limited. He was also dependent on the Husseinis politically, having been elected with their support. For that reason he decided at the last minute against setting up a moderate political party, as he had planned to do. But a similar analysis, together with criticism of the Husseinis' way of conducting business, led others to collaborate. A prominent example was Muhammad Tawil, who worked as a publicist for the United Bureau in 1929 and 1930.

Tawil was born in Acre in the 1880s into a well-off family and reached officer rank in the Turkish army. After the British conquest he joined the British civil service, but he resigned a short time later to travel in Transjordan and Anatolia. In 1923 he returned to Acre and in 1926 he opened a clerical services office in Tiberias.[67] There he developed contacts with Zionist figures in the region, in particular Tiberias's Jewish mayor, Zaki Alhadif, a member of the United Bureau. After the disturbances of 1929 he testified against Palestinian nationalists who had incited the murder of Jews in Safed. But he invested most of his energy publishing articles and pamphlets condemning the Supreme Muslim Council and favoring Zionism. One of his first publications, in 1930, was the booklet *Tariq al-Hayah* (Way of Life), in which he attacked Hajj Amin al-Husseini. As mentioned earlier, he argued that the mufti had failed as a leader and was bringing on the loss of Palestine.[68]

Hounded by agents of the Supreme Muslim Council, Tawil knew that he was looked on as a traitor. In one of his pamphlets he explained his views, which were shared by other "traitors" whose concept of nationalism lay outside the Palestinian consensus:

> My principle is reform. Reform of the land, reform of our religious life, because religion has weakened and the moral level of many of us has gone bad. That is my goal and that is my principle. Am I a traitor? . . . I am not a traitor, my people. The traitor is he who deceives you and plays with you in order to rob you of your money. And you know who that traitor is. The traitor is he who incited you in the days of the strikes, and there is a reason why dozens of your young men were sentenced to death and for the rest of the judgments.[69]

In another booklet, Tawil described himself as follows:

> I am not a Zionist and I have no contact with the Zionists. Scrutinize my booklets and articles and you will not find in them anything to arouse suspicion. I am more nationalist than others. Our national demands are equivalent but our means differ. Your method will lead you to destruction and to expulsion. A man has a right to criticize, and criticism should not be obstructed. I cannot blindly follow the leaders of the Arab Executive. I cannot believe in a doctor who has not cured our illness after ten years of treatment. I cannot recognize Hajj Amin al-Husseini as the leader of Palestine because his direction has brought no benefit to the country.[70]

Tawil's declaration that he had no contact with the Zionists is hard to take seriously; his letters to the United Bureau have been preserved. What is important in his statements, however, is his conviction that his activity is an alternative path of nationalism. Furthermore, his prediction was correct. Palestine was indeed destroyed and its inhabitants uprooted, partly as a result of Hajj Amin's policies.

Tawil's ties with the United Bureau did not last long. His contact person, Alhadif, described him as "a disreputable man . . . [who] milked the Zionist Executive."[71] In any case, he did not supply the goods; his books and manifestos did not succeed in mitigating Arab opposition to Zionism. And Alhadif was angry that Tawil declared his opposition to land sales to Jews.

In contrast to leaders like Tuqan, al-Shuqayri, and Hasan Shukri, the propagandists who worked for the United Bureau had no social or economic backing. When the Bureau severed its relations with them, they found themselves ostracized from the society in which they lived and pariahs among the people they had sought to become close to. In despair, Tawil tried to settle in Syria, but he was deported by the French authorities there, who suspected that he was a Zionist agent. Crushed and defeated, he returned to Palestine and wrote to the Jewish National Council a letter similar to the grievances that would be voiced by hundreds of collaborators in the generations that followed:

> I can take no more. I have become a man who despises all and is despised by all, and all the gates to making my livelihood are locked. Human decency requires you to take an interest in my plight. I did not testify before the commission of inquiry [on the events of 1929] for any reason other than the internal urging of my conscience, and I did not write my books with the goal of or because of dependence on what you paid me. I relied on your honor and I believed that you would certainly not allow me to suffer and that you would extend a helping hand in time of trouble. . . . If you abandon me and withdraw your hand from me, it will mean that you push me to suicide. And if you want that, that is, if you decide not to help me and not to take an interest in my plight, believe me that I will kill myself, but before I do so I will record the reason for the deed and will publish it in all the newspapers in Europe and the Orient so that the world will know that you are the reason for my death.[72]

Such correspondence went on for several months, during which Tawil traveled to Europe. There he tried to promote the publication of a pro-Zionist newspaper in Arabic and to meet Weizmann, both without success. He submitted an expense account that prompted no response, and in January 1931 he wrote to "Lord Ruler Yitzhak Ben-Zvi" and begged to receive four and a half pounds "because it is the month of Ramadan and the fast and I have not a penny." His letter concluded: "I hereby notify you that if you continue to abuse my rights and refuse to pay this sum after I have proved to you my right, you will cause a bomb to explode."[73]

Ben-Zvi responded dryly. "Since your last letter contains threats and is not written politely, and since information has reached me that you have already commenced hostile actions against me and against the Jews, and you abuse and insult the Jews, etc., I think that it would be beneath my honor to enter into a polemic with you."[74] Tawil, whose prophetic abilities (with regard to the mufti) would later be proved, did not remain silent but summed up his relations with the Zionists with sentiments that many collaborators with the Israeli security agencies could identify with in years to come:

> O leaders, O Jews! You whom I have risked my life to defend, you who do not acknowledge favors and who do not display gratitude. You make friends with people when you need them, and if evil befalls them because of you, you shake off their hands as you did with me. And what would you do to the Arabs if you reached an agreement with them? I think that you would plague their sleep and push them to their deaths. Is that not so?[75]

THE MORALISTS

Another type of collaborator developed good relations with Jewish neighbors, whether Jews of the old established community or of the first *aliya,* the initial wave of Zionist immigrants to Palestine in the late nineteenth century. These Arabs did not view Jewish immigration as a catastrophe. Among them were some who worked in Jewish farming villages and had been treated fairly, who had been treated by a Jewish doctor, who had had business dealings with Jews, or who became personal friends with them. They ignored the rules of the game that came into play with the rise of the Arab national movement, and political changes did not cause them to view Jews as enemies. Zionist activists would later recall a few individual Arabs who identified absolutely with the Zionist enterprise. Moshe Goldenberg, KKL's representative in the Beit She'an Valley, said this of Sheikh Rashid Hasan, one of the mukhtars of Beisan:

> He said the time has come when the Jew must receive his land. Once when I had negotiations with an Arab over the price of land he broke in and said, "*Khawajah** Musa, you are not buying dunams, you are buying a homeland, and that has no price." This Arab simply recognized that the time had come for us to buy the land, and he helped us with that with all his heart.[76]

But even in cases where identification with the cause was not quite so complete, social ties led Arabs to provide assistance in areas forbidden by

*A polite form of address used when speaking to a non-Muslim.

the Arab Palestinian ethos. Several Arab families lived, for example, within the bounds of the Jewish farming village of Nes-Tziona. The best known of these was the Taji al-Farouqi family. Some members of it, such as Shukri Taji al-Farouqi, joined the national movement, while 'Abd al-Rahman "did favors for the moshava and assisted in the redemption of the land around it, and not always only for profit. He was a friend of the settlement in thought and in action," members of the community wrote.[77]

In the first years of British rule this was a fairly common phenomenon, the best evidence being the many attacks on the "Jews' friends" printed in the Palestinian Arab nationalist press. Not all those who held these views cooperated with Jews actively. Most of them kept their beliefs to themselves and did little more than maintain neighborly relations even in tense times. But some chose to collaborate actively, sometimes even openly. One such person was Ibrahim 'Abdin of Ramla, who headed that city's branch of the Muslim National Associations.

'Abdin belonged to a family that for years had had good relations with the Jews. Immediately after the British conquest and establishment of the Zionist Executive in Palestine, he attached himself to its members. Among his activities was the establishment of an espionage network in the service of the information office (Murshid Shahin of Hebron, mentioned above, was also involved), the founding of the Muslim National Associations branch in Ramla, and promotion of the elections to the legislative assembly in 1923 on behalf of Zionist institutions. When Chaim Weizmann visited Palestine in 1922, 'Abdin, like many other Arab figures, asked to meet with him. The Zionist Executive recommended him as worthy of being honored with a visit by Weizmann. 'Abdin took advantage of the opportunity to make a formal speech in which he held forth on his view of good relations based on a recognition of Jews' right to live in Palestine. Like other collaborators, he skirted the Arab national question. His speech indicates that he did not ask himself about the future of the Arabs in Palestine, and the Zionists who benefited from his services did not, for their part, bother to point out this omission.*[78]

---

*Another example of Zionist activists hiding their real goals while speaking to Arabs who were ready to cooperate with them is Ben-Gurion's speech to the rail workers' council, a joint Jewish-Arab body, in January 1925. Avraham Khalfon, who was translating the speech into Arabic, changed and softened Ben-Gurion's rhetoric. He assumed that if the Arabs present understood Ben-Gurion's statements on Jewish immigration and settlement, they would resign from the union. See Zachary Lockman, "'We Opened the Arabs' Brains': Zionist Socialist Discourse and the Rail Workers of Palestine, 1919–1929" (in Hebrew), in Ilan Pappe, ed., Aravim vi-Yhudim bi-Tkufat ha-Mandat [Arabs and Jews in the Mandate Period] (Givat Haviva, 1995), 113–114.

Disregard of the "big" national questions was characteristic of many who helped the Zionist movement out of friendship, although 'Abdin himself took pains to stress that he was not a traitor to his people.[79] Even so, as friction between the two sides increased, so did the need to compensate the collaborators. For years 'Abdin received, for various reasons, not insignificant sums of money. He applied to the Zionist Executive before holidays and asked for money to host his associates, and when he or his family became burdened with debt he asked Colonel Kisch for relief.[80]

Most of 'Abdin's activity was in the fields of politics and intelligence. In many other cases, friendship or neighborliness led Arabs to pass on warnings. An early example can be found in the diaries of Yosef Trumpeldor, the leader of Jewish defense forces in the Upper Galilee after World War I. Diary entries from the days leading up to the attack on Tel Hai in 1920, in which Trumpeldor was killed, indicate that contact between Tel Hai and nearby Jewish settlements was maintained with the help of Arabs from nearby villages. These Arabs also told the garrison at Tel Hai about the plans to attack them.[81] About a decade later, during the riots of summer 1929, the Jewish farming village of Migdal, on the shores of the Sea of Galilee, was in much the same situation. Pinhas Grobovsky, the village guard, described it:

> We sit in Migdal's central yard and an Arab friend passes information on to me. Why an Arab friend? Because I advised him not to join the robbers. In the end the robbery won't take place and order will be restored and why on the day of judgment should he be taken among the ruffians. That is what I said to that Arab and changed his heart to respect me. One day the Arab told me that that night a large crowd would attack us.[82]

Thanks to this friend's warning, the people of Migdal were able to prepare for and repel the attack. Guard Alexander Zeid, whose family lived alone on Sheikh Ibriq hill between Haifa and the Jezreel Valley, received from his friend Sliman al-Qteishi information that the hill was about to be attacked. Al-Qteishi invited Alexander's family to be his guests in his tent until the danger passed, but Alexander refused. In the end, al-Qteishi took only the children, who were thus in a safe place during the attack.[83] A similar example is that of Sheikh Yusuf al-Heib, who sent some of his men to defend Kibbutz Ayelet ha-Shahar, Kibbutz Mahanayim, and other Jewish settlements.[84]

Friendly relations with Arabs also helped Jewish military and intelligence personnel defend and secure other Jewish settlements. The mukhtar

of the village of Battir, whose alias was "Na'aman," was a friend of Yitzhak Ben-Zvi, A. H. Cohen, and other Jews and worked for the United
Bureau. He presented his thinking at a meeting of mukhtars in 1930 in the
home of the sheikh of the Bani-Hasan *nahiya*, Sa'id Musa Darwish, in the
village of al-Maliha. A transcript of his talk survives and provides a rare
glimpse into the internal world of a collaborator. It should be kept in
mind, however, that the talk was recorded by Cohen, who attended the
meeting in Arab dress.

The mukhtars discussed the situation in the country, and Darwish
turned to "Na'aman," who was under his protection, and asked to hear
his opinion. The form of address reveals the relations between the two:
"And you, the Jew [as he was known because of his ties to Jews], will
you remain silent, speak you as well and slay your father in his grave,
speak and we will hear your words." "Na'aman" replied:

> Before I voice my words I know that you will treat my words with con-
> tempt, because I am known to all of you as a traitor. And I admit and
> confess that I am a traitor, I am a traitor to the twisted ways that the
> leaders of the Supreme Muslim Council have chosen for you, and so
> I will always be. The day will come when you will slaughter me like
> a sheep, but that is a different matter. I will continue in the same direc-
> tion. I cannot under any circumstances betray people in whose salt I
> have dipped my bread. Let those who sit here with us, the mukhtars
> of Walaja, Sir'a, Dir Aban and Ishwa', please say, what have the people
> of Har-Tuv sinned against you that we have brought this catastrophe
> on them [the attack in 1929]? Let them [the mukhtars] swear in the
> name of the saint 'Uqash, may he rest in peace, and see whether they
> can tell of any evil that the Jew "Qaqun" (Levi) and his partners did
> to them. Have they done evil to you by employing you in their hyssop
> production . . . answer me, you elders. I have sworn you by your
> maker, answer!
>
> *The elders:* No, by God, they have done us no evil. The prophet forbade
> lies.
>
> *"Na'aman":* And you, the elder from Beit Safafa [Hajj Ibrahim al-Khalil,
> mukhtar of Beit Safafa], please tell me — in the name of the angels I
> have sworn you, what evil have the poor Jews of Mekor Hayyim done
> to you? Please tell me and we will put out their eyes. And on the other
> hand please be so good as to enumerate before us the good things that
> our brothers have done for you, those who call themselves the leaders
> of the nation, so they say.[85]

These vigorous arguments were much the same as those in the manifestos of the pro-Zionist Muslim National Associations: the Jews have
brought only blessings, and they should not be fought. But "Na'aman"

added a personal, moral note: Our neighbors should not be harmed, because they are people who have helped us in our livelihoods and hosted us in their homes and have done us no evil. Hurting them is a violation of human morality and the commands of the Prophet, and these values are greater than the so-called national duty. These ideas (in combination, of course, with additional factors such as his competition with his village's other mukhtar, Mustafa Hasan, and his economic ties with Jews) led him to tie himself to A. H. Cohen and serve as one of his major sources of information. In this capacity he traveled throughout the country to collect security and political information.

Yehoshua Palmon was acquainted with collaborators of this type: "They thought the greatest benefit to Arabs would come from living at peace with Jews. I would not say that they saw the political picture, but they were people who were in fact identified with us in daily life, involved, integrated, and thanks to us they became decent human beings." Ezra Danin, one of the founders of the Haganah's information service, spoke of one of the guards who worked at his citrus grove who was also involved in land sales: "He believed in the return to Zion and wanted cooperation with the Jews. That he in the meantime received some money makes no difference. I remember an instance in which I once said to him: You do it for the money, of course. Why do you get so angry if they tell you that you are a hired spy? He said: I for money? I work only for the idea."[86]

Of course, the idea was not just the return to Zion. More frequently it was the simple principle of neighborliness. In the case of the Bedouin, this principle was well grounded in tribal common law, which imposed much more severe penalties on a person who hurt a neighbor than on a person who hurt a stranger. The elders of 'Arab al-Turkeman, a Bedouin tribe that lived in the Jezreel Valley and the Iron Hills, told a woman research historian from the tribe that in the 1920s and 1930s they hesitated to join the national struggle because they felt that by doing so they would violate the sacred principle of neighborliness. The principle seemed all the more sacred because they had good relations with the inhabitants of Pardes Hannah and other Jewish settlements.*[87]

This may cast light on why some of Hebron's Arabs supported the return of Jews to the city after the massacre of 1929, in contradiction to

---

*The tribal elders said that before joining the rebellion of 1936 they moved away from the environs of Binyamina to free themselves of the obligation to observe *huquq al-Jar,* the law of neighbors. This testimony was given to an Arab researcher, Ulya al-Khatib, outside the borders of Israel. Such claims are thus not voiced only to please Israeli audiences. They constitute part of the reality and discourse of the Arabs of Palestine.

the position taken by the Arab national leadership and despite its intimidation. Though the support for return of the Jews largely reflected economic needs, the Arabs of Hebron, including those who helped Jews during the massacre, also cited the social and moral aspect of the initiative.

In May 1931, A. H. Cohen met the president of Hebron's chamber of commerce, Ahmad Rashid al-Hirbawi, who voiced his support for the Jews' return to the city. Cohen asked him how that could be reconciled with the Supreme Muslim Council's position. Al-Hirbawi replied that a representative of the national institutions had already attacked him for his opinion, but that his answer had been, "The Jews have a claim to be natives of this city no less than we do. The Jews have lived on our land for more than three hundred years and no one may deny them their right to live in the city of their birth."[88]

On the evening of that same day, Cohen visited Sheikh Shaker al-Qawasmeh. Several other of the city's dignitaries also came to his house. They spoke of their meeting with the king of Hejaz and Najd (today's Saudi Arabia), 'Abd al-'Aziz Ibn Sa'ud, while on their pilgrimage to Mecca:

> When 'Abd al-'Aziz learned that his guests were Hebronites, he reprimanded them: Is this the way you observe the word of God? And how will the Prophet pray for you when you have washed your hands in the blood of women and babies who have no power and no valor. Please bring me the six books of God and show me in one of their pages the verse that says it is permitted to slaughter Jews! And who permitted you to make innovations in the religion and speak in the name of the Prophet and say that the Prophet commanded the slaughter of Jews? Shame, shame and disgrace for you leaders of the city. This cup shall pass to you because God will not absolve those who do such deeds.[89]

Ibn Sa'ud's position seems to have derived also from his pro-British tendencies and his overall political outlook.[90] But his religious terminology and the morality that lies behind it should not be dismissed. The context in which he was quoted indicates that at least some of those present agreed with the king's sentiments. They did not enlist in the Zionist movement's intelligence apparatus, but some of them were reinforced in their opposition to the Supreme Muslim Council and supported the return of the Jews to their city. For many other Palestinians, this was enough to brand them as traitors. The process of bringing the Jews back to Hebron, however, was cut short by the Arab rebellion that broke out five years later, which utterly changed the fabric of relations between Jews and Arabs in Palestine.

PART II

REBELS AND TRAITORS,
1936–1939

CHAPTER 4

OLD COLLABORATORS,
NEW TRAITORS

On 15 April 1936, armed Arabs, apparently acolytes of Sheikh Izz al-Din al-Qassam of Haifa, murdered two Jews on a road near Tulkarem. In response, members of Haganah Bet, a militant Jewish group that had broken from the Haganah, murdered two Arab workers near Petah Tikva. During the workers' funeral, Arabs in Jaffa attacked Jews and murdered nine of them. So began the great Arab rebellion. For Palestine's Arabs, the military option passed from theory into practice.[1]

On the day of the funeral, nationalist activists (most of them members of al-Istiqlal and supporters of the Husseinis) assembled in Nablus and declared a general strike. The strike quickly spread throughout the country. In cities and villages national committees organized to supervise the strike. Within a week, Palestinian political parties had established a joint leadership, the Higher Arab Committee, to coordinate and direct events. At the same time, combat units (called "gangs" by the Jews and the British) organized and began to attack British and Jewish targets as well as Arab collaborators.[2]

The general strike lasted for 175 days and was later considered the first stage of the rebellion. It ended only after the British sent major military reinforcements to Palestine, threatened to impose military rule, and pressed rulers of Arab countries to exert their influence to end the uprising. For the next nine months (October 1936–July 1937) the country was relatively calm as a royal commission headed by Lord Peel examined ideas for solving the Palestine problem. The commission published its recommendations in July, proposing partition of the country into an independent Jewish state and an Arab state to be united with Trans-jordan. After the recommendations were published, Arab forces commenced attacks on potential Arab supporters of partition. In September 1937, after an attack on Lewis Andrews, acting governor of the Galilee district—and after the aggressive measures the British took in response—the uprising broke out again, now in full force.* Thousands of villagers joined the rebels in the spring, and there were renewed attacks on Jewish settlements and institutional targets representing British rule, such as police stations, courthouses, banks, and British vehicles. The rebels also struck out against Arab "traitors." At the peak of the uprising, in summer 1938, rebels controlled most of the country's rural areas and had partial sway over the cities. A concerted British military effort on the eve of World War II forced many rebel commanders to retreat over Palestine's borders. The rest were killed. By the end of 1939 the rebellion was largely over.

The revolt led to two significant changes in collaboration between Arabs and the Zionist movement. For one, the scope of the term "treason" was broadened in Arab public discourse. Actions previously considered legitimate or tolerable were now outside the pale, and the number of "traitors" rose accordingly. Additionally, sanctions against traitors became much more severe. A society at war requires solidarity. A person who balked at taking an active role in the uprising, all the more so a person who violated the new norms, was thus seen to be thwarting the collective will and preventing the nation from attaining the objectives it was paying in blood to achieve. This explains the Arabs' willingness to use the ultimate weapon—murder—in their struggle against deviators. It was only natural that the leadership encouraged such deeds. If it allowed violators to act as they wished, the leadership could not present itself as the representative of the nation as a whole.

The Arab military leadership also had a vested interest in wiping out collaboration; popular support improves the quality of combat operations. Collaboration with the enemy not only reduces the chances of success but also places fighters in danger. It is hardly surprising, then, that

---

*Andrews seems to have been an intentional target. Among the district governors, he was one of the most enthusiastic supporters of Zionist settlement. Aharon Danin related that Andrews was a good friend of the land buyer Hankin: "He admired him. . . . Andrews helped Hankin considerably in the purchase of the Hula [Valley]." Testimony by Aharon Danin, 23 April 1971, OHD-HU 57–9. See also the testimonies of Moshe Goldenberg and Yosef Weitz, ibid.

the murder of collaborators (true or imagined), rare before the rebellion, now became a matter of course.[3]

But attacking traitors does not always create unity. In the Palestinian case, it did the opposite, alienating important people and groups, who refused to accept the new norms and distanced themselves from the leadership. Social and political unity actually declined, and new forms of collaboration appeared, including actual combat against Arab rebels.

PUTTING NATIONALISM TO THE TEST

When the riots and general strike began, Arab political parties established the Higher Arab Committee as a symbol of unity. "Because of the general feeling of danger that envelops this noble nation, there is a need for solidarity and unity and a focus on strengthening the holy national jihad movement," the founding declaration stated.[4]

The parties united to fight on behalf of generations to come. An al-Istiqlal manifesto stated that present sacrifice would prevent the future loss of Palestine. The editor of *al-Jami'ah al-Islamiyya*, Suliman al-Taji al-Farouqi, stressed the danger to the mosques on al-Haram al-Sharif (the Temple Mount), which could be lost forever. The Higher Arab Committee issued declarations calling on the people to persist with the strike.[5] It took no time at all before someone took it upon himself to oversee observance of the new rules. On the strike's tenth day an underground group called "the Lightning" organized in Jerusalem. They published their goals on placards they pasted up throughout the city:

> To fight imperialism and Zionism with all our might.
> To fight any person who does not surrender to the will of the people or who thinks of stepping out of bounds.
> To fight any person who schemes to do anything against the interests of the nation and the homeland.
> To fight every man who does not help his homeland and who helps cause it damage.[6]

This was an attempt to create a consensus, and it hints at what is to come. Of the four missions formulated by the group, three were directed inward at Arab society, only one at external forces. The placards contained the seeds of mayhem because of the broad definition of targets. The group placed in its sights not only those who acted against Palestinian interests but also those who "schemed," as well as those who remained passive and who did not help the homeland.

This way of thinking was not unique to the Lightning. The Moham-med's Youth Association, a group organized around students of Sheikh al-Qassam in Haifa (the cities were at the time the focal points of the rebellion and the strike), issued a declaration that defined the enemies of the nation as follows: "1. Muslims who betray the homeland who are: robbers of the *zakat* [charity funds], the *samasirah* [land speculators], in-formers, sellers of land, and civil servants; 2. hypocrites among the Chris-tians; 3. British and all other imperialists; 4. Jewish dogs who dream of a national home and Jewish kingdom."[7] Here, too, it was treasonous Arabs, not the British and Jews, who were the principal enemies. Similar messages were disseminated extensively in mosques and in the national-ist press.[8]

As we have seen, land speculators and sellers, informers working with the British and Jews, and those who provided political assistance to the Zionist movement were already considered traitors before the uprising. But with the start of the rebellion, sanctions against them were made much more severe. The most important change, however, was the inclu-sion of a new range of actions under the rubric of treason.

Strikebreakers

Toward the end of April 1936, the face of Palestine's cities changed. Businesses closed, both public and private Arab transport halted, and schools shut their gates. Schoolchildren were on the streets, either on protest marches or warning storekeepers who did not observe the sanc-tions. Striking workers congregated outside. The newspapers counted off the days of the strike on their front pages, creating an expectation that it would achieve its goals in short order. In such an atmosphere, nationalists viewed strikebreakers as acting against the nation's vital interests. Strikebreaking was the first new violation to be added to the definition of treason.

The nationalist press was one of the most important means for instill-ing this idea in the public mind. The Husseini party organ, *al-Liwaa,* which commenced publication just a few months before the rebellion broke out, led this campaign. It printed letters of support for the strike from various bodies, such as the 'ulama of Acre, villagers in the Ramla district, and village dignitaries of the Bani-Hasan *nahiya.* The newspaper also publicized lists of people who had donated to the strike fund, and they became the new national heroes.[9] In parallel, the newspaper worked to make public opinion hostile to those who deviated from the nationalist line. On 26 April, *al-Liwaa* published an advertisement under the headline "Exceptions to the National Consensus on the General Strike." It declared that from that point forward it would print the names of people who opened their stores: "Beware lest you find yourself on the list," it warned.[10]

Publication of strikebreakers' names was not systematic and did not encompass the entire country. But attacks on strikebreakers became a national sport. "Some small schoolboys were wandering the streets and wanted to do something to demonstrate their national feelings. When they saw some people who had placed themselves outside the general public by opening their stores, they threw stones and poured [filthy] liquid on them," *al-Liwaa* reported.[11] The Haifa bureau of Shai, the Haganah's intelligence service, saw the phenomenon differently. It reported that juvenile delinquents were running through the open-air markets with clubs, thrilled at the opportunity to vandalize and beat up produce merchants and laborers.[12]

These schoolboys may have acted spontaneously, as the newspaper implied. If so, it would be evidence that the nationalist principle of fighting traitors had percolated down to the younger generation. But most of the activity against violators was accomplished by men hired by the national committees.[13] The methods varied. The first was an appeal to the violator's conscience. Young nationalists offered food to storekeepers who broke the strike. "We know that you work so that you can bring food home," they said. "Strike and we'll see to it that you don't go hungry." There were those who closed their stores out of shame, *al-Liwaa* wrote.[14] Humiliation and threats were used in other cases. A driver from Nablus who broke the strike was banned by the drivers' union, and children in the city mounted a dog on a donkey and hung a sign on them condemning the driver. A Jerusalem storekeeper refused to close his shop and the national committee sent boys to dump a bucket of sewage on his head. Arabs who worked as laborers or guards for Jews received threatening letters and were warned that they would be punished if they did not strike.[15]

The next stage was the destruction of merchandise and physical attacks. In Haifa, Arab women destroyed the goods of merchants who broke the strike.* In Acre, schoolchildren broke into a sugar factory and

---

*Later, women were appointed to oversee the strike in other cities as well. George 'Azar, an informer in Jaffa, reported that "Arab women patrol the streets of Tel Aviv" for this purpose. In Jerusalem, three of the eight strike enforcers were women. See Eshel, *Ma'arkhot ha-Hagana*, 134; Jewish Agency's intelligence reports, 10 and 12 August 1936, CZA S25/22460.

emptied sacks of sugar. A storekeeper in Far'oun, near Tulkarem, was beaten. These were individual instances of actions of a sort that occurred daily during the strike's first weeks.[16] Most of the public participated, and violators placed their livelihoods, sometimes their lives, in jeopardy. Arabs who worked for the telegraph and train systems, for example, did not strike, and at the beginning of June a rail worker was murdered. The next day his colleagues joined the strike.[17] The move to define strike-breaking as treason was complete.

Economic Traitors

Maintaining economic contact with Jews was viewed by Palestinian Arab nationalists as even worse than breaking the strike. The common label for violators of the boycott was *khawarij* (deviants, dissenters, viola-tors). The term was a heavily charged one in Muslim history; it was the name of a sect that split away from both the Sunnis and Shia after the battle of Siffin in the year 657 and was considered heretical by both major streams of Islam. The nationalists viewed the *khawarij*, many of whom were fellahin whose livelihood was selling their produce to Jews, as a double threat: they ignored the strike and also helped the Jews with-stand it. Moreover, violation of the boycott while making a profit was liable to tempt others to ignore the directives of the national leadership and so subvert the strike.[18] That was another reason to use drastic mea-sures against the *khawarij*.

Here, too, the press represented the national interest. So, for example, *al-Liwaa* reported, under the headline "*Khawarij* News," about mer-chants from Tulkarem who sent merchandise to Jerusalem by train. It published other articles, for example, about a Jerusalem attorney who continued to work with Jews while flagrantly ignoring the strike, and about the residents of Arab neighborhoods in Jerusalem who continued to use Jewish public transportation. "Apparently their delicate bodies cannot bear the burden of walking," *al-Liwaa* sneered. Along with such jabs, it proposed sending activists to indoctrinate villagers.[19]

Harangues, attacks, and the risk of being branded a traitor did not prevent all collaboration. So the nationalists soon resorted to more dras-tic means of enforcement. They began confiscating the merchandise of violators, beating them, and humiliating them. The ways of degrading vio-lators grew more sophisticated after the strike's first month. A livestock trader was apprehended near Petah Tikva as he tried to smuggle twenty head of cattle into a Jewish farming village. According to *al-Liwaa*, the cattle were slaughtered and the smuggler was beaten and half his beard shaved off.[20]

Threats, humiliations, mild beatings, and the destruction of merchandise brought no real change. These same methods had been used in 1929–30,[21] but this time the rebels did not stop with them. The rebellion was seen as a matter of life and death. Soon the nationalists began to use arms against strikebreakers and collaborators.

The first attacks were with light weapons. At the beginning of May an Arab who smuggled vegetables into Jewish neighborhoods in Jerusalem was stabbed. *Al-Liwaa* wrote that the results were positive: "The lesson given to the few *khawarij* proved itself effective. Only one storekeeper in [the Jerusalem Arab neighborhood] Musrara opened his store yesterday."[22] But a few days later firearms came into use, a major ratcheting up of the sanctions against "traitors." Until then, it was extremely rare for even blatant collaborators to be shot.

The first victim was an Arab laborer in a quarry near Givat Shaul, in western Jerusalem. On the night of 12 May 1936, at midnight, a band of twenty armed Arabs descended on the quarry and attacked the Arab workers there. The laborers claimed in defense that the factory was an Arab one (a lie), but to no avail. "You are dogs and deserve death," the attackers said. They shot two of the workers. The tracks they left led to a house in Lifta, a village in a valley not far from the factory. The owner of the house was a nationalist activist who spoke out in favor of the strike. He was arrested by the police.[23] Two days later, shots were fired at produce merchants in Jerusalem, and the body of another Arab was found in the Old City. Everyone assumed that he had been killed for violating the strike.[24]

A Muslim legal ruling permitting such murders was disseminated openly in early July.[25] The public responded accordingly. During the course of that month the body of an Arab turned up near Hadera, alongside merchandise he intended to smuggle into the Jewish village. It turned out that he had been cautioned several times not to do business with Jews but had not heeded the warning. His fellow villagers applied the age-old sanction reserved for murdered traitors, refusing to bury him in his family plot.[26]

At this time rebels, most of whom were villagers and fellahin who had migrated to the cities, were active throughout the country. They attacked government institutions and Jewish settlements, set fire to fields, and chopped down orchards. By the end of May, twenty-nine Jews had been killed, and during the four months that followed sixty-two more were murdered.[27] The Arab press reported, with considerable exaggeration, that Jews were abandoning small settlements and moving to the cities, because of both the attacks and the shortage of food and other necessities. More than ever, Arabs who did business with Jews were seen to be delaying victory. Sometimes they were sentenced to death. In many other cases the rebel units imposed less severe punishments. The owner of a watermelon patch who sold his produce to Jews was warned, and when he did not desist armed rebels killed his three horses. They confiscated cows from boycott violators in the Jerusalem area and used the animals to feed the guerrillas.[28] In all these cases the message was unambiguous.

Putting Friendship to the Test

On a clear spring day in mid-May 1936, an Arab boy set out on a trip from Jerusalem. With him in his car were two Jewish girls. The boy's name was Victor Lulas. To the nationalists he was a criminal two times over. He was driving a car, in violation of the leadership's strike orders, and he had maintained his social ties with Jews. When he reached the turn in the road by the village of Abu-Ghosh, a group of young men stopped him. They dragged him out of the car, beat him, and then sent him on his way. In another such instance a young man from Beit Jala who was romantically involved with a young woman from the Jewish neighborhood of Rechavia in Jerusalem was rescued from a beating but received threats and had his love life written up in the press.[29]

These were the new traitors. Without changing their ways and their habits, they suddenly found themselves outside their society's norms. Patronizing a Jewish doctor or employing Jewish workers also became illegitimate: "We do not want to see Jews in our village," the Husseini newspaper declared unequivocally.[30]

The rupture between Arab and Jewish populations widened as the strike continued and the demand for ending all contacts with Jews grew more pervasive. People who were once friendly with Jews were forced to sever relations; those who did not were attacked. In the Beit She'an Valley, Arabs were afraid to be seen with Jewish friends in public, thinking that rumors would spread that they were passing intelligence to the Jews.[31] Yosef Nahmani of KKL wrote to Yitzhak Ben-Zvi about Sheikh Ahmad Salih of Zawiyya, who had friends in Kibbutz Kfar Giladi and had openly taken their part in 1929. After the rebellion broke out, the veteran Jewish defense figure, Nahum Horowitz, visited Salih and heard the following confession from him:

Listen, Nahum, we have been friends for many years, and I hope that after this period of rage passes we will again be friends. But now, I am sorry to tell you, the black times we are in do not allow me to carry on my friendship with you. . . . I must act this way. I cannot separate myself from my nation. People in the village are starting to shun me and they will soon leave me.[32]

In these "black times," any expression of friendship with the Zionists was viewed as aiding the enemy. National values had to be given precedence over family ties, friendship, traditional social structures, and personal opinions. Arab friends of Jews risked not only social banishment but also death. That was the fate of Hasan 'Omar, the son of the village sheikh of Huseniyya in the Upper Galilee. The sheikh and his family had close ties with the Jewish settlements in the area and did not sever them when the rebellion broke out. At the beginning of July a group of rebels attacked his home and shot his son dead.[33]

Law and Order

Rebel units and militant groups such as the disciples of Sheikh al-Qassam tried at this time to establish norms that forbade cooperation with the Mandate government. The Husseini leadership was hesitant about this, because Hajj Amin himself was a senior civil servant and had brought many of his close associates into the British administration as well.

In May and June 1936, attacks on government buildings, police stations, and Jewish settlements became routine. The nationalist demand that Arabs sever ties with the British administration grew louder. Leaflets issued by rebel forces called, with the backing of the press, for the mukhtars to resign first.[34] In mid-June the press reported that the mukhtars in the villages around Ramla, Jenin, and Haifa had resigned en masse. The judges of the tribal court in the Negev also announced that they no longer functioned on the basis of their government appointments. Here, too, *al-Liwaa* played an active role, threatening to publish the names of mukhtars who did not obey the resignation order.[35]

At the beginning of June anonymous placards pasted on the walls of government buildings in Nablus called on civil servants to join the general strike. It gave them a month's grace period and warned that those who did not obey would be sentenced to death. Another poster accused two Nablus opposition leaders, Taher al-Masri and Ahmad al-Shak'a, of treason because of their contacts with the government. This poster was signed by the Black Hand, a name adopted by several underground groups, not necessarily related.[36] This was an indication of events to come. Public accusations against the Nashashibi-led National Defense Party had ceased with the establishment of the Higher Arab Committee, but it was only a matter of time before they resurfaced. At the same time, the poster criticized the mufti and his circle, who continued to hold on to their government jobs. The mufti was losing room to maneuver between the rebels and the government.

The general public's view was, however, that not all service in the British administration could be considered treason—only those positions involved in keeping public order or fighting the rebels. It was not long before social sanctions were imposed on policemen. When the leader of al-Aqsa mosque's boy scout troop joined the police force in May 1936, he was fired from his scout position. This was a clear statement about the dominant Arab attitude to the police force and service therein. Most Arab anger was directed at policemen who were overly diligent in investigating the terrorist acts of rebels or in dispersing demonstrations. At first such policemen were merely banned socially. Police officer Hasan Makkawi, who served in Acre, came down hard on demonstrators there. On more than one occasion he had opened fire on Arab crowds and desecrated the Arab flag. At this point no retaliatory action was taken against him, but members of the Makkawi family in Nablus published notices declaring that they had severed contacts with him and bore no responsibility for his actions.[37]

This was the situation as of mid-May, but when the campaign against collaborators escalated, Arab policemen became a main target. On 21 May one in Acre was shot and wounded, and on 28 May rebels attacked and wounded a Christian Arab policeman, making off with his gun in the process. In June rebels murdered an Arab guard at a Jewish citrus grove near Ekron and threw his body into a well.[38] Haifa saw the fiercest fight against Arab policemen, led by the disciples of al-Qassam. Toward the end of July an Arab police detective was shot and wounded as he pursued a suspect. The detective fired back at his attacker and killed him. A few days later nationalist and religious activists assembled in Haifa with delegates from Hebron and Gaza and decided to murder the detective and prepare a list of other traitors to be executed. The list included police officer Ahmad Na'if, who had been involved in the capture of Izz al-Din al-Qassam's band less than a year earlier. Na'if, like Hasan Makkawi, had continued to fight terror after the strike broke out.[39]

On 2 August, gunmen shot and killed Na'if and wounded another policeman who was with him. It was a heavy blow to the British police;

Na'if had been one of the pillars of the fight against the rebels. But public reaction to the murder was no less important than the bullets that killed the detective. Every mosque in Haifa locked its doors during the afternoon prayers in order to keep the British from bringing them the body for burial, and not a single Muslim cleric was willing to conduct the funeral service. When police officer Muhammad Ja'ouni tried to persuade one sheikh to allow the service in his mosque, an angry crowd gathered around him and shouted, "All those who aid traitors—are traitors." Ja'ouni gave up trying. "Such is the fate of the traitors who brought about the death of the martyr al-Qassam," declared the underground Communist newspaper *Jabha Sha'biyya*. "It is a lesson to all those whose conscience has died, to all those who have lost their honor." The Islamist sheikh had become a national symbol whom even the Communists adopted. Na'if was finally buried in the village of Yajour, and the police had to station a guard at his grave to prevent the exhumation and defacement of the body.[40]

Ten days later Sergeant Shafiq al-Ghussayn was shot and killed in Jerusalem. His body was unearthed and burned after his burial. In Safed a police detective from the 'Abd al-Hadi family was shot dead. "He was one of those called *jawasis* [spies] and caused much damage," Izzat Darwaza of al-Istiqlal noted in his diary.[41] Mukhtars who refused to resign, not to mention those who closely collaborated with the security forces and with Jews, were murdered. The mukhtar of Tirat-Haifa, Muhammad Sheikh-Yunis, was one of the first. Sheikh-Yunis was accused of treason (and had also feuded with 'Abdallah Salman, an associate of the mufti).[42] His body was found in his village toward the end of August.[43]

The assassinations seem to have been carried out in accordance with the decision made at a gathering of representatives from all over the country. An intelligence report from mid-August stated that a decision had been made that month by rebels from Jerusalem, Haifa, Jenin, Tulkarem, and Nablus to execute all Arabs who gave aid to the government or the Jews, including those who did business with Jews.[44]

The Doubters

The widening circle of assassinations testified to the existence of militant groups that viewed murder as a legitimate political act. But even more so it indicated the growing opposition to the general strike. This showed that the Palestinian Arab national consensus was beginning to unravel.

One salient sign that some circles were dissatisfied with the rebellion was the opposition's support for Emir 'Abdallah's mediation initiative. The emir of Transjordan attempted, with the consent and encouragement of the British, to find a compromise that would allow the rebels to lay down their arms in exchange for the release of prisoners and the establishment of a royal commission of inquiry. Contacts between 'Abdallah and the Higher Arab Committee began in early May, but in August the Committee rejected the compromise because the British would not agree to stop Jewish immigration.[45]

Another reason the mufti and his associates rejected the compromise was their antagonism toward 'Abdallah, whom they saw as a rival. Palestinian Arabs who were aware of his close contacts with the Jewish Agency sent him hostile letters; their depiction of the emir as a traitor became fixed in the public mind: "If you, Emir 'Abdallah, continue to make love with the Jews, we will be compelled to topple you from your throne and also put an end to your life," one of them threatened. 'Abdallah's personal secretary showed the letters to Haganah intelligence operative A. H. Cohen.[46]

Despite this, there were opposition figures who continued to support 'Abdallah's mediation effort. On 5 August some of them met again with 'Abdallah. The mufti was furious and wrote the emir an angry letter.[47] This diplomatic reaction was accompanied by an act of violence. Ten days after the delegation returned from Transjordan, two of its members were assaulted. One, the acting mayor of Hebron, Nassir al-Din Nassir al-Din, was head of his city's national committee and considered one of the largest donors to the strike fund. On the evening of 14 August, as he left a meeting of the strike committee, he was shot dead. The second victim was the editor of *Filastin*, 'Isa al-'Isa, who was beaten by unknown assailants on the day he returned. A few days later a bomb went off in his house.[48] Al-'Isa still did not change his opinions and published an article demanding that representatives of the national committees conduct a serious discussion of the strike's advantages and disadvantages. He was shot but survived this attack as well.[49]

These were not the only such attacks. On August 18 a bomb was thrown at the mayor of Nazareth's house, and Hajj Khalil Taha, chairman of the national committee in Haifa, was murdered at the end of September. So came yet another aspect of the definition of treason. The assassins were not carrying out the will of the people or acting in their interests. Rather, they were doing the bidding of the leadership. For them, any attempt to take a stand against Hajj Amin al-Husseini or to make practical proposals for ending the strike was considered an act of treason. Taha's murder demonstrated this. According to one interpretation, he was murdered because he suggested that orange growers be allowed to market their produce in exchange for paying a tax into the strike fund. Taha believed that this would prevent damage to a central sector of the Palestinian economy and strengthen the strike as well.[50] His murder ended any consideration of this idea.*

There is no reliable way of knowing what the public at large thought of the assassinations. *Filastin* came out against them, but that is hardly surprising given that its editor was a victim. Hebron's traditional national leadership placed a notice in the same newspaper claiming that Nassir al-Din was murdered for personal, not political, reasons. The murder was classified as *khiyana*, treason.[51] This was the first example of an interesting phenomenon: The supporters of a man murdered on charges of treason themselves defined the murder as treason, ignoring the real motives behind it. In doing so, they were seeking first and foremost to absolve the victim of the accusation against him. At the same time, they granted legitimacy to the national leadership by refraining from accusing it of the murder.

Moshe Shertok, then head of the Jewish Agency's political department, believed that the opposition's disregard of the murder's political motives did not indicate real acceptance of the national leadership. It was motivated by fear. "There have been attempts to explain this murder on personal grounds so that [the opposition] would not need to respond to it," he said at a meeting of the central committee of his political party, Mapai, a week after the murder. "On all matters in dispute in the Higher Arab Committee the mufti had his way, and the opposition displayed its powerlessness."[52]

Ironically, one person who did not ignore the political background to the murder was Izzat Darwaza of Nablus, a member of the al-Istiqlal who was close to al-Husseini. He wrote laconically in his diary that Nassir al-Din's life was taken "because of his public support and dissemination of the idea of agreeing to a royal commission and damping down

---

*As with other murders, here too there were different theories about the motive. Some argued that the motive was political and that the mufti ordered the murder; others maintained that the murder was the result of a property dispute between Taha and a resident of Shefaʿamr. It is important to keep in mind that Taha was one of the most powerful people in Haifa and that the Husseinis, Nashashibis, and Istiqlal all sought his favor. His large property holdings allowed him to maintain a private band of thugs. The CID report obtained by the Haganah stated that "he was involved in unpleasant incidents, including murders" (see n. 50).

violence and the strike, in coordination with Emir ʿAbdallah, the Defense [Nashashibi] Party, and *Filastin.*"[53]

Nevertheless, despite attacks on several of its senior figures, the opposition was still active in this part of the revolt. Several of the rebel bands were led by pro-Nashashibi families, such as the Irsheid family of the Jenin region, the Nimer family of Nablus, and the ʿAbd al-Hadi family of ʿArrabet. Furthermore, when Arab officer Fawzi al-Qawuqji arrived in Palestine on 22 August with his militia to assist the Palestinian revolt, he established especially close contacts with these opposition rebel units.[54]

Standing Aside

In spring 1936, the regional nationalist leadership called on the inhabitants of the village of Tira, south of Haifa, to take up arms and join the rebel units that were then organizing. The villagers tried to evade the orders. The rebels gave them an extension until after the grain harvest. In June 1936, when the harvest ended and they continued to refuse, emissaries arrived from Haifa and threatened: "If you do not act, you will be destroyed for your treason."[55] George Zahlan, one of Tulkarem's wealthiest citizens, refused to contribute to the strike fund. He received a threatening letter in June. When he failed to respond to the letter, shots were fired at him. A Haifa merchant, Saʿid Nabi, also refused to contribute to the rebels. At the beginning of July a bomb was thrown at his home. Nationalist forces posted placards on mosque doors in Haifa warning against failure to support the rebels.[56] In Beisan the rebels distributed leaflets addressed to the town's inhabitants: "You must supply men and money to the rebels, or your fate will be like the Jews'." Residents of the village of Qalunya, near Jerusalem, were beaten "because they refused to join the bands or buy exemptions for five liras a man."[57]

The rebels were not simply trying to extract money from innocent villagers. For political, military, and social reasons they sought to involve all of Palestine's Arabs in the struggle. They knew that in this kind of uprising success required popular backing.[58] Under these circumstances, it is hardly surprising that veteran collaborators with the Zionists found their situation worsening.

The Veteran Collaborators

The first attack on a known collaborator took place in Haifa on 11 May. The target was the pro-Zionist mayor, Hasan Shukri. A homemade bomb was planted near his house and only by luck failed to kill him. The bombing came after Shukri visited the Jewish neighborhood of Hadar ha-Carmel to demonstrate his solidarity with Jews who had been forced to flee Haifa's Arab neighborhoods after they were attacked.[59]

Treatment of land agents also became more severe. The boycott against them, which had at times been observed only loosely, now became active. Sheikh Mahmoud al-Dajani, who had been a close associate of Hajj Amin until the early 1930s, died in July 1936. Toward the end of his life the ties had been severed and al-Dajani made his living selling land, to Jews among others. After his death, the mufti ordered the imam of al-Aqsa mosque not to pray for him and forbade his funeral party to take out the holy flags that, according to custom, are flown at the funerals of clerics. Some people viewed the mufti's ruling as improper. They did not take very seriously the fatwa he had issued a year before in which he forbade praying for land sellers. Others believed that al-Dajani had been poisoned by the mufti's agents.[60]

Verbal assaults on land sellers intensified, and the mosques became the principal arena for the fight against land sales. At the end of April before a large gathering in the Lydda mosque, Hasan Hassouna, a city dignitary, declared that "each Palestinian Arab should know that if he sells even an inch of his land, he kills himself."[61] Hassouna's message bore a double meaning: that land sellers would be dispatched by the nation's emissaries, and that selling land to Jews was equivalent to committing suicide, since it rendered the sellers unable to live honorably in their country. In the Nablus area, the city's mufti and qadi went from village to village preaching that anyone who killed a land seller would reside in paradise in the company of the righteous people of the world.[62]

Attempts to murder land agents did indeed increase. In the middle of July a bomb was thrown at Kamel Shanti in Jaffa. He was wounded by shrapnel.[63] Shanti, as noted, was one of the biggest land agents in the Sharon area. He was married to a Jewish woman and was involved in a large portion of KKL's land deals in the region. From the point of view of the Palestinian national movement, it was essential to attack him and his colleagues. It had tried for years to fight the land brokers and now made the cessation of land sales to Jews a fundamental demand for the end of the strike.

Nor were informers left unscathed. At the beginning of June there was talk in the Istiqlal mosque in Haifa (a stronghold of al-Qassam's supporters) of the need to punish police informers who frequented the mosque and reported on what was done there. Islamic activists in the cities passed out leaflets announcing that it was permitted to kill traitors, including informers.[64] Violence was not long in coming. In mid-July the Abu-'Awad home in Tulkarem was attacked. The family was suspected of passing information to the British. *Filastin*, which reported the incident, wrote that this was vengeance against people who acted against the nation.[65] That same month a bomb was thrown at the home of 'Isa Bandak, mayor of Bethlehem, a day after he held a party in honor of an officer in the British secret service.[66]

Supplying information to the British or Jews was considered treason in an earlier period as well, as we have seen. But it did not lead to murder. Nor were suspected spies harmed during the strike's early weeks. In the first week in May, for example, *al-Liwaa* published the name of a resident of 'Ilut in the Galilee who was suspected of passing information to the Jews. The newspaper did no more than call on him to mend his ways so as not to be considered a traitor.[67] But as the fighting continued, and as the rebel bands grew stronger, punishment also became more severe. Suspected informers were executed.[68]

THE COLLABORATORS' DILEMMA

The rebellion, liquidations, and internal political changes obligated collaborators (and the "new traitors") to reexamine their habits and ideas. They faced three basic options. One was to repent and join the national movement. Another was flight; as the rebellion spread, ever-growing numbers of so-called collaborators preferred to move to a neighboring country to wait out the storm. A third option was fortitude—continuing to collaborate with Zionist intelligence and with Zionist land purchasers despite the tense environment.

The Penitents

In the first half of May 1936, a few weeks after the strike began, hundreds of family chieftains and notables convened in the village of al-Maliha, near Jerusalem. The meeting was similar to other gatherings conducted at around this time throughout the country, all of them devoted to national unity. 'Abd al-Fattah Darwish, one of the leaders of the local *nahiya* and one of the largest speculators in land in the Jerusalem region, was a main speaker. "I call on Allah, may He be exalted, to bear witness and swear before those gathered here that I will be a loyal soldier in the service of the homeland," he declared. "I call on Allah and the angels and the prophets and the knights of Palestinian nationalism to bear witness that if I violate this oath, I will kill myself with my own hands." To underline his declaration he donated, on the spot, 50 Palestinian pounds to the strike fund.[69]

Darwish, one of the mufti's bitterest rivals in the Jerusalem region, decided to atone for his past. But his speech revealed the contrary forces acting on and within him. Even as he announced his return to the bosom of his nation, he mentioned the possibility that he would violate his oath. And in the same breath he declared that he would be the one to punish himself. This was a rare expression of the subconscious ambivalence of a collaborator, but we have no way of ascertaining his motives. Did he join the strike and rebellion in response to the call of his nation, out of a sense that at this fateful time he could not stand against the majority of his people? Was his announcement the product of a profound conviction that power and its perquisites would be divided in a more egalitarian way between the mufti and his opponents, between the urban elite and villagers? Did his political instincts perhaps tell him that, at this point in time, land sellers were doomed to a bitter end? Whatever the case, Darwish joined the strikers and rebels until the British arrested and incarcerated him, along with other Arab political leaders, in the detention camp at Sarafand. He also bolstered his ties with the rebellion's military leadership. When rebel commander 'Abd al-Qader al-Husseini was arrested after being wounded in a skirmish near Solomon's Pools, south of Bethlehem, in summer 1936, Darwish demonstrated his family's allegiance to the rebel leader from the Husseini clan. The man who put up bail to obtain al-Husseini's release was no other than Sa'id Musa Darwish, 'Abd al-Fattah's uncle. Ironically, it was another of Darwish's close associates, the collaborator code-named "Na'aman," who had revealed 'Abd al-Qader's whereabouts to the British.[70]

Darwish's assistance in freeing the rebel commander symbolized the establishment, during the rebellion's early months, of unity between rural and urban Arabs in the Jerusalem region. Other village leaders who had tended to stray from the nationalist line and refused to accept the dictates of the urban leadership now joined the national consensus; the same was true of land speculators. The day after the gathering of Bani-Hasan leaders, village leaders in the Lydda region also convened. There the leaders of the Khawajah family, who had offered their lands to KKL and maintained close contact with the neighboring Jewish farm village of Ben Shemen, declared their loyalty to their homeland. The land speculator Hasan Muhammad 'Ariqat of Abu Dis did the same. After selling land in his village to Jews, 'Ariqat appeared at a gathering of the Wadiya *nahiya*, comprising villages east of Jerusalem, and expressed his regret. He promised to abstain from such acts in the future.[71] On these lands in Abu Dis that he was involved in selling, now, seventy years later, Israel is planning to build a new Jewish settlement.

The picture would not be complete without noting Abu-Ghosh's response to the rebellion. This village, which had been the center of the Bani-Malek *nahiya*, came out against al-Husseini leadership at the beginning of the 1920s. During the riots of 1929, the villagers defended their Jewish neighbors, and some of them sold their land to Jews. Muhammad Mahmoud Abu-Ghosh, one of the village's most prominent men, was a leader of this pro-Jewish line. In 1930, Tuvia Ashkenazi of the Haganah described him as "fifty years old or more, fat, clean-shaven, dressed half *madani* [city-style], a pious type, generally resides in Jerusalem. A person who sells himself easily (kissed Balfour's hands in Kiryat Anavim and took part in the reception). Married. He has lands near the village and lands in the area. In Abu-Ghosh only a house. In Jerusalem he has property. Speaks with utter sympathy about the Jews, and he can be worked with!"[72]

The new circumstances caused a change in Abu-Ghosh as well. The village split into three camps. Mahmoud reversed himself and took the side of the rebel forces, lending them "financial and moral aid and providing the gangs with information on events in the region," as a later report stated. Others maintained their ties with the Jews, while many chose neutrality.[73]

Some of the "penitents" did not stop making political declarations. They actually joined the rebels, even if in support roles. So, for example, Rabbah 'Awad of the village of Ghabsiyya in the Western Galilee had been involved in land sales but now became a rebel commander in his area.[74] The national leadership encouraged such about-faces, especially when the people involved were local leaders who had previously been its opponents. These were acknowledgments of the national leadership's hegemony and of the justice of its cause.

The rebellion's early months were, in this sense, the Palestinian national leadership's greatest hour. For the first time in Palestinian Arab history, all factions united under a single flag. The Nashashibis participated along with the Husseinis in the Higher Arab Committee and played an important role, as was proved by the arrest of Fakhri Nashashibi. Former supporters of the farmers' parties, *nahiya* leaders, and other opposition figures also joined the struggle. Other collaborators who did not become active in the rebellion nevertheless voiced their support for the uprising and its commanders, if for no other reason than to protect themselves. One such person was the great land speculator Salameh (the "Hunchback") al-Hajj Ibrahim, who gave three wristwatches as presents to senior rebel commanders.[75] To protect themselves and their reputations, people previously branded as traitors now made sure to be seen with rebel fighters and to support them in myriad ways.*

The Émigrés

Many of the "old traitors" could not find a place for themselves in these new circumstances. The same was true of the "new traitors"—merchants and businessmen whose lives had been complicated by the new norms, people who had doubts about the strike's efficacy or maintained economic ties with Jews, and those who were critical of the rebel or national leadership. As the strike went on and the number of rebel bands increased, daily life became more and more difficult for these people. They were required time and again to make sizable financial contributions to local rebel commanders. Anyone who refused to do so became, under the new norms, a traitor to the nation. As acts of violence increased, hundreds of people chose to leave the country.

A. H. Cohen tracked the process that led to flight and concluded that it resulted from a combination of financial pressure and a sense of peril. In a report, he described the national movement's mechanism for collecting money and the changes it underwent. At the beginning, he wrote, the Higher Arab Committee conducted collections through mukhtars and religious preachers, and this was well received. But

> a few months afterward signs of opposition to this collection appeared here and there. Many merchants, government officials, and businessmen

---

*The new bonds between collaborators and Arab forces understandably caused concern among Zionist intelligence operatives. They assumed that known collaborators who were in contact with militants were liable to commit acts against Jews in order to clear their names. This practice indeed became common in later years. An early example was a Jewish Colonization Association worker named Amin, about whom Haganah intelligence reported: "Very dangerous, wants to show that despite his ties with Jews he remains loyal to the Arabs"; report dated 19 July 1936, HA 8/39. On the other hand, establishing close ties with rebel commanders did not necessarily mean that collaborators stopped working with Jews; some succeeded in maintaining good relations with both sides. This also was true in later years, for example, after the establishment of the Palestinian Authority in the mid-1990s, when collaborators established contacts with officers in the Palestinian security forces who came from Tunisia and elsewhere but did not always disconnect themselves from the Israelis.

refused to pay their assessments. The Husseinis thus decided to institute a method of compulsion and coercion. The first victim of this method was the well-known citrus farmer from Jaffa, Zuhdi Abu-Jabin. Through intermediaries, the terrorists demanded 500 Palestinian pounds and received them. Afterward they doubled their demand and received 1,000 Palestinian pounds. But when they returned a few weeks later and demanded 2,000 Palestinian pounds, he refused and informed them that he could not afford to pay such large sums. The terrorists conveyed to him that they would take revenge. Zuhdi did not leave his house after that, but the terrorists penetrated his home in broad daylight and, threatening him with pistols, obtained 2,000 Palestinian pounds from him. Zuhdi was one of the first to flee the country and in doing so served as an example to others.[76]

This man's sin was that he did not want to donate large sums to the rebels (although Abu-Jabin was suspected of selling land and was on the rebel commanders' liquidation list). Active collaborators faced a similar danger. Cohen stated in his report: "The terrorists have also started spreading rumors that anyone who sells land to Jews and every speculator or spy must atone for his transgression with money and pay the terrorists the ransom assessed on him." Some chose to pay the money and buy their lives, but the sums they paid did not always satisfy the rebels. In some instances different commanders or bands demanded money again and again. When people in such situations saw they could not bear the burden, they left the country.

Hajj Taher Qaraman, one of the most prominent businessmen in Haifa (a partner of David Hacohen, of the Haganah and Solel Boneh, a Histadrut construction company), was one of many who abandoned the city as early as summer 1936 after receiving threatening letters demanding large sums. Like others, he felt that the rebellion was directed in part against him and others like him. He feared that his life was in jeopardy. These fears worsened after unknown assailants threw rocks at his home.[77] A short time later he left for Beirut. The day after he departed, rebels murdered a leading Arab leader in Haifa and a close friend of Qaraman's. His fears were thus justified. When Hacohen visited Qaraman in Beirut, the latter accused the Palestinian national movement of producing criminals and murderers. He expressed his acute frustration at the social change brought on by the rebellion, which was being steered by members of the lower classes rather than by men of his own class.[78] Far from the eye of the storm, within the Palestinian exile community, Qaraman and others hoped to gain tranquility and escape the peril they had felt in Palestine. When the general strike ended, they had some sense of relief and went home—but not for long. When the rebellion was renewed at the end of 1937, they again faced threats and danger, in many cases more severe than those during the strike.

The Stalwarts

The third group of collaborators, and the most interesting, was made up of those who remained stalwart and continued to act in concert with the Zionists even in this difficult time, the high hour of Palestinian national-ism. As with the "penitents," we cannot always know what their motives were. It may well be that some of them assumed that the Jews, with British assistance, would be able to subdue the rebellion and that it would be best to support the winning side from the start. Others may have hoped for financial compensation. Still others were probably moti-vated by social ties or ideology.

Zahed Shahin was a Nablus propagandist who worked in the frame-work of the United Bureau at the beginning of the 1930s. In June 1936 he wrote to Yitzhak Ben-Zvi: "As a peace-loving person I find myself obliged, after reading all the pamphlets being sent to the villages, to bring it to your attention that the situation now requires propaganda among the Arabs that will halt the activities of the anarchists. Now, as in 1929, I am at your service."[79] Ben-Zvi did not respond to his offer, per-haps because he lacked confidence in Shahin's abilities, or perhaps because he realized that such propaganda had proved ineffective. Still, Arabs in the Palestine Labor League were drafted into propaganda and information-gathering activities and into establishing useful contacts. They published their propaganda openly. A booklet issued by the League opposed the strike and attacked the "counterfeit" national leadership, which, they charged, was sacrificing the common people on the altar of the politicians' personal and economic interests.[80]

It was not just members of the labor unions and over-the-hill propa-gandists who expressed an interest in cooperating with the Jewish Yishuv against the Arab national leadership. Sheikh Muhammad Zeinati of the Beisan Valley, chief of the Ghazawiyya tribe, told acquaintances in Zionist intelligence that he would continue to work alongside them. In a conversation with Yosef Davidesko, Zeinati reported that he was sabo-taging efforts to unite the Arabs of the Beisan area under the national leadership and requested money for his operations.[81] Zeinati, it may be recalled, had been in contact with Zionist figures since the early 1920s.

Other veteran collaborators who were accustomed to working by the old methods—bribery, propaganda, and fomenting conflict—renewed their contacts with Zionist institutions and proposed ideas for common efforts. So, for example, one of the members of the Higher Arab Committee (apparently one of the veteran members of the Nashashibi opposition) contacted the Yishuv leadership at the beginning of the strike and offered to use his influence to end the strike in exchange for a large sum of money. The Zionist decision makers were divided on how to respond. Chaim Weizmann and Pinhas Rutenberg favored accepting the offer, while Shertok and Ben-Gurion were opposed—more out of their lack of confidence in the efficacy of the move and the influence of the man who had made the offer than out of opposition to the method itself. The offer was rejected.[82]

During the first days of the strike, it seems that both Arabs and Jews believed that the economic boycott and strike might achieve political gains for the Arabs of Palestine. Jewish Agency officials sought a way to undermine it. Farid Shanti, a member of a family of land speculators, offered his services to disrupt the strike at the Jaffa port. He organized sixty longshoremen and sent them to the local strike committee to demand food and work and to express their resentment at having lost their livelihoods because of the strike at the port. He claimed that the action was effective and that it produced real unrest among the strikers. Shanti worked on this with Re'uven Zaslani and A. H. Cohen. A similar action, of proven effectiveness, was carried out in Haifa via payments to drivers, owners of automobile repair shops, and shopkeepers. The same was done in Jerusalem and Jericho, with less success.[83]

In these cases the motive was largely financial. For others, the declared and perhaps real motive was ideological. At the beginning of the rebellion, Jaffa journalist George 'Azar told his Jewish acquaintances that he wanted to help and be helped in fighting the strike. 'Azar had once been the editor of the newspaper al-Aqdam, which had taken a pro-Zionist line. As editor, 'Azar had been in touch with Kalvarisky, Shertok, and others. He now wrote to Ya'akov Shlush: "For every well-mannered, thinking man, every man who keeps his distance from extremism, who has a free and true conscience, the primary duty is to act with the intention of restoring peace to the country and to put an end to the acts of killing, to the spirit of rebellion and to the emotion of hatred, because we believe that these events are being conducted by provocateur terrorists." He claimed that a group of Arabs "who have consciences and who think freely" wanted to work to halt the strike and violence and were in need of money so that they could commence work. A. H. Cohen proposed to enlist 'Azar in the writing of pro-Zionist propaganda (as he had done in the past). In addition, 'Azar was asked to provide information on events in Jaffa. He began to convey intelligence on a regular basis, as he continued his work as a journalist.[*][84]

The mayor of Haifa, Hasan Shukri, was another stalwart. He survived two assassination attempts during the rebellion's early months and then left the country. When he returned there was another attempt on his life. Moshe Shertok was swift in writing him a personal letter:

> I was shocked by the vile attempt to kill such a noble personage. . . . I express, in the name of the public that I represent, our sincere blessings and our admiration for your courage as a citizen and the spiritual courage that you express in these difficult days. I hope that we will all know how to bear through until the time comes when we can reach an honorable agreement between the two nations, the Jewish and the Arab.

Shukri replied in Hebrew, stating unequivocally that the attacks had only made his resolve firmer and expressing hope that the security situation in Palestine would improve.[85]

This dramatic assertion was in keeping with Shukri's character. Of course, there was no improvement in the security situation. The only change was in Shukri's personal security, since the British provided him with two paid personal guards. The Zionists, for their part, searched for ways to improve their community's security, among them by collecting intelligence. Some Arabs participated in this effort during the rebellion's first stage.

"Na'aman," the mukhtar of Battir who had collaborated with Zionist intelligence since 1929, worked enthusiastically in the Zionist cause during the great rebellion. He adhered to his belief that no harm should be done to his Jewish neighbors and passed on information about villagers from the Jerusalem area who had organized bands to attack the Jewish neighborhoods of Bayyit va-Gan and Romema. In summer 1936, "Na'aman" provided information on the location of an important rebel unit under the command of 'Abd al-Qader al-Husseini and Sa'id al-'Ass.

---

[*]Another journalist who maintained ongoing contacts with Zionist intelligence officials, but out of a completely different view of the situation, was Bulus Shehada, editor of *Mirat al-Sharq*. He reported to A. H. Cohen about opposition groups and from time to time received financial compensation. In July 1936 he met with Shertok and presented his positions on the solution to the conflict. Among his demands was that the Zionists halt Jewish immigration. Shehada seems to have thought of himself as a politician searching for a solution to the crisis. For the Zionists he was a source of information; in the eyes of the Palestinian mainstream he was a collaborator. See Sharett, *Yoman Medini*, 240–241.

The unit was attacked by a large British force and suffered many casualties; al-Husseini himself was apprehended. "Na'aman" continued to provide intelligence throughout the rebellion and survived several assassination attempts.[86]

An additional source who provided intelligence because of his personal connections and his convictions was Abu-'Oda, an elderly man who taught Moshe Shertok Arabic when Shertok lived with his parents in the village of 'Ayn Sinya, along the road from Ramallah to Nablus. Abu-'Oda was not a real intelligence agent like "Na'aman," but when the rebellion broke out he rushed to meet Shertok, who afterward wrote about their meeting:

> The old man entered the room and broke out crying. Warm tears fell from his eyes and he was barely able to control himself. He had put his life at risk to come to me from the other side of the front. From the enemy camp. During the entire time he had received no news from me. I explained to him that I had not wanted to place him in danger, but he claimed that he had been unable to endure the thought that I might suspect him of helping our adversaries. His village is small and destitute and its people were not enough to make up a gang, but some of them had bought rifles. They had also demanded that he buy one and he had refused. They were goading him about his friendship with Jews, and once one of the young men tried to mock him by declaring, where the village elders sat and read the newspaper, that Musa Shertok had been killed. Abu-'Oda rushed at the boy to beat him, but the others separated them.[87]

Despite the general atmosphere in the village after the rebellion broke out, Abu-'Oda refused to view the Shertok family (and perhaps the Jews as a whole) as enemies. He rejected the new norms and the militant attitude toward Jews, and his meeting with Shertok was not simply one of friendship. He also passed on military information:

> In recent days Abu-'Oda went to stay with his daughter in the village of 'Anata close to Jerusalem. There he heard of a plan to attack Jews walking to the Western Wall on the fast day. He himself saw nearby four camels from Transjordan loaded with bombs and bullets, sent to a certain person in the village of A-a ['Anata] near Jerusalem for distribution to the city's young men. He decided to come warn me not to go with my family to the Western Wall this year.[88]

These events turned Abu-'Oda into an active informer. In his case he actually stepped up his collaboration with the Jews, and thus the level of his "treason," after the rebellion began. In the weeks that followed the old man continued to pass on to Yishuv intelligence operatives information on forthcoming attacks.[89] Other Arab friends of Jews underwent a similar process and turned into active informers. Field guard Aryeh Shliman wrote in his memoirs:

> One day, when I was riding through the citrus grove guarding workers, I was met by a Bedouin named Jerbi who lived next to Tira, a lone Bedouin among fellahin whom I knew well. We always talked about horses, about races—which for the Bedouin is a very important subject. . . . I met with the Bedouin as I always did and he told me: "You approached me in a not O.K. way." I said: "Jerbi, we're friends, what do you want? That I see you as an enemy? How should I approach you?"
> "Listen," he says. "Always be cautious. Don't trust friends and beware of strangers. You should have approached me with your rifle pointed at me, if only so that others will see from afar and not suspect there is friendship between us." As we spoke I saw him scanning the surroundings to see if there were not strangers watching. He whispered to me: "Listen, tonight they are planning to attack Herut; know what is before you." I tried to dismiss what he said, but he was apprehensive about talking too much. He bade me farewell and quickly disappeared.[90]

That same evening there was indeed gunfire on Moshav Beit Herut, as Jerbi had warned. He turned from friend to informer. We may presume that he did not want to lose his friendship with Shliman (perhaps because, as a Bedouin, he himself was a stranger in the area, just as the guard was). Since friendship with Jews was considered treason, he had no reason not to go one step further and supply security information to the Jewish guard. Another Jewish guard, Shraga Sahar, had a similar experience. An Arab friend who was ostracized in his own village, but whom Sahar treated with respect, told him about an armed band that had arrived there. He had been present at the group's meeting place and heard them planning to kill the Jewish guard and give his rifle and horse as a present to Hasan Salameh, the rebel commander in the Lydda region. The Arab acquaintance rushed to tell his friend the guard, who took the necessary precautions.[91]

Not a few Arabs kept up friendly relations with Jewish guards and supplied them with information, despite—perhaps because of—the strain of the conflict.[92] And not only friends of guards did this. In Haifa an Arab told his former employer about a planned attack. At the request of his friend and boss he agreed to meet with members of the armed band that planned the attack and to turn them in. When another Haifa Arab heard of an impending assault on Jews who visited crowded Arab areas, he reported the fact to his Jewish friends and asked that they spread the word.[93] In other words, many Arabs (and a small number of Jews; rebel commander 'Aref 'Abd al-Razeq hid several times with Jewish friends)[94] took seriously their personal, human relations when they faced a decision and sometimes gave these priority over their national struggle. Yishuv intelligence operatives then took the further step of "tying the knot" with these one-time informers and enlisting them into the service of the Zionist security apparatus.

The growing willingness to help Jews can be seen as testimony to the opposition of individuals within Palestinian society to the militancy of the Arab national movement. It can also be taken as a portent of the increasing collaboration of later years. It was not the collaborators, however, who brought the strike to its end. The damage the rebellion did to the Palestinian Arab economy was a much more important factor, as were Arab military failures and the news that the British were sending military reinforcements to quell the uprising. The Higher Arab Committee sought an honorable way out. On 10 October 1936, it announced that it would accept the appeal of Arab rulers (which the Higher Arab Committee had itself initiated). It called on the Arabs of Palestine to end the strike and the state of combat. In exchange, the British promised to send an independent royal commission to reexamine the question of Palestine. The rebel units laid down their arms and disbanded, and al-Qawuqji and his volunteers left the country.[95]

CHAPTER 5

UNITY ENDS

PURGING THE COMPROMISERS

The Peel Commission commenced its work in November 1936. Its members traveled through the country, heard testimony from both sides, and could see that the British administration had reasserted control. Yet the most prominent Arab collaborators were still being pursued. A Haifa police officer, Halim Basta, was murdered. He had contacts in the Yishuv and had trailed Sheikh al-Qassam's followers. Bullets and explosives were aimed—yet again—at Haifa's pro-Zionist mayor, Hasan Shukri, and at his son-in-law. A bomb was thrown at the house of the longtime informer "Na'aman" in Battir.[1] These were, however, exceptional cases. The hundreds of exiles in Lebanon and other neighboring countries returned to Palestine to rehabilitate their businesses, and it looked as if the public had returned to its normal routine.

But unrest continued under the surface, manifesting itself in threatening letters and placards.[2] On the eve of George VI's coronation in 1937, militants ordered Arab public figures to boycott the celebrations in Palestine. They told the members of the Nablus city council that participants would be executed.[3] Threatening letters were also received by Arabs who employed Jews. The owner of the Marina Café on Princess Mary Street in Jerusalem faced a dilemma. The members of the band that played music for his clients were Jews. With a heavy heart he dismissed them.[4] Tensions rose as the country waited for the commission to issue its recommendations. Here and there underground gangs resumed their operations, and bombs were thrown at merchants who refused to give them money.[5]

During the month preceding the publication of the Peel Commission report, the threats and attacks focused on opposition figures, as if to warn them how to react to the coming report. In mid-June 1937 a bomb was thrown at Salah 'Abduh, the Nashashibis' most prominent field activist in Jerusalem. He was not hurt. Two weeks later, on the last day of June, came the first attempt to kill Fakhri Nashashibi, nephew of Mayor Ragheb Nashashibi and the actual leader of the Defense Party organized around the family. He survived miraculously; he raised his hand to scratch himself and the bullet aimed at his head lodged in his arm.[6] At the beginning of July, unknown assailants arrived (for the second time) at the home of Bethlehem's mayor, 'Isa Bandak, a member of the Defense Party. They opened fire, wounding Bandak's wife and daughter and a housemaid.[7] The message was clear: anyone who leaned toward compromise or disputed Hajj Amin's leadership was a traitor whose life was forfeit. It was the end of national unity. The Higher Arab Committee refused to discuss the attacks, and the Defense Party's representatives resigned.[8]

The Peel Commission issued its report on July 7, 1937. It recommended partitioning Palestine into three parts. The Jews would receive territory on the coast and in the Galilee (comprising some 15 percent of western Palestine between the Jordan River and the Mediterranean). Another area would remain under the British rule (including Bethlehem, Jerusalem, Lydda, and Jaffa port). An Arab area would include the rest of the country, some 80 percent, which would be united with Transjordan and gain independence.[9] The Higher Arab Committee, now under exclusive al-Husseini control, rejected the proposal. Apparently the Committee's rejection did not derive only from national considerations; there was also concern that attaching the Arab region to Transjordan might mean acceptance of Emir 'Abdallah's rule. The emir, for his part, declared his support for the plan. The Defense Party was split.[10]

The propaganda campaign, threats, and murders accelerated. Just two days after the publication of the Peel Commission report, the Husseini newspaper *al-Liwaa* wrote that "anyone who supports the idea of partition is a traitor." The newspaper of al-Istiqlal said the same thing. Dozens of religious leaders issued a declaration stating that supporters of the Peel proposal were heretics.[11] Assemblies and protest meetings were organized throughout the country and sought to swing public opinion against partition, this in response to the guarded support various people and groups had expressed for the plan.[12] A resident of the village of Isdud told Zionist intelligence agent Meir Hirschfeld of Rishon le-Tzion about an assembly in his village. The crowd, he said, swore by Muhammad that they would fight partition and declared: "Any man who sells land to the Jews will be put to death. Any man who serves the government will be put to death. Any man who destroys Jewish property will be a saint."[13] As in the past, most of these belligerent declarations were directed inward, at other Arabs.

It took only a few days for talk to become action. On 19 July, Muhammad al-Qasem was murdered in Haifa. Al-Qasem was a land speculator who got Arabs to sign a petition opposing restrictions on land sales to Jews. The next day, in Jaffa, the *simsar* Muhammad Sa'id Shanti was shot. He was a member of the well-known land agent family. At the end of July the mukhtar of Lifta, a Nashashibi supporter, was shot and wounded.[14] In mid-August, Hasan Hanun was shot dead in Tulkarem, and his brother 'Abd al-Majid was injured. Both dealt in land, and Hasan had also been active politically in the opposition. The man suspected of masterminding the murder was, ironically, a competing land speculator, 'Ali al-Qasem, whose sharp political instincts sensed which way the wind was blowing.[15] The primary motivation for this murder is not altogether clear.*

The battle against partition and its potential advocates grew fiercer. On 8 September 1937, the Higher Arab Committee convened a pan-Arab convention in the town of Bludan in Syria. Its purpose was to unite all Arab forces against partition. The conference delegates swore "to carry on the struggle for Palestine until it is liberated and under Arab sovereignty."[16] The convention's finance and economics committee decided to broaden the boycott of Jewish goods to the entire Arab world and to boycott British products as well. It was also decided that violators of the boycott, as well as those who refused to contribute money to the

---

*Chaim Weizmann told the British that the motive for the murder was Hanun's support of the Defense Party; see Porath, *Palestinian Arab National Movement*, 361n105. Several of Hanun's family members made the same claim. They added that the murderer was 'Ali al-Qasem, and that he had been sent by Dr. Daud al-Husseini and the mufti. They denied that Hanun was involved in land sales; see report dated 13 October 1937, CZA S25/3539. Al-Qasem was brought to trial at the end of 1937, after the authorities found a witness who testified that he had heard al-Qasem order the murder of Hanun because he was a traitor and sold land to the Jews. But the trial ended in acquittal because of doubts regarding the evidence. Hanun's brother, Kamel, admitted that the two brothers had planned to sell a large parcel of land to Yehoshua Hankin so that they could repay debts. On the trial, see the protocol in ISA 66, 176/36. Ultimately, then, it is not clear whether the murder was political or was committed because of competition between *samasirah*.

struggle, would be ostracized and humiliated until they understood their national duty. At the same time, secret decisions concerning operations against traitors and collaborators were ratified.[17]

The liquidations continued. 'Abd al-Salam Barqawi, a senior opposition figure in the Jenin district, was murdered immediately after the Bludan convention. Jewish sources claimed that before dying he managed to accuse the mufti of his murder. The reason: Barqawi had sent a telegram to Bludan stating that the mufti did not represent Palestine's Arabs.[18] Toward the end of September a land speculator from Dammun in the Western Galilee was murdered, and collaborators became even more alarmed.[19]

The liquidations achieved their goal. No one dared support the partition plan openly. Ahmad al-Imam, a close associate of the mufti who under the alias "the Cantor" worked for the Shai, the Haganah's intelligence service, reported: "The opposition, which was prepared to agree to partition, had to go along with the opponents of partition after they learned of the decision to murder everyone who supported that opinion, even if they were among the greatest [leaders]."[20]

The rebels were euphoric; their opponents were in panic. Businessman Hajj Taher Qaraman of Haifa described daily life in the city at that time:

> Terror in full force. If not so much in the victims it knocks down, then in its force to cast fear over large circles of the Arab public. No man dares lift his head up and fight. The power of the secret terrorist gangs is not in their letters but in their very existence. A man does not wait to receive a letter, but instead wanders the streets and seeks out the gang members so as to pay them their levy in advance and so ensure that he will live. The organization is becoming ever more enveloped in fanatic Arab ideology and is not built on money. The people live in an ecstasy of extremist idealism. [Mayor] Hasan [Shukri] has survived so far only because of the two British guards who protect him day and night, but he has no hope other than a miracle from heaven.[21]

This, as it turns out, was also how Shukri saw it. He called in Haganah official David Hacohen and told him that he had decided to leave the city. According to Hacohen, Shukri looked "traumatized to the bone, crushed, broken, and despondent." He was haunted not by the convention but rather by the renewed wave of liquidations. That week in mid-September underground militants had murdered his brother-in-law, Ibrahim Bey Khalil, a long-serving former mayor, head of one of Haifa's wealthiest families, and a member of the Nashashibi opposition. Of Qaraman, who was staying put for the meantime, Hacohen reported:

He does not sleep through the night in the same bed. He switches cars each day. He has no regular days and hours for his everyday work, retains in his home the three sons of Sheikh Nimer Sa'adi, the brother of Sheikh Farhan [Sa'adi, one of the Qassamites' leaders],[22] supports at his own expense the family of Sheikh 'Atiyyah from Balad al-Sheikh [commander of a rebel unit],[23] frequently visits Hajj Amin and contributes to his funds and prays next to him in the mosque, does not refuse even a single demand for money, and despite all this fears for his life each day and makes energetic preparations to liquidate his affairs and flee the country.[24] *

In this way the rebels again took control of the private and public lives of Palestine's Arabs, even before the rebellion recommenced in full force. The police force was helpless; fear spread through its ranks as well. The previous year's murders of policemen, among them Ahmad Na'if in Haifa, Shafiq al-Ghussayn in Jerusalem, and 'Abd al-Hadi in Safed, were still fresh and painful memories.

The opening shot of the rebellion's second stage resounded on 26 September 1937. Assailants shot dead Lewis Andrews, acting governor of the Galilee district. This was the boldest attack so far, the first bullet fired at a high-ranking British official. The British saw the attack as a declaration of war and reacted accordingly. They outlawed the Higher Arab Committee and the national committees that functioned in the cities. Hajj Amin was removed from his position as president of the Supreme Muslim Council, and senior members of the Higher Arab Committee were arrested and exiled to the Seychelles Islands.[25]

The mufti hid out on al-Haram al-Sharif (the Temple Mount) for several weeks and then slipped out of the compound disguised as a Bedouin. He made his way by sea to Lebanon, where his boat was intercepted by the coast guard. The French authorities allowed him to remain in Lebanon but restricted his movements. Some two weeks after his flight, rebels staged a wave of attacks on Jewish settlements and British targets, actions that were apparently planned in advance. Several members of the Higher Arab Committee who were not under arrest managed to join the mufti in Lebanon. Some of them proceeded to Damascus, where they established the Central Committee of the Jihad, which served as the rebel-

---

*Qaraman had good reason to fear. Nationalist circles knew of his ties with the Jews and suspected him of dealing in land. Newspaper coverage of his contributions to nationalist groups did not help him: "It looks as if the attacks in Palestine scared him," Izzat Darwaza jeered in September 1937; see Darwaza, *Mudhakkarat*, 3:31. Contributions by collaborators to nationalist groups were well known in later periods, including after the establishment of the Palestinian Authority in 1994.

lion's high command. Its office was headed by Izzat Darwaza, who received his instructions from Hajj Amin.[26]

Hajj Amin's flight created an opportunity for the opposition to assume leadership of Palestine's Arabs. To achieve this, its members asked for Zionist help. Ragheb Nashashibi conveyed to Shertok an unprecedented message in which he stated his full willingness to cooperate with the Jewish Agency and to agree to whatever policy it proposed. He added that he had broad public backing, but that the time was not ripe for open cooperation. His nephew, Fakhri Nashashibi, laid out his position in a meeting with Hacohen: Now, after the mufti's fall, the opposition needed to engage in a major campaign to win public support—and then conclude a three-way peace agreement among the Jews, Arabs, and British. All this would be accomplished with funding from the Jewish Agency.[27]

The opposition's grand plan was never put into action. Hajj Amin may have been absent himself, but his associates were able—mostly by violent means—to prevent any manifestations of independence from the mufti's dictates. Sheikh 'Abdallah Tahboub of Hebron chaired a public meeting that resolved to oppose terrorism. Hajj Amin's accomplices sent him threatening letters and shot at his house. When he stuck to his position, his house was fired on again. The mukhtar of Tirat-Haifa, who opposed his villagers' participation in armed actions, was shot and wounded.[28] The message got across in both places, and the residents of Hebron and Tirat-Haifa thereafter took a more active role in the rebellion.

Nevertheless, in November 1937 the opposition decided to elect a representative body that would negotiate with the British in the name of the Palestinian nation. When word of this got out, opposition leaders such as Ragheb Nashashibi, Suliman Tuqan, Hasan Sidqi al-Dajani, 'Omar al-Baytar, and Ahmad al-Shak'a received threats from the mufti's men. Gunfire was directed at the opposition leader in the Tulkarem area, Hafez Hamdallah from 'Anabta (who, in addition to his political activity, was involved in land sales to KKL).[29] The mufti's order, according to intelligence sources, was to fight the opposition and the idea of a convention because "it would serve the English and the Jews."[30] The alternative leadership never rose.

At the same time, the mufti ordered his men to refrain from attacks on the British and to concentrate on Jewish targets and Arab traitors. He was obeyed. Warning shots were fired at the homes of the mayor of Nablus, Suliman Tuqan, a noted opposition leader, and of his partner Ahmad al-Shak'a. From this point forward Tuqan was provided with police bodyguards, and he ceased to receive guests other than his closest loyal associates in his home.[31]

For Tuqan it was a bitter surprise. During the early months of the rebellion he was viewed as a patriot. Despite his association with the opposition, most of his city's young people, from all parties, supported him. But the mufti's propaganda had done its work, and overnight Tuqan was branded a traitor. For a short while he still tried, along with Fakhri Nashashibi and other oppositionists, to organize and fight back. Nashashibi even proposed creating armed opposition units. But it did not happen at this stage.[32]

By the beginning of 1938 the opposition was nearly mute. The pro-Husseini newspaper *al-Liwaa*, which began appearing again in January 1938 after a three-month closure by the government, proclaimed triumphantly: "Two months of official [British] terror have gone by, and the government stands there waiting for a band of people from the nation to betray it—but for naught."[33] The mufti himself explained to a journalist in *al-Jami'ah al-Islamiyyah* how he saw the fight against collaborators: "Human beings are like metal blasted in a forge," he said. "The false parts of the metal [the traitors] melt away from the heat of the fire [nationalist fervor], while the original parts [those faithful to the homeland] grow brighter with the increase in the blazing heat under them." What the mufti did not know was that his interlocutor was one of the "traitors" and that he was conveying the substance of their meetings to the Jewish Agency. This deep intelligence penetration did not, however, change the intra-Palestinian balance of power.[34]

In mid-1938 the leaders of the opposition were preoccupied with their personal survival, and the rebels were at the height of their power. The Woodhead Commission arrived in the country to examine the prospects for implementing the Peel partition plan. Placards printed by the Higher Arab Committee called on Palestinians to boycott the commission, and the rebels were instructed "to kill every Arab who communicates with the commission in any form." A blacklist naming traitors was put up in Haifa's mosques. Actions soon followed words. Four followers of Sheikh Izz al-Din al-Qassam set out from Haifa for Nablus with the intention of murdering opposition leaders Suliman Tuqan and Ahmad al-Shak'a. The plan was foiled, but only thanks to a police dragnet involving a large number of arrests.[35] Hasan Sidqi al-Dajani planned to testify before the commission. The mufti learned of this, and al-Dajani received a letter: "Those who go to meet the partition commission should take their shrouds with them." Al-Dajani changed his mind.[36]

The silencing of the opposition and humiliation of its leaders continued in the months that followed. In July 1938 an armed squad appeared
at the home of a family of Nashashibi supporters in the village of Beit
Rima, northwest of Ramallah. The guerrillas demanded that the family
remove a photograph of Ragheb Nashashibi from the wall and spit on it.
Then they commanded one of the family's young men to curse all the
opposition's leaders as he stood with a Qur'an in his hand, forced him to
the ground, and gave him fifty lashes. Before they left, the gang offered
an explanation for their behavior: The jihad, they said, was directed
against any person who did not obey the mufti.[37] In the passion of the
moment, they revealed the militants' fundamental tenet: Their national
struggle was a religious holy war, and the incarnation of both the
Palestinian Arab nation and Islam was Hajj Amin al-Husseini. Anyone
who rejected his leadership was a heretic and his life was forfeit.

The rebellion's leadership operated on the same premise. Its hit list,
which was obtained by the Jewish Agency's intelligence personnel, promised a reward of 500 Palestinian pounds to anyone who succeeded in
killing Ragheb Nashashibi, Suliman Tuqan, and Hussam al-Din Jarallah,
who was slated to assume Hajj Amin's position as chairman of the
Supreme Muslim Council. Lesser rewards were offered for the deaths of
other opposition figures.[38] The mayor of Jaffa, 'Omar al-Baytar, was also
in the rebels' sights. At the beginning of September a former fortune-
teller named Sheikh Muhammad al-Ghazzalah appeared at his office and
emptied a gun at him at close range. Al-Baytar hit the ground and survived—but from then on he made no move without bodyguards.[39]

Nablus mayor Suliman Tuqan was given an opportunity to repent.
Because of his dominant position in the city and surrounding villages, the
mufti preferred to entice him into his camp. Hajj Amin repeatedly sent
emissaries to Tuqan in an attempt to persuade him to support the rebellion. But Tuqan stood his ground and the mufti finally ordered his people
to attack—but not to kill him. One day, reported one of A. H. Cohen's
sources, Tuqan entered his bedroom and found a letter pasted on the wall
above his bed: "If you do not make amends with the rebels and work
together with them for the homeland, you will be sentenced to death." A
short time afterward four bombs were found in his house. A note was
attached to one of them: "We could have killed you but we had mercy;
come over to us immediately." Tuqan lost his confidence and began ex-
hibiting signs of mental deterioration. He refused to eat before one of his
companions tasted his food and began to suspect all those around him.
At this point the mufti sent his senior commander, 'Abd al-Rahim al-Hajj

Muhammad, to make another attempt to persuade him. This time Tuqan ended his opposition to the rebellion. He was, however, still strong enough to say that Hajj Amin's political positions were not acceptable to him.[40]

At the same time, the mufti's men continued their battle against the new religious leadership that was seeking to establish itself with British help. This group was headed by Sheikh Hussam al-Din Jarallah, who had been Hajj Amin's opponent in the elections for mufti in 1921. In that first confrontation Jarallah had been accused of being in the Jews' pockets and of having promised to hand over the Aqsa mosque to them.[41] Now, after the mufti's departure, he agreed to serve on the committee that oversaw the Muslim Waqf, with its large holdings of property in Jerusalem and throughout the country, and was also offered by the British as a candidate to head the Supreme Muslim Council.* These were reasons enough for the mufti's men to try to kill him.

During 1938 there were several attempts to assassinate religious leaders who opposed the rebels. Sheikh 'Aref Yunis al-Husseini, the sheikh of al-Haram al-Sharif, supported the establishment of a police station on the holy site and escaped assassination twice. The imam of al-Aqsa mosque, 'Ali Nur al-Khatib, did not have the same luck. He was shot dead in July 1938. "He had for some time been under suspicion of ties with British intelligence," Darwaza noted, "and during the strike rebellion of 1936 he was warned not to continue to pray before the public and refuse was thrown at him—until he resigned his position and hid from the public eye. Recently, it seems, he renewed his ties, and the rebels dealt with him in the appropriate way."[42]

In November 1938 one of the rebel commanders, 'Aref 'Abd al-Razeq, sent a letter to Jarallah and two other senior members of the new Supreme Muslim Council in which he demanded that they resign within eight days. This was the same month that the new British colonial secretary, Malcolm MacDonald, announced that Britain was withdrawing the partition plan and convening a Jewish-Arab-British conference in London. The mufti and his supporters sought to prevent their opponents from putting together an independent delegation.[43]

---

*Jarallah received a senior post—mufti of Jerusalem—only in December 1948, under Hashemite rule and in the framework of King 'Abdallah's process of taking control of the West Bank and installing the mufti's opponents in leadership positions. See Aharon Layish, "The Religious Establishment in the West Bank," in Rafi Israeli, ed., *Eser Shnot Shilton Yisraeli bi-Yehuda ve-Shomron* [Ten Years of Israeli Rule in Judea and Samaria, 1967–1977] (Jerusalem, 1981), 25 (in Hebrew).

Jarallah was convinced, and not only by the letter. Immediately after the British announced their decision, 'Abd al-Razeq's men threw a bomb close to the police station in the Old City of Jerusalem and afterward pasted up placards at the Nablus and Jaffa gates threatening death to anyone who entered into negotiations with the government without the mufti's sanction. The week was capped with the murder of an opposition leader in Jerusalem, Sheikh 'Abd al-Rahman al-Khatib, a teacher at the city's Rashidiyya school—"a brave fighter against the mufti and his family," according to A. H. Cohen.[44]

This murder was preceded by the killing of Hasan Sidqi al-Dajani in mid-October. Al-Dajani was a prominent political activist from a high-placed Jerusalem family and did not hesitate to express independent opinions. Among other things, he had organized a joint Jewish-Arab drivers' strike in 1931. He also had contacts with the Jewish Agency Executive, presenting a moderate position on the question of Jewish immigration. He offered to organize an Arab labor party that would not oppose Zionism.[45] In 1936 he was one of the leaders of the general strike and was arrested in the great roundup of that year. When the rebellion resumed, he served as liaison between the rebels and his family and conveyed frequent contributions from the family to the fighters. As a result, he developed ties with 'Abd al-Razeq, who had become fond of him. Their relations were so good, a Zionist intelligence source related, that 'Abd al-Razeq refused to carry out the mufti's order to murder al-Dajani. The mission was imposed instead on 'Abd al-Rahim al-Hajj Muhammad (who, compared to his colleague, carried out few executions).

On October 12 a messenger arrived at al-Dajani's office and invited him to a meeting with 'Abd al-Razeq. He set out accompanied by two members of his family. On his way back to Jerusalem from Ramallah, armed men stopped his car, removed al-Dajani, and sent his companions on their way. His body was found nearby the next day. Both hands were broken and there were two bullet holes in his forehead.* His funeral demonstrated his popularity; representatives of all Jerusalem's leading

---

*Opinions differ as to the reason for his murder. The high commissioner reported that all al-Dajani's activities, from politics to drug dealing, were aimed at personal profit, and he could have been killed by half a hundred enemies for half a hundred acts of betrayal. But, the high commissioner wrote, the public believed fervently that he was killed because of his friendship with Emir 'Abdallah and because of his record of not always toeing the line of the mufti's party. Public opinion, the high commissioner thought, was not baseless. See High Commissioner to the Minister of Foreign Affairs, 12 December 1938, PRO CO-932/21. Al-Dajani's family had a somewhat different view of the reason he was murdered: one relative, Khayri al-Dajani, said in an interview I conducted with him in the presence of other

families (except the Husseinis) attended, as did many other people. When the funeral procession passed his office, his pallbearers raised the coffin on the tips of their fingers, an honor reserved for the most respected leaders.[46]

The Arab press reported the murder laconically. The only newspaper that wrote of it at length was the pro-mufti Beirut newspaper, which said the killing was justified—"since in all wars of national survival fall the heads of people whom the fighters see as obstacles in their way."[47]

Al-Dajani was one of the most prominent opposition figures to be murdered. Soon afterward, a member of the oppositionist Jarallah family was murdered in Jericho, and Rafe' al-Fahoum was killed in Nazareth. Two years earlier al-Fahoum had been identified as an organizer of the rebellion and the British demolished his house. Now he was shot by a rebel band.[48] Opposition figures who were able to avoid assassination suffered nevertheless from harassment. Local rebel commanders seized control of their property and land or found ways to harm them publicly. Hamed Zawatah, 'Abd al-Razeq's deputy, commandeered the lands of Ahmad al-Shak'a, who had left the country, and sold the crop while it was still on the trees. He thus brought the production of soap in the Shak'a family factory to a standstill. He leased the lands to fellahin from the region. The same was done with the property of other wealthy opposition figures, such as Shukri al-Taji, Jawdat Nashashibi, and Mahmoud al-Madi.[49]

There was hardly a person close to the opposition who remained in the country without being at least humiliated. Attorney Isma'il al-Khatib of 'Ayn Karem, a supporter of the oppositionist Sheikh As'ad al-Shuqayri, had been involved in the farmers' parties of the 1930s. Now he became a scapegoat. When 'Abd al-Qader al-Husseini returned to Palestine in autumn 1938 after a two-year absence, he shored up his status as a rising force by harassing "traitors" like al-Khatib.[50] Immediately on returning he organized a force of about 150 fighters and took control of the Jerusalem region. One night in Ramadan, the month of his return, he arrived in 'Ayn Karem at the head of his men. He ordered al-Khatib and other suspected traitors to be brought before him, then tied their hands and ordered the villagers to flog them. A delegation of village

family members in November 1993 that "the situation reached the point that Hasan Sidqi's leadership overshadowed that of Hajj Amin. He was an excellent attorney, a graduate of Cambridge, and his popularity came from the people, not from wearing the cap of a religious official."

teachers pleaded with him for mercy for al-Khatib. 'Abd al-Qader lined up the members of the delegation and slapped each one, on the grounds that whoever asked for mercy for a traitor was himself a traitor. Afterward he collected all the villagers and ordered al-Khatib to walk among them barefoot, carrying his shoes between his teeth. Before leaving the village at dawn he demanded—and received—a breakfast meal *(imsak)* for himself and his men. Al-Khatib suffered several similar incidents in the months that followed, until he was murdered.[51]

Along with such attacks, rebels occasionally made efforts to win over their opponents. In September 1938 a large assembly of rebel commanders gathered in the village of Dir Ghassanah in southern Samaria. The leaders of the rural opposition in the Jerusalem and Hebron areas were also invited, led by 'Abd al-Fattah Darwish, his uncle Sa'id Darwish, attorney Isma'il al-Khatib, and 'Abd al-Rahman al-'Azzi of Beit Jibrin (who was suspected of turning over a rebel commander, 'Isa Battat, at the beginning of that year). Other than al-'Azzi, who sent his regrets, all those invited came, declared allegiance to the rebellion, and paid tribute to atone for their past sins. Then the two most senior of them, 'Abd al-Fattah Darwish and 'Abd al-Rahman al-'Azzi, were asked to take command of the rebel bands in their home regions.

Darwish preferred not to take the post, both because the fighters he was to command opposed it and because of his own reluctance. He suggested appointing one of his sons instead, but the rebels refused to accept him. They suspected him of having ties with the authorities and were in any case hostile toward the family because of the aid it had rendered to the Zionists and British.[52] Since the family failed to organize a rebel band and join the rebellion, the guerrillas took 'Abd al-Fattah to task for his past sins. They ordered him to pay a sum of 1,000 Palestinian pounds and one hundred rifles as recompense for his real estate dealings with Jews. He refused to pay and holed up in his house, armed. The rebels responded immediately, although not directly. Assassins shot dead 'Abd al-Fattah's son, Mustafa, a police officer who served in Jaffa. The aid the son had supplied to rebels from his position in the police force was of no use to him. He paid with his life for his father's activities.[53]

The continuing violence impelled the opposition to conduct its own military actions, some of them successful, with British and Zionist cooperation. These did not, however, propel the opposition into national leadership. The London conference, held with the participation of British, Zionists, and Arabs in February 1939, perpetuated its inferior position. The opposition had only token representation in the Palestinian delegation, and even that was achieved only after a tenacious struggle. Fakhri Nashashibi himself traveled to London on Zionist funding; it was his friend Pinhas Rutenberg who gave him 4,000 Palestinian pounds to pay for his trip.[54] Jamal al-Husseini headed the delegation, but his title was vice-chairman. The British had forbidden the mufti's participation, but the Arabs nevertheless designated him their delegation's chairman. The rebel commanders, who were of course not present, also influenced decisions. They vetoed any compromise with the British that did not include an amnesty for prisoners. The difficulties facing an accommodation were expressed in procedural issues; the Palestinian Arab delegation refused to negotiate directly with the Jewish delegation, and the British representatives were forced to shuttle between the two groups.[55]

The British did not accept all the mufti's demands and were unable to bridge the gaps between Arab and Jewish positions. On 17 May they issued their new policy, the White Paper of 1939, based on the understandings they had reached with the delegations from the other Arab countries. The principal points were severe restrictions on Jewish immigration to Palestine and Jewish land purchases and agreement in principle to the establishment of an independent Palestinian state within ten years—if Jewish-Arab relations would allow proper administration of the country. On the following day the Higher Arab Committee discussed the proposal. Hajj Amin chaired the meeting, which was attended by five other members. They decided to reject the White Paper, despite the fact that it included significant gains for Arabs. The four members who were absent from this meeting favored acceptance of the British decision; they remained in the minority. The Nashashibis' announcement that they supported the new British policy was of only marginal significance because of their political weakness. So, despite the White Paper's many benefits for Arabs, and even though most of the Arab public in Palestine viewed it as an achievement, the official Palestinian Arab leadership rejected it.[56]

The campaign against the opposition and its leaders continued after the promulgation of the White Paper, and it did not end when the rebellion ended. Ihsan al-Nimer, an oppositionist in Nablus, discerned after the fact that there was a pattern to the rebel actions—they killed a prominent opposition figure in each of the country's regions: Rafe' al-Fahoum in Nazareth, Dr. Anwar Shuqayri in Acre, Ahmad and Muhammad Irsheid in Jenin, Hasan Sidqi al-Dajani in Jerusalem, Nassir al-Din Nassir al-Din in Hebron, and prominent leaders in the villages.[57] This was in addition to the death sentences passed on figures such as Fakhri Nashashibi and Fakhri 'Abd al-Hadi, which were proclaimed publicly. In this way the Husseini leadership silenced opposition political voices (although oppositionists continued to extend military and intelligence aid to the British and Zionists).

The fight against the opposition was largely political. At the same time, rebel units fought against real or imagined Arab informers as well as Arabs who enlisted in the police force. The political leadership considered the two levels of struggle to be linked. According to Izzat Darwaza, the leaders of the Nashashibis' Defense Party encouraged informers, incited villagers and village leaders against the rebellion, and encouraged enlistment in the police.[58] In any case, for the rebels it was a life-or-death struggle, especially after the British established military courts and imposed emergency military regulations that stipulated the death penalty for anyone who was caught with illegal weapons or shot at another human being.[59]

FIGHTING INFORMERS AND POLICEMEN

When Hajj Amin fled to Lebanon in October 1937, Palestine experienced two weeks of bloody combat followed by relative calm. Armed bands called on villagers to join their ranks, but the villagers demurred and even helped the British in their efforts to subdue the rebels. At the beginning of December 1937 the newspaper *Filastin* reported that, since the establishment of the military courts some three weeks before, there had been a significant rise in Arabs turning rebels over to the police. Darwaza also noted in his diary that the British were having great success seizing weapons and suggested that the reason was that so many Arabs were providing the authorities with information. This was a pernicious disease infecting the rebellion, one that had not been widespread just a year before, he discerned. It was indicative of Palestinian society's ambivalence about restarting the revolt. Naturally enough, nationalist circles turned to attack those who opposed the revolt. They viewed them as "people who sell their souls and honor and their ancestors' graves and the honor of their descendants," to use the words of *al-Jami'ah al-Islamiyyah*.[60]

Informers were not just vilified in the newspapers—they were pursued in the field as well. In mid-October 1937, rebels shot and wounded 'Abd al-Fattah Bal'awi, an informer who worked for the British in Acre. The same day the mukhtar of the village of Ja'uni, who had contacts with Jewish intelligence agents, was murdered. Sheikh Mahmoud Joda al-Ansari of Jerusalem was shot in early November: "Our friends in Beirut say he was accused of espionage," Darwaza wrote in his diary.[61] In December two police informers were killed and one wounded in Acre. The body of an Arab named Ahmad Yunis was found in Wadi 'Ara with his tongue severed and a note on his body: "These are the wages of treason."[62]

The murder of suspected informers and policemen became a nationwide phenomenon. Toward the end of December 1937, a Christian Arab policeman named Jamil 'Aziqi who served in Taybe was slain. A. H. Cohen was told: "This marks a new line of activity the gangs intend to take. They are calling to open a general attack on adjunct policemen in order to cast fear into their hearts and to force them to resign from government service."[63] Unlike the first stage of the rebellion, in which policemen were attacked according to their involvement in countering the revolt, now all policemen became targets.

And the manhunt continued. In Beit Ummar, north of Hebron, rebels executed a man who tracked the movements of a rebel commander, 'Isa Battat, for the police.[64] In January the police station in Sukhmata was attacked. Rebels relieved the nine policemen of their weapons and killed their commander, Qasem Da'ib. The Arabs of Safed boycotted his funeral. These messages were no less effective than the threatening placards rebels plastered on city and village walls.[65]

When Sheikh Farhan al-Sa'adi was turned in to British authorities on November 22 and executed five days later, it seemed to cause violence to escalate. Now, more than ever, informers were seen as a threat. The elder Farhan had been a direct disciple of Izz al-Din al-Qassam and had headed an armed band active in Samaria that had set off the rebellion of 1936. Many viewed him as a saint, and his execution caused much unrest. It should, however, be noted that he was captured after a report from relatives of a man Farhan's men had murdered. This was their revenge.[66] The same thing happened in other places. Betrayal led to murder, which led to another betrayal and another murder in a continuing cycle of revenge.

During the winter months, the rebels did not enjoy broad public support. In December 1937 they were again routed in battles with the British. Some rebel commanders were forced to flee to Syria with their remaining men. Palestinian villagers refused to give them refuge. When they returned, they tested themselves in direct combat with the British— and failed. Sheikh 'Atiyyah 'Awad and 'Abdallah al-As'ad, two northern rebel leaders, were killed one after another in March 1938 in battles against the British.[67]

These military defeats increased the tension between the rural population and the rebels. The latter attributed their failures to villager informers and searched for the guilty parties. When an ambush was set for the band of one rebel commander, 'Abd al-Rahim al-Hajj Muhammad in Shweikah, the rebels suspected one Abu Rummanah and summoned him for interrogation. According to one version of the events, he was promised a pardon on condition that he tell about his connections with the police. Then, after he confessed, they killed him. Another version has it that the rebels shot nine bullets into his mouth as soon as they captured him. Afterward the rebels murdered two other suspected spies. One was Muhammad Othman, who as early as 1921 had passed on to Jewish friends, at risk to his own life, information about a planned attack on Hadera, a moshava on the coastal plain between Tel Aviv and Haifa. During the current rebellion Othman had continued to maintain his contacts with Jews. One day, when he got off a bus, a man dressed as a woman got off with him, drew a gun, shot him, and fled.[68]

The rebels continued their activity at a lower level and without much success until mid-May 1938, when the rebellion became more popular. Villagers freed up from their farming formed fighting bands or joined existing ones. Attacks on British and Jewish targets became more frequent, as did actions against "traitors." Attacks on Arab notables, policemen, and mukhtars became almost daily affairs. The latter received warnings to resign their positions or face execution. Many policemen were shot dead. At the end of May, rebels attacked the guesthouse (madafah) of the Radwan family of the village of 'Azzun in western Samaria. Eleven Arab policemen were staying there at the time; six were killed, and the rebels commandeered the weapons of the rest.[69] That same month the mukhtar of Saniria was murdered, as were the mukhtar of Umm a-Zinat, a sheikh of the Bedouin tribe 'Arab al-Turkeman, policeman 'Aayesh Zu'bi, and police sergeant Salah Zu'bi. Muhammad Zeinati of the Beisan Valley and Hafez Hamdallah of 'Anabta—who were tied to Zionist intelligence and also sold land to the Jews—were fired at. They survived, but two of their close associates were killed.[70] An updated blacklist was posted in Haifa's mosques with the names of informers and a religious ruling permitting their murder.[71] The hunting season was well under way.*

---

*The term "hunting season" is borrowed from Israeli parlance, where it refers to the period, eight years later, in which the Haganah attacked its more extreme rival, Etzel (and to a lesser degree, Lehi). There are two differences, however, between the Jewish and the Arab situations. One is that among the Jews the "season" involved a more moderate majority acting against a more militant minority, whereas among the Palestinians the

The rebels and their supporters grew stronger. They hoped their actions would lead to the liberation of the country from British and Zionist invaders. Their opponents, and along with them members of the silent masses, lived in constant anxiety. Armed rebels would appear and demand to be hidden, fed, armed, and paid. Refusal led to revenge. Providing assistance to rebels led to punishment by the British.[72] Living conditions in the villages worsened, and national pride was not always enough to compensate for day-to-day difficulties. The situation was not much different in the cities. Toward autumn 1938, rebels, most of them villagers, began to act openly in urban centers. Many Arabs supported them, sometimes for ideological reasons and sometimes just paying lip service. But their presence was not problem free. They demanded money from the people[73] and told them how to dress. Men were forbidden to wear fezzes and shorts and were required to wear the *kufiyya*, the traditional fellah head cover. The goal was to make it harder for British authorities to recognize rebels while in the cities but also to enforce rural norms on the urban population. The prohibition against social ties with Jews was renewed, and carrying an official Mandatory identity card was also forbidden.[74] The usual power relations, in which city Arabs ruled the villagers, were turned on end.

The rebel command deployed a special force, called *fasil al-tathir* (purge unit), to kill "traitors," informers, and political opponents.[75] These liquidations produced compliance in the short run but increased resentment against the rebels and set off cycles of revenge. In summer 1938, signs of waning support for the rebellion became more and more salient. In an attempt to shore up support, the rebel command issued instructions that mukhtars who provided information to the police should not be murdered, only warned. They should be killed only if they ignored the warning. 'Abd al-Razeq issued a similar order in November.[76] It is difficult to estimate how effective these orders were, given the independence assumed by regional commanders. In any case, the kidnapping of suspects for interrogation became more frequent.

Rebel courts, to which many people took internal disputes (the rebels forbade citizens to use government courts),[77] served also for investigating crimes against the nation. This category included informing, selling land,

moderates were the target. On the Jewish side the compromisers had the upper hand, whereas among the Arabs these figures became ever weaker. The second and more significant difference is that in the Zionist "season" the Haganah for the most part turned the men it captured over to the British instead of executing them.

and having relations with Jews or the British. Hasan Salameh, the rebel leader in the Lydda region, sent a man to track land transfers in the property registration office in his district. Land sellers were brought to trial, fined, or ordered to buy rifles for the rebels.[78] 'Aref 'Abd al-Razeq followed the same policy. Two residents of the village of al-Haram, where north Tel Aviv now stands, were brought to trial before him for selling land to Jews. Official documents were presented to the court proving that the sale took place. The convicted men were held in a pit for several days, fined some 100 Palestinian pounds, and then released.[79]

Some convicted violators who were released told their stories to Yishuv intelligence. These reports provide much information on rebel conduct toward collaborators. The father of one of Abba Hushi's Palestinian agents recounted:

> While I was sleeping at home, at the edge of the village, after midnight, an armed man woke me up and ordered me to follow him. When I wanted to put on shoes and a headdress, he beat me with the butt of his rifle. I went out in a nightdress and underpants. Outside my house I saw eight armed men encircling the house. They immediately blindfolded me and called me after them. Three other bands did the same to three of my friends, and we all walked after them. When one of us tripped on a stone or dead animal, they beat us intensely. We walked that way for two hours, and when they removed the blindfolds we were in a pit two meters deep and an armed man guarded us. We remember that we did not jump and they brought us through a cave until we reached the pit.
>
> After a short time one of the armed men appeared at the edge of the pit and said that in an hour we would be executed, and that we had been tried in our absence. A second one appeared and announced that we must wait until the commander arrived. A third one announced that the commanders had arrived and we were to come out. We began climbing. One of the old men refused to go up, saying it would be better for him to be killed here, but the guard mollified him and said that we would be brought before a "rebel court-martial." Small comfort, we said to ourselves. In one of the caves sat three commanders dressed nicely and armed from head to foot. All around dozens of armed men were walking and guarding us, wearing khaki shirts with riding pants. I was the first brought to trial. They asked me why I had recently sold land in Beisan to the Jews. I replied that I didn't sell any and that I had no land there, but that the owners of the land owed me money and that the heirs' trustees sold the land and paid me some of what I had coming. There was a big interrogation about the question, and when they realized that what I said was correct, they said but your son R comes and goes and is a friend of the Jews. I answered: It has been more than ten years since my son left the village and I have no connection with him and you can ask the people here. They were about 100 meters from me. They asked the people. When they came back they

brought Evanglion and told me to swear that I pledge all my mind, my strength, and my property for the Palestinian Arab rebellion. I swore three times, and two sentries dragged me to one side and brought my brother. They asked my brother about the land sale in Beisan. On the spot they flogged him and his shrieks could be heard far off. When they finished with him he could not walk. Two of them dragged him over to us.

The third they sentenced to one month's imprisonment.

But when they brought the mukhtar they asked him three times if he was guilty, and he answered that he was not guilty. They informed him that he was sentenced to death. They returned him to the pit and we stayed until evening fell and we had not yet had any food. Afterward they asked us what we wanted to eat. We thought that they were apparently doing to us as is done with those who are going to die and they ask them. We answered that we had no appetite for food. Without any further talk they brought us chicks and told us to eat.

At close to midnight they blindfolded us again and three armed men led us. When we arrived at the place, they took the blindfolds off all three of us and asked us if we knew where we were. We answered in the affirmative. The sergeant whistled and two others took up positions and shot their rifles at the mukhtar's head without him knowing. He fell down dead. We were horrified. We sat. We could not and did not want to get up, but they told us that they wouldn't do anything to us, and they sent each of us to his home.[80]

This testimony shows, first, that the rebels controlled the countryside, or at least were easily able to act there without interference. It also shows that they viewed executions as a valid judicial function. Furthermore, they used controlled violence, viewing themselves as possessing the legitimate right to use it.

The courts were meant, among other things, to grant the liquidations at least an appearance of judicial review. To guarantee public support, the rebels issued placards in which they justified their death sentences. A placard issued by "the information office of the Arab Rebellion" in summer 1939 set out the reasons for five executions carried out at that time. Two of the dead men were called "traitors . . . who worked in tandem with the army in the villages of the Ramallah district." One of the two, the placard claimed, "bragged that he was the one who caused the defeat of the holy Arab rebellion." Another man was sentenced to death and shot because "he spied against people in his home town and extorted their money on the claim that he would obtain a pardon for those who were arrested." With regard to one other man they simply noted the fact that he was "a spy and traitor." The most senior of them, so it seems, was Fahmi Sufan, who was shot dead in Jerusalem on August 15, 1939. Sufan had served for many months as 'Aref 'Abd al-Razeq's personal secretary. At the beginning of 1939 he defected and went to live in Jerusalem under British protection.* He then established contact with Jewish Agency officials Eliahu Sasson and A. H. Cohen. In 1939 he wrote—anonymously—two articles against the rebellion for the Histadrut's Arabic newspaper, *Haqiqat al-Amr*, in which he attacked the rebel leadership and called for Jewish-Arab coexistence with respect for the rights of both sides.[81]

The reasons for the killing set out in the placards were nationalistic. Sometimes a religious rationale was added. Such was the case in a placard pasted up in the village of Balad al-Sheikh, near Haifa, where a policeman named Nimer had been killed. The headline read: "God Is Above Any Traitor."

> From the fighters to all the residents. We hereby inform you that on 8 March 1939, Nimer the policeman was executed in Balad al-Sheikh as he betrayed his religion and his homeland for the sake of the oppressive government and who thought himself in the right. But the supreme God revealed to those who preserve their religion and their homeland that he betrayed them, and they did to him what Muslim law commands. Because the supreme and holy God said: "Fight the heretics and hypocrites; their dwelling-place is hell."[82]

The placard went on to warn the villagers against reporting what they knew about the murderer to the authorities, but it was principally concerned with defending the murder and creating sympathetic public opinion. Additional means were also used to achieve this goal. In Jerusalem a local assassination contingent organized a group whose job was to appear at the place where a collaborator was killed to praise the attackers and slander the victims: "May the hands of the killer be blessed. . . . [T]he murdered man was a traitor, a base man who committed subversion against his nation and its sanctity."[83]

It is difficult to estimate to what extent these actions influenced public opinion. In some cases the public expressed its revulsion for the trai-

---

*Sufan, as it happens, was arrested a few months before his defection by 'Aref 'Abd al-Razeq men, who suspected him of being a traitor. But then one of the commanders, Fares al-'Azzouni, released him. This demonstrates that there was internal dissension within the rebel ranks as well as a lack of clarity about who was a traitor and who was not. Al-'Azzouni was sentenced to death as a result of this incident (and other instances of disobedience) by 'Abd al-Razeq, but the sentence was not carried out. In the end he was captured in Syria, handed over to the British, and hanged by them in Acre. See Danin, *Te'udot*, 66n133. According to 'Abd al-Razeq's son, Sufan was planted by the British to breed dissension among rebel leaders. He was murdered by rebels when he went to visit a girl in Jerusalem's Old City. See 'Abd al-Razeq, *Amjad Thawriyya*, 116.

tors by preventing their burial or other such postmortem sanctions. Opponents of the killings, if there were any, generally had no way of expressing their opinion—at least not at the height of the rebellion. An informer who lived in Jaffa, George 'Azar, told of a Christian named Sayyid Gharbiyyah who was murdered in broad daylight because of his ties to the authorities. His body was left untouched in the street in a pool of blood for more than an entire day, with a shoe shoved into his mouth. A Jaffa policeman, also a Christian, was killed that same week. The rebels forbade the Christian clergy to conduct a funeral service, and the guards at the cemetery refused to allow his burial. Police officers had to crowbar the cemetery gate open and dig him a grave themselves. A few hours after the burial, a group of armed men arrived and found the dead man's mother mourning him. They admonished her not to lament and not to dress for mourning. If she did not obey, they would "lay down" her other sons alongside their dead brother.[84]

David Hacohen of Haifa was familiar with this atmosphere. Identifying with those who suffered from it, he wrote:

> The terror inside has encompassed the entire nation and no one dares say a word or make a sound. There is no chance to avenge or to criticize, because the man closest to the victim does not know whom he is talking to and what his end will be. A man does not accompany his brother to the cemetery. The closest people, who know the victim for decades and who weep in their hearts about his death, do not dare write a condolence letter to his family lest the long arm of terror reach them on this act of treason.[85]

THE PURGE: HOW MANY?

The second stage of the rebellion was characterized by a more extreme turn in the fight against traitors. Rebels again demanded that villagers and city dwellers fund their actions. Those who refused were punished, sometimes cruelly, and were vilified as traitors. Muggings and robberies in the name of the rebellion became daily events.[86] The newspaper al-Jami'ah al-Islamiyyah declared, "O, Arabs of Palestine, do not destroy your homes with your own hands . . . fear God and remember the homeland . . . repent your deeds."[87] But it was a lone voice in the wilderness. The atmosphere of unity that had prevailed during the rebellion's first months gave way to confusion and dread. The constant struggle among rebel leaders, often with noncombatants as victims, reinforced this condition.

Attempts to reduce the level of internal violence were fruitless. Ahmad Shuqayri related this in his memoirs:

Every time an innocent man was killed, I would set out for Hajj Amin's mansion and warn him of the destructive consequences of anarchy and its negative impact on the progress of the rebellion, and each time he would express his regret for these incidents. But I would tell him firmly that expressing regret is not sufficient, and I would implore him to forget feuds and take action for national unity. . . . But Hajj Amin did not do a thing.[88]

There seems to be no reason to attribute Shuqayri's criticism of Hajj Amin solely to the fact that his brother, Dr. Anwar Shuqayri, was one of the terror campaign's victims.* Many other people also tried to persuade Hajj Amin to put an end to the murders, but none was successful.[89] This does not mean that the rebel leadership was behind all murders of Palestinians. To be precise, it lost control of them. In October 1938, rebel headquarters in Damascus sent Mahmoud 'Ala al-Din, a native of Ramla, from Syria to Palestine to prepare a report on the murderers, with the aim of rooting them out. He spent twenty-five days in the country, met with the leaders of the large rebel bands (al-Hajj Muhammad, Hasan Salameh, and 'Abd al-Razeq), and wrote a scathing report. But the murders did not cease.[90]

Nevertheless, the numbers generally cited in Israeli research about Palestinian internecine murders are higher than the evidence supports. Ya'akov Shimoni wrote that the number of victims of "this ferocious terror war . . . reached the thousands."[91] In his book on the rebellion, Yuval Arnon-Ohana cited a similar figure:

This terror was the harshest measure used by the fellah gangs in the cities, and it took on dimensions unprecedented in the Mandate period. According to Fakhri al-Nashashibi, one of the leaders of the mu'aradah [opposition], the number of Arabs murdered in the years of the Arab rebellion in Palestine reached 3,000. But it is likely that Fakhri related in this number only those murdered in the internal terror. According to another source, some 6,000 Arabs were killed during the rebellion's three years, and only

---

*The principal suspect in Shuqayri's murder, a police officer in Acre named Yussuf Ahmad, had been involved in land deals with Jews; see the letter of Yosef Fein, secretary of Kibbutz Hanita, to Moshe Shertok, 10 June 1938, CZA S25/22527. The files of the investigation of the Shuqayri murder are in ISA, sec. 66 (Arab attorneys), 176/56 and 190/14. This is one more example of people's actions following not necessarily from their values or ideology (nationalist, antinationalist, or otherwise) but rather from a variety of motives that may include fear, avarice, and economic, social, and political interests. A possible motive for the murder was Ahmad's desire to divert suspicion from himself. It is still not clear whether he acted of his own volition or at the behest of someone else. The fact that Shuqayri, a physician, used to treat wounded rebels placed another question mark over the murder. For additional details on this complicated affair, see Swedenburg, *Memories of Revolt,* 157–164, who interviewed people who had been involved in the affair.

1,500 of them were killed by those against whom the Palestinian Arab population conducted its rebellion—the British and the Jews. The decisive majority of the Arab dead, some 4,500, were killed during the internal terror conducted by Arab bands against their Arab brothers.[92]

The "other source" cited by Arnon-Ohana is Haviv Cna'an, who served as a policeman under the Mandate and wrote some books on the period.[93] Cna'an presented no evidence to support his claims and cannot be taken as a reliable source. Even more important, Arnon-Ohana incorrectly interpreted his principal source, Nashashibi. First, Nashashibi himself stated in the same document Arnon-Ohana cites that it is impossible to deny "that more than a hundred Arabs have been murdered by Arabs." He later updated this figure to 292.[94] The figure 3,000 relates to all those killed as a result of the mufti's disastrous policies from the time he commenced his political activity. In other words, it includes all the Arab dead in the riots of the 1920s as well as rebels killed by the British from the outbreak of the rebellion (more than 2,000 by the end of 1938, according to British reports).[95] It can thus be stated with certainty that the number of Arabs killed by other Arabs numbered, at the time Nashashibi wrote, only in the hundreds.

It is interesting to note that Shimoni himself, in an article written before the one quoted above, gave a lower estimate. "Internal Arab terror took, in the years 1936–39, hundreds of victims—many more than fell at the hands of the British, the police, or the Jewish defense forces," he wrote in 1962.[96] Note the order of magnitude: hundreds rather than thousands. This article was, however, imprecise with regard to another piece of data: the number of Arabs killed by the British was about 4,000.

The smaller numbers published by Nashashibi are consistent with other sources. The material gathered by Izzat Darwaza (largely from open sources but with the addition of field reports), the periodic summaries printed by the Hebrew press, British reports, and—no less important—the count kept by Haganah headquarters all indicate fewer than 1,000 Arabs killed by rebels. According to a report submitted by the high commissioner in 1938—the rebellion's peak year—the rebels killed 498 Arabs—467 civilians and 31 policemen.[97] These figures are similar to those published in the Hebrew daily *Davar*, according to which 1,997 people were killed in the conflict that year, among them 1,624 Arabs (along with 69 British subjects and 292 Jews). Among the Arabs, 1,138 were "gang members," as the newspaper called them, and only 486 were civilians or policemen. Similar statistics appeared in the daily reports collected by Haganah headquarters.[98] In 1937, during most of which there was no combat, *Davar* counted 97 people killed—33 Jews and the rest British and Arabs, both rebels and others. An examination of Darwaza's and other data indicates the number of people murdered by the rebels that year as not more than thirty, and the same for 1936. In 1939 the wave of murders continued, and by the midpoint of that year 260 Arab civilians had been killed, as well as nine Arab policemen.[99] In the second half of 1939 the number of murders declined significantly, to a few dozen.

All the documented cases of Arabs killed by rebels through all the years of the rebellion thus total about 900. Presumably there were also victims whose deaths were not reported, but not many. An estimate of 1,000 Arabs killed by rebels seems to be quite reasonable.[100] This contradicts the common claim that more Arabs were killed by Arabs than by the British and Jews. As we have seen, in the rebellion's peak year, 1938, a total of 1,138 Arab rebels were killed by their rivals, whereas 498 "traitors" and innocent bystanders were killed by the rebels. In other words, the number of Arabs killed by the rebels was less than half the number killed by the British.

The exaggerated numbers that appear in Israeli scholarship on the rebellion are worth examination as part of a discussion of the writing of Palestinian history by Zionists. In any case, even those who accept the smaller estimate cannot ignore the fact that the rebels killed more Arabs than Jews and cannot deny that the murder of Arabs by other Arabs testifies to the existence of significant Palestinian opposition to the national movement led by Hajj Amin. And one cannot ignore the serious implications of these executions and murders, the most important being the development of intense antipathy toward the rebels, both in the field and among political circles. This antipathy catalyzed cooperation among all elements that fought the rebels—the British, the Jews, and the Arab opposition—in ways and to an extent that were without precedent.

CHAPTER 6

THE "TRAITORS" COUNTERATTACK

ORGANIZED POLITICAL
AND MILITARY COLLABORATION

On a dark and rainy night in winter 1938, three men set out for Jerusalem's Sheikh Jarrah neighborhood: the Haganah's commander in Jerusalem, Ya'akov Pat; Eliahu Sasson of the Jewish Agency's Arab department; and Eliahu Elyashar of Jerusalem's Jewish Committee. They bore crates of weapons for the antirebel force led by Fakhri Nashashibi. After unloading their cargo and transferring it to a hiding place, the men proceeded to the Nashashibi residence for a toast. You will soon see that your confidence in us is not misplaced, their hosts promised.

Elyashar was the broker of the alliance. He had known the hotblooded young Nashashibi since their student days together at a university in Beirut. For him, it was an opportunity once again to put his connections and talents at the service of the Zionist establishment (from which Elyashar felt, to his dying day, that he had been ostracized because he was an Oriental rather than an Ashkenazi Jew). In his memoirs he wrote that the operation was approved at the Haganah's highest levels, but only after considerable misgivings.

> We returned home in the early hours, each man with his bodyguards, our hearts heavy from the risk and responsibility we had assumed. Especially from the responsibility I had taken on myself, to trust a young man who was known to be rash, frivolous, and sometimes a womanizer and

drinker. . . . Not 24 hours had passed and the entire communications media was reporting that three of the mufti's men in Jerusalem and its environs had been assassinated by their opponents. It was the first manifestation of the Nashashibi group's armed defense against those who had violated the honor of their family and the honor of all the other moderate and peace-seeking Arab families.[1]

Fakhri Nashashibi was the most senior, but not the only, member of the opposition in the Jerusalem region who decided to fight back against the rebels in coordination with the Jewish Yishuv's defense forces. The Dajani family also received arms from the Haganah.[2] A similar phenomenon was evident in the region's villages. The strongman of the Bani-Hasan *nahiya*, 'Abd al-Fattah Darwish, had "repented his ways" at the beginning of the rebellion. But when the general strike ended, he once again began coordinating his moves with the Zionists.[3]

The opposition's principal motivation for security cooperation was the assassination campaign pursued by the rebels at the behest of the Husseini leadership. In March 1938, Ragheb Nashashibi revived a proposal that Ben-Gurion had previously rejected: the establishment of armed Arab units with Jewish funding.[4] He conveyed his proposal through the secretary of the Jerusalem municipality, Avraham Franko:

> I don't lack men, and I won't lack weapons either. The government has indicated that it will be prepared to give my men the quantities of weapons they need for their defense. But I lack money to buy these people. It is essential to provide each one of them with a cloak ['abaya], and in the event of death it is necessary to give the family a sack of rice and a sack of sugar. With a sum of 2,000 Palestine pounds I could roll back terror. We know where the weapons are and where the Syrian terrorists are coming from, and we have the capability of capturing them before they enter the country, and if necessary to make war against them as well.[5]

Nashashibi had cooperated with the Zionists in only a limited way before the rebellion.[6] He now made a critical, three-part decision: not to join the rebellion, despite the assassinations; to wage a military campaign against the rebels and the Husseini leadership; and to accept aid from and provide assistance to the rival Jewish national movement. Only the combination of personal mortal danger and the threat of political extinction could have produced such a radical choice.

Fakhri's uncle, Ragheb Nashashibi, handled the politics. The nephew focused on operations. Fakhri met with Sasson and the Lebanese prime minister, Kheir al-Din al-Ahdab (who had just submitted his resignation), to draw up a plan of action against the mufti. It included increased supervision of the Lebanese border to prevent weapons smuggling; provision of information to the French government about how the mufti was harming its interests; and organization of actions against the mufti's supporters in Beirut. Fakhri Nashashibi promised to pass on information on the rebel commands, and Sasson emerged with the impression that "he is prepared to devote himself to us, to work with us loyally and honestly, and to act according to our instructions." Sasson requested and received funding for his activity.[7]

Fakhri began working openly in autumn 1938. He commenced an exceptionally sharp media offensive against the mufti, paid for by the Jewish Agency. Jewish newspapers and journalists gave him prominent play.[8] His propaganda was directed at the Palestinian public, the Arab world, and the international community. In an interview with the *Yorkshire Post,* he attacked the mufti harshly for diverting the "noble Arab revolution" to his own purposes. A month later he published a pamphlet in Arabic titled "A Voice from the Graves of Palestine," in which he accused the mufti of being responsible for the deaths of thousands of innocent people. He further claimed that 'Aref 'Abd al-Razeq, a rebel commander who also carried out the mufti's death sentences, was a criminal who had sold land and arms to the Jews. He sought to strip both men of public legitimacy.[9]

Fakhri Nashashibi did not restrict himself to propaganda. In September 1938, as an immediate response to the murder of Ibrahim 'Abd al-Razeq, his ally in the villages west of Ramallah, he established fighting forces under his command. These forces were called "peace units" by the British and Zionists, for they fought alongside the British and Zionists against the rebels in order to achieve what the British saw as a "restoration of peace and order" in the Ramallah region. Fakhri tried to make these a model for other such groups throughout the country, and in the following months similar units were established in Samaria, the Hebron area, and the Galilee by Nashashibi and others. Seeking to gain influence, Nashashibi first held two large public meetings of his supporters. The first, held in his home in the presence of the press, was attended by notables from forty-five villages in the area of Jerusalem, Ramallah, and Hebron. The second, held in the village of Yatta, was attended by 3,000 people from the Mt. Hebron region. The sheikh of sheikhs of Mt. Hebron, Shehadah 'Arram, stated in his speech to the local residents and their guests (including Gen. Richard O'Connor, commander of the 7th Division and military governor of Jerusalem) that they represented 60,000 people of Mt. Hebron, all of whom rejected the rebels' actions.

He thanked the army for acting against the rebellion and promised co-operation in the ongoing struggle.[10]

The rebels called Fakhri's men a gang of traitors without any popular support. They attributed the extensive foreign press coverage the opposition campaign received to Nashashibi's connections with foreign journalists and the Zionists. They utterly dismissed Fakhri's claim that 70 percent of the population supported the opposition.[11] They could not, however, ignore the campaign's victories in the field and in public opinion. During one of Nashashibi's visits to Mt. Hebron, three rebel units arrived in the village of Bani Na'im, most of whose residents supported the opposition. The rebel commanders, who included 'Abd al-Qader al-Husseini, intended to force the villagers to declare their support for the rebellion and to punish them if they refused. But Nashashibi learned of the rebels' arrival from the villagers and alerted the British army, which attacked the rebels with air support. Dozens of them were killed and the rest fled, casting their rifles into a nearby well.[12]

Nashashibi and his men proved to the army that they could be valuable allies. The Zionists complemented the military success with a media campaign. In addition to the boost in morale the battle of Bani Na'im provided and the military beating the rebels took, the event reinforced the claim—whose importance increased as the London conference approached—that the mufti and his men did not represent the Arabs of Palestine. And, in fact, a few days after the battle Fakhri Nashashibi met with Eliahu Sasson to discuss upgrading their common propaganda effort.[13]

Another example of three-way military cooperation among the Arab opposition, Zionists, and British army was the Abu-Ghosh family. The Abu-Ghoshes had long been close to both the Nashashibis and the Zionists. When the rebellion broke out, some members of the family joined the fighters, but one of the family's branches maintained a neutral stance at the beginning of the rebellion, sympathetic to Zionism. As the rebellion's problematic manifestations increased, this branch strengthened its ties to the Zionists.

The family's long-standing links to the anti-Husseini opposition were soon supplemented by another powerful motive: revenge. In mid-1938, Yussuf Abu-Ghosh was murdered in Jaffa; he had been bodyguard to Jaffa district officer 'Azmi Nashashibi. As long as 'Azmi was in the area and maintained correct relations with the rebels, they would not lay a hand on his bodyguard. But when the district officer received death threats and left the country, apparently for Lebanon, Yussuf Abu-Ghosh was cruelly murdered. According to A. H. Cohen, his body was handed over to his family "hacked to pieces with a hatchet."[14]

His family wanted revenge. Nimer Abu-Ghosh was close to a band of fighters under the command of Hasan Salameh, the rebel commander in the Ramla-Lydda region. He began reporting to the British on the movements and hideouts of Salameh and his men. The rebels learned he was informing on them, blew up his home in the village of 'Emwas, and informed him that a rebel court had sentenced him to death. They also set fire to the home of the family elder, Sheikh Jalal Abu-Ghosh, in the village of al-Qubab.[15] The Abu-Ghoshes ratcheted up their level of retaliation and contacted the Jewish Agency. A Haganah intelligence agent, Yosef Yakobson of Rechovot, invited to his home members of the family—who had prepared a list of suspects to be apprehended—and introduced them to the commander of the British 19th Brigade stationed at Sarafand. A detachment from the brigade set out under the guidance of Sheikh Jalal, who made no attempt to conceal his identity. The sheikh pointed out the suspects, who were arrested on the spot. Among them were several of Hasan Salameh's deputies in possession of important rebel documents.[16]

The tension between the Abu-Ghoshes and the rebels increased. In contrast, Jewish Agency officials already felt at home in the village. They felt even safer after the family linked them up with the village leaders of Jallud and Nebi Saleh in Samaria, who also declared their desire to work together against the terrorists (they, too, it turns out, were connected with Fakhri Nashashibi).[17]

Jewish Agency officials used their contacts and meetings with these Arabs for both propaganda—as proof that the Arab public was fed up with the rebellion and its leaders—and operational purposes. At the Haganah's request, Sheikh Nimer and his men located, apprehended, and turned over to the police a rebel detachment that had shot a Jewish driver on the Jerusalem–Tel Aviv road. They also captured men who had murdered five workers at Kiryat Anavim in late 1937 (the neighboring kibbutz, Ma'aleh ha-Hamisha, was named in their memory).

"We learned that the murderers were from the nearby village of Qatanna. We surrounded the village and captured the murderers and turned them over to the authorities," the leaders of Abu-Ghosh wrote more than a decade after the event. "When the inhabitants of the village opposed our actions, we were forced to open fire, and we killed two of them. One of them was connected to the murder of the five."[18]

Abu-Ghosh family ties with the Haganah were so close that it is necessary to reiterate that they were not just pursuing Jewish interests or solely seeking revenge for their family. They were also pursuing their own interests, as inhabitants of the village that headed the *nahiya* of Bani-Malek. After the outbreak of the rebellion, the people of Qatanna, who were previously subordinate to Abu-Ghosh and some of whom worked as laborers in the Abu-Ghosh fields, began to attack their former masters.[19] The village rebels' ambition to overturn the social order was another incentive for Abu-Ghosh to cooperate with the Zionists.

Fakhri 'Abd al-Hadi, who was active at the same time in northern Samaria, coordinated some of his moves with Fakhri Nashashibi. 'Abd al-Hadi, from the village of 'Arrabet in the Jenin district, was the man of action and violence in his extended and wealthy family. Although he had been in contact with the Zionist Executive in the 1920s, he had no compunctions about serving as Fawzi al-Qawuqji's right-hand man in summer 1936. In October 1936, when the rebellion was suspended, he left the country and wandered through Syria, Lebanon, and Iraq. When the rebellion broke out again, the revolt's headquarters in Damascus refused to give him a command because his allegiance to the leadership was suspect. Bereft of a specific function, he tightened his ties with opposition figures and was enthusiastically courted by the Zionists.[20] According to Darwaza, in early 1938, 'Abd al-Hadi ("who was and remains a gang leader and was never a nationalist activist, even when he took part in the rebellion") established contact with Nashashibi, and the two exchanged ideas on how to act against the rebels. Later that year the British consul in Damascus as well as opposition figures in Nablus and Emir 'Abdallah tried to persuade him to assume command of the counter-rebellion. Toward the end of 1938, when Nashashibi embarked on his campaign and won Jewish and British support, 'Abd al-Hadi returned to Palestine and commenced military action against the rebellion.[21]

'Abd al-Hadi based his combat against the rebels on British aid. Robert Newton, deputy Jenin district officer, met with 'Abd al-Hadi secretly in December 1938 to take stock of him. His impression was that 'Abd al-Hadi had no interest whatsoever in politics and had no sense of loyalty to the government. He termed the counter-rebel leader "an aristocratic bandit" whose pride had been wounded when rebels from the lower classes gained prominence. Newton decided that there was reason to assist 'Abd al-Hadi and receive assistance from him but warned him that he should not instigate superfluous blood feuds or commit extortion or robbery in the name of the government. Soon after the meeting, 'Abd al-Hadi issued a placard in which he called on villagers to rise up against "the counterfeit rebellion" and announced that he would aid any village that did so.[22]

The circumstances that played into Nashashibi's hands, and that drove people into the arms of Zionist intelligence agents, were also fertile ground for 'Abd al-Hadi's activities. Village elders who felt that they had lost their status, villagers who suffered from the iron fist of the rebels and the army, and many who noticed that some rebel leaders put their personal interests first joined up with him or with other forces that fought the rebels.

The rebels, for their part, tried to cope with the new situation in several ways. First, they quickly declared that the lives of Nashashibi and 'Abd al-Hadi were forfeit.[23] At the same time, they tried to fight against the trend Nashashibi was encouraging, the estrangement of village Arabs from urban ones. A placard that appeared in Mt. Hebron in December 1938 stated that hatred between fellahin and urban Arabs was against God's will: "We say: a single nation, a single people, a single language." But its authors could not restrain themselves from closing with a grim warning: "And as the Prophet said: Rise up first to kill he who rises to kill you."[24]

Along with their propaganda efforts and attempts to enlist leading oppositionists into their ranks, the rebels continued to attack and kill their opponents. To neutralize negative public reaction to their executions, they pasted up placards detailing the crimes of the men they killed. But another aspect of the revolt caused the public's repugnance of the rebels. The armed bands were plundering, blackmailing, and robbing more than ever before. They made no effort to justify these actions and instead tried to deny responsibility. Those who extort money in the name of the rebellion are not *mujahidin,* holy warriors, the placards stated. They were in fact felons acting at the behest of the British secret service or the Zionists, with the goal of defaming the rebellion and creating dissension within the Palestinian community.[25] This was the beginning of a practice still common today—blaming collaborators for the ills of Palestinian society. Indeed, there is a grain of truth in the charge, but the national leadership and its supporters were no less responsible for these maladies.

Internally, the rebel leadership occasionally attempted to root out unacceptable practices by rebels in the field, but they had little success. Attempts to establish peaceful relations between rebel units and villagers who had suffered damage at their hands were generally unsuccessful. Resentment against the rebels, and the blood feuds that began between them and some villages—and some dominant families—kept the public from uniting behind them. The army's success, with the opposition's help, also lowered the level of support. As time passed, a growing number of Arabs were willing to turn their backs on the rebels and offer direct assistance to the British or Zionists.

This atmosphere penetrated the rebel ranks as well. Internal dissension increased, and suspicion that comrades were informants, even within the same unit, became routine.[26] 'Abd al-Rahim al-Hajj Muhammad of central Samaria, one of the rebellion's most talented commanders and a claimant to the title of commander in chief, decided to leave the country. He concluded that "many of the participants in the gangs are spies, and that made him despair of continuing his activity."[27] Yusuf Abu Durra, commander of the Haifa region, did the same.[28] When al-Hajj Muhammad returned to Palestine in March 1939, bearing his commission as supreme commander of the rebellion, several blood feuds from the recent past awaited him. The blood of the Irsheid brothers, Ahmad and Muhammad, who were killed in May 1938, still demanded revenge.[29] Their brother Farid, one of the most important local leaders in the Jenin area and a friend of 'Abd al-Hadi, the Zionists, and the British, founded a peace unit and a network of informers and tracked the movements of al-Hajj Muhammad and his men. Toward the end of March 1939, he learned that the commander had returned and was staying in the village of Sanur in Samaria. He passed the information on to the British and on March 26 arrived in the village with them. The force located al-Hajj Muhammad's hiding place, opened fire, and killed him on the spot.[30] The rebellion had lost one of its important leaders.

And so, slowly losing the sympathy of the people, under attack from the British and Jews, and disintegrating from within, the rebel units grew ever weaker. The peace units gained strength, even though not all parts of the British administration encouraged them, and those that did support them did not do so all the time.[31] The greater part of their activity was directed by Fakhri Nashashibi, who advised, maintained ties with the British, and organized joint missions. He had a network of contacts all through the country, coordinating actions with Fakhri 'Abd al-Hadi of 'Arrabet, Farid Irsheid of Jenin, the Fahoum family in Nazareth,[32] Kamel Hussein of the Hula Valley, Ahmad al-Shak'a of Nablus, Sheikh Hussam al-Din Jarallah of Jerusalem, 'Abd al-Fattah Darwish of the Bani-Hasan *nahiya*, Isma'il al-'Azzi of Tel al-Safi (near Beit Jibrin), the Abu-Ghosh clan, and the mayors of Jaffa, Gaza, and Bethlehem. He and they lent each other support and cooperated in military operations.[33]

A central source of Nashashibi's strength was his links to the British military, especially in air force intelligence, which had been assigned the task of gathering information that could be used in repressing the revolt. On occasion this allowed him to obtain the release of prisoners, creating a debt of gratitude that brought former rebels into his ranks. Several Haganah intelligence operatives had similar relations with British forces at this time and used the same tactic. The freed prisoners conveyed high-quality information to their benefactors. Yosef Yakobson reported on one rebel activist, Yehia al-Natour, who turned himself in to the army and began working with it closely in the antiterror campaign. He also worked as a guard in Jewish citrus groves in the Beit Dajan area. Like the leaders of the peace units, he began to believe the rebellion was counterfeit and served only the interests of its leaders. This did not mean that he accepted the Zionist enterprise, but he saw that the rebellion had caused great harm to Palestinian society in general and to the rebels themselves in particular.

Kamel Hussein Effendi, one of the most influential men in the Hula region, was one of those who joined the antirebel campaign. He had a personal reason—rivalry for dominance in the valley. In particular, the Bedouin emir Sam'an and Musa Hajj Hussein, chief of the village of Talil, whose inhabitants were of North African ancestry, wielded rebel detachments under their influence against Kamel and his men.* They even succeeded in compelling the rebel command to sentence him to death for collaboration. He realized "that he had to get closer to the authorities and work together with them and in this way he would secure his life and his position in the region," Nahum Horowitz of Kfar Giladi reported in November 1938.[34] Within three months Kamel succeeded in persuading the inhabitants of his region that "the way of terror would destroy them utterly." Half a year later he distributed British weapons to villagers so that they could block the rebels from entering their lands.[35] During that

---

*Hajj Hussein himself was a classic example of a man who tried to dance at everyone's wedding. When the early Zionist settlement of Yesod ha-Ma'alah was established in the late nineteenth century, he defended the moshav against attack. In exchange, however, he pressed to receive the job of guarding the village. In spring 1938 he met with Re'uven Zaslani, who tried to recruit him as an informer. But Hajj Hussein agreed to political activity only and refused to provide information on the rebels. He also organized rebel units and was connected to the rebel command. But at the end of 1938 he warned Yosef Nahmani that he had been chosen as a rebel target. See Mordechai A. Harizman, *Nahshonei ha-Hula* [The Pioneers of the Hula] (Jerusalem and Yesod ha-Ma'alah, 1958), and additional information in Feitelson's report to Zaslani, 16 December 1938, CZA S25/4960, and in Zaslani and Sasson, "Report on a Visit in Beirut and Damascus," April 1938, CZA S25/3639.

entire time he maintained contact with Yosef Nahmani, the KKL land purchaser, and with Haganah intelligence agents.

Sheikh Hussein al-Heib headed one of the divisions of the Heib Bedouin tribe and had maintained good relations with the region's Jews before the rebellion. He joined the rebels but recanted at the beginning of 1939 and once again cooperated with his Jewish neighbors. The transition was not a smooth one. He and his brother were first arrested by the British, on the basis of a report from Jewish intelligence about his hostile activity. In February the British deputy district commissioner, E. R. Reeves, suggested releasing al-Heib on condition that he join Kamel Effendi's efforts to calm tempers in the region, and al-Heib accepted the deal.[36]

At the beginning of August 1939, Farid Irsheid hosted Abba Hushi, the union activist and intelligence operator from Haifa, in his home in Jenin. At that juncture, Irsheid had at his service a force of 200 men and had defeated most of the rebel bands in his area. The meeting took place just a few months after the British government published the White Paper that placed severe restrictions on Jewish immigration and land purchases. Irsheid was well aware of the Zionist anger at the new policy and proposed to Hushi that they work together to thwart it. He added that the only way to achieve peace in Palestine was an agreement that would respect the rights of Jews. He proposed selling land to the Jews in order to demonstrate his opposition to the land law. If the law forbade him to sell the land, he said he would lease it indefinitely.[37]

Hushi met later that same day with 'Abd al-Hadi, who also expressed his readiness to cooperate with the Yishuv, with or without the Nashashibis and the government. 'Abd al-Hadi reiterated that he was no traitor, because he believed that accommodation with the Jews would serve the interests of the Palestinian homeland and its inhabitants.[38]

Institutionalized collaboration thus had four sources: the Palestinian opposition's sense that it had reached a dead end and must choose between dissolution and accepting help from the Zionists; the desire for revenge on the part of people whose relatives had been murdered by the rebels; local leaders' fears of changes in the existing social order; and an alternative view of Palestinian nationalism and Jewish-Arab relations. Fakhri Nashashibi and Fakhri 'Abd al-Hadi were among the leaders of this institutionalized collaboration, along with local leaders like Farid Irsheid and Kamel Hussein. Some of them had been amenable to political cooperation with the Jews even before the rebellion, and during the uprising they cooperated in both intelligence and military activities. They were not motivated by identification with Zionist interests; rather, they sought to further their own interests, to save their own lives, and to promote their political agenda. After the rebellion they continued to oppose Hajj Amin's leadership and to advocate accommodation with the Zionists.

POLICEMEN, AVENGERS, AND INNOCENTS

More and more Arabs supplied information to Zionist intelligence as the rebellion wore on. Sometimes the peace units served as intermediaries. More often, these were independent local initiatives. The result was the Haganah's regional information networks, which in some cases continued to operate even after the rebellion was over. An important factor in the Haganah's successful intelligence operation was the great investment it made in intelligence gathering. With the declaration of a state of emergency, the Haganah called on everyone who had any sort of contact with Arabs—Jewish policemen in the Mandatory police force, merchants, field guards, kibbutz secretaries (in popular parlance, the kibbutz secretary was called the mukhtar), residents of the established Jewish farming communities *(moshavot)*, and others—to gather information constantly. These people used a variety of methods to coax and persuade their Arab acquaintances—and the effort bore fruit.

Those who were motivated principally by a desire for vengeance often took their information to the British, but some preferred to work with the Yishuv's intelligence operators. There were three reasons for this. One was personal contacts. In many cases it was easier for potential informers to work with Jews they knew rather than with nonnative British officials and officers. Another reason was lack of confidence in the British administration, and especially in the police. Yosef Yakobson told A. H. Cohen that many Arabs in his region suspected that their compatriots in the British police force were in league with the terrorists. Additionally, some informers felt bonds of friendship or were grateful for help they had received from Jews.[39] Jewish intelligence passed information on to British officials and on occasion also went out into the field with them. The mukhtar of the Bedouin tribe 'Arab Zbeidat in the Jezreel Valley suspected that some of his villagers who belonged to the Black Hand had been involved in the murder of police officer Halim Basta. He reported his suspicions to a member of Kibbutz Sha'ar ha-Amakim, who arranged a meeting with the regional British police commander.[40] Even an Arab officer in the British police force who wanted to convey information about the rebels chose to do so through Haganah intelligence.*

Nadav Baskind, a Haganah operative in Rishon le-Tzion, provided a vivid description of three-way collaboration on the local level. In testimony he gave to the Haganah archives, he told of Arab informers who aided him and his fellows: "One of them, an old Bedouin, was a good and dedicated friend of ours over many years and provided us with much important and valuable information. . . . He was a sharp old man and did it because he thought it was worthwhile for him to live with us in peace." Information from this man was passed on to the British army:

> We contacted Captain Miller, an army officer stationed in Sarafand. We took the best advantage we could of the guy, and indeed he helped us. He destroyed several houses in Arab villages for us, and once we entered Sarafand al-Harrab with him, took out the mukhtars, and he demanded that they turn over the terrorists and as part of that beat them to a pulp. Our relations were so good that I would sit on a tank and go out on missions with two or three other light tanks and armored cars.[41]

This was the golden age of cooperation between Haganah intelligence and the British army. In this symbiosis, the British contributed the muscle and the Jews the information. In a small number of instances, such as the one described here, the Jews intimidated hostile Arab neighbors of theirs under British sponsorship, entering their villages and beating them up. More often, the information was used by the British to round up terrorists and to identify prisoners who could serve as informers if released.

Haganah intelligence agents became specialists at recruiting informers and binding them to long-term relationships. Ezra Danin, a Jaffa-born citrus grower and one of the founders of the Haganah's Arab intelligence service, was one of those who honed these skills. Danin wrote an account of his work. He lived in Hadera and began his intelligence activity in 1936, after the outbreak of the rebellion. But he had for years maintained contacts in Arab settlements throughout the country, as did his brothers Hiram and Aharon, who were active in land purchases. After accepting the post of regional intelligence coordinator, Ezra found Jews who had Arab contacts and briefed them on how to recruit informers.

---

*The officer was Amin Nabhani. Like other informers, he spied for more than one side, including the rebels. So, for example, Nabhani frustrated British plans by informing a rebel unit in Tulkarem about a large-scale search the army was preparing to conduct in their area. See report of 27 January 1939, HA 8/2, where the writer noted: "I wrote previously several times on the talent to betray [of Nabhani and a colleague of his]."

You've got no Arab village that is not brimming over with personal, family, or clan feuds [*fasad*], large and small, about wayward children, women, land allocation, and cattle theft. There is always bad blood in a village and sometimes there are murders and then a chain of reprisals. In many cases of this sort, the murderer emigrates to another settlement, where he receives protection under Muslim custom. You can always get information from such a pursued, protected man in need of succor. The refusal to give a girl to a given man can lead to harsh conflicts. A man who asks the hand of a girl and is refused by her parents feels himself abused, especially if he is the girl's cousin. Types generally exploitable for intelligence work are rebellious sons, thieves who have brought disgrace on their families, rapists who have acted on their passions and fled the avengers of tainted honor. An intelligence agent with open eyes and ready ears will always be able to make use of these personal circumstances and exploit them for his own needs.[42]

Danin's working hypothesis was that to get the most reliable picture possible one must operate a large number of sources, collect every scrap of information, and cross-check each one. His men opened their eyes and began recruiting informers. Sometimes these sources provided only general information, for example, about relations within their villages. This sort of information was put on file and used to recruit additional agents and to provide more in-depth knowledge of events in each region. Sometimes informers reported the movements and actions of rebels. This information was not always operational, but it was of great importance in putting together a body of knowledge about the rebels, their commanders, and the interests guiding their actions. In other cases the informers provided early warnings of impending actions or other operational intelligence.

Danin recruited one of his first agents, in summer 1936, through Kibbutz Givat Hayyim's shepherd, Parneto Klein. When out grazing the kibbutz's livestock, Klein occasionally encountered a middle-aged Arab shepherd. He learned that the man had never married because he lacked the money to pay a bride price. One day Klein made a proposal: "You, a miserable beggar, will never be able to save enough money to buy a young woman like you want, and in the meantime you, God forbid, commit the sin of bestiality. . . . But if you provide us with news about what goes on in al-Qawuqji's camp, over there on the mountain across the way, we will give you money and you can finally buy a woman." The shepherd accepted the offer and asked first for money to buy a donkey and two crates for vegetables.[43]

The conversation between the two sounds simplistic and testifies to the attitude toward this collaborator and others like him. But Danin said that from that moment on the shepherd became a produce merchant who regularly visited al-Qawuqji's camp and passed information about what he saw there to Klein. Once he brought news of an attack al-Qawuqji was planning. The information was passed on immediately to Danin, who forwarded it to his contacts in British intelligence. A British force set out to meet the rebels and inflicted serious losses on them. Afterward, when the shepherd–produce merchant had saved up money, he married. To his dismay, however, he was unable to consummate his marriage with his young bride. Danin sent him a Jewish doctor on the wedding night, who gave him an injection to improve his performance and preserve his honor. This, of course, only reinforced the man's loyalty to his operators.[44]

This shepherd was recruited in the rebellion's first phase and agreed to collaborate with the Zionists mainly because of his personal need. His inexperience and political naïveté were an aid to his recruiters. As hostilities continued, the Zionists increasingly used manipulation and financial and material inducements to recruit Arabs. Abba Hushi, for example, used his contacts with Arab workers established through his position in the Histadrut to collect information during the early stages of the rebellion. In February 1937 he received a warning about a plot to incite riots and kill Jewish longshoremen at the port: "With the help of four or five of my friends among the Arab port workers, I was able, last night, to uncover this web of intrigues as well as the place they met and from which the orders are handed down," he reported to the Jewish Agency Executive. His informants were members of the Palestine Labor League, the Histadrut's Arab arm. They brought the information to him despite the curfew and double jeopardy of entering a Jewish neighborhood—an act that made them a target for both Jewish and Arab thugs.[45]

Such informers acted out of friendship and appreciation, and they were aware of Hushi's power and influence in the port city. Hushi skillfully cultivated this awareness. When the thirst for vengeance was added to this mix, the road to fruitful collaboration was even smoother. A report he wrote about a group of Samarian fellah informers casts light on his methods:

On 8 February 1939, six fellahin from the Jenin area contacted me. Some were from 'Arrabet and the rest from other villages, among them the mukhtar of one of the villages. They told me: One of our friends advised us to come to you because you are known as a faithful friend of the Arabs and you have more than once come to the aid of people in trouble. . . . Our sheikh is mortally ill; his days are numbered if he does not receive immediate help. He was taken prisoner by one of 'Aref 'Abd al-Razeq's gangs and spent five or six days in a deep pit without light, air, and food—he lost blood. Please help us save our leader and we will not forget the favor all our days. . . .

I sent the sick man, accompanied by two friends, to the clinic. There they examined him and decided that it was vital to send him immediately to the hospital for a blood transfusion and injections, and if it were delayed by another day the man would die. . . . I asked the Red Magen David for people with the right kind of blood for a transfusion. . . . Providing aid, to the point of donating Jewish blood to an Arab, who just a short time ago may have been a member of the gangs, made a huge impression on the other five Arabs, especially since we made no conditions and demanded no payment or compensation for the humane act we performed.

They offered us their help in the war against terror and the terrorists. I asked them why they were doing this. They answered: We have suffered enough from the terror—we have suffered more than you—in our village there is almost no family in which one or two or three have not been killed. We have all descended into poverty, our property has been destroyed. Between us and Yusuf Abu Durra and 'Aref 'Abd al-Razeq there is a blood feud [gom]. . . . We want to prove our friendship to you and "pay for blood with blood," to avenge our murdered relatives and together with that prevent the spilling of innocent blood. We are prepared to show you, or whomever you tell us, the terrorists in the city and also to give you information that will prevent murders in the city.

After I investigated and checked the identities of the people and confirmed that they would indeed be able to help because they knew almost all the terrorists in the city and its environs, I contacted an influential man so that he could offer the army the services of these people.[46]

Indeed, it did not take long for Hushi to bring these seeds to harvest. These men mingled with the city's Arabs (in particular, immigrants from rural areas, who were the central core of the rebels) and began providing Hushi with tips. They had little difficulty obtaining news—thanks, as it turned out, to their previous active role in the terror campaign. One piece of intelligence, about two Arabs bearing a bomb with the intention of throwing it at a Jewish bus, arrived just in time. Hushi immediately passed the item on to the police, who got on the rebels' trail. When the bombers realized they were being followed, they hid the bomb in a café and fled. The police found and defused it.[47]

A no less significant achievement of these collaborators (whom Hushi split up, leaving two in Haifa and sending four back to their villages) was their report that the rebellion's supreme commander, 'Abd al-Rahim al-Hajj Muhammad, had returned to Palestine. As mentioned above, he left the country for Syria because of conflicts among rebel commanders and increasing incidence of Arabs informing on their compatriots. In Damascus he met with the rebellion's high command and received an official appointment as supreme commander. Hushi's plants learned of his return and immediately passed the news on to Hushi, who gave the information to the army—resulting in the killing of al-Hajj Muhammad.[48] This was the collaborators' way of avenging the imprisonment of their sheikh and of expressing their thanks for the assistance they received from Hushi. They added that they were also motivated by moral considerations. They wanted to prevent "the spilling of innocent blood." It is difficult to estimate what weight this consideration had in this particular instance.[*]

Moshe Feitelson of Tiberias also directed a network of local informers. Revenge was also a motive for his Arabs, and he also received assistance from the British military. He wrote to Re'uven Zaslani of the Jewish Agency's Arab bureau:

> I am now taking advantage of the resentment that has built up in the family of Sheikh Mutliq against the gangs for our benefit. I have asked the military authorities, with the help of our men, to arrange for searches in Majdal and the surrounding villages to capture the activists among them, and so to cleanse the area of bad elements and along with this to help the family and restore its prestige, which declined disastrously over the last year, and in doing so to win it over to our side. I explained to the army that if we do this we will be able to receive help from the family, even to the point where they themselves will guide us in searches in Arab villages in the area. This was accepted by the army commander and a search was conducted on 22 November in Majdal, in Ghweir Abu Shusha, and in the farm of the Tabha Hospice. The results were excellent.[49]

The humiliation experienced by Sheikh Mutliq's family when the rebels, some of them simple fellahin, ceased to obey them created an alliance of common interest among them, the local Jews, and the British. In an attempt to restore their lost honor, the family cooperated with the Haganah in locating arms in Arab villages around Tiberias. One of them served as a regular paid informer for Feitelson and the British district officer, and they conducted arrests in the villages together. Sheikh Mutliq himself provided Feitelson with information about rebel plans to assassinate prominent Jews and Arab collaborators in Tiberias.[50]

Sheikh Mutliq took revenge on the rebels because his leadership had

---

[*]As previously noted, Farid Irsheid and his men also pursued al-Hajj Muhammad. It is not clear whether the Samarian group worked in concert with both Hushi and Irsheid (the two men met several times), or whether the British received the information independently from more than one source.

been challenged. The Miqbal family of Sindiana had even better reasons to seek revenge. They had friendly relations with Jews of nearby Zikhron Ya'akov but nevertheless took part in the rebellion. But when the regional rebel commander, Sabri Hamed, and his men wanted to uproot the Jewish town's vineyards, the Miqbal family persuaded them not to do so, explaining that the army would take retribution on them. Hamed agreed but demanded that they pay him and his men for their trouble. The Miqbals equivocated, and so Hamed and his men returned to the village on January 1, 1939, and murdered the sheikh and his eldest son. Ten days later they returned and murdered the sheikh's wife and another son. The rest of the family, led by a remaining brother, Miqbal Ahmad Miqbal, had no choice but to flee to Zikhron Ya'akov and then to seek revenge.[51]

"They are ready to go out on operations openly. They aren't afraid and don't need to hide. They are not taking action against Sabri's gang because they don't have arms. . . . If we armed them they would go into the villages and clean out Sabri's men who control the area," Danin wrote to the Jewish Agency Executive after meeting the Miqbal family. "I asked them why they do not link up with Fakhri 'Abd al-Hadi. They replied that it is hard for them to get there. They haven't met for technical reasons. If we think they ought to meet, we can help them and they will meet. . . . They are [also] prepared to testify in court about all the murders that took place in the area."[52]

Danin put them in touch with the regional British command. The Miqbal clan's forces put most of their energies into pursuing Sabri Hamed. One of their most successful operations came at the end of May, when they led a British detachment to a rebel hideout. Three of Hamed's men were killed in the ensuing battle and one of his family members was taken prisoner, badly wounded.[53] In the meantime, the Miqbals helped the British track down other members of the gang. They testified against the rebels and helped apprehend two who had taken part in the murder of a Jewish guard in Binyamina.[54]

Such cooperation derived from a confluence of interests. Both sides wanted to kill or capture rebels who were threatening them. The rebels viewed the Miqbals and their like as traitors, but the Arabs who fought the rebels viewed the situation in an entirely different light. From their perspective, the British and Jews were collaborating with them in a revenge campaign against their enemies. For them, the rebels represented not Arab nationalism but rivals who harmed Palestinians in general and their families in particular. So the Mutliq and Miqbals and others like them saw no reason not to participate in actions against the rebels.[55] The Miqbals said as much in a letter to the Jews of Zikhron Ya'akov: "Such actions [murder of innocent people by the rebels] violate the honor of Islam and the good name of the Arabs." They portrayed themselves as the real defenders of traditional values.[56]

Nevertheless, most collaborators did not overtly cross the line. Ongoing intelligence work was based on a large number of informers who went on with their lives and from time to time conveyed a scrap of information. Nathan Fisch of Yesod ha-Ma'alah, who served as a Mandatory policeman, provided testimony on how he manipulatively gathered information from Arabs he befriended. In the course of duty he once heard from a Jewish policeman at the Rosh Pina police station about a search the police were planning for the nearby village of Talil. Fisch forwarded the information to an Arab he worked with by the name of 'Ali. 'Ali had an expensive antique sword that had belonged to his father and that he was forbidden to possess under the Mandate's antiterror statute. He feared that the police would confiscate it. Fisch offered to keep the sword in his house during the search, after which he returned it. From that time on, Fisch related, "'Ali sought to prove his appreciation and devotion, and from time to time brought me information about what was going on in the Arab camp and the rebel forces." One of his reports was about sixty armed men who had just crossed the northern border. Fisch conveyed it to the authorities.[57]

In Fisch's testimony, it is not clear how the friendship developed or if 'Ali's sole motive in providing intelligence was to demonstrate his friendship to the Jewish policeman. There may well have been additional reasons, perhaps a personal or family rivalry with local rebels, economic dependence on the Jewish settlement, or a recognition that the Jews were strong. The story of the sword may have been an opportunity to collaborate but not the real, sole motive.

Many of the men who guarded the fields of Jewish farming communities also gathered intelligence, and some of them continued to work in Israel's intelligence community after independence in 1948. The memoirs some of them wrote tell of a wealth of information they received as a result of their contacts, their talents, and the gratitude they were able to foster among their Arab acquaintances. Some of the information they collected touched on thefts from Jewish settlements (which the guards viewed as another face of the terror campaign), and some touched on acts of violence.[58] Giora Zeid, son of the legendary guard Alexander Zeid, told of a spinster from a respectable family who was caught stealing. He decided not to press charges against her and instead chastised the leaders of her tribe for not supporting her. She was grateful and reported to him about thieves who stole crops from the fields in the region.[59] Zeid scouted out the suspects and confirmed that the woman had told the truth. Another guard from the same area, Yosef Havkin, also turned a Bedouin woman who lived nearby into an informer:

> A. had a young and beautiful sister who was married to a well-known thief and smuggler in the region. Halima was different from all the other women of her race, with her golden hair and big blue eyes, but she was no different from them in her love of chatter and gossip, and I would on occasion take advantage of that weakness. I owed to her most of my knowledge about what was going on in her tribe and in the other nearby Bedouin tribes. More than once she thwarted her husband the thief and took violent beatings from him for it. The beatings made her do the opposite of what the husband wanted. Instead of frightening and restraining her, they amplified her anger and her desire to get back at him. After the beatings she would be sick and go to the clinic in the moshav, our regular meeting place, and in the presence of the doctor provide me with all the news and information I needed.[60]

Setting aside Havkin's romantic and sexist imagery, the relevant point is how he exploited family dynamics to encourage the woman to give him information. The reaction of the beaten wife, by the way, can be compared to the reaction of the opposition at the national level. Giora Zeid also used his ties with a local woman in one of the most important investigations he conducted during the rebellion, a concerted effort to find out who murdered his father in summer 1938. Zeid related that a young, crippled Bedouin woman who was in love with him provided the initial tip that led him to the murderer. Oded Yanai, Zeid's friend and himself a guard (both later enlisted in Israel's General Security Service, popularly known as the Shin Bet), provided details:

> There was a 16-year-old girl named Shinara. Her brother was a frequent visitor at Zeid's house and she herself was in love with Giora. She was crippled. One day they forced one of the young men in her tribe to take her as his second wife. The reluctant husband tried to get out of it and attacked her. We knew about it and saved her. Shinara felt obligated to us and told what she knew about [the senior Zeid's murderer] Qasem Tabash.[61]

A detachment from the Palmach, the Yishuv's elite military organization, found Qasem Tabash and killed him next to his tent.

Ya'akov Barazani, a guard in the Sharon region whose nickname was "the Trumpeter," also used his female acquaintances to gain information and recruit agents. He made a habit of bringing small gifts to the two wives of one of his neighbors, who was nicknamed "Shorty." They met frequently, and little by little Shorty began providing information about impending attacks on Jewish settlements and the placement of land mines. Since he was a member of an armed band, the information he provided was precise, and on occasion it saved lives in Jewish settlements.

It was not only the silk stockings Barazani gave Shorty's wives that led him to reveal his comrades' secrets and place his own life in danger. Additional details of Shorty's story suggest another motive—his personal accounts with rivals within his band and in other bands. That, Barazani recounted, was why he asked for no payment for the information he provided.[62] Shorty ended up dead; his bullet-ridden body turned up near Khirbet Beit-Lid.[63]

Ironically, Barazani claimed that Shorty's rival and murderer, Abu Khalifa, himself a veteran rebel, also provided him with valuable information. Barazani even sent him to Jenin to kill the murderer of a Jewish wagon driver from Kfar Vitkin. Abu Khalifa became, toward the end of his life, a bodyguard for al-Hajj Muhammad and was killed with him in Sanur in March 1939. Fares al-'Azzouni, commander of one of the larger rebel bands in the Sharon region, met with Jewish intelligence operatives on occasion and at least in once instance helped them purchase weapons.[64]

Friendships between Arab rebels and Jews were not rare. Some rebels made a point of not harming their Jewish acquaintances, even though they took part in attacks on Jewish settlements. Some warned Jewish friends about impending attacks or other operations. Hasan 'Ali Dib, who headed an armed band in the Mt. Gilboa region, was friendly with a guard at Kibbutz Beit Alfa, Kuba Lans. The two had become acquainted some years before the rebellion; as a boy, Dib had impressed Lans with his agility and intelligence. After their friendship grew stronger, Dib would provide Lans with information about thefts from the kibbutz. Later, when he became commander of a rebel band that repeatedly sabotaged the Iraq–Haifa oil pipeline that ran through the Yisakhar highlands, he was careful to avoid damage to Beit Alfa's fields and attacks on its guards. One day, after several members of his family were killed, he changed his mind and went to the kibbutz's fields to kill some Jewish farmers. Lans arrived and stood between him and his intended victims. Dib would not shoot Lans, but he informed him that their friendship was over, then went on his way, in search of another target. That same night, when he and his men approached the pipeline, British officer Orde Wingate's special night squads killed him in battle.[65]

Sparing acquaintances or friends was not perceived as proscribed collaboration. But when the friendship also involved passing on information about the plans of other rebel bands, that was treason. Both phenomena had a similar origin. National interests were not always at the top of rebels' agenda. Sometimes personal and class rivalries affected decisions, sometimes personal relations, and sometimes competition between different rebel groups. In any case, the fact that the national cause was not always the only or central motive of armed Palestinian Arabs made it much easier for Jewish intelligence operatives to do their work. As the rebellion deteriorated into corruption and crime, the national interest became more and more marginal and Jewish intelligence had greater success—not only in cooperation with opponents of the rebellion but also in recruitment of informers within the rebel bands.

DRUZE AND CHRISTIANS

Zionist institutions and prominent members of the Druze community forged good relations at the beginning of the 1930s. During the rebellion, some Druze strengthened their ties with Jews to the point of collaboration with the Zionists. Here, too, the rebel bands' fervor worked against their own interests. Many Druze viewed rebel aggression against them as directed at their religion. The result was that their identification with Arab nationalism, tenuous in the first place, weakened further. The fact that one part of the Druze community viewed the Druze as a distinct national entity, and that the Druze in Palestine received support from the Druze leadership in Syria and Lebanon, helped those who chose to eschew Palestinian nationalism and collaborate with the Jews. All the same, then as now, there was a range of Druze attitudes toward Zionism.[66]

In 1936, Druze from Syria and Lebanon as well as the Galilee and Mt. Carmel fought alongside the rebels. The unit commanded by Fakhri 'Abd al-Hadi, who served that year as deputy to al-Qawuqji, included Druze fighters from the Mt. Carmel villages of Daliat al-Karmil and 'Isfiya, and a rebel band commanded by Qasem al-Diban was composed of Druze from Syria and Lebanon.[67] This was in keeping with the spirit of national unity that prevailed then in the Palestinian Arab community. Senior Druze figures were not, however, comfortable with this. Zionists involved with the Druze—Yosef Nahmani in the Galilee and Abba Hushi in the Mt. Carmel region—prepared leaflets proclaiming that the Druze had benefited from Zionist settlement. They stressed that the Druze were a minority among the Muslims, just as the Jews were.* They assigned Druze acquaintances to distribute the leaflets, which were meant as a counterweight to the Higher Arab Committee's efforts to bring the Druze into the rebellion.[68]

The result was an antirebel group centered on members of the Abu Rukun family of 'Isfiya, which provided information on the rebels and tried to mediate between the Jewish Agency and Sultan al-Atrash, the senior Druze leader.[69] At the end of the first stage of the rebellion, the same people helped Abba Hushi and his associates in Haifa meet with Druze fighters who had arrived from Syria and Lebanon. At the beginning of 1937, Hushi and David Hacohen met with al-Diban, who promised to cooperate if doing so would help the Druze of Palestine. He also offered to help the Jews procure arms, to provide information on rebel plans, and even "to turn on the Arab bands in battle and kill them."[70] There is no evidence of such actions by al-Diban and, in any case, there was no significant Druze involvement in the rebellion's second stage. On the contrary, among the first people killed by the rebels in winter 1937 were two Druze mukhtars, one from Sukhmata and one from Kufr Sami'. Izzat Darwaza remarked that they were killed because they opposed the rebellion, indicating that opposition to the rebellion had spread in the Druze community.[71] A few months later, the Druze in the Mt. Carmel region and the Galilee decided not to join the rebel ranks, and Druze religious leaders from Hasbaya declared that Lebanese Druze who joined the rebellion would be interdicted and excommunicated.[72]

As a result, during 1938 the rebels frequently attacked Druze villages. The climax came that November—an attack on Daliat al-Karmil and 'Isfiya. The rebels kidnapped the mukhtar and desecrated holy books, which outraged the community. Three months later, Sheikh Hasan Khneifes of Shefa'amr and two other Druze village leaders were murdered. These events contributed to Druze willingness to assist Jewish and British intelligence. This was evident, at least in the case of the Khneifes family, largely at the end of the rebellion and during the 1948 war.[73]

This does not mean that all Druze opposed the rebellion and joined the antirebel campaign. Officially, the community remained neutral during

---

*The Zionists tried to convey to the Druze a sense that the two minorities had a common fate. This was not necessarily cynical manipulation. "Migdali," a Shai operative, sent his headquarters a report on the Druze in the village of Mghar after a Bedouin raid. Mghar, he wrote, looked "like a Jewish town after a pogrom," and he compared the eyes of the victims to those of Jews in the Diaspora, "full of envy and vengeance." See Migdali report, 11 September 1940, HA 105/2.

the rebellion, but there were individuals who joined the rebellion and others who took part in the fighting against the rebels alongside the Haganah. Tuvia Umani, who commanded a joint Druze-Jewish unit in the Haganah, said that his Druze soldiers joined up because the rebels had attacked their villages, and also for money or "other things." The unit was composed of ten Druze and ten Jews. They conducted ambushes on Mt. Carmel and chased down Yusuf Abu Durra, the local rebel commander. The Druze also accompanied British armed patrols in the villages, identifying suspects and assisting in their arrest.[74] According to a report from early April 1939, they enjoyed considerable success. The same report states that they displayed a greater motivation to enter into battle against the rebels than did the commanders of the British army in Haifa.[75]

Despite the neutrality of most of the community and the cooperation of some with the British and the Haganah, the rebel command treated the Druze as loyal sons of the Palestinian nation. A notice issued at the end of April 1939 stated that the Druze "vigilantly defend the unity of the sacred homeland and are prepared, whenever they are given an opportunity, to aid the homeland and those who act for its sake." Apparently the authors of the declaration assumed that exacerbation of Muslim-Druze conflict was liable to strengthen the pro-Zionist Druze camp, something they sought to prevent. The declaration, issued by the rebel command of the northern region, stated that anyone who slandered the Druze community would suffer "the harshest punishment."[76] The conciliation efforts were not successful. The proclamation did not halt the attacks on the Druze, who were pushed into acting directly against the rebels.

Like the Druze, Christians played only a marginal role in the rebellion at first. Of the 282 rebel leaders studied by Yehoshua Porath, only four were Christians. This was the cause of ongoing friction between Muslims and the Christian minority. The Muslim claim that Christians received preferential treatment from the government reinforced antagonism between the communities.[77]

As the definition of treason broadened, all those who opposed the rebels came to be perceived as traitors. A fierce leaflet distributed at the end of 1936 called the Christians violators of the national interest. Here, as with the Druze, nationalist leaders intervened to prevent division in the ranks. The Higher Arab Committee issued a counterstatement that denounced "reprehensible propaganda conducted by mercenaries in order to divide this country's Muslims and Christians." Christian-Muslim unity assemblies were conducted throughout the country.[78]

The Higher Arab Committee's presumption that mercenaries were seeking to divide the Arab public was hardly baseless. Zionist intelligence had sought to create dissension between Christians and Muslims as early as the 1920s, as documented in chapter 1. The same strategy was pursued during the rebellion. In December 1938, when Christian policemen were killed and Christian tempers flared, A. H. Cohen suggested "assigning our Christian people in Haifa and Jaffa to fan the flames."[79] But not everything was a result of Zionist conspiracy. The rebels themselves tended to treat Christian policemen more harshly than Muslim ones, and, when rebels took control of Jerusalem at the end of summer 1938, young Muslims planned reprisals against Christians whom they suspected of helping the army hunt down rebel leaders.[80]

The perception that Christians were closer to the government than Muslims were prevailed in Zionist intelligence as well.[81] Yet no entire sectors of the Christian community collaborated, as was the case with the Druze. Most of the aid the British and Zionists received in suppressing the rebellion came from Muslims—members of the peace units, villagers, Bedouin, and urban Arabs throughout the country.

PART III

WAR IN EUROPE,
WAR AT HOME

CHAPTER 7

WORLD WAR, LOCAL CALM

The great Arab revolt disintegrated late in 1939. The rebel leadership tried to cope with its military and political failure by initiating a new round of attacks on "traitors." In June an intelligence source reported that the mufti had ordered the liquidation of all *suspects,* even those in his own family. This repealed his previous directive to murder only proven turncoats. A month later the rebel leadership in Beirut issued an updated list of head prices. Top rewards were for the murders of opposition leaders and commanders of the peace units, whose deaths would enrich their assailants by 100 Palestinian pounds each. The rate for lower-level traitors was 25 pounds. In comparison, murdering a Jew was worth only 10 pounds. Shortly thereafter the Shai learned that Sami al-Husseini of Jerusalem, 'Abd al-Qader's brother and leader of the attack on the Jewish moshav Har-Tuv in 1929, had organized a team whose principal mission was the murder of traitors.[1]

A few assassinations were carried out after World War II began in Europe. Two police detectives who served in Haifa, Yusuf al-'Aqel and Elias 'Adas, were ambushed and shot in mid-October 1939. A policeman, Shafiq Sadeq, was gunned down in Balad al-Sheikh at the beginning of November. Liquidations of traitors also continued in Beirut. At the end of December, rebel agents killed Mahmoud al-Karami, a journalist, opponent of the rebellion, and brother of 'Abd al-Ghani al-Karami, himself a man with close ties to the Jewish Agency.[2]

These were the rebellion's final gasps. As the signs of its passing became concrete, more and more Arabs from all walks of life began reestablishing their ties with Jews. The strictures imposed by the rebellion were no longer obeyed.

A TIME FOR RECONCILIATION

The circles associated with the Nashashibi opposition were the first to reestablish ties with the Jews. In July 1939 the mufti of Hebron, Sheikh 'Abdallah Tahboub, set up a meeting with A. H. Cohen in Jerusalem's Baq'a neighborhood, at the home of one of Tahboub's supporters. A year earlier the rebels had issued a death sentence against the sheikh and fired at his home several times. Now Tahboub spoke to Cohen of the importance of understanding between Jews and Arabs and proposed that the Jewish Agency assist "materially and spiritually" in the establishment of an Arab organization for cooperation.[3]

Some members of the oppositionist Fahoum family, which controlled large tracts of land in Nazareth and its environs, had continued to speculate in real estate during the rebellion. Now the family renewed its unabashed political alliance with the Jews. In December 1939, Muhammad Tawfiq al-Fahoum, director of the Acre *waqf* (endowment), invited Eliahu Sasson of the Jewish Agency's political department to a dinner party at his home. Muhammad's brother Ahmad was also in attendance. The guests conversed about the political situation and recent difficult times. The Fahoum brothers promised that they would avenge the blood of their relatives whom the rebels had killed, the most senior being Rafe' al-Fahoum. They also discussed business; the brothers proposed to sell the Zionists tens of thousands of dunams. Their impression, like that of many others, was that the British took a dim view of the improving relations between Palestine's Arabs and Jews.[4]

Whether or not this was indeed the British attitude, the reconciliation was unaffected. The change in atmosphere was evident throughout the country. Here is but one example, from Beisan. During the long period of the rebellion, even as old a friend of the Jews as Muhammad Zeinati was compelled to support the rebels, if only outwardly. Now the picture completely reversed itself. Emir Bashir al-Hasan, head of another faction of the Ghazawiyya tribe and Zeinati's rival, contacted Re'uven Malhi, a Jew serving in the town as a Mandatory policeman. He asked that Malhi set up a meeting with a senior Jewish official. "He said that Jews had contacted him about twenty years previously and asked his assistance in the Zionist enterprise. In exchange for his agreement, they had sent him

1,000 Palestinian pounds and a very fine mare, but he did not agree," Malhi wrote. "Today his opinion has changed entirely (apparently for financial reasons). He carped considerably to me that the Jews were paying him no attention, apparently because they wanted to protect their relations with Muhammad Zeinati. . . . He is now old but thinks that he can still help and be at our service."[5]

The heads of the 'Azzi family, centered in the Beit Jibrin area, took similar action. In the early 1930s they sold some of their large holdings to Jews and were involved in the establishment of a farmers' party with Zionist support. During the rebellion they were in a delicate position. Their history was problematic, and so was their conduct in the uprising's early days. The Husseini faction suspected them, not groundlessly, of turning over to the British the popular regional commander 'Isa al-Battat. The 'Azzi leaders were required to prove their loyalty by founding and commanding a combat force. They did as they were told. 'Abd al-Rahman al-'Azzi was appointed the commander responsible for the Beit Jibrin area, and Isma'il al-'Azzi was the field commander. Everything went fine until the end of the rebellion. Ezra Danin met with them in July 1940; they told him of their interest in establishing closer ties with the Jews. We are disillusioned with the Husseinis, they told him, and are tired of being hounded by the Nashashibi-led peace units.[6]

The rural elite, with their large landholdings, were accused of opportunism by fellahin, who declared: "They, the effendis, sold their lands to the Jews, they are the intermediaries between us and the Jews in the sale of land, they exploit us with usurious interest and head the gangs that abused us."[7] But it was not only the effendis who wanted to get close to the Jews. A report on Jewish Mandatory policemen in train stations noted that "their relations with the Arabs are very good." Jewish policemen play backgammon with local Arabs, the report noted, in a place that just months earlier had been a regular rebel target.[8] The same was true elsewhere. David Ben-Gurion concluded that "on the Arab side there is a desire to return to normal relations with the Jews, as before."[9]

In summer 1940 it was almost impossible to imagine that there had ever been armed conflict between the two peoples. Kibbutz Mishmar ha-Emek invited children from nearby Arab villages to meet the kibbutz children (though in the end only one kibbutz child showed up). The Maccabi Netanya soccer team played an away game against the Tulkarem team. After they won, the Jewish players were invited to a party also attended by senior town personages, including the qadi, the district officer, and the mayor's brother.[10] Members of kibbutzim in the Beit She'an

Valley celebrated the Muslim holiday of 'Id al-Fitr with local Bedouin sheikhs. One of the guests summed up his impressions: "The wish was expressed that friendly relations not be impeded from now on."[11]

The new atmosphere allowed Jews once more to visit places that had been inaccessible during the rebellion. Many of them felt a sense of relief. In January 1940 a group of 150 students from the Hebrew University went to watch the Armenian Christmas celebration in Bethlehem "for the first time since the disturbances." In the spring, members of Kibbutz Dalia toured the nearby Arab villages and reported that "the days of siege are behind us."[12] A group from Jerusalem organized a bicycle trip to Solomon's Pools, north of Hebron, and on the way saw dozens of armed Arabs marching together. They did not feel threatened. They asked the Jewish Agency's Arab experts about the armed men and learned that they were under the command of 'Abd al-Fattah Darwish, who had organized a peace unit from the villages south of Jerusalem.[13] Jews rented houses in Arab villages along the Gedera–Gaza road and opened restaurants and stores with the consent of the villagers.[14] The Nablus municipality opened talks with Re'uven Zaslani, Eliahu Sasson, and Pinhas Rutenberg about linking the city to the Zionist electricity grid.[15] The tranquil atmosphere was disturbed only by a handful of incidents—and by the news from Europe, which was falling, country by country, to the advancing columns of the German Reich.

A Shai agent code-named "Eiloni" (Dov Yermiah from Kibbutz Eilon) conducted an extended expedition in his territory, the Western Galilee, and returned with a similar assessment. Former rebels welcomed him as a guest and told him how happy they were with the good fortune and calm that now prevailed. These allowed them to fraternize freely with Jews, "which would have meant certain death just a short time ago." Here and there he met individual Jews building bridges and roads in the area and living in Arab villages. "They are treated very well and they live in complete security," he reported. His general impression was that the region was entirely quiet and that only a major effort and a change in the political situation could lead to any significant unrest.[16]

In September 1940 a Jewish Agency informer in Jaffa analyzed the reasons for the renewed ties between Jews and Arabs:

> The growing closeness between these two peoples is following a completely normal path. The attack on Tel Aviv [by Italian bombers]; the fact that the entire country is vulnerable to this peril, as well as the threat of occupation; the Arab surmise that thousands of Jews will leave Palestine for other countries—all these impel the Arabs to view the Jews as the second most

important danger. For example, the condolences conveyed by 'Ali Musta-qim and others to the people of Tel Aviv [after the bombing] were not disparaged in Jaffa, as they would have been in the past, but were rather construed as excellent propaganda for the Arabs and as a matter of human decency. For the same reason, Gaza and other cities have encouraged this trend and expressed their condolences to the victims of the attack. The fact that the Arabs see new personages and not just the Nashashibis involved has made a good impression.[17]

In this analysis, one important reason for the reduction in animosity was the Arabs' sense that Jews were no longer a threat to them. There was also a sense (albeit limited) of solidarity with their suffering. This was not the only sentiment; another informer reported "great joy in some extreme Arab circles" at the bombing of Tel Aviv, and many hoped that Germany would win the war.* Paradoxically, however, the barrier between Jews and Arabs in Palestine disappeared.[18]

The hope for an improvement in the standard of living was also a central reason for the changed atmosphere. This was especially notable in the cities, which after years of tension now felt relief. A Shai observer reported how tranquil Jaffa was but took a somewhat sanctimonious attitude about the self-indulgence that came along with the calm:

> In my opinion, Jaffa is languishing. The young people engage in good times, sex, and sport. The sons of the effendis, and indeed of all the well-off families, dress in the latest fashions, cultivate moustaches, and try to look like movie stars. When they talk among themselves they insert words and nicknames from English. They buy photo magazines from Egypt, ardently peruse them, and have a great interest in Hollywood stars. Prostitution is almost open. In accordance with intimations from on high, the police ignore it. There is also a dancehall and everyone tries to learn the craft.[19]

According to veteran Jaffa informer George 'Azar, the Arabs of Jaffa were not just motivated by a desire for an easy life. They were also disil-

---

*Opinion surveys conducted at the time (apparently the first ever conducted among the Arabs of Palestine) showed widespread support for the Germans. Sari al-Sakakini, the son of writer and political activist Khalil al-Sakakini, conducted surveys in the course of his work at the U.S. consulate in Jerusalem. He asked hundreds of Arabs about their attitudes on the war and the opposing camps. In February 1941, 88 percent of those polled expressed support for Germany, while only 9 percent supported England. The principal factor affecting their opinion, the people surveyed said, was the future of Palestine and the chance that it would be handed over to the Jews. In other words, they believed that Great Britain would continue to act in favor of a Jewish homeland in Palestine, up to and including the establishment of a Jewish state, and that Germany would not do so. Some of the consulate's documents reached the Jewish Agency and can be found in the Central Zionist Archives. On this specific survey, see "Poll," [February 1941], CZA S25/9226.

lusioned about the use of violence. After the rebellion ended, he claimed, people understood that terror would do them no good, and they began to acknowledge that the country had benefited from the presence of Jews. The Arab press published less incendiary material, in part because of the more stringent censorship instituted as a wartime measure. So it was easier for Arabs to focus on their personal affairs and resume normal relations with Jews.[20]

Reconciliation was not restricted to the wealthy and the "silent majority." There was a third and even more significant group—rebel commanders and fighters, including those who had attacked "traitors" but now themselves initiated contact with Jews. Muhammad al-As'ad was a close associate of well-known rebel commander 'Abdallah al-As'ad. During the rebellion he had been arrested by the British, tortured, and released. In mid-1939 he was again sought by the authorities and fled to Iraq, where he joined a fairly large community of insurgents and fugitives who lived off the rebel support fund. When al-As'ad returned to Palestine after a year and a half in exile, the mukhtar of a village on the coastal plain introduced him to a Shai agent code-named "Noah." In his report "Noah" wrote: "The conditions for the meeting were clear: If he spoke openly and freely—he would receive payment. If he was evasive—better he not show up." Al-As'ad showed up. He provided fine detail about the lives of the Palestinian exiles in Iraq, how they were financed, the embezzlement by those responsible for the money, and, most important, specifics about military training, operative plans, and weaponry. He also offered his evaluation of the chances that the rebellion would resume: "I am convinced that all those who were in Iraq will never again play at rebellion. Cut off my hand if I repeat my foolish actions. They broke us, tortured us, our families suffered, our property was damaged, and so on. No, we will not repeat those childish deeds."[21]

In the Jerusalem area, veteran collaborators, among them members of the Abu-Ghosh family, mediated between the British army, the Shai, and former rebels with whom they had developed relations after the end of the uprising. An insurgent detachment commander named Jaber Abu-Tbeikh became an informer among his former comrades. For example, after shots were fired on a British military vehicle in March 1941, Abu-Tbeikh went to the Hebron region, met the gunmen, then proposed to the British that he lead them into a trap—all this through the mediation of Mahmoud Abu-Ghosh. He passed on the information to the Shai as well.[22] As in the final days of the revolt, participants hoped that when it ended they would be pardoned if they collaborated.

This was the state of affairs in Palestine from the final months of 1939 until just before the end of the world war, with significant variations depending on the balance of power between the Allies and the Axis.[23] Regular contact with Jews was no longer viewed as treason, demonstrating again that the definition of collaboration varied in light of circumstances.

THE BUSINESS OF INTELLIGENCE

The Arabs who resumed their ties with Jews acted as individuals. The Jews, in contrast, generally acted at the behest of their national institutions. Of course, there were also Jews who desired no more than friendship or good business relations, and some of these operated on their own. But they too were identified by the Shai, which tried to use them to collect information and recruit Arab informers. The process demonstrated the Yishuv's high level of mobilization and organization in comparison with that of the Arab community.

The Jewish sense of mission was especially notable in the Jews' contacts with former rebels, some of whom were armed and in hiding in the mountains, still sought by the police. The Shai wished to use these contacts to keep current on events in the Arab villages, especially in order to make realistic evaluations of the chance that armed struggle would be renewed. The meetings were conducted under the direction of senior Shai officials, and the Jewish participants steered the conversations to points that interested them. In this way the rebels, sometimes even without being aware of it, became Haganah informers.[24]

It was only to be expected that the Shai would seek to extract information from rebels. Former insurgents had access to information and ties to people who were liable to reignite violent resistance. It was also only natural for Jewish settlements to demand intelligence from the Arab guards they employed.[25] Much more important, however, was that the Shai and Jewish Agency's Arab bureau increasingly supervised and directed Jewish-Arab relations at all levels so that the day-to-day ties could be exploited for intelligence purposes.

In organizing the Shai's work among the Arabs after the rebellion, the Agency's chief, Ezra Danin, identified twenty-five areas in which Jews and Arabs were in contact. The list included, for example, offices of the British administration, employees of Solel Boneh, gasoline tank truck drivers, workers at the ports and in the train and telephone systems, journalists, Jewish-Arab municipalities, and prisoners in jails. He proposed that the Jews in these venues enlist Arab collaborators. "I presume that such activity should be similar to the way the Nazis worked in Denmark, Norway, and Holland—touching on every area of life," Danin wrote.[26] This was different from the British approach, according to which only political and military organizations and subversive bodies were intelligence targets and a pool for the recruitment of informers.

In January 1941, Danin assembled the Shai's intelligence controllers from the entire country, listened to reports on their ties with Arabs, and reached a conclusion: "How unfortunate is the fact that we do not completely take advantage of all those cases of joint commerce, joint contracting, common office and other work." He instructed his people not to allow relations with Arabs to develop without guidance, and to make sure that the Yishuv extracted useful intelligence from every such connection. His axiom was that every personal contact had to be exploited for information gathering. He explained to the controllers how that could be done: "The informer's economic dependence is the most convenient way. Arrange a regular job for him, as a guard, use him as a construction subcontractor, and give him preference over others. Partnership in planting fields, medical assistance in cases of distress, and so on."[27]

Today, sixty-five years later, this approach seems obvious, but in the early 1940s it was revolutionary. Just a decade before, in an effort to obtain international support as well as the collective cooperation of the Arabs of Palestine, the Zionist movement claimed that it was benefiting all the country's inhabitants. That dream, or at least that claim, had evaporated. Enjoyment of Zionism's benefits would henceforth be conditioned on active collaboration.

The Jewish Agency's Arab bureau also advocated the exploitation of every friendly contact for intelligence and propaganda purposes. "The Jews need a large number of Arab friends in this and neighboring countries. These friends can provide assistance in the realization of our goals," Eliahu Sasson wrote. The objective, he explained, was successful propaganda and information collection. Among his proposals was to improve relations with Arab women: "Attention to this field is a duty of young Jewish women, especially educated young women and those who have contact with young Arab women through their work, such as teachers, university students, nurses in hospitals, office workers in the government and with lawyers, assistants to private doctors, troop leaders in the scouts and coaches in sports, and so on." The Neighborly Relations committees established at this time in many Jewish settlements operated on this basis. The Jewish Agency initiated and financed their activities, which included the study of Arab language and culture, mutual visits, and joint projects—for example, pest control and petitions to the government.[28] In the background was a desire not only to enhance mutual understanding and promote coexistence but also to recruit collaborators.*

The near totality of the Yishuv's focus on defense must be seen in its historical context. As a result of the Arab rebellion, Palestine's Jewish population shifted, in Anita Shapira's formulation, from a defensive to an offensive ethos. Or, as Uri Ben-Eliezer wrote, for the Yishuv's younger generation the use of military force was transformed from a necessity into an ideology. The belief that the Jewish national home could be established by peaceful means had eroded and was replaced with a realization that Jewish-Arab confrontation was an inescapable reality.[29] In this strategy, the collection of information was of vital importance. Early news about the fate of European Jewry under the Nazi regime, along with the threat of a Nazi invasion of Palestine, sharpened the sense of danger. The alliance between Hajj Amin and the Axis reinforced the view that Palestine's Arabs were in every sense an enemy.

So, even as the two sides resumed their routine life together on the surface, the Yishuv's intelligence apparatus acted to establish and expand its penetration of Arab society. The Arab nationalists, for their part, continued to hope that they would soon, with German assistance, be able to put an end to Zionism.

COLLABORATION AFTER THE REBELLION

Peace Units

Weariness and economic distress were the most notable motives for Arabs to reestablish ties with Jews. But one distinct group increased its cooperation with Jews after the rebellion for manifestly political reasons. This was the loose coalition of local leaders who were close to Jews before the rebellion and harassed by rebels during the uprising. During that time they provided moral support, and sometimes manpower, to each other. When the rebellion faded, they continued to coordinate with the Shai to track down and capture rebels. Like the Jews, they also feared

---

*One can suggest that this method has affected Jewish-Arab relations in Palestine and Israel ever since the Mandate period; Israelis who develop personal relations—or even take part in joint political activity—with Palestinians are often suspected of being agents of the Israeli intelligence.

the implications of a German victory, a renewal of the rebellion, and the return of the mufti. Their goal was to maintain the three-way cooperation with the British and Zionists that had consolidated during the rebellion's final year. This group's top men—Fakhri Nashashibi in Jerusalem and the mayor of Nablus, Suliman Tuqan—voiced public support for the British in their war against the Nazis. At the same time, they ratcheted up their cooperation with Zionist institutions.[30]

In summer 1940, fearing that rebellion might break out again with the aid of the Axis, several of these men went so far as to conclude a compact with the Jewish Agency.[31] The Arab participants were Muhammad Zeinati of the Ghazawiyya Bedouin tribe, Kamel Hussein Effendi of the Hula Valley, and Fakhri 'Abd al-Hadi of 'Arrabet-Jenin. They were joined by other opposition figures such as Mahmoud al-Madi of Haifa (originally from Ijzim, a village at the foot of Mt. Carmel) and Midhat Abu-Hantash of Qaqun, in the Tulkarem district. The five met in August and agreed: "We must walk hand in hand with the Jews. Our situation is like theirs. So that we can work against the gangs that seek to infiltrate the country, we must each work in his own place and follow everything that happens in his surroundings, and to do everything to break the power of the gangs from the start and not allow them to develop." That same day, Fakhri Nashashibi and the mayor of Jaffa, 'Abd al-Rauf al-Baytar, also met. They too agreed that the opposition had to unite and cooperate with the Jews.[32]

They did not keep their opinions a secret. At a large assembly held in 'Arrabet—the base of the 'Abd al-Hadi family—opposition spokesmen declared that the armed forces at their disposal would respond immediately to any attack on Jewish settlements. They also decided to assassinate their rivals if they plotted any attacks and to respond harshly to any assault against themselves.[33]

Because they lived on the border, Kamel Effendi and Zeinati played an important role in preventing the infiltration of rebels and weapons. Others functioned in the interior. There was symbiosis with the Zionists. The Shai needed current information and a fighting force that could battle the remnants of the rebel bands, and the Arab oppositionists needed Zionist support because their own public standing was at its nadir at the end of the rebellion. Their attempts to enlist Arabs into the British army had failed, and the British were no longer as supportive as they once had been. The opposition leaders feared more for their own lives as the chances of rebellion at home and invasion from without increased.[34] The mood was best expressed by Hafez Hamdallah, "the Watchman," who told Ezra Danin that Husseinis hated the members of the Nashashibi-led Defense Party more than they hated the Jews or British. "If they could slaughter them, they would happily do so."[35]

Farid Irsheid of Jenin was in a similar predicament. He joined the counter-rebellion after his two brothers were killed by men under the command of 'Abd al-Rahim al-Hajj Muhammad in 1938. In coordination with Fakhri 'Abd al-Hadi he established a military force in northern Samaria that pursued the rebels. When they had completed that task, the British began restraining them. In May 1941, just a few weeks after Rashid 'Ali al-Kilani incited rebellion in Baghdad, Irsheid met with the Shai agent "Noah." The British and Zionists feared that the Iraqi rebellion would spread to Palestine, and Irsheid intimated that the end was near. His only request was for help in obtaining weaponry, before it was too late.[36]

In summer 1942 the Yishuv's sense of danger rose to new heights. Nazi commander Rommel was on the offensive in the North African desert, and a Nazi conquest of Palestine seemed a very real possibility. This situation resulted in an ambitious plan for cooperation. The British again sought out the Palestinian opposition. Via the leadership of the Palestinian peace units and Jewish Agency officials, the British chose a mountain next to the Samarian village of Jallud to serve as a communications center in the event of a German invasion. Most of Jallud's inhabitants had supported Fakhri Nashashibi during the rebellion. The Arab oppositionists also tightened their ties with the Jewish Agency, and the two sides established a joint weapons procurement fund. On the Jewish side, these contacts were conducted by Eliahu Sasson, Re'uven Zaslani (Shiloah), and Ezra Danin, and on the Arab side by Irsheid, 'Abd al-Hadi, and Tuqan. "All of us, Jews and Arabs, were convinced that the mufti's men would arrive at the head of the German forces and would do their best to destroy their Arab opponents from the opposition as well as the Jews," Danin wrote in his memoirs. He estimated, as he told Ben-Gurion, that even if he didn't in the end need the agreement, it had guaranteed that "the conduits of contact and mutual supply of information remained open."[37]

Beyond these emergency plans and long-range strategies, ongoing intelligence and military cooperation continued. Members of the peace units supplied information about armed infiltrators, tried to block infiltrators from passing through their regions, and prepared lists of people likely to be involved in a future uprising.[38] In addition, they organized joint actions to purge villages in their regions of remaining rebels. The British were not always eager to cooperate in such initiatives.[39]

These British reservations helped bring the Arab opposition and the Shai somewhat closer. Time and again the oppositionists asked the Shai for assistance in providing contacts, money, or equipment. Some of the Arabs owed their positions within their community entirely to their connections with the Zionists. Shai agent Gershon Ritov reported that the British had severed their ties with the emir of the Ghazawiyya tribe, Muhammad Zeinati, and that Zeinati could not retain his influence without Zionist money.[40] Hafez Hamdallah of 'Anabta, who coordinated the peace units in the Tulkarem region, needed the Jewish Agency to mediate a dispute between him and a hostile British administration.[41]

As the three-way alliance unraveled, Zionist institutions were unable to provide significant support for the Arab opposition. The Arabs had a hugely inflated impression of world Jewry's influence and wealth. That paved the way for discontent and complaints about the Jews' impotence. "You've become like the government," said Hamdallah to Danin when the latter was unable to help him win a government contract. At a meeting of Irsheid, Hamdallah, and Shai agent Ya'akov Barazani, Irsheid lashed out, he said, in the name of all those who had made agreements with the Jewish Agency: "You are evading us. You tied us, pushed us into actions, we have made deals with people, spent money—and now, silence. The money you gave us, you said it was a small advance, a beginning of what was to come. The continuation hasn't come and we need it very much."[42]

Zionism's limited abilities and British reservations about their activities were not the only barriers that kept the opposition from gaining strength. Another important source of its weakness was its internal divisions and personal squabbles among its leaders. Suliman Tuqan had a low opinion of Fakhri Nashashibi: "He has become a British agent and does everything they demand of him. He chases after money and status and spends his time getting drunk, sleeping with women, and attending loud parties that do nothing at all for the Arab cause. . . . He brings disgrace upon himself and on anyone who joins him." Hamdallah, for his part, opened a front against Fakhri 'Abd al-Hadi: "He's all pose. Erratic and you can't depend on him. He wants to be at the top." Zeinati did not escape Hamdallah's critique, either: "We all agree that he won't be of much use for regular work."[43]

The Shai continued to make use of the opposition despite its weakness. When the Zionist intelligence agency needed an armed guard to conduct a trip through Samaria, or when KKL functionary Yosef Weitz wanted to visit the area, Hamdallah provided the required assistance.[44]

Along with his associates, he continued to convey information about developments in the area under his influence. But the illusion of building up a significant pro-Zionist Arab force was soon dispelled. The two paths that remained open to Zionist institutions were the use of opposition leaders to collect information and the identification, recruitment, and management of new informers.

The Politics of Intelligence

In summer 1941, Ahmad al-Imam returned to Palestine. Al-Imam had been an intimate associate of the mufti and an infrequent informer. At the beginning of the rebellion he leaked information to the Jewish Agency on developments in Arab political circles. When Hajj Amin was exiled to Lebanon, al-Imam joined him and became one of his closest advisors; he subsequently followed the mufti to Iraq.[45] At this point his link with the Jewish Agency seems to have been severed. But immediately on his return to Palestine, Ezra Danin and Eliahu Sasson reestablished contact with him. The go-between was a Haifa businessman, Taher Qaraman, a partner of David Hacohen. Qaraman made a point of staying in touch with all possible sources. He provided financial assistance to the national committees in charge of the general strike, worked and exchanged information with Jews, and took in and supported the orphans of al-Qassam's men.

During the tempestuous years of the rebellion, Qaraman took refuge in Lebanon. From time to time he passed on information from there to Hacohen. After returning to Palestine he was again in contact with all the forces around him. Danin surmised that he was principally interested in advancing his own economic interests, but also that he believed in a politics of conciliation—that is, he believed that conflicts could and should be resolved nonviolently.[46]

Al-Imam had good reasons for meeting with Jewish intelligence figures at Qaraman's house. He had joint business ventures with his host, a past of supplying information to the Jews, need of a source of income, and disappointment with the mufti. Al-Imam viewed himself as a staunch nationalist, just as many collaborators did. He therefore proposed to Danin and Sasson that they work together in "a war against violence in all its forms." Sensitive to his self-image, the two Jews stressed that they had no intention of turning him into a collaborator who would "sabotage the general Arab interest."[47]

At first, al-Imam and Qaraman were unwilling to help hand over former rebels or even to provide the names of rebels who had left the country to undergo military training by the Germans. In their view it was better to let these men return to Palestine to conduct peaceful lives, so that they would have no interest in engaging in acts of terror.[48] This position was a corollary of their view of the rebellion. The Palestinian national movement, al-Imam claimed, opposed violence in principle. But, in the wake of the riots of summer 1929, Arabs realized that only violence brought results. He added that al-Qassam's men had assassinated acting Galilee district governor Lewis Andrews without coordination with the Higher Arab Committee, and that it was the harsh British response that forced the Arabs to take up arms.

After presenting his nationalist ideology and defending the rebels, al-Imam went on to provide a list of names of people who should be kept under surveillance. From that time onward he maintained contact with the Jewish Agency's Arab bureau and provided information on nationalist circles in Palestine and neighboring countries.[49] His initial opposition to naming names can be understood in two ways: real reluctance to aid the enemy, or a tactic in his negotiations with his future operators. An important point to keep in mind is that, unlike the opposition figures discussed above, al-Imam worked secretly, without presenting any immediate political demands.

Al-Imam can be viewed as a collaborator who had his limits or, alternatively, as one who wanted to have the best of both worlds. In any case, he and Qaraman tried to get the British to release political and security prisoners. Such an achievement would have enhanced their standing in nationalist circles. In later periods, it became common for collaborators to seek to gain credit for the release of prisoners.

Sheikh 'Abd al-Qader al-Muzaffar established even clearer limits. He was a pillar of Palestinian Arab nationalism, having denounced traitors before the legislative assembly elections in 1923. After the outbreak of the rebellion he became one of the mufti's sharpest critics and supported a political resolution of the conflict in which Emir 'Abdallah of Transjordan would receive sovereignty over Palestine. Since then, the mufti's men had viewed him as a traitor. In February 1941, Eliahu Sasson met with him, and al-Muzaffar said he was delighted by the conciliation between Arabs and Jews. For both sides to benefit from the new situation, he maintained, the British must state unambiguously that they would have no more dealings with the mufti and his circle. The British, he pointed out, were taking the opposite approach—appointing supporters of Hajj Amin to senior positions in the religious hierarchy.

Sasson tried to take advantage of the opportunity to receive from al-Muzaffar current information on the mufti's pro-Nazi activities. Al-Muzaffar said he would provide the information gladly, but he feared that doing so would be detrimental to the Arab national cause. To be perfectly frank, al-Muzaffar said to Sasson, the Jews could use reliable information of this sort to prove, now and after the war, that the Arabs were opposed to democracy. Better for the Arabs, he added, to suffer the mufti's intrigues and try to obstruct them on their own than to provide such proofs to a rival force. If one or another Arab public figure himself were to warn the authorities about the treasonous behavior of one of his community's leaders, he explained, that would bring honor to his people. But that would hardly be the case if the person who brought the warning to the British was a Jew. That would besmirch the honor of all Arabs.[50]

This conversation shows that al-Muzaffar (who said he was willing to meet Shertok as well) had lines that he would not cross. It also shows that an Arab leader who did not feel bound by the strategy of the accepted leadership of the time, and who had even been declared a traitor, did not necessarily prefer the fortunes of the opposing nation to the fortunes of his own. This was characteristic of many "political collaborators"—not that it saved them from the fate of others like them, as was the case with al-Muzaffar, who was hit by a Molotov cocktail not long after his meeting with Sasson.[51]

Another religious figure who cooperated closely with Jewish Agency officials was Sheikh Fawzi al-Imam. Born in 1905, he was a graduate of al-Azhar University in Cairo and a prominent clergyman. At the beginning of the rebellion, the mufti ousted him from his position as a preacher in Jaffa on the grounds that he had been involved in unspecified immoral acts.[52] After his dismissal, al-Imam joined the opposition. According to another source, the order of events was the reverse of this: "In 1937, when terror against Arabs, Jews, and the English was on the rise, Sheikh Fawzi sought to influence the mufti to abandon his criminal ways. After his efforts failed, he resigned all his religious and political positions and traveled to Transjordan." Two years later he returned to Palestine, preached in villages against violence and the terrorist gangs, "and helped the government impose order." In 1940, al-Imam again became a mosque preacher, ranting with passion in favor of the British and against the Axis powers. He made a big impression, according to a report written after a sermon he delivered in a mosque in Jaffa. But the mufti's supporters walked out in the middle, asserting that al-Imam had been bribed by the British.[53]

Such a man was a natural target of recruitment by the Zionists, and Eliahu Sasson met with him several times and gave him various assignments. They considered founding a partnership to battle Nazi propaganda and deal with any riots that might break out during the war. There is no evidence that such an association was ever established, but al-Imam did provide evaluations of the mood in Palestinian Arab society and information on religious leaders. In spring 1941, Sasson sent him on a trip through southern Palestine. On his return, al-Imam provided the names of preachers who were speaking in support of Germany and of arms dealers in southern villages. In a second report he listed the names of the mufti's supporters who had been restored to posts as preachers in mosques, adding who in the British administration was behind their return. He also suggested possible replacements for the pro-German preachers.[54]

We have no account of al-Imam's motives. He may have wanted to receive a senior post in the religious establishment and perhaps thought that working with the British and Jews would help him get an appointment. He may well have believed that the welfare of his people required supporting the British in wartime. And perhaps his desire for revenge against the mufti overcame all other considerations.

Local Informers

The Mutliq family, which dominated the village of Majdal near Tiberias, was part of the rural leadership the rebels had attacked. As noted above, they began helping the Shai during the rebellion and continued to do so during the war. Khaled Mutliq, the village's mukhtar, reported to his operators about armed exercises conducted by Arabs in the region, about a plan to attack the Jews of Tiberias, and about a rebel activist who had entered the country carrying large amounts of money with the purpose of reviving the rebellion. Another informer from Majdal working alongside Khaled was 'Ali Saleh, who was rated an exceptionally reliable source.[55]

Khaled Mutliq was used largely to gather intelligence, but he also helped stabilize relations between the region's Jews and Arabs. After an incident in which Haganah soldiers from Kibbutz Ginnosar killed the mukhtar of the village of Ghweir Abu Shusha (apparently as a result of a misunderstanding), Mutliq and his veteran operator, Feitelson, intervened. Together with sheikhs, notables, and British officers, they led the two sides to an alliance of peace (sulha).[56]

Anyone who acted this way revealed himself. Other informers tried, as much as they could, to camouflage their activity. They passed on the information they collected covertly to Shai agents, who in turn relayed it, when necessary, to the British police. One interesting case of this sort was that of an informer code-named "Blacky," who worked as a guard in KKL forests and was considered reliable. He suggested the arrest of two of his cousins from the village of Manshiyya, near Acre, "because they cause a lot of trouble in the area."[57] It is not clear whether he was at odds with them for family or other personal reasons or really did want to stop violence.

An old friend of Danin's reported on arms in the villages around Qalqilya. In the town itself, he said, a British operation to round up weapons had left only a few dozen guns. In Tira there were also several dozen and in Taybe about 200, he estimated. Another informer told his operators about a resident of 'Arab al-Nafi'at who had purchased stolen British arms. The police found the guns and arrested the buyer.[58]

The nephew of the Qassamite leader Farhan al-Sa'adi served as a secret police detective. He was shot but rescued, and he maintained contact with a Shai agent code-named "Aloni." In spring 1941 he told "Aloni" that he had been offered three months of training in Syria: "When I'm with the *shebab* [the young men] and see their enthusiasm, I'm with them, but the minute I get out of there and begin to think about my wife and children, all the enthusiasm fades and I don't want to go at all," he related. He went on to say that if he were to decide in the end to go to Syria, he would pass on information about the training camp through his younger brother.[59]

Among the regular tasks the Shai assigned informers was the compilation of lists of Arab activists to be arrested in emergencies. George 'Azar of Jaffa prepared an inventory of supporters of the mufti and Nazis in thirty villages around Jaffa. He made note of those who held unlicensed weapons (generally purchased from British or Australian soldiers, or from Bedouins) and of government workers "who in their hearts oppose the British and who might act against the government at an appropriate time." Others reported on the movements of rebel commanders, public assemblies, and similar activities. Some informers took the opportunity to settle personal scores, as informers have done down through history. Their reports therefore had to be vetted to separate authentic information from private vendettas.[60]

Other collaborators were field operators, hunting down wanted men or investigating murders committed during the rebellion. Some set up sting operations to capture insurgents. A man from the village of Samakh on the southern coast of the Sea of Galilee offered to turn in 'Atiyyah al-Rutni, a former rebel who was a regular dinner guest at the collaborator's house. Al-Rutni was wanted for repeatedly sabotaging the oil pipeline. For his services, the collaborator asked for 50 Palestinian pounds but consented to being paid only after al-Rutni was brought to trial. A man from Wadi 'Ara agreed to go undercover as a fugitive and infiltrate an armed band and then turn in its cohorts. After the killings of two Jewish members of the Ma'abarot ha-Yarden commune on the north end of the Dead Sea, Arab informers were sent to find the murderer. An individual of the Shibli Bedouin tribe brought in the information. After the killing of a member of Kibbutz Mishmar ha-Yarden, a man from the village of 'Ayn Zeitun offered to apprehend the murderer—whose identity he knew—and to turn him over to the police, dead or alive.[61]

Arabs also took part in Jewish revenge operations. The common (but mistaken) wisdom among the police and many Arabs was that Qasem Tabash, slayer of Alexander Zeid, was liquidated by Muhammad Abu Soda, known as a friend of Giora Zeid and other Jews.[62] An Arab police officer went even farther in serving the cause of Jewish vengeance. He told the Shai that he had met a Druze man who was willing, for pay, to assassinate Hajj Amin. The proposal was conveyed to British security officials.[63] The Shai was also able to use its sources to track the mufti's dealings. The son of one of its Arab informers, from the village of 'Ayn Karem, was one of the mufti's bodyguards during his exile. Whenever his son told him where the mufti was and what his plans were, the man passed the information on to A. H. Cohen.[64]

Local informers also took part in an important intelligence enterprise initiated by the Shai's Arab department after the end of the rebellion—preparation of a database on Palestine's Arab settlements. As part of the project, executed in three stages, the department composed assessments of 720 Arab villages and Bedouin tribes. The material was collected in two ways. Shai agents questioned informers and spoke with inhabitants of the settlements, taking advantage of the conciliatory atmosphere that allowed social contacts between Jews and Arabs. Additionally, a small number of informers themselves specialized in writing these reports. Three such individuals stood out in this part of the project: one in Samaria, one in the Jerusalem hills, and a third in the Haifa region and the Galilee. The three were instructed to collect information of interest to the Shai, and the material they supplied was cross-checked with data from other sources. These surveys were updated over the years, extending into the war of 1948.[65]

Real Estate

During the rebellion, land sales dropped appreciably because of attacks on sellers and the reluctance of Jewish investors to put their money in real estate. Nevertheless, during the uprising's four years, Arabs sold about 140,000 dunams to Jews. This was some 30 percent less than sales in the previous four years but still quite a respectable figure.[66] When the rebellion ended, more land was put up for sale, largely because of the economic crisis. The land brokers—*samasirah*—returned in full force. The fact that sellers put their financial interest before the national interest indicated that the national leadership had failed to achieve a fundamental shift in Arab mores on this issue. After all, the prohibition on selling land to the Zionists had been the centerpiece of their campaign before and during the rebellion.[67]

George 'Azar analyzed the real estate market for his Zionist contacts near the end of the rebellion. The two variables that were working in the Jews' favor, he noted, were the fall in the price of land and the weakness of the national forces. He suggested that the Jews obtain large sums of money because "there can be no doubt that many parcels of land will be put up for sale at the beginning of next summer, and it is certain that the Arabs will be unable to buy them, so they will in any case fall into the hands of the Jews."[68] The war shut down trade routes, shrinking citrus exports, thus reducing the liquid capital of Arab citrus farmers. This and the desire to have cash available for an emergency encouraged the sale of land.[69]

But in April 1940 the British imposed a legal impediment to further transactions. The Land Transfer Clause, issued to put the White Paper's policies into effect, came into force and divided Palestine into three regions. One, in which land sales to Jews were entirely forbidden, constituted 63 percent of the country. A second, in which sales could be effected only with a special permit from the high commissioner, constituted 32 percent. Only in some 5 percent of the territory, mostly along the coastal plain, were purchases allowed without restriction.[70] A delegation from Abu-Ghosh met with Emir 'Abdallah in an exceptional attempt to quash the law but failed.[71] Nevertheless, Yosef Weitz wrote:

> Wonder of wonders. Just as the land law came into force and Zionism faced a wall that closed it off from most of the country's land, closed off its redemption and so also its settlement project—there was a decisive change for the better. The inertia that marked the Zionist movement in the period under discussion above came to an end. This "law," illegal according to the

Mandate and the country's constitution, which took from the Jews most possibilities for purchasing land, seems to have awakened new powers in them, powers of resistance to it—not in words but rather in deeds and actions. From that point onward we have witnessed a heartening phenomenon of penetration beyond the wall of the law, into forbidden areas, of the redemption and settlement of important tracts of land. . . . KKL's augmented activity in this field is increasing by the year, and its result: expansion of land holdings in the three years 1940–1942 by 137,000 dunams, granting us a standing in the south, in the Judean highlands, in Samaria, and in the Upper Galilee.[72]

KKL needed collaborators to accomplish this "penetration beyond the wall of the law." It found them. Landowners who feared that their property would lose value because it was in areas where sale to Jews was forbidden put their holdings on the market as soon as the law was published but before it went into effect.[73] Many villagers now needed money and consented to sell their land; lawyers and government officials agreed to help conclude the deals under the table. Mukhtars and agents organized potential sellers and brought them together with KKL's purchasers, and the real estate market flourished, as Weitz noted, more than it ever had.

The movers of the deals were the old-time *samasirah*. Sharif Shanti continued to operate in the Sharon region: "In the Tulkarem block we purchased much land through him, that was in the years 1942, 1944, even 1945," recollected Avraham Gissin, who worked with Gad Makhnes. Members of the Samara family of Tulkarem also continued to be active. Although one of the family's leaders, 'Abdallah Samara, had for years headed the nationalist forces in the city, other members of the family had no compunctions about working with the Zionists.[74]

Local leaders, in particular members of the opposition and those close to them, were also involved in land transactions. One was Isma'il al-'Azzi, who had begun working with the Zionists in the 1930s. His business partner was a Christian Arab from Jaffa, George Sayegh, who was married to a Jewish woman. Al-'Azzi, a leader in the Beit Jibrin area, lived in the village of Tel al-Safi. Along with Sayegh, he bought lands from the Negev villages of Hoj and Breir on which Kibbutz Dorot was built. The property was registered in their names, and they provided KKL with power of attorney that enabled the Jews to settle on it. From that time on, until the war of 1948, al-'Azzi continued, like others in his family, to be a central figure in Zionist land purchases in the northern Negev. Farid Irsheid of Jenin also went into the real estate business. He tried his hand at a huge undertaking in northeast Samaria, between Tubas and Jenin, though without success.[75]

These local leaders redoubled their land operations at this time for much the same reason that had motivated them before the rebellion; they needed money to shore up their social and political standing. "His [al-'Azzi's] problem was how to hold on, not to let the family decline politically," Danin explained.[76] Hamdallah faced the same problem. He opened a large *madafah* (guesthouse) in his village and lobbied to release people from prison—and he also worked as a land agent. This fit in with his intelligence and political activity, and he justified it on the grounds that the money received from selling part of his land would allow the cultivation of the rest.[77]

Mukhtars all over the country cooperated with Jewish land purchasers, sometimes even initiating sales. Yosef Sharon shopped for property in the Gush Etzion area (between Bethlehem and Hebron) for Marom, a Zionist land purchase company. He was also a Shai agent. To obtain parcels from the village of Nahalin, he related, he hired the village's two mukhtars and the mukhtar of the adjacent village of Jaba'. "He was as cunning as a snake. A very seasoned and shrewd person," Sharon said of the latter. They organized the landowners in their villages and had them sign the necessary papers. An Arab officer named Yussuf from the Bethlehem police accepted cash in sealed envelopes and proceeded to ignore any complaints brought to his attention. The mukhtars also earned their share. "I can't say that they did anything out of or for the love of Israel," Sharon said. "What they did, they did for money, for lucre."[78]

A critical stage in transferring ownership after a sale was the removal of the tenant farmers who lived on the land. Sometimes the mukhtars assumed this task. For example, the mukhtar of Beit Naballah would, for a fee, "arbitrate between us and the tenants," as Gissin put it.[79] Sometimes agents arrived from distant areas and used their connections and status to do the job. This was the case with 'Ali al-Mustaqim, deputy mayor of Jaffa. He helped KKL and a group of Jews from Tel Aviv remove tenants from land purchased in the Beit She'an district. He went out with attorney S. B. Sasson, "and thanks to his personal influence with Halusi Khayri [later a government minister in Jordan] and on sheikhs from the area arranged the matter easily, and the land was transferred to KKL," Sasson wrote in 1949.[80]

KKL's man in Tiberias, Shalom Svardlov, had a different method. He sent Bedouin acquaintances to raid the homes of the tenants "in order to intimidate them and urge them on." In one case he planned to burn a granary containing a village's entire year's crop "so that they understand that it's worth their while to sell." This scheme, unlike the harassment and robbery Svardlov orchestrated, was not carried out.[81]

The process during this period was different from that before the rebellion. On the one hand, the job was easier; the punitive campaign against land dealers and sellers had ended, and most of the people who had led it were no longer in the country. On the other hand, the sellers and buyers had to cope with the prohibition on land sales imposed by the British. KKL lawyers found a loophole that allowed the organization to continue to purchase land, but taking advantage of this dodge required the use of collaborators and a high level of mutual trust between them and their operators.

The gambit took advantage of exceptions to the areas in which Jews were forbidden to buy land. For example, such purchases were permitted when the land was offered for sale by the courts because of the landowner's debts, or when the landlord owed money to Jews and wished to repay his debt in real estate rather than in cash. KKL found ways to take advantage of these provisions. One fairly simple method was to locate Arab landowners who were debtors and had open files in the executor's office. KKL representatives contacted these debtors and offered large sums of money for their land. Once the property owner agreed, the sellers applied to the executor's office and put the land up for auction. In some cases KKL offered larger sums than other bidders, and in other instances there were no other bidders; the two sides in the deal would conclude it in the presence of Jewish officials in the executor's office in Tel Aviv before anyone else got involved.

In spring 1943, the assistant to the chief of British police in Palestine reported to the Mandatory government's chief secretary that Jews had, since the publication of the restrictions, used this method to purchase more than 20,000 dunams in the Gaza district alone. Some in the British administration disputed this estimate, but not the fact that the method was in use. The assistant noted that Zionist institutions took advantage of the fact that the law did not limit the proceeds of debtor land sales to the sum of the debt itself. The debtors were free to sell as much as they wished—and some did. It was clear to all that these were voluntary transactions, and that the Arab sellers were no less interested in them than the Zionists. But the governor of the Gaza district maintained that the administration nevertheless had to take steps to halt the practice.[82]

Another method was enlistment of Arabs who were in debt to Jews (or to KKL itself) as strawmen to purchase land. These people received funds from KKL to buy parcels in the forbidden areas. After the land was registered in their names, KKL would produce their promissory notes— and the courts had no choice but to rule that the land should be registered in KKL's name.

One of these professional debtors was Darwish Dahudi al-Dajani, member of a leading Jerusalem family. In the 1930s he had worked with Moshe Smilansky on the purchase of land in the area of Rechovot and the northern Negev. He had been involved, together with his brother Sheikh Mahmoud, in some particularly large transactions.[83] Some of his Jewish acquaintances viewed him as extremely reliable, while others termed him a swindler. At the beginning of the 1940s he was about 50 years old. He owned a flour mill and land close to Motza, just west of Jerusalem, but he was deeply in debt to both Arabs and Jews. After the Land Transfer Clause was promulgated, the Zionists needed people like him. KKL's representative in the south, Yoav Zuckerman, did not know Dahudi personally but was aware of his history. Zuckerman suggested that KKL employ Dahudi as a front man. Aharon Malkov, who arranged a meeting between the two in Jerusalem's Eden Hotel, recounted Dahudi's reaction to the proposal: "He said to me: Please, may it be, may it be, may it be. If you can do such a thing for me then I will never ever forget you."[84]

From then on, Dahudi served as an important agent for land purchases in forbidden areas. He bought tracts from Arabs and, as a debtor, immediately put them up for public auction in coordination with the executor. At this point KKL (or another Jewish organization) would purchase the land. "We took advantage of old judgments handed down against him," Hiram Danin related.

> At first it was mostly Zuckerman who worked with him and purchased the debts of debtors. He received an appropriate power of attorney from them, and then the machine worked to put the land up for auction. Dahudi would appear before the presiding judge and give his consent to the sale of the land to KKL, to the point that it became a routine matter and they used Dahudi not only in the south; also in the north land was registered in his name.[85]

The Mandatory government and land department of the Higher Arab Committee became aware of Dahudi's activity in the later 1940s.[86] Arab nationalists began to pursue him. The Zionists spirited him from one hiding place to another and sent his children to Egypt. In 1947 he left Palestine for Turkey, where he died.[87]

As noted, in the first half of the decade there was relatively little activity against land dealers. Another member of the Dajani family, Ibrahim al-Dajani, entered the business. He was instrumental in 1944 in the transfer to the Zionists of some of the land of Jabal Abu-Ghneim, the hill between Jerusalem and Bethlehem where the controversial Jewish neighborhood of Har Homa was built in the late 1990s.[88]

The weakness of the Arab national movement also worked to the benefit of 'Ali al-Qasem of Taybe. He became an informer for the Jews and British and was suspected of carrying out contract murders. At the same time, he maintained ties with the Arab national leadership. Al-Qasem was the brother-in-law of Salameh 'Abd al-Rahman, the famous land agent from the Sharon and son-in-law of the mayor of Tulkarem. They brought him into their business at the end of the 1920s, and right at the start of his career he received money from Yehoshua Hankin for a transaction he promised to make but never actually did. This left him a debtor to the Zionist institutions, and after the promulgation of the land law it was decided to make use of him. Al-Qasem agreed, and he brokered deals in exchange for large sums of money.[89]

Al-Qasem was then one of the most powerful men in the Sharon region. His influence came from his family connections and his wealth. His relations with the British also worked in his favor; they appointed him inspector of the Faliq (Poleg River) swamp in the Sharon. He also took protection money from Jews who bought land in his area of influence.[90] Slowly, he expanded his business into other regions. In Abu-Ghosh, for example, he cooked up a scheme to transfer land to KKL. The plan came to light because al-Qasem and one of his partners forged bills of sale and tripled the amount of land registered in their names. The sellers discovered the fraud and demanded in court that the original land registration be restored. They understood that al-Qasem was a front man.

Another deal of his involved real estate on the southern coastal plain. Al-Qasem, it was charged, transferred land to Jews without the knowledge of its owners. Arab nationalists decided to teach him a lesson. When he learned that they planned to murder him, al-Qasem mobilized fifteen bodyguards, armed them, and trained them in defensive and offensive tactics.[91] As noted above, in the end he was killed by Israeli intelligence, not by Arab nationalists.

Yet another central figure in land sales during this period was Yusuf al-Jarushi. His family, which originated in Libya, had settled near Gedera. Two of its members, Muhammad and 'Omar, were guards of the

Jewish moshav and its fields. "They were loyal to the moshava, spoke fluent Hebrew, and cooperated with the Jews even during the disturbances and the struggle."[92] Yusuf was put in charge of the land business. "A great deal of property was registered in Yusuf al-Jarushi's name, but his loyalty to us was complete," Hiram Danin related.[93]

The gallery of front men, or "borrowed names," as they were called in KKL, also included Ahmad Miqbal of Sindiana. This is the same Miqbal who took part in the rebellion and crossed the lines after his father and brothers were slain by rebels. Miqbal, it will be recalled, sought refuge in Zikhron Ya'akov but later took up residence in Ezra Danin's citrus grove near Hadera. When the rebellion ended, he began purchasing land for the Zionists. Danin recalled the relationship:

> Ahmad Miqbal was a guard in my orchard. He knew the purpose of the action [the purchase of land]. For that he received small sums of money as did the other one [another front man who lived on Danin's land]. But they were tied to us. We gave them protection, we gave them help. They were not Zionists. In that, we did [them] a favor, because we kept very careful watch on Ahmad Miqbal. He was in the orchard and they [the rebels] could not reach him. We would transport him each time, and in general, until we taught him how to sign his name, then he would go to the land registration office and in the end became a millionaire. That black nigger who lived in a miserable tent.[94]

Danin, so it seems, patronized Miqbal in no small measure. Neither did Yehoshua Palmon think much of the front men who worked for KKL:

> That guy [Miqbal] was not the same type as 'Ali Qasem or Sayf al-Din Zu'bi. They were well-heeled, respected among their people. They were public figures, people who looked impressive, you know. That was their livelihood during that period. . . . It should also be noted that all those borrowed names, with the exception of Ezra's [Danin's] two guys, they were serpents, they were leeches. They were not decent people, and forgive me Deputy Speaker of the Knesset Sayf al-Din Zu'bi or 'Ali Qasem and all those [decent] types. They were leeches and it cost us a lot of money.[95]

Leeches and serpents perhaps, but ideal for KKL. Not only did they help register land; they assisted in purchasing land from Arabs who were hesitant about selling directly to Jews. They allayed sellers' concerns by allowing those who needed such solace to persuade themselves that they were selling to Arabs. Of course, anyone who wanted to know knew full well what the ultimate disposition of the land was going to be, but in certain pressured situations people can convince themselves of totally

groundless propositions. With the help of these shills, KKL land purchases spread to areas in which there was only a small Jewish presence
before the Land Transfer Clause came into force. The Zionists' hold on
the land thus grew in parallel with their greater intelligence penetration
of the Arab community.

Partners in the Hebrew Rebellion

Arab arms traffickers had been an important Zionist source of weaponry
from the inception of the Yishuv's military organizations.[96] Purchases
were generally made on a local basis, by direct contact with Arab sellers
or through intermediaries. Toward the end of World War II the need for
arms increased. In February 1944 the Jewish militant underground Etzel,
under the command of Menachem Begin, declared an armed struggle
against the British. In October 1945 the Haganah joined the struggle in
the framework of the "Hebrew Rebellion." The common wisdom was
that the fate of Palestine would be decided by force of arms. The purchase of weapons from Arabs became institutionalized.

Arab arms merchants worked outside the law. Sometimes they were
involved in other criminal activities, such as drug sales. They were not
concerned with national issues and certainly did not favor one Jewish
organization over another for ideological reasons. Some worked with the
Haganah, others with the smaller and more militant Etzel or Lehi. Others
dealt with whoever bid the highest. The choice depended largely on previous connections or economic considerations.[97]

The most prominent of the Arabs who aided Lehi was Yusuf Abu-
Ghosh. His involvement in the movement grew over time and, among
other exploits, he participated in the operation that freed Lehi operative
Geula Cohen (later a member of the Israeli Knesset) from a British prison
in April 1947. The force's chief of intelligence, Yitzhak Hasson, recruited
him for that operation. He later related that the two of them had been
brought together by the Lehi member whose code name was "Re'uven,"
"a man who had a hand in everything and who had everyone's hand
raised against him, a past and present criminal who worked as a smuggler and whatever else came to hand, and who was friendly with Arabs
for that purpose." The report of the British police's Criminal Investigation Department of June 1947 contains accounts (of varying degrees of
reliability) of Abu-Ghosh's work with Lehi, including the purchase of
arms and explosives and operations in Arab territories, as well as criminal activities. Lehi's ideologue and member of its high command, Yisrael

Eldad, knew only of his role in the Jewish underground: "Jewish blood flows within him; it can't be that he is an Arab . . . a wondrous phenomenon in the murky sea of hypocritical Levantinism," he marveled.[98]

Abu-Ghosh bought materials for explosives from Arab quarries. Another source, used also by Etzel, was British army camps. Arabs, mostly Bedouin, stole mines and other munitions from bunkers and camps. They passed the goods on to Jewish underground operatives who had ordered them. One such delivery was intercepted in September 1945 not far from Khan-Yunis on its way to the center of the country. According to one source, Etzel had paid the Arab smuggler with narcotics.[99]

A central Etzel weapons supplier was a drug dealer named Muhammad Abu-Yasin of Jaffa. According to information obtained by the Haganah, in the year after the end of World War II, Abu-Yasin sold Etzel several tons of TNT and more than 200 Thompson submachine guns. In June 1946 relations soured after Etzel operatives loaded up two tons of explosives from a storeroom in Abu-Yasin's citrus orchard but, instead of paying, threatened him with their guns and left. A few months later Etzel realized that it had made a mistake and sought to reestablish the business connection.[100]

Arab collaborators also took part in the Hebrew resistance against the British after World War II. Some of them helped Etzel and Lehi in robberies carried out to fund their activities, some provided covering fire in operations against British targets, and some concealed kidnapped British personnel in hideouts in Arab areas where the British never thought to look. Haganah sources reported that a man named Rashid, a close associate of 'Ali al-Qasem, joined Etzel operatives in three robberies—in Nablus, Jaffa, and Tel Aviv. This same Rashid was also sent, according to a British police investigation, to throw a bomb at Palestinian Arab public figures with the aim of causing dissension within the local leadership.[101] The British also suspected that Arabs aided Etzel in blowing up the King David Hotel in July 1946.[102] Another case was that of a Bedouin of the Sawarke tribe, which dwelt near Yahudia. He joined Etzel in attacks on British targets near Petah Tikva, was trained in laying mines, and was sent to sabotage the railroad line to Jerusalem. Some Arabs helped distribute leaflets issued by the Jewish underground organizations,[103] and others offered humanitarian assistance—hiding Etzel men in the Dajani hospital. This cooperation was also motivated by family ties. Havva Rechtman of Rechovot, daughter of a well-known revisionist right-wing family, married a member of the Dajani family, the brother of the hospital's owner. Haganah sources related that she was also involved in purchasing arms from an Arab dealer in Gaza. In 1990 one of their sons became a member of the central committee of the Likud.[104]

It is difficult to estimate the number of collaborators involved in arms sales. The reports contain a handful of names of people who sold weapons to Jews on a regular basis. But, as in land sales, there were also many Arabs who purveyed arms to Jews when the opportunity arose. Bedouin found mines, dismantled them, and sold the explosives. Others came, in one way or another, into possession of rifles or pistols they did not need.

Like other collaborators, arms dealers did not see themselves as absolutely bound by the rules of the national cause. Had they wanted to, they could have justified their actions ideologically. The weapons they sold were directed almost entirely against the British at this stage of the conflict.

CAUGHT IN THE WEB

During World War II, collaborators' ties with their operators became institutionalized and the pool of them increased as veteran collaborators continued their work and new ones were recruited. Geopolitics was not the only factor; the personal histories of informers and their operators were also highly significant.

After the rebellion, the men who had led the peace units found that they had painted themselves into a corner. Halting their collaboration with the Zionists would have been difficult even if that is what they had wanted to do. The armed struggle they had carried out against the rebellion had tainted them in the eyes of many Arabs (even though no few Arabs waited anxiously for the end of the rebellion), and death sentences hung over them. They had little choice but to continue to battle the national movement's leadership and to try to reestablish their preeminence, each in his own region. In this life-or-death struggle they needed allies, and the Zionists, who shared their general view of the situation, were the obvious candidates. This was true both on the political level and in the field. After all, armed bands that still roamed the country threatened the members of the peace units no less—perhaps even more—than they did the Jews. In their case, collaboration clearly resulted from a double confluence of interests.

Relations with the veteran "minor" informers were based on a different kind of common interest. During the revolt their motives, as noted, included vengeance, alienation from their own community, and friendship with Jews. For these people the end of the rebellion was a relief. They were no longer in constant mortal danger, and the connections they had developed with the Zionists became more useful because of the retribution policy adopted by the Shai. It was only natural for them to continue to aid Jews with whom they had maintained contact. In those cases in which the thirst for vengeance had not been quenched, they continued to work to capture rebels. Some of them, who were still in danger, were under the protection of their Jewish operators, hence no longer active. Miqbal of Sindiana, for example, adjusted himself to changing conditions. He had been a guide for the Shai and the British; now he assisted in land purchases.

Aharon Danin spoke from his experience with collaborators who worked with him on land deals, but his description applies just as well to other areas of activity. Danin explained how personal connections could turn both money and nationalism into marginal issues:

> The people who worked with us began at first for financial benefit. Afterward they got into the groove. They saw it as part of their personal relations with us. Then they got into the swing of working with us. At the beginning it was for financial benefit. That was only the first factor, but not the only one. They didn't deal with Zionism, but in a later period—after all, people live their lives—we had connections with them and not just for work. Very close personal relationships developed, and they instructed us in how to work there. . . . They received a certain sum for each operation. But aside from the money there was also a drive to succeed.[105]

This drive to succeed is an important factor in the operating of collaborators, one that has not received the attention it deserves. This is a fundamental psychological mechanism that played into the operators' hands. Once the collaborators accepted a mission, it was important to them to prove that they could carry it out. This was the case both with land brokers sent to persuade people to sell their property and with informers sent to investigate an incident.

This was all the more true when positive personal relations developed between an operator and a collaborator. As Danin notes, extremely close relations can generate mutual obligations. The operator invests in his collaborator (at least for as long as he needs him), and in exchange the collaborator puts out maximum effort. "When you work with an Arab, you need to know, you don't finish things at the table with him. You go to his home, he visits your house, when his son is ill you need to help take him to the doctor," related Mordechai Shakhevitz, a KKL and Shai operative.[106]

The sense of a shared fate also deepened relations, as Shalom Svardlov of KKL said: "They also felt—if I already sold [land to the Jews] I've already been sold to the Jews, and I must be in constant touch with them and live near them. Partners in fate. After I have taken the first step, I can make myself out to be a nationalist on the outside, but in practice I am already tied to that Jewish circle that attends to such matters and continue to work with them at all times."[107]

This is how Jewish operators viewed it. Yet there remained a dissonance between, on the one hand, the collaborators' identification with and ties to their operators and their desire to earn money, and, on the other, their perception of themselves as members of the Palestinian Arab community. Aharon Danin of KKL told of an interesting conversation he had at the beginning of the 1940s with Khaled Zu'bi (brother of Sayf al-Din), who helped him buy land in the Zu'biyya villages east of Nazareth:

> He [Zu'bi] said, "Look, who knows better than me that your work is pure. You pay money for everything, top dollar, many times more than what the land is worth. But that doesn't change the fact that you are dispossessing us. You are dispossessing us with money, not by force, but the fact is that we are leaving the land." I say to him: "You are from this Zu'biyya tribe which is located here, in Transjordan, and in Syria, what difference does it make to you where you are, if you are here or if you and your family are there? . . ." He said: "It's hard for me to tell you, but in any case the graves of my forefathers are here. I feel that we are leaving this place. It's our fault and not yours."[108]

Zu'bi accepted the Zionist version of events—that the Jews were acting morally. The Arabs were guilty of not managing to hold on to their land. There were, of course, things he did not know (or chose to ignore) that Danin knew. There were Jewish land buyers who took men to bars and prostitutes to induce them to sell their land. There were collaborators who fomented feuds within villages to create conditions in which they could buy land.* But in the view of Zu'bi, who identified with the Zionist land-buying system that he had become a part of, the Arabs, him-

---

*Aharon Danin said: "Can you force a person to sell? Whoever wants to sell, sells. We had our plants among them; [the *samasirah*] could also, using the odd ways of our cousins [the Arabs], induce certain people to sell. But you can't call that an unfair or dishonest way." In a subsequent interview he added: "That he [Zeinati, 'Arsan, Shanti, or Abu-Hantash] forced them to sell—that's clear. We know about the relations among them. But we were not, we did not deal with that and we did not indicate to anyone that they should go that way." And in the previous conversation, he said: "They [certain Jews] used the American method; they accustomed the Arabs to drink liquor and to use prostitutes and so on. We [KKL] did not use those tactics." OHD-HU 57–9. He and others also referred to other methods used by collaborators—fraud, usurious loans, and the incitement of feuds.

self included, were fully responsible for their situation. Zu'bi internalized the Zionist discourse to such a high degree that we would be justified in concluding that he was the ideal collaborator. That is why we should not ignore what he said in another conversation with Danin: "I have no complaints against you, but deep inside I'm against you."[109]

Zu'bi did not specify precisely whom he was against: Zionism (for nationalist reasons), or perhaps those who had caused him to act against his people and himself. Apparently both were correct. Either way, his statement betrays nationalist sentiments within even him, the most loyal of collaborators. In this he was not exceptional. But these misgivings did not dictate collaborators' actions.

The war years were a relatively easy period for Zionist intelligence and for land purchases. True, collaborators continued to be hounded by Palestinian nationalists, and even dominant figures could not move without bodyguards. But the major harm they suffered was in the social sphere. A significant change took place toward the end of the war, when the Palestinian Arab national movement reorganized itself.

CHAPTER 8

PRELUDE TO WAR

STAMPING OUT COLLABORATORS

Early in the evening of 9 November 1941, Fakhri Nashashibi left a meeting at a Baghdad residence and headed for his nearby hotel. The distance was short, so he told his bodyguards that he would walk alone. A young man named Ahmad Nusseibah, whom Nashashibi had first met a few days earlier, awaited him at the hotel entrance. When Nashashibi approached him, Nusseibah drew a pistol and fired several shots. So ended the life of the most prominent member of the Palestinian Arab opposition, the high-living libertine who had founded the peace units during the rebellion, maintained contacts with both the Zionists and the British, and, more than any other man, personified the opposition to Hajj Amin al-Husseini.

Nusseibah fled, but not before passing his pistol to a waiting motorcyclist. The motorcyclist was apprehended. He turned in Nusseibah, who told his interrogators that 'Abd al-Qader al-Husseini had ordered the murder. Al-Husseini himself was arrested but was released a short time later. The assassination proved once again that, in the long-standing rivalry between Nashashibis and al-Husseinis, the latter had the upper hand.

Nashashibi had been in Baghdad on business. The British had asked him to counteract German influence in the Arab world. But there were stronger forces than he at work. Baghdad of November 1941 was a haven for Palestinian exiles from the mufti's camp—among them Akram Zu'itar, 'Abd al-Qader al-Husseini, and Mu'in al-Madi—who were working actively for the Germans against the British. The mufti himself had been in Iraq just before Nashashibi's arrival but had to flee after the abortive al-Kilani revolution. He arrived in Berlin a day before the murder, welcomed by Germany's Arabic-language radio station, while Nashashibi had been meeting with pro-British Iraqis. Between Nashashibi's official meetings, many Palestinians came up to his room and asked for his help obtaining British permission to return to Palestine in exchange for abandoning their hostile activities. Young Nusseibah, who had been involved in political murders in Palestine and underground activity in Iraq, was one of these petitioners. A few days before the murder he had told Nashashibi that he wanted to abandon terror, and Nashashibi believed he was sincere. Nusseibah took advantage of this trust to get close enough to kill Nashashibi, who had survived at least two previous assassination attempts.[1]

Nashashibi's murder was more than just a painful reminder of the hostility between the two Palestinian camps. It was also a severe moral and organizational blow to the mufti's opponents. That could be seen at the funeral. Some 800 guests came to pay their last respects, but the great majority of them were British and Jewish friends. The British representative was a low-ranking official. Observers pointed out that the Arab guests were mostly villagers, not city dwellers, and that no representatives of Jerusalem's leading families showed up. The only exception—hardly a surprising one—was the Dajani family, who had suffered a similar blow with the murder of Hasan Sidqi three years previously.

After the burial, the Nashashibi family considered how to react. They debated among themselves whether they ought to avenge Fakhri's blood, and if so whose blood should pay for it and who should be assigned the mission. No decision was made, so nothing was done. The general feeling was that, without Fakhri, the already weak opposition had become a shepherdless flock.[2]

The dramatic murder, along with the mufti's successful escape from British clutches and his warm welcome in Berlin, strengthened the Husseini camp. Reports came in from around Palestine about the joy that greeted the death of the "chief traitor." Only card-carrying members of the opposition dared express their regret at the murder and, in doing so, voice fear for their own lives.[3] For some the message was clear: they must strengthen their ties with the Jews. "In times like these, it is vital that we work together with you, in case something happens," said the brother of

Muhammad Zeinati of the Beisan Valley to his Shai operator, Gershon Ritov.[4]

The murder was part of a concerted campaign against the opposition that continued, in low gear, after the end of the rebellion. In October 1940, 'Abd al-Rahman al-Huneidi was murdered in Lydda—two years after the slaying of his brother, who had been the town's mayor. In revenge for that earlier killing, 'Abd al-Rahman had in the months before his death helped the British capture several rebels. Some of the apprehended men were hanged. A 14-year-old boy, a relative of one of the rebels, managed to get through al-Huneidi's bodyguard and shoot him at close range. A third brother, who had connections with the Shai, reported that the British had asked him not to seek vengeance.[5]

In August 1941 assailants attempted to murder two leaders of the peace units in Samaria, Hafez Hamdallah of 'Anabta and Farid Irsheid of Jenin. The attack failed because the conspirators tried to enlist one of Hamdallah's former bodyguards, on the mistaken assumption that he held a grudge against his old employer. The bodyguard quickly reported the plot to Hamdallah, and the latter alerted the police. They organized an operation to apprehend the suspects, hoping to use them to reach the most senior level of the mufti's supporters. Two plainclothesmen contacted the conspirators who had ordered Hamdallah's murder, presenting themselves as former rebels who were prepared to commit murders on order. The suspects explained to the undercover policemen how important it was to kill traitors and added that, if they were injured or lost their lives in the operation, the rebel command would cover all their needs in this world and the next. The police agents immediately arrested the men, but in interrogation they did not reveal the identity of those above them.[6]

On the local level, the focus was on mukhtars. So, for example, the village leaders of Qatanna and Lifta west of Jerusalem were warned about their ties with the opposition. Lifta's mukhtar, Mahmoud al-'Isa, also received death threats.[7] Everyone knew that the warnings were not empty; two Samarian mukhtars, from the villages of Talluza and Qaddum, were murdered by rebels. Information that reached Haganah intelligence indicated an intention to slay more mukhtars and opposition figures in the Nablus highlands.[8] The murders reminded those who had managed to forget that, despite the rebellion's failure and the relative calm, the spirit of the rebels and the mufti still hovered over the political arena.

In addition to attacks on opposition leaders, in which the motive was largely political, the mufti's faction also acted against "treason" on two other levels. They attacked and threatened Arabs who maintained social and economic ties with Jews in a futile attempt to uphold the norms established during the rebellion.[9] They also pursued informers, seeking to deter them or take revenge for acts they had committed during the rebellion.[10] But this activity was marginal compared with that in the rebellion. Propaganda against land sales also continued, but at low volume. In general, the mufti's men were on hold, waiting for a German victory. Sometimes they told their opponents that after the victory they would settle accounts with all those who had joined forces with the British and Zionists.[11] Only when Rommel was defeated in the North African desert and the Axis lost decisive battles in Europe did the Palestinian national forces lose hope that the war would advance their program. As they came to realize the implications of Nazi Germany's defeat, they understood that they must revive Palestinian Arab political activity and reorganize its public arena. This included the reestablishment of boundaries and norms regarding Jewish-Arab relations.

ARAB POLITICS AWAKENS

The first signs of Palestinian Arab political reorganization appeared at the end of 1943. Independent leaders, led by Ahmad Hilmi Pasha along with al-Istiqlal leaders 'Awni 'Abd al-Hadi and Rashid al-Hajj Ibrahim, reestablished the Nation's Fund (Sunduq al-Umma).[12] The Fund operated in three channels: propaganda against selling land to Jews, rescuing land that was in danger, and direct action against sellers.

At the same time, the entire Palestinian Arab political system shook itself awake. The Communist National Liberation League ('Usbat al-Taharrur al-Watani) was also founded in 1943, and in 1944 the Husseinis reactivated their Arab Party.[13] In winter 1946, Jamal al-Husseini returned from a British prison camp in Rhodesia and Hajj Amin escaped trial for war crimes in France and made his way to Cairo. One of the principal reasons for the stagnation in Arab politics had been the leadership vacuum left by these two men. Now they injected new momentum, setting off a flurry of activity.

But this new activism had fatal flaws—internal dissension and institutional redundancy. The Higher Arab Committee, reestablished by Jamal al-Husseini in March 1946, garnered but little support. His opponents established the Arab Front, composed of representatives from five opposition parties. Musa al-'Alami, an independent oppositionist, established the Constructive Enterprise (al-Mashru' al-Insha'i) as a counter-weight to the Nation's Fund. The Higher Arab Committee founded the Arab Treasury (Beit al-Mal al-'Arabi) for the same purpose. Two para-military organizations operated in parallel: the Najjadah, established after the war at the initiative of Jaffa attorney Nimer al-Hawwari, which was independent but inclined toward the opposition; and the pro-Husseini Futuwwa, which did its best to sully the Najjadah's prestige.[14] A plethora of competing organizations and lack of central political leader-ship accepted by all Palestinian Arabs became the most salient features of Palestinian Arab politics.

These internal divisions weighed down Palestine's Arabs as they con-fronted a convoluted set of adverse circumstances. In the West, public opinion and the Allied governments were reeling from the Holocaust. Ships full of Jewish refugees were sailing for Palestine with the goal of smuggling in illegal immigrants. The United States was lobbying Britain to allow the refugees into the country, even as the Jewish underground was carrying out widespread sabotage and attacks against British per-sonnel. On top of all this, Zionist institutions continued to purchase land. To frustrate the growing pressures for the establishment of a Jewish state, the Palestinian Arab leadership had to function in the international arena, within the Arab world, and locally.

The mission could not be accomplished without public backing. To ensure it, the national leadership tried to institute severe restrictions on ties with Jews, to reinstitute a strict definition of treason, and to neutral-ize those who opposed these rules. Its partner in this effort was the Arab League, established in 1945 by the seven independent Arab states, which assumed guardianship of the Palestinian problem.

The Palestinian leadership, in coordination with the Arab League, worked on two fronts: a general boycott of Zionist merchandise and all economic cooperation with the Zionists, and an escalation of the battle against Arabs who sold land to Jews. It called on the entire Arab public to take part in this great struggle. Anyone who disobeyed these strictures or acted contrary to the instructions of the Higher Arab Committee was accused of treason.

Back to the Boycott

The idea of an economic boycott was as old as the conflict itself. It was, however, put into practice only in times of tension. Its first widespread application was in 1929, after which it faded away. Another boycott was declared at the time of the general strike of April 1936. That one continued, at one or another level, throughout the years of the rebellion. The boycott again rose to the top of the Arab agenda in the crisis that followed World War II.

At this point, however, it changed from a Palestinian Arab to a pan-Arab project. On 2 December 1945, the Arab League decided that, beginning in January 1946, all its member states should "take the appropriate measures, in accordance with their administrative and legislative principles, to prevent the entry of Zionist merchandise into their territories." The justification was that helping the Zionist economy would allow the Jews to achieve their political objectives, which were opposed to Arab interests.[15] The *iftaa* (religious legal) council of al-Azhar Institute in Cairo issued a ruling in the same spirit, stating that economic aid to the enemies of Islam was one of the most serious crimes against God. All who trade with Jews are heretics, with all that that implies, the council declared.[16]

Palestinian Arabs publicly welcomed the Arab League decision. The Haifa boycott committee thanked the League effusively, defining the sanctions as a matter of life and death. "This is the opportunity to paralyze the Zionist hand," declared one of its leaflets.[17] Another leaflet, which appeared in Jerusalem, offered a weighty argument for the boycott: "It is neither manly nor logical for us to pay our enemies money so that they can buy arms and use them to murder us, and which will help them conquer our homeland and uproot us from the Holy Land. . . . Every Arab should swear to shun all that is Jewish, from this moment onward."[18] The armed struggle then being conducted by the Jewish underground, which included attacks on police stations, bombings of government offices, and ambushes of British soldiers, turned the equation "money to the Zionists equals arms for the Zionists" to one that was concrete and frightening. The obvious conclusion was that whoever aided the Zionists economically was helping murder his own compatriots.

Nevertheless, the boycott was far from universally observed. A leaflet posted in August 1946 by the Higher Arab Committee's economic department bluntly addressed the political implications of breaking the boycott. In doing so, it depicted the actual state of compliance:

> The National Economic Organization Committee regrets that it must accuse the Palestinian Arab people of demeaning its rights and failure to carry out the boycott decision. Every Arab's duty is to consider that God alone is the best inspector and that each person's conscience must serve as his chief inspector. But those who have forgotten God, betrayed the trust,

sold their religion for this world, and put their consciences in their hands
and in their pockets, all such will be cursed by Allah and history and the
nation will judge them and impose the appropriate punishment. O noble
Arab nation! The enemy has constantly said *that he is a people without a
homeland and that he wants to conquer the homeland that has no people.
Do not prove that, as he argues, you do not exist* [emphasis added]. Will
land sellers, speculators, and all those who do not boycott the enemy's
merchandise heed this call?[19]

The text opens with a typical attempt to rally the public's spirit: "[The
boycott] operates like bombs at the foundations of the [Jewish] national
home." Both the press and the Higher Arab Committee from time to
time published news of the damage the Zionists were suffering as a result
of the boycott.[20] But the leaflet's central message was an accusation
against uncooperative Palestinian Arabs. The Higher Arab Committee
realized the significance of this disobedience. The attempt to unite the
Arabs of Palestine in a battle against Zionism was not succeeding, and
this lent credence to the Zionist contention that there was no Palestinian
people. It also supported the Zionist argument that the national leadership was cut off from the Arab public at large, who were prepared to live
alongside the Zionists.

During the next year, the leadership printed more leaflets in this spirit
and conducted assemblies around the country to publicize the duty to
boycott Jewish goods. A large national gathering was held in Haifa in
July 1947; in attendance were Muslims and Christians, representatives of
the Negev Bedouin, and emissaries from the Muslim Brotherhood in
Egypt and from churches in Jerusalem. Jamal al-Husseini declared there
that open hostilities were likely to break out very soon and threatened
that merchants who did not observe the boycott would have their homes
destroyed and be the targets of blood revenge. Detailed instructions
about sanctions against boycott violators were sent to the chambers of
commerce.[21]

The leaflets and assemblies reflected the national leadership's point of
view, but they also show that part of the Arab public ignored both the
arguments in favor of the boycott and the pathos of the appeals. The
leadership thus set up municipal boycott inspection committees to
enforce the sanctions. In central Jerusalem squads of inspectors prevented Arabs from entering Jewish stores and places of entertainment. In
Qalqilya the boycott committee tried to compel all merchants to observe
the ban, which caused tensions in the town. Even soldiers of the Arab

Legion who were stationed in northern Palestine* took part in the struggle against boycott violators.[22] The inspectors confiscated merchandise purchased from Jews or, alternatively, forced buyers to return the goods to their sellers. According to Shai sources, the Jerusalemite inspectors belonged to "the lower strata of the underworld in the Old City," and in addition to confiscating merchandise from buyers they used violence to enforce the boycott.[23] The major problem was Arab shopkeepers who sold Zionist goods. They received warnings from the boycott committee:

> We have requested your attention several times and have asked you to respect your nation's decisions and protect your homeland and the heritage of your fathers and to cease working with your nation's enemies, who attack your homeland and threaten to expel you from it—namely, the Jews—and you have not complied. Therefore, the committee has issued you this final warning and enjoins you in the name of the threatened homeland to halt these base actions and refrain from collaborating with your enemy—and if you do not, we will be compelled to disseminate your name as being outside the nation, and to consider you one of its enemies.[24]

Those who received these warnings were directed to sign them, and so to accept responsibility for their behavior and its consequences. Yet even this did not bring about total compliance—even by those who signed. At the end of 1946 there were twenty to thirty inspectors working in Jerusalem, but the feeling was that this was insufficient. The boycott committee asked the Higher Arab Committee for additional funds to enlarge the force and broaden the scope of its work.[25] Subsequently, the nationalist forces began using arms to enforce the boycott. At the beginning of August 1946, bombs were thrown at two Arab cafés that employed Jewish women, and in October there were four incidents in which bombs were hurled at houses, warehouses, and businesses of Arabs who worked with Jews. In December a contingent of the Futuwwa, the al-Husseini paramilitary organization, lobbed a bomb into al-Is'af market in Haifa in order to frighten boycott violators. In Jerusalem a purchaser of Jewish goods was shot at.[26] Words, it seems, were not enough.

In summer 1947, after several more months of the ineffective boycott, the pressure increased. In Safed, however, the inspectors behaved with moderation and consideration. The notebook of one inspector, 'Izz al-Din al-Khadra, preserved in the files of the Higher Arab Committee, dis-

---

*Units of the Transjordan Arab Legion were seconded to the British army and served as garrison companies in Palestine.

plays a propensity for well-mannered enforcement. A woman from a village near Safed arrived in the town with a can of olive oil she offered for
sale in the Jewish quarter. Al-Khadra wrote in his notebook that "she
said she did not know that the nation forbids this, and she is also very
poor. I let her be." A fellah from Salahiyya was seen exiting the store of
a Jewish clockmaker with a wristwatch. The watch was confiscated and
the fellah detained for questioning. He told the boycott committee that
he had come only to have his watch repaired, and that he had not bought
it after the boycott was declared. The committee returned the watch to
him, with an admonition not to do business with Jews. The same was
done with a boy who was sent to bring medicine from a Jewish phar-
macy. In other cases al-Khadra confiscated the merchandise.[27]

The combined militant approach and propaganda did not bring about
full acceptance of the boycott, and the failure of the Higher Arab Committee led to the establishment of more militant forces. One, based in
Jerusalem, took the name al-Huriyya (Freedom).* It began its campaign
early in July 1947 by issuing two leaflets. One called on Arabs to avoid
any violation of the boycott, and the other made threats: "We will
severely punish every merchant who continues to deal with Jews. Every
merchant who so continues puts his good name, his money, and his life
on the line. . . . Let no person blame anyone but himself if he falls under
the weight of our punishment. Traitor, do not expect us to establish a
court for you; we will judge you in your absence, issue a verdict, and
carry out the punishment." The leaflet also contained a list of merchants
who were not adhering to the boycott. It called on Arabs close to them to
pressure them and not to intervene if the violators were punished for
their treasonous acts.[28]

It was not long before the Higher Arab Committee's economic committee was itself accused of treason. In mid-July 1947, al-Huriyya issued
a leaflet that stated: "We will settle accounts with the ineffective economic committee for its indolence and indifference. We will fight it because some of its members have committed treason and taken bribes. We
will soon publish some names of its treasonous members, and they must

---

*One of the leaders of al-Huriyya was Sheikh Yasin al-Bakri, who in the 1948 war com-
manded a Holy Jihad detachment. It is interesting to note that al-Bakri did not refrain from
meeting Jewish Agency officials. At a meeting with Asher Lutzky at the beginning of March
1947, he declared that he aspired to an understanding between Jews and Arabs and was
"angry" at his city of birth, Hebron, for the slaughter of Jews in 1929. It is not clear what
al-Bakri wanted to achieve in this meeting, which is mentioned in a report dated 4 March
1947, HA 105/18.

resign or catastrophe will befall them."[29] So not only the people who refused to participate in the boycott rejected the authority of the leaders.
As in the case of many national liberation movements, militant Palestinian nationalists also defied the national leadership. Another al-Huriyya
leaflet accused the boycott committee of treason because in special cases
it granted Arab merchants exemptions and allowed them to use Jewish
products.[30]

These warning leaflets were the prologue to al-Huriyya's subsequent
operations. In June members of the group lobbed bombs at the homes of
three Jerusalem merchants who violated the boycott and shot at the
home of a fourth. They also set fire to the warehouse of a leather dealer.
A leaflet they printed named the victims and warned: "From here on we
will open fire on everyone who interferes with our actions."[31] This was
tantamount to mutiny against the leadership; any state, even a would-be
one like the Palestinian Arab state, has to maintain a monopoly on the
use of violence and the authority to pass judgment on its citizens.[32]

Circles close to the mufti also initiated a social boycott of Jews, both
for propaganda and for security and political reasons. One justification
was expressed by the mufti-aligned newspaper al-Wahda, which called
on Arabs not to rent homes to Jews: "Through the creation of mixed
neighborhoods, the Jews seek to prove that coexistence is viable." A lack
of mixed housing would make it clear to the world that Jews and Arabs
could not live together in the same country.[33] Another justification for
severing social ties with Jews was that these liaisons gave Jews an opportunity to incite their Arab acquaintances against the leadership or to
recruit them as collaborators.[34] In 1947, it seems, the Arabs of Palestine
were already well aware of Zionist methods.

In the area of social relations the leadership had more success than it
did in the economic field. The efficacy of the antisocial campaign is illus-
trated by the following incident. In June 1947 a group of young Druze
from Daliat al-Karmil attended a party at the neighboring Kibbutz Dalia.
A villager immediately notified the Higher Arab Committee, and a few
days later some of the village notables (wujaha u-makhatir) issued a condemnation. To absolve themselves of all responsibility, they began by
stating that they had not been in any way aware of the young people's
plans, which had come out of "a desire to see Jewish girls dancing, and
out of lust, and without appreciating the harmful national implications
of their actions." Nevertheless, the authors wrote, "We, the inhabitants
of Dalia [Daliat al-Karmil], consider them as having separated themselves from their nation and consider this act of theirs a crime against the

nation, even if its motive was youth's weakness of mind and the lust of the flesh."[35]

Trade Union Rivalry

The economic prosperity of the war years was accompanied by internal migration from villages to cities and work camps. This process brought on significant socioeconomic changes, among them a rise in the proportion of salaried employees.[36] In response, labor unions became more active in the Arab sector. The Palestinian Arab Workers Society (PAWS), headed by Sami Taha, recruited new members in significant numbers. The Federation of Arab Trade Unions, founded by members of the Communist Party, split off from Taha's group.[37] Neither of these unions was subordinate to the Higher Arab Committee or the Husseini party. At the same time, the Histadrut-sponsored Palestine Labor League continued to be active. According to Aharon Cohen, a Histadrut official, the Arab auxiliary had 1,500–2,000 members.[38]

The national awakening intensified antagonism toward the Palestine Labor League and its members. The Arab unions had refused to cooperate with the League even before this time, but they now went on the offensive. On May Day 1944, members of PAWS came to Jaffa and threatened countrymen who had gathered to celebrate the workers' holiday in the League's local chapter headquarters. The Histadrut's Arab department reported that, from that time on, League members were afraid to show their faces there. PAWS tried something similar in Jerusalem, but the police intervened and prevented the League's assembly from being disrupted. The League chapter in Qalunya, near Jerusalem, was also closed under PAWS pressure. According to the Arab department, PAWS first tried to work through the village mukhtars, but when that was unsuccessful it incited the villagers against the League.[39]

The central forces in the Palestinian Arab community viewed membership in an organization established by the Zionist Histadrut a blow to their national project. They knew that some of the League's members also served as Zionist informers, but that was not the only reason for their objection to the organization. The mere fact of Arab participation in a common labor front under Histadrut leadership abetted Zionist propaganda, which sought to project an image of coexistence. Nevertheless, PAWS, under the leadership of Sami Taha and Hanna 'Asfour, did coordinate its actions with the Histadrut in matters that served purely labor interests. Such was the case, for example, in the Jewish-Arab civil service strike of April 1946. This cooperation was criticized in many Arab circles but was supported by the workers.[40]

Sami Taha's independence in making such decisions led him to become increasingly active in politics. For a time he was considered to be close to the mufti's camp, but he nevertheless had no hesitation about differing from Hajj Amin in public. He opposed the Higher Arab Committee's boycott of the UN Special Commission that visited Palestine in summer 1947. He did not support the partition plan, but he maintained that Arabs could not ignore international forces. Consistent with this, he sent the UN secretary-general a telegram rejecting the partition concept. The Husseini camp was beside itself at Taha's diplomatic activity as well as at his ability to organize thousands of workers throughout the country. The pro-Husseini newspaper *al-Wahda* launched a smear campaign against him and termed him a traitor. His opponents criticized his support for the right of Jews who had lived in Palestine before 1918 to remain in the country as citizens with equal rights (even though this was the official position of the Higher Arab Committee as well). He did not live long— unknown assailants dispatched him on 11 September 1947. The Higher Arab Committee issued a condemnation of the murder, but the conventional wisdom was that the mufti was behind it. Many people thought what Bayan al-Hout later wrote—that Taha's sin was not his opinions but the position of power he occupied through the support he enjoyed in the Arab working class, the largest organized Palestinian sector.[41]

The labor union controversy thus typifies the campaign against "traitors." The attacks on the Palestine Labor League were brought on by its refusal to play by the national movement's rules. The League was intolerable both because of its defiance and because it offered an alternative to the dominant national movement.

According to contemporary sources and al-Hout's study, the antagonism to Taha derived only from his refusal to obey the leadership. However, additional information makes us aware of how complicated a business it is to investigate the murder of "traitors" at a distance of many years. David Hacohen reveals in *Et le-Saper* (A Time to Tell) that Taha had collaborated with him on a few critical matters. Taha, with his colleague 'Asfour, and under the protection of police officer Halim Basta (who was murdered in the rebellion), helped place Jewish workers in the quarries of the Nesher company in Haifa during the general strike of 1936. Such an action ran entirely counter to the national norms that prevailed during the rebellion, even if it was motivated by concern for the interests of the company's Arab workers. Moreover, Taha continued to maintain contact with Hacohen in the 1940s, despite his strictly anti-Zionist image. Their contacts were close enough that Hacohen looked after Taha's widow—who fled penniless to Damascus with her baby—and provided her with a pension through a Solel Boneh subsidiary.[42]

Land Dealers: A Wave of Murders

The *samasirah* harmed the national movement on three levels. They enabled the establishment and expansion of Jewish settlements, which were the foundation of the embryonic Jewish state; they demonstrated that there were Arabs who did not oppose the Zionists and were even willing to help them; and they flouted the authority of the national leadership. Together, these behaviors marked the land dealers for death. Yet neither the rebellion, nor the murder of dealers, nor the British Land Transfer Clause was able to halt the sale of land. When Palestinian Arab political activity resumed, the fight against land sales gained considerable momentum. It was of twofold importance. Internally, it was a tool for inculcating the Palestinian public with the principles of the national movement. Externally, it aimed at delivering a blow to the Zionists.

The institutional expression of the campaign against land sales was the Nation's Fund, reestablished at the end of 1943. Public discussion of the issue also resumed at this time. *Filastin, al-Difa'*, and other newspapers began publishing articles that laid out the danger of selling land to Jews. They began reporting deals in the making, and placards threatening land sellers popped up in many locations. Schools put on plays condemning land brokers and sellers.[43]

Like the economic boycott, the land issue became a pan-Arab one, just as the problem of Palestine became a pan-Arab problem. The Muslim Brotherhood sent representatives to Palestine, and the Arab League's Bludan conference resolved that the sale of land to Jews should be criminalized in all Arab states. The delegates also resolved to use "all means" to save Palestine's lands and to establish a fund to aid Palestine's Arabs—with half the aid designated for rescuing and cultivating land. Money was also collected in Palestine. Donors' names were published in the press and on placards in an effort to grant them prestige and so draw others into contributing.[44]

The disputes over control of the aid money are not germane to this work. The money was in fact used to halt the sale of land. In May 1946 a court prevented the removal of the Arabs of Nafi'at, near Hadera, from land purchased by KKL, thanks to the Fund. The decision was appealed to the Privy Council.[45] A month later the Fund saved land in the Beisan area, in Buteimat (next to Kibbutz Dalia), in Zbuba and Tubas (Jenin district), in Abu-Ghosh, in Bir 'Adas (next to Jaffa), and elsewhere. The strategy was legal; the Fund filed suits in the names of owners of adjacent plots, seeking first refusal in the purchase of land that was up for sale. This local legal principle, called *awlawiyya* in Arabic, granted precedence to the owners of contiguous fields. Such a suit could be filed even after a contract had been signed, before the land transfer was registered. It could delay the registration and even void the transaction. In several cases in which land for sale was identified before a contract was signed with Jews, the Fund offered the sellers an alternative deal.[46]

The case of Buteimat is typical of how the Fund worked. In 1938, Tawfiq Bey al-Khalil sold hundreds of dunams to KKL via an irrevocable power of attorney that he gave to KKL's legal counsel, Aharon Ben-Shemesh. Al-Khalil's brothers, Mustafa and Ahmad, were partners in the sale. Mustafa was killed in Haifa during the rebellion, and Tawfiq Bey fled to Sidon, where he died in 1939, before the land was transferred to the Jews. His son, 'Ali, who now held title to the land, remained in contact with KKL. Information on the proposed deal reached the Nation's Fund, which in 1946 commenced a legal campaign to keep the land in Arab hands. The Fund first made contact with the inhabitants of Umm al-Fahm, whose lands bordered those of the Khalil family. In their name the Fund petitioned the Supreme Court on the grounds that they held first refusal rights to buy the land. Under pressure from the Fund, 'Ali al-Khalil joined the suit that asked the court to rule against him and in favor of the Fund and the people of Umm al-Fahm. The Fund also transferred monies to al-Khalil so that he could pay off his debts to KKL.[47]

The Arabic press lauded the Nation's Fund for its activity. But the Fund was controlled by members of al-Istiqlal and so aroused the ire of the Husseini party, which did all it could to take it over. In April 1947 the Husseinis succeeded, thus concentrating all activity against land sales in their hands. They called on the public at large to participate in the campaign. This involvement included reporting on *samasirah* and their activities to the Higher Arab Committee's land division. Some of the reports were anonymous, and in some cases there was no way of knowing whether they were truthful. Collating the letters sent to the Higher Arab Committee with the testimonies of KKL land purchasers does, however, show that the information was usually reliable. It allowed the Higher Arab Committee to put together a general picture of land sales throughout the country.

For example, the information the public provided on the activities of 'Abd al-Rahman al-'Azzi, a *simsar* who was one of the leading KKL collaborators in southern Palestine, seems to have been pretty reliable. The information came from one of Battir's mukhtars, Mustafa Hasan, who specialized in tracking land purchasers in the area south of Jerusalem.[48] When he learned of a deal al-'Azzi was about to conclude in the Beit Jibrin region, Hasan approached him and offered to be a partner in the transaction. Al-'Azzi invited him to his home, where Hasan saw a large oil painting of the mufti on the wall—meant to mislead potential land sellers into thinking al-'Azzi was a nationalist.[49] Hasan reported this, and in the years that followed the national leadership kept tabs on al-'Azzi—although they never succeeded in halting his activities.[50]

Reliable information also came from the north. 'Ali Zu'bi, an attorney, wrote of a transaction involving 1,500 dunams being sold by the Qa'war family (which in public advocated the national cause). This seems not to have been mere defamation. The Qa'wars owned large tracts in the north. According to KKL official Aharon Danin, the family had amassed its property by lending at usurious rates to fellahin in the region's villages. When the Qa'wars were unable to repay their debts, they had no choice but to sign over their land to the lenders. Danin reported that in the 1940s the Qa'wars sold many of the parcels they had obtained in this way in the Na'ura area to Zionist institutions.[51]

The Higher Arab Committee also received reports on current transactions on Mt. Carmel and in the Zevulun Valley. "The *samasirah* are extremely active in the 'Isfiya area," stated an urgent letter to the Committee's land department. "They betray their homeland out of avarice, and not a day passes without them carrying out a sale. We call on you in the name of Allah and the homeland to save what little remains of our village's lands." KKL's man in the area was Mordechai Shakhevitz, who also coordinated Shai activity in the region. He spoke of thousands of dunams that were bought in that period and mentioned that the Nation's Fund made a ruckus about the deals. But he remembered no case in which they succeeded in preventing a transaction.[52]

Another anonymous letter reported on Bedouin sheikhs who traveled to Beersheva, Tel Aviv, and Hebron to close deals. A deed was transferred, according to the letter, with the help of the director of the land registration office in Hebron, 'Omar al-Ansari. Al-Ansari, related Aharon Malkov of KKL, was his personal friend and confidant and cooperated with him closely in land purchases in the south.[53] Reports also came in about a deal concluded by 'Abd al-Fattah Darwish in the village of al-Qastel in the Jerusalem mountains and another involving George Sayegh in the south. Darwish's involvement in land speculation had been common knowledge since the beginning of the 1930s. Sayegh, in contrast, was new in the field and worked with Isma'il al-'Azzi (a relative of 'Abd al-Rahman). According to a letter sent by a resident of Majdal (Ashkelon) to the Higher Arab Committee, Sayegh concluded a purchase of some 1,500 dunams in the village of Barbarah south of Majdal at the beginning of 1947. It said that he and other brokers were doing a brisk business in southern villages.[54]

Some of the letters to the Higher Arab Committee contained analyses of the situation and proposals for solving the problem. Zaki al-Tamimi of Jerusalem wrote a long memorandum in which he considered the reasons why Arabs were continuing to sell land. An anonymous writer addressed the importance of obtaining the assistance of all the Arab states. Muhammad al-Khatib of Majdal, who reported on land sales in his vicinity, also suggested solutions: Speeches and conferences and aid to needy fellahin were not sufficient, he argued. What was needed were secret vigilante squads that would execute the *samasirah*.[55]

That was hardly a new idea, of course. The press could not put it before the public for open discussion because of strict British censorship.[56] But a seal of approval was provided by the clergy and political leadership. Hajj Amin again issued his fatwa forbidding the sale of land, and the mufti of al-Azhar, 'Abd al-Majid Salim, also issued a fatwa stating that the *samasirah* were worse than open enemies. He decreed, hardly innovatively, that they be shunned and economically boycotted, refused burial in Muslim cemeteries, forbidden access to their wives, and considered *murtaddun*, Muslims who had abandoned their religion. The legal implication of this decree was that they should be executed.[57]

This ruling was highly popular. The climax of the large boycott and anti-land sale demonstration held in Haifa in July 1947 came when Jamal al-Husseini called for the murder of land sellers. Delegations from all over the country had gathered in the city for a unity rally (although some claimed that they saw only the Husseini leadership there), and Jamal al-Husseini made the main speech. A Shai informer reported:

"There is a group of Arabs that has stained us and blackened our faces before foreigners and before our Arab brothers," al-Husseini began. "What punishment will we mete out to them?" All those present answered: "Death, death to them." Jamal continued: "Yes, death! And I say to you: Murder them, murder them. Our religion commands this and you must do as the religion commands."[58]

Perhaps out of fear that his words were being reported, al-Husseini added: "I am not telling you to kill them with bullets, but rather to kill them morally. When you hear that someone has sold his land, you must ostracize him and distance yourself from him and call at him: 'Hey, traitor; hey, traitor.'"[59] Not that he objected to murder. A week later, for example, a large rally was held in Jaffa. An informer code-named "the Farmer" ("ha-Yogev"—perhaps 'Abd al-Ghani al-Karami) was present and reported that in his speech al-Husseini demanded that a son murder his father if he were a land speculator, and that a father have no mercy and slay his son for the same reason. "He also demanded that the forty to fifty speculators and informers in the Arab community be killed, to get rid of those who were sabotaging the efforts of the Higher Arab Committee." Al-Husseini was not the only one to raise the issue. Mahmoud Sharbawi, of a small and short-lived organization, the Village Congress, did so also. At the Jaffa rally he called for the murder of four types of traitors: samasirah, land sellers, buyers of Zionist merchandise, and informers.[60]

The theoretical discussion and the shrill calls for execution were voiced at the height of a murder campaign. A wave of killings was signaled in March 1945 with the murder of a land agent from Jaffa named Foteih Sarruji. This was the only political murder that year, but the Zionist leadership believed—and told the British Mandatory administration—that it was a test case, and that if measures were not taken against the murderers a wave of killings would begin.[61]

The hypothesis was soon proved. Although there were no more murders in 1945, the Shai received reports that the Husseini party and the Nation's Fund were planning a purge. Nationalist activists went to local land registration offices and prepared lists of land speculators. Suspects were summoned to mosques or offices of the Nation's Fund and required to pledge to halt their activity. In October shots were fired at Muhammad Zeinati, the major land seller in the Beisan Valley.[62]

The great purge began when Jamal al-Husseini returned to Palestine. He seems to have had a double goal: to fight land speculators as part of the struggle against Zionism and its collaborators, and to take control of the intra-Arab political arena by leading the apparatus that fought against traitors. During this time, Jamal tried, as shown above, to keep his involvement hazy and to claim that his calls for murder referred to spiritual murder. Such rhetoric was meant to prevent the government from filing criminal charges against him, but a quarter-century later he said openly: "We acknowledge our responsibility. We carried out the attacks first and foremost to put an end to land sales, after all other means of persuasion did not succeed. We bear responsibility for thirty to forty dead men, among them my cousin, whom we advised [to halt his actions] but who did not accept our advice, and we were compelled to send a man to kill him on his doorstep."[63]

Jamal al-Husseini referred here to attacks both during the rebellion and subsequently. The murdered cousin was apparently Fawzi Darwish al-Husseini, who was slain in November 1946. We do not know if he was dispatched because of land dealings or because of his political contacts with Jews.[64] In any case, about ten murders can be attributed to the purge campaign in 1946.[65] The first victim was Taleb Subh of Safed (son of Na'if Subh, mayor at the time of the British conquest and a business partner of the Jewish 'Abbu family). In May 1945, Shai coordinator Hillel Landesman of Ayelet ha-Shahar received information from an Arab district officer that "a death sentence has been handed down against Taleb Subhi, an Arab of Safed, who works for the KKL office in Tiberias." The report was not sufficient to prevent the murder. In February 1946, Subh was shot at home by a team of four men. Killed with him was Muhammad Suliman al-Baytar of Jaffa, who was staying with him. People in Safed reported that "a secret organization has been founded to murder land speculators and those who sell land to Jews." The organization sent warning letters to a member of the prominent Murad family and to Muhammad al-Khuli, both suspected of land speculation.[66]

The next month an anonymous assailant attacked one of the major land dealers in the Sharon region, Salameh al-Hajj Ibrahim. Salameh's brother, Salim, a nationalist activist, returned from exile and was appointed secretary of the Nation's Bank. But Salameh continued to mediate land purchases for the Jews. His life at risk, he decided to move to Jaffa, where he set up a citrus export firm. In March 1946 a young man with a pistol appeared in his office. Salameh shouted at the young man and unnerved him to the extent that when he fired he hit another merchant and fled. The assailant looked as if he had been drugged, Salameh told the police, adding that there was no need for an investigation. He and his friends would settle accounts with those who had sent the killer.[67]

Salim al-'Omar, a *simsar* who was a business partner in land deals with Jaffa's mayor, 'Abd al-Rauf al-Baytar, was not as lucky. The assassins that failed to murder Salameh succeeded in killing him. Placards pasted up around the city proclaimed: "Know each of you that in the end every Arab who sells land of the Arab patrimony or who pimps for the Jews will soon receive his due, which is certain death." The placards were signed by an organization calling itself "Revenge." "Our problem is the outcome of the sale of our land. The amazing thing is that we sell to the Jews and then scream and wail and ask for the government's help," the placard stated. Like some boycott posters, this one had no compunctions about specifying the real problem: the public's reluctance to adopt the nationalist stance. Its authors were well aware that the process of building an Arab nation had not been completed. They saw themselves as the emissaries of a nation that was still under construction. The way to accelerate the process, in their analysis, was to fight noncompliers to the death.[68]

Throughout the country people established posses and gangs to kill land brokers. A month later, in Nazareth, a member of the Khuri family was shot. He had been accused of selling land to Jews. The attack caused tension between Muslims and Christians. The latter claimed that al-Khuri's guilt had not been proved and that Muslim dealers were making even bigger deals with Jews yet had not been attacked.[69] As an example, they pointed to the Fahoum family, which had sold some 1,000 dunams in Daburiyya, causing hardship to the villagers. In fact, however, Muslims were hardly spared. Muhammad Hajj Amin Murad, of a large Safed family that had sold some of its holdings to KKL, was murdered in mid-May, as the Safed underground had threatened.[70] In July, As'ad Taha of Birwe in the Western Galilee was slain. More purge squads were formed and engaged in additional attempts to kill land dealers throughout the country.[71]

The assassins scored another success in August, when they murdered Muhammad (Abu Shafiq) Buqa'i of the village of Dammun in the western Lower Galilee. Muhammad and his son Shafiq were among KKL's most important collaborators in the area and helped the Zionist organization locate plots that were up for sale, purchase them, and pursue the subsequent legal battle. Attorney Yermihahu Feiglin said of Shafiq:

> [He] is an Arab who was in fact devoted, let's say to us, with all his heart and soul. They themselves, his family, had much land. . . . Shafiq Buqa'i was of course tied to the KKL office in Haifa. . . . Shafiq Buqa'i was the living spirit in connection with negotiations with various Arabs. . . . I had to get material on these lands in the framework of this suit, and the knowledge about this land was in the possession of this Abu Shafiq. It was almost impossible and undesirable to enter Dammun at that time. . . . I arranged with Shafiq that he send his father from the village into the field, a long ways from the village; there on a hill, behind a boulder, I sat with him and there I received all the details I need to receive regarding the case. A few days later he [the father] was murdered.[72]

The liquidation campaign continued. Hafez Mahmoud, an associate of Hafez Hamdallah who helped KKL with purchases in the Sharon region, was shot to death in 'Anabta. Ibrahim al-Tayyeb of the eastern Galilee was murdered after he testified in KKL's favor and against the Nation's Fund in a lawsuit. In Jerusalem anonymous assailants tried to kill the leaders of the Abu-Ghosh family. The *simsar* Muhammad Nassir al-Bashiti escaped an assassination attempt; Fawzi Darwish al-Husseini was shot and killed. At the end of 1946 the sheikh of the Ghazawiyya tribe, Emir Muhammad Zeinati, was murdered in Haifa.[73]

Zeinati's murder was preceded by attacks on two of KKL's lower-level collaborators in the Beit She'an Valley, 'Abdallah Kurdi and 'Abd al-Ra'ouf.[74] Yehoshua Barouchi, a KKL agent and mukhtar of Kibbutz Tirat Tzvi, later recalled that everyone knew that the assassins had Zeinati in their sights. The Shai received concrete intelligence on a plan to murder him and sent Barouchi on horseback to Zeinati's encampment to warn him. Zeinati took precautions but they were not sufficient. A month after he received the information, Zeinati went to the barbershop he regularly frequented in Haifa. After his haircut, he stepped out into the street with his bodyguards, and attackers shot him down on the spot. This murder, Barouchi related, "worked better than all the thousands of speeches that Hajj Amin al-Husseini made."[75]

Zeinati's killing was significant for two reasons. For one, he was the first senior figure to be killed in this wave of terror. Until then the victims had been professional land brokers or KKL collaborators; not one of them was a public figure or local leader. Furthermore, at the time of his death Zeinati was close to concluding a unique transaction with KKL; he had undertaken to sell all his land and emigrate with his tribe to Transjordan. This was a rare case of "voluntary population transfer" that had been initiated by the Zionists and reached fruition. Even Emir 'Abdallah had given his consent and granted Zeinati's people citizenship in Transjordan.[76] The murder was thus a warning not only to low-level land dealers but also to the most senior of them, as well as to the Palestinian leadership's rival east of the Jordan. It meant that the Palestinian Arab nationalist movement intended to pursue its struggle across borders and would give no quarter.

The purge continued in 1947. For a time the Jerusalem hills became the focus of the battle against "traitors." In January there was an attempt to kill Yussuf and Musa Abu-Ghosh, who worked on land deals and with the Jewish underground; Yussuf, as noted earlier, had helped free

Lehi radio announcer Geula Cohen from the Bethlehem jail. April brought the murder of Anton 'Abis, the Christian mukhtar of 'Ayn Karem, who had signed over land to Jews. He took seven bullets in his abdomen and died on the spot.[77]

The assassins then tried to reach Sheikh 'Abd al-Fattah Darwish and his son Hasan, who were considered the leading *samasirah* in the Jerusalem area. Assailants fired on the two men as they drove with their bodyguards on the road that ascends from 'Ayn Karem to Bayyit va-Gan. The Darwishes, suffering wounds from shattered glass, returned fire. They told their Jewish acquaintances that some weeks before they had received a threatening letter that demanded that they cut off their contacts with Jews.[78] Nor was the 'Azzi family spared. The family's leading *samasirah*, Isma'il and 'Abd al-Rahman, remained unharmed. But in June 1947, Hajj Mahmoud 'Abbas al-'Azzi and Mahmoud Salameh al-'Azzi were killed while driving home from Tel Aviv. The press reported the deaths without comment, as it reported the abortive attack on Darwish. But KKL official Aharon Malkov said that Hajj had been killed on his way to a business meeting.[79]

The picture is thus one of a methodical campaign against land sellers, especially the forty to fifty *samasirah* al-Husseini referred to time and again.[80] The campaign was not entirely successful, just as the economic boycott was enforced only in part.

THE WAR AGAINST THE TRAITORS: SUCCESS OR FAILURE

Before the rebellion many members of the Arab public did not subordinate themselves to the national movement, even if they opposed foreign rule and a Zionist takeover of Palestine. Some were cut off from the political arena; others (in the villages, Bedouin encampments, and cities as well) viewed the national movement as an elitist, alien clique that sought to impose a new order on them. This was the source of the "treason" of many Arabs. But this was not the case during the rebellion and afterward, when it was impossible to ignore the nationalist discourse. The continuation of collaboration and treason in those years was, in part, a reaction to the violence employed by the rebels and the national movement as a whole. Other reasons for collaboration, especially "hard" and conscious collaboration, like selling land and providing intelligence, were the finely honed system of recruitment and "binding" developed by the Zionist institutions. Most important was that many Arabs felt that the Palestinian leadership was pursuing a wrongheaded strategy—that the fight against the Zionists was counterproductive. The attempt to fight these views by stigmatizing collaborators was not always successful. Sometimes it led to the creation of an alternative normative system.

All this was true of those who collaborated with the Zionists intentionally. But we must also seek to understand why many Arabs who were not routinely classified as traitors and certainly did not see themselves as such nevertheless did business with Jews. Such people sold land and traded with Jews even when this was defined as treason. Why did the national movement have such limited success in inculcating its public with nationalist norms? Even the Higher Arab Committee sensed that Arabs were, in their ineffective response to the threat they faced, proving the Zionist claim that the Jews had arrived in a "land without a people."

Basically, many Arabs did not associate their negative feelings toward Zionism with their daily contacts with Jews; they did not connect the political and the personal. This was a result of the contradiction between the individual's interest and the interest of the nation as portrayed by the leadership. In addition, for the national movement to succeed in instilling its code of behavior, people had to feel that the sacrifices they were being called on to make were indeed being asked of and made by all. If they were to give up convenience, money, sometimes their lives, it had to be for the good of the nation, not for the benefit of the leadership's particular interests, whether concealed or open. The people had to believe that they could trust their leaders and that the leaders were acting equitably.

This was, however, not the general feeling in Palestinian Arab society in the 1940s. The leadership indeed used a rhetoric of unity, but the public did not believe it. Previously existing fissures in Arab society widened when the boycott was declared. This was true of both the religious and the geographical divide.

A few examples relating to the economic boycott serve to illustrate this point. In October 1946, boycott inspectors in Shefa'amr discovered Jewish merchandise in two business establishments. One was owned by a Christian named Mazawi, the other by a Muslim named Kanafani. According to a report to the Higher Arab Committee, the Christian was humiliated in public and forced to pay a fine to the local boycott committee. No action was taken against the Muslim. The inhabitants of Shefa'amr and the surrounding villages, so wrote one resident to the Higher Arab Committee, were convinced that this constituted discrimination on a religious basis and feared that the religious split of the rebellion was returning. For the struggle to succeed, the Arab people had to be united, the writer reminded the Committee. The Shai also received reports of discrimination on a religious basis in enforcement of the boycott. One of its informers reported a wave of thefts against Christians, justified on the grounds that the Christians' merchandise came from Zionist sources.[81]

Such conduct made some groups view the boycott as a partisan rather than a national effort. This prevented the public from rallying to the boycott and making it a focus of national identity. At the same time, it led to distrust of the local boycott committees and of the national leadership as a whole. Instead of developing a sense of common destiny, in which each individual would give up some of his wealth but the community as a whole would benefit, people saw that some people were profiting from the boycott. There were Arabs who sent extortion letters to others and forced them to pay protection money, and there were boycott inspectors who levied fines, then took the money for themselves. Even worse, there were inspectors who themselves did business with Jews. Arabs sent complaints to the Higher Arab Committee, but there is no evidence that they were taken seriously—perhaps because the inspectors had been appointed from within al-Husseini circles.[82] Even if much of the Arab public was willing to make sacrifices, the conduct of the bodies that oversaw the boycott failed to create public confidence in the leadership and did not encourage people to unite around it.

The campaign against land sales faced similar problems. Nationalist activists reported to the Higher Arab Committee that Nation's Fund officials in Khan-Yunis and Jaffa were using public funds for personal gain, getting drunk, and behaving violently. Some said that all the Fund's offices were corrupt and needed to be cleaned out.[83] It goes without saying that this situation was hardly conducive to the success of the campaign. Here, too, people sensed that some parts of the country were benefiting at the expense of others. When the Arab League allocated money for agricultural development in Palestine, Musa al-'Alami's Constructive Enterprise received about a quarter of a million Palestinian pounds. All this was invested in the country's north, to the chagrin of sheikhs from the Negev, who claimed, with justice, that the land sale problem was no less severe in the Negev than in other areas.[84]

Many Palestinian Arabs believed that the cause was not an authentic national one in which all of society's sectors and individuals had equal standing. Instead, it seemed like the cause of the Husseinis and their allies. Evidence of this was the lenience accorded to abuses committed by people close to the Husseinis (even if there were one or two exceptions) and the banishment of Arabs from outside the camp from positions of influence (even if their nationalist record was spotless). A letter sent to Arab newspapers, but never published, contained information on land transactions conducted by Qadri Hafez Tuqan (whom the writer called "a bogus nationalist") with Muhammad Zeinati. Zeinati was murdered at the end of 1946, but Tuqan continued to proclaim his nationalist credentials. Similar criticism was voiced after Yussuf Sahyun of Haifa was appointed to the Higher Arab Committee despite persistent rumors that he had sold land to Jews, and similar voices were heard after the celebrations surrounding Mu'in al-Madi's return to Palestine for the same reason.[85] The assumption was that al-Madi's sins had been forgiven because he had joined Hajj Amin during the latter's time in Baghdad. Land deals carried out by men close to the Husseinis, such as Saleh 'Awnallah of Nazareth, were consummated relatively quietly. It was only a short leap to the conclusion that people were being judged not on the basis of their deeds but on their connections. Nationalist principles and values seemed to be but a cover for the Husseini thirst for power.

At the same time, the members of al-Istiqlal were being shut out of decision-making centers. They were not invited to the large assemblies organized by the Higher Arab Committee against land sales and in support of the boycott. Critics of the Higher Arab Committee concluded that the Husseinis themselves considered these rallies to be partisan events rather than national ones. But any attempt to warn the public of the implications was immediately silenced. Muhammad Nimer al-Hawwari, who headed the Najjadah, took the microphone at a rally in Jaffa and said, "For twenty years we have heard talk against land brokers and land sellers, yet here they sit in the front rows at every national gathering." The rally's organizers reacted swiftly; they turned off the loudspeakers.[86]

On the other side were the Zionists, who used the division and mistrust in the Arab camp for their own purposes. Such was the case with the rivalry between the Husseini Futuwwa and al-Hawwari's Najjadah, which enabled the Shai and Jewish Agency to meet with al-Hawwari and receive from him information about his various rivals.[87] In the case of the Nation's Fund, the Shai received the information it required from the Husseini camp because of its rivalry with the founders of the Fund, who were independents or supporters of al-Istiqlal. The contact was the mufti's assistant, Ahmad al-Imam, with whom the Shai had been in touch for many years. Yehoshua Palmon, a top figure in the Shai, testified about the relations with al-Imam: "We reached an understanding with him on the following basis: That we have common interests and opposed interests. We won't touch the opposing interests. With the common interests, we will endeavor to work together. Our common interest was to halt the advancement and strengthening of [Istiqlalists] Rashid al-Hajj Ibrahim and Ahmad Hilmi Pasha at the expense of the influence and status of the mufti's men."[88]

The latter helped the Zionists stay current on doings at the Nation's Fund and block its activities. The Shai also succeeded in planting an informer at the highest levels of the Fund. "Ovadiah," as he was codenamed, provided detailed information about developments in the mufti's camp and in Arab political circles as a whole. In mid-June 1944 the Shai already had a list with the names of forty of the forty-two members of the Fund's governing board, organized according to place of residence and party affiliation.[89] And if that were not enough, some members of the board themselves ignored or even facilitated land sales—this in addition to their questionable personal behavior and honesty.

Such was the case in a transaction near Mt. Tabor that the Fund was unable to prevent. The Fund decided to allow the deal to go ahead in exchange for part of the money that KKL paid the owners. This was not an isolated incident. "The people who worked with us were very successful people. They knew how to arrange matters with the Nation's Fund and the government," Aharon Danin testified.[90] Avraham Gissin offered the example of Isma'il al-'Azzi: "[He] was a well-known and very brave Arab. He was not afraid, and George [Sayegh] took cover under him so that they were covered with regard to the Nation's Fund with all kinds of shenanigans that they did."[91] The public was aware of this and reported it to the Higher Arab Committee, which did nothing. That too contributed to a lack of faith in the national leadership and gave more people a basis for acting contrary to its instructions.[92]

The public thus perceived the rhetoric of national unity largely as hypocrisy. This is one of the reasons that Druze activists with connections to Zionist institutions disregarded the Higher Arab Committee's attempt to recruit them for the national struggle. In February 1946 leading Druze from Mt. Carmel were summoned before the national committee of Haifa, which demanded that they sever their ties with Jews. In May of that year the national movement's leaders in Acre summoned Sheikh Saleh Khneifes of Shefa'amr to appear before them. Khneifes had direct ties with the Shai after his father was murdered during the rebellion. They demanded to know what the Druze position would be in the upcoming struggle. He avoided an answer on the grounds that he had to consult with the members of his community and evaded a planned meeting with Jamal al-Husseini. A few months later, Khneifes and Labib Abu-Rukun of 'Isfiya received threatening letters and were commanded to appear before the Muslim National Associations branch in Haifa to answer questions about land deals in which they had had a hand. The Druze leaders reported these events to the Shai. They had not forgotten the harassment they had suffered during the rebellion, the attacks on Druze villages, and the murder of mukhtars. They assured their Jewish contacts that they were committed to carrying on and strengthening the Druze-Zionist relationship.[93]

The Druze were not the only ones to maintain their ties with Zionists in the face of pressure and threats. Najjadah commander Nimer al-Hawwari carried on his relations with the Haganah and Jewish Agency despite an attempt on his life in April 1947.[94] The same was true of Kamel Hussein of the Hula Valley. As nationalist activity swelled, he received several death threats but nevertheless continued to mediate land sales to Jews in the Galilee panhandle.[95] After the killing of Zeinati, Hussein tried to encourage Zionist figures to retaliate with force against the murders of Arab land dealers.[96] He himself kept up his ties with KKL and the Shai. KKL's representative in the Galilee, Yosef Nahmani, made much use of Hussein but said he was mercurial: "I am afraid that the end will be bad. Don't believe his opponents [who offered him rehabilitation in return for severing his contacts with the Jews]; at the first opportunity they'll finish him off." The prospect presented itself only in 1949. Hussein, who had moved to Syria with his family, was shot dead a few days after he returned to the Galilee with the consent of the government of the new state of Israel.[97]

Hussein sought to avenge Zeinati's blood both because of the long personal connection between them and also because in his estimation only acts of vengeance could bring an end to the assassinations and the threat to his own life. His approach was accepted. In March 1947, three months after Zeinati's murder, the first effective revenge operation was carried out against a member of the Husseini party.[98] Farid Fakhr al-Din of the Arab Party, thought to be the mastermind behind Zeinati's murder, had gone to Cairo after the attack. When he returned to Beisan, his family organized a dinner in his honor. An assailant entered the home and shot into the family. Six of them were wounded, with one dying the next day. The British police surmised that behind the attack were either Jews or Arabs seeking to avenge Zeinati's death. They arrested Zeinati's son-in-law, Mit'ab al-'Arsan. He was convicted on the basis of testimony from his uncle, Sheikh Nimer al-'Arsan, who testified at his trial. He said that his nephew had told him that the attack had been planned by Kibbutz Tirat Tzvi's mukhtar, Yehoshua Barouchi, who was also involved in land purchases in the Beit She'an Valley.* According to Sheikh Nimer, Mit'ab and his two codefendants had received large sums of money to kill Fakhr al-Din and other nationalist figures.[99]

During this period there were several more attacks on Palestinian nationalist figures and members of the Husseini party. The best-known victims were 'Abdallah Sammara and Zaki Safarini of Tulkarem, Mustafa al-Dajani of Jaffa, and Muhammad Yunis al-Husseini of the Nation's Fund in Jerusalem. Rumors circulated of an attempt to kill Jamal al-Husseini himself.[100] There were many contradictory theories about these deeds. Some believed that the Zionists were using Arab proxies, others that an oppositionist Arab group was behind them, and others that the victims were being punished internally for corruption or for selling land to the Jews. Zionist groups were certainly behind at least some of the attacks. Ezra Danin, who headed the Shai's Arab department, wrote in his memoirs that Ben-Gurion and Shertok themselves approved the tactic in 1946. In his account, the meeting where the decision was made was also attended by Yosef Weitz and Avraham Granot of KKL. One of its main objectives was to strike at the "leading rioters" and those who were attacking collaborators.[101]

The Arab community was thus not at all certain who was behind the killings, and this confusion was exacerbated by a new wave of political murders launched by the mufti's supporters. Together, these put on the public agenda the question of the legitimacy and efficacy of internal terror. The Communist National Liberation League led the opponents of the terror campaign but did not succeed in stopping it.[102]

Land sales continued and the Higher Arab Committee failed to subordinate all Palestinian Arab institutions and organizations. Jamal al-Husseini thus convened, in coordination with the mufti, a pan-Palestinian Arab congress under the promising slogan "peace among brothers." In summer 1947 his delegates asked opposition figures—among them Suliman Tuqan of Nablus—to participate. They refused. The oppositionists blamed the mufti and Jamal for the murders and attacks during the rebellion, and for accusing them falsely of treason and

---

*In testimony, Barouchi did not say whether he had indeed been involved in planning the attack; 30 December 1970, OHD-HU 57–10. None of his living relatives or friends are able to cast light on the affair, except for the fact that soon afterward the Jewish Agency ordered Barouchi to leave the country, out of fear for his life. We know that during this period the Zionist institutions used collaborators for attacks on militant Arab leaders.

land sales. Their condition for participation was a public apology by Jamal. No such apology materialized, and a congress was not held that summer—the last summer before the war, the last summer before the Palestinian defeat—the Nakba.[103]

On the eve of war, the Palestinian national institutions were thus unable to unite the country's Arabs. They were vulnerable to intelligence penetration by the Zionists, whom each faction and leader helped in his own way in order to harm his opponents. Terrorism and counterterrorism had taken the place of persuasion and national consensus. Many Arabs continued to maintain social and economic ties with Jews in violation of the Higher Arab Committee's instructions. Zionist intelligence recruitment was becoming more and more sophisticated. And the Arabs of Palestine were facing a war that commenced immediately after their leadership announced its rejection of the UN General Assembly decision to partition Palestine into two countries.

CHAPTER 9

TREASON AND DEFEAT:
THE 1948 WAR

The war of 1948 ended with the severe defeat of the Arabs of Palestine and the Arab countries that came to their aid. Palestinian Arab political institutions collapsed. Hundreds of thousands of Arabs were uprooted from their homes. Hundreds of Arab settlements were laid waste. The Palestinian Arab state envisioned by the partition plan was aborted. Instead, the greater part of Palestine became a Jewish state that encompassed a much larger territory than that decreed by the United Nations. Though the collaborators could not have predicted the outcome, they did slightly contribute to this crushing defeat, termed in Arabic the Nakba. On the other hand, they also contributed to the ability of some 130,000 Palestinians to remain on their land, within the borders of the new Jewish state.

Accusations of treason were made by, and directed at, almost everyone who took part in the political or military aspects of the war. Palestinian political circles accused the Arab League, especially King 'Abdallah of Transjordan. 'Abd al-Qader al-Husseini accused the League's military committee. 'Abdallah al-Tal, an officer in the Arab Legion, Transjordan's army, joined those accusing his own king as well as his prime minister, Tawfiq Abu al-Huda. King 'Abdallah, for his part, accused the League of betrayal and the Higher Arab Committee of irresponsibility. Most important, many in other Arab countries pointed their fingers at the Arabs of Palestine. Some said that, if the Palestinians had not sold their land to the Jews, the Zionists would not have been able to establish their territorial foothold in the Middle East. Others pointed to the low level of local enlistment in the campaign. They also said that many Palestinian Arabs had provided information to the Jewish forces.[1]

There was a measure of truth in these claims. In considering them, however, it is important to remember that treason is in the eye of the beholder. Its definition depends on the definition of the national interest at any given moment, and this is usually a matter of debate, as is the question of who has the authority to define that interest. This is true in all places and all times. In the case of Palestinian society in 1948, the Husseini approach, which rejected the UN partition decision and demanded that the Arabs of Palestine mobilize against it, was ostensibly nationalist and patriotic. As the mufti declared, "A vital, self-respecting nation does not accept the partition of its homeland."[2] Accordingly, anyone who opposed the war, passively or actively, was defined a traitor to his people. But others maintained that, even if they did not always express their opinions openly, war with the Jews would bring catastrophe to the Arabs. Avoidance of war and even agreement with the Jews were, in their view, best for the Palestinian Arab nation. As far as they were concerned, those who tried to prevent fighting were the real patriots, while the mufti, who declared an open war against the Jews, was self-centered, detached from his people. This view was an important motive for collaboration during the war.

PASSIVITY, REFUSAL TO FIGHT, AND PEACE ALLIANCES

On the last day of November 1947, three days before hostilities broke out, the Higher Arab Committee reiterated its established policy on ties with Jews: "The Arab nation is called on to remain steadfast in an absolute boycott of the Jews and to consider any connection with them a severe crime and great betrayal of religion and the homeland." It called on the Arabs of Palestine to enlist in the struggle, which was to begin with a three-day general strike beginning December 2.[3] It quickly became clear, however, that Arabs were in no hurry to heed the Committee's call. Only a few thousand enlisted in the combat forces—the Holy Jihad, which was under the mufti's control; the guard forces of the Arab cities; and the auxiliary of the Arab Liberation Army (Jaysh al-Inqadh).[4] Nor was severing ties with the Jews accepted by the public at large. What the Higher Arab Committee called "a great betrayal" did not appear that way to many Arabs. Furthermore, not only were they passive, but some resisted (at various levels) the fighters and military activities.[5]

This unwillingness to do battle pervaded the country. In December 1947 the inhabitants of Tulkarem refused to attack Jewish towns to their west, to the chagrin of the local Holy Jihad commander, Hasan Salameh. Sources in Ramallah reported at the same time that many were refusing to enlist, and reports from Beit Jibrin indicated that 'Abd al-Rahman al-'Azzi was doing all he could to keep his region quiet. The villagers of the Bani-Hasan *nahiya* southwest of Jerusalem decided not to carry out military actions within their territory, and the people of al-Maliha refused a request from 'Abd al-Qader al-Husseini to attack the Jewish neighborhoods of Mekor Hayyim and Bayyit va-Gan. That same month, at the end of January, the inhabitants of 'Ayn Ghazal, on the coast below Mt. Carmel, refused to blow up Jewish-owned lime kilns adjacent to the village. Three weeks later the residents of Ramla and Lydda were told to take part in an attack on Jews; they ignored the order. At the end of March men under the command of Hussein Hassouna of Lydda disarmed mines near the Jewish agricultural school of Ben Shemen laid by volunteers from the Arab Liberation Army. Similar incidents occurred in villages in the Lower Galilee.[6] Only a minority of Arabs were involved in offensive, as opposed to defensive, combat. This minority established its own fighting forces or joined volunteers from Arab countries and operated against Jewish settlements and Jewish transportation.

This unwillingness to fight was frequently buttressed by agreements with Jews in nearby settlements. Sources in many parts of the country reported that local Arab representatives had approached their Jewish neighbors with requests to conclude nonaggression pacts. The members of the 'Arab al-Hawarith and 'Arab al-Shumali tribes made such an approach to the Jewish farming village of Kfar Vitkin; the Arabs of al-Mughayer, Mansuriyya, and Manshiyya contacted Tel-Mond and Givat Hayyim; the residents of Qatanna appealed to Ma'aleh ha-Hamisha; Sheikh Na'if al-Tabari made overtures to the Jews of Tiberias; and the inhabitants of Beit Hanina did the same to their Jewish neighbors in Neve Ya'akov. All these Arabs sought mutual nonbelligerency agreements. Representatives of Lifta and Abu-Ghosh coordinated their moves with their Jewish neighbors, and the Arab village of Deir Yasin and the Jews of the Jewish neighborhood of Givat Sha'ul concluded a pact.[7] The villagers of Yajour made a similar request of Kibbutz Yagur, but only after the Haganah's offensive in Balad al-Sheikh. Kufr Qara' made its appeal to next-door Kfar Glickson.[8] This trend continued through March and April. Fares Hamdan, a prominent resident of Baqa al-Gharbiyyeh (later a member of Israel's Knesset), proposed a peace agreement to the Jewish settlements in his vicinity, and the Arabs of Fajja and ʿArab al-Quz, who dwelt east of Petach Tikva, made a pact with Kfar Sirkin. Bedouin tribal chiefs in the Negev made similar offers to the Jewish settlements near them. Muhammad Nimer al-Hawwari, head of the Najjadah organization, went so far as to organize guard contingents to man Tel Aviv's southern border so as to prevent attacks from Jaffa on Jewish neighborhoods. These are only examples.[9] Palestinian Arab interest in fighting the Jews seems not to have been very high.

To the Arab national leadership, this was out-and-out treason. Moreover, Arabs who made agreements with Jews, and many others as well, often refused to provide assistance to Arab military forces and even tried to prevent them from operating in their vicinity. In several cases Arab detachments could not find a village that would quarter them or allow them to deploy. The mukhtar of ʿAyn Karem prevented Arab forces from firing from his village at the Jewish quarry near Suba. An armed band that reached Qalunya was told by the villagers to leave, and in Tarshiha local activists prevented a village resident from laying a mine on the road leading to a nearby kibbutz. Qalandiya expelled a band of fighters that wanted to attack the Jewish village of Atarot, and the village of Taʿnak expelled fighters who asked for help attacking a Jewish bus that served the Jezreel Valley settlements. An assault on the Jewish Jerusalem neighborhood of Romema was foiled by the residents of Lifta, from which the attackers had hoped to launch their operation. Holy Jihad irregulars who arrived in Subbarin (near Zikhron Yaʿakov) were told to leave. The Arabs of Subbarin, like their neighbors in Sindiana and Faradis, seem to have wanted to turn themselves over to the Jewish forces, but none of the villages wanted to be the first to surrender.[10]

So it was in the first months of fighting, and so it was thereafter. The inhabitants of Deir Yasin, who made a pact with Givat Shaʾul, kept their word. They refused to allow Syrian and Iraqi volunteers to enter. Sindiana and Sharkas also kept foreigners out. Residents of Kababir, near Haifa, went one step further. When they realized that Arab combatants intended to enter the village, they contacted the Haganah and asked that it occupy them first. Maʿlul refused the Arab Liberation Army's demand that they take part in an attack on Nahalal in June 1948. They also refused to allow one of the army's companies to deploy in the village—and the soldiers expelled the villagers. Other combat forces that tried to draw the public into the struggle also failed, time after time.[11] Many Palestinian Arabs thus not only refrained from fighting themselves but also did their best to prevent foreigners and locals from carrying out military actions.

Senior figures in the Shai and Jewish Agency concluded that the Arabs of Palestine were not interested in fighting. They also deduced that Jewish offensive actions had increased the ranks of Palestinian fighters.*

The fighters from Arab countries were, of course, witnesses to this conduct, which became the origin of the charge that the Palestinians were traitors to the Arab cause. The foreign volunteers could not but be cognizant that, while they had come from afar to save Palestine and fight for its Arabs, some of the Palestinian Arabs themselves were making alliances and maintaining social and economic ties with Jews. Some were even seeking to negotiate a peace agreement.

Local pacts and passivity were just one part of the picture. Palestinian Arabs were also involved in wide-ranging hostilities that cost hundreds of lives on both sides, including during the "civil war" that preceded the invasion by the regular Arab armies. Furthermore, beyond the few thousand that enlisted in the militias, there were many who took part in the fighting in the form designated by the Arab word faz'a—appearing on the battlefield, to defend or attack, in response to an immediate call to arms. Our interest here is not, however, in the fighting forces but in the "traitors" and their motives.

• • •

The decision to avoid the fighting and collaborate with the Jewish forces was sometimes a personal matter motivated by individual or family considerations; in other cases it stemmed from public motives and was influenced by a political tendency or affiliation; yet other times such a decision was made by community leaders. On the political-public level, the rivalry between the Higher Arab Committee and the organized political opposition was of central importance. The opposition, composed of the Nashashibi-sponsored Defense Party and its allies and the veterans of the peace units, contested the Husseinis throughout the Mandatory period, and we have seen how the Jewish Agency and Shai worked to exploit and deepen this split. When military tensions rose in Palestine in autumn

---

*Yoram Nimrod argues in his study that even in the spring of 1948 most Palestinian Arabs abstained from fighting (he bases his contention on Ben-Gurion's statement to this effect); see Nimrod, *Brerat ha-shalom ve-Derekh ha-Milhama, 1947–1950* [War or Peace: Formation of Patterns in Israeli-Arab Relations, 1947–1950] (Givat Haviva, 2000), 63–65, 126 (in Hebrew). Benny Morris maintains that at this time the entire public was united behind the Husseinis. But Morris quotes Danin and Palmon to the effect that this was the result of excessive and indiscriminate Jewish retaliations; see Morris, *The Birth of the Palestinian Refugee Problem, 1947–1949* (Cambridge, 1987), 36–41.

1947, even before the outbreak of hostilities, the Jewish Agency wanted to make decisive use of these ties. At Ben-Gurion's orders, Shai agents met in October 1947 with Farid Irsheid, a peace unit leader in the Jenin region, to coordinate action. Irsheid argued that he could organize anti-Husseini groups throughout Palestine to cooperate with the Jews against the mufti and the forces that were liable to invade. He referred to the Jewish Agency's ties with Suliman Tuqan of Nablus, Kamel Hussein of the Hula Valley, the Fahoum family of Nazareth, the 'Abd al-Hadi clan in 'Arrabet, the Zeinatis in the Beit She'an Valley, 'Adel Nashashibi in Jerusalem, and 'Abdallah Bashir in Hebron. Each of these, Irsheid proposed, should receive a large sum of money to enable them to enlist men and buy arms.[12] This went far beyond anything the opposition had ever proposed before—joint combat against the Higher Arab Committee based on a common interest.

In light of the public campaign the mufti's supporters had conducted against the opposition, both during the rebellion and afterward—branding it traitorous and encouraging murder of its members—the oppositionists reached the obvious conclusion. If the mufti succeeded in establishing an independent state in Palestine, they would lose all political power and perhaps their lives as well. They were so certain of this that they preferred collaborating with the "enemy" to subordinating themselves to rival compatriots. This is a classic case of sanctions leading to a result that is the opposite of what was intended.

Irsheid's plan was never put into practice,[13] but the very fact that he proposed it testifies to the intensity of the opposition's hostility to the Higher Arab Committee. It is not the only piece of evidence. Opposition figures maintained contact throughout the war with operatives from the Shai and Jewish Agency, and they sought to prevent their followers from participating in the fighting, demonstrating unambiguously that the last thing they were interested in was an independent Palestinian state under the mufti's rule. Many also read the political and military map and concluded that the pro-Husseini forces had no real chance of achieving anything on the battlefield. It was far more likely, they concluded, that the Arab parts of Mandatory Palestine would be annexed to Transjordan.[14]

Although these leaders did not support the partition plan publicly, they indubitably viewed with favor 'Abdallah's effort to take over those parts of Palestine the partition plan designated as Arab. When the Husseinis ensured that, before and during the fighting, only their own supporters would receive money and arms,[15] they reinforced the sense that the fight was partisan, not national. They also confirmed the opposition's fears that the mufti would take revenge on them if he achieved power. This apprehension seeped from the political opposition into other parts of the public, who had felt much the same during the great rebellion of 1936–39 and the economic boycott that followed World War II. Even a man like ʿAbd al-Rahim Nashef, one of the most influential figures in the village of Tira and not at all close to the opposition, maintained that the mufti and his men were motivated by personal interests.[16] And Musa al-ʿAlami surmised that the mufti would agree to partition if he were promised that he would rule the Arab state.[17]

Long years of retroactive construction of Palestinian memory has to a certain extent obscured the fact that some Arabs supported partition. In his monumental book on the Nakba published in the mid-1950s, ʿAref al-ʾAref took note of them. Their central argument, according to al-ʿAref, was that the fight against partition was futile because the Arabs had no arms and the Jews had the support of the United States and Britain. True, he added, this was a minority view not voiced openly by its supporters (with the exception of some Communists, who advocated a two-state solution, but for other reasons). But it certainly was a factor that influenced the public's willingness to fight. Some chose to strengthen their contacts with the Zionists, others to side with King ʿAbdallah, who had supported partition as early as 1937.[18]

These high-level political considerations did not necessarily preoccupy the masses, who were simply striving to survive. The severe drought of 1947 left many on the verge of starvation. They knew they could not endure another season without a harvest. For them, remaining on and working their land were more important than abstract national ideas. A Shai informer in the south stated this explicitly: "The fellahin of Gaza [district] as a whole are trying, the informer says, not to get tangled up in operations against the Jews, since the most vital thing for them today is to preserve their crop and ensure a proper harvest."[19] What was true of the fellahin was also true of the tens of thousands of laborers who advanced the Jewish economy, especially by working in the citrus groves. Urban businessmen who dealt with Jews were also interested in calm and in sustaining economic activity.[20] The Neighborly Relations committees sponsored by the Jewish Agency, as well as the Histadrut's Arab bureau, continued to organize Jewish-Arab meetings before and during the hostilities, sometimes even helping participants to reach agreements.[21]

As the fighting continued and it became clear that the Jewish forces had the advantage, local Arabs' willingness to take up arms declined still further. Some felt this relatively early, others after a few months of fighting. "The Bedouin in the western Negev region are explicitly dubious about combat," a Haganah report of February 1948 stated. One of the reasons given was "fear of the Jews." The inhabitants of Samakh near Tiberias, another Haganah intelligence report said, "have no intention of intervening in political affairs" because they are a minority in the midst of Jewish settlements. The villagers in the area west of Jerusalem—in Sataf, Khirbet al-Loz, Suba, and Umm al-Mis—sought negotiations with the Haganah immediately after it conquered the village of Beit-Makhsir. They assumed they were next in line.[22] Sure enough, the Arab successes in the battles of March 1948 helped the Husseinis recruit more fighters, but this was reversed in April that year, when 'Abd al-Qader al-Husseini was killed in the village of al-Qastel, the first to be occupied by Jewish forces. It is hardly surprising, then, that Israel Defense Forces (IDF) operations carried out later that year in the Negev and Galilee met almost no resistance from Palestinians.

Before the scale of the defeat and the dimensions of the Palestinian catastrophe became clear, collaborators and opponents of the Husseinis in general were pleased with Jewish military successes. One of the Shai's Arab informers in Jaffa was still saying in February 1948 that "the Arabs have to be struck with heavy and severe blows." He explained that in Jaffa and its surrounding villages "there are many moderate forces waiting for a convenient opportunity to come on stage, but they are waiting for action on the part of the Jews." Similar sentiments were expressed by others.[23]

Memories of the rebellion were also a factor. When 'Abd al-Qader al-Husseini arrived in 'Ayn Karem and requested the villagers' assistance, they remembered that Ramadan evening a decade earlier in which al-Husseini had humiliated and accused the village elders and residents of treason. Neither had they forgotten the murder of Isma'il al-Khatib, an attorney and one of the village's leading citizens. A Shai informer reported that when 'Abd al-Qader appeared in the village of Surif, in the Hebron district, to speak before the village elders, "there were some who said to him: 'You murdered eighty mukhtars and you should be fought before we fight the Jews.' 'Abd al-Qader replied that he killed traitors. He was told: 'You are a criminal and your uncle [Hajj Amin] is a criminal and you are all an assembly of traitors.' "[24]

If these words were in fact uttered, it is worth noting that they came from people in a Muslim village where support for the Husseinis was ostensibly strong. Druze and Christians presumably had even harder feelings. These were the two populations that had suffered most during the rebellion, sometimes for no reason other than their minority status and their marginality in the national movement. Christians also felt discriminated against during the economic boycott declared at the beginning of the war. When the battles began, interfaith tension worsened.[25] It reached the point that the Christians in Haifa were accused by the local national committee of treason, and a battalion commander in the Arab Liberation Army ordered that only Muslim volunteers be allowed into his unit. There were Druze and Christians who feared that, after an Arab victory, the Muslims' weapons would be directed at them. That was sufficient reason for them not to take part in the fighting.[26]

Many Arabs refrained from taking part in the hostilities, but a small number went one step further and actively aided the Jewish war effort.

ACTIVE COLLABORATION

Informers

Throughout the war, Arab informers continued to provide Zionist intelligence agents with political and military information. In the political field these were veteran informers who maintained their contact with officials in Zionist institutions. Their motives were sometimes broadly political (preferring the Hashemite option), sometimes personal, sometimes a combination of the two. Prominent among them were 'Abd al-Ghani al-Karami and 'Omar Sidqi al-Dajani. Both had close ties with King 'Abdallah and were from families that had been victims of the rebels' assassination campaign. Al-Dajani actively promoted partition while continuing to provide Jewish Agency officials with information.[27]

Political intelligence gathering and anti-Husseini political activity were generally engaged in by political figures with political purposes in mind. They were in the purview of the Jewish Agency's political department. At the same time, the Shai continued to operate field informers. It is notable that in many cases Arabs became more willing to provide intelligence after hostilities broke out. A central reason for this was their desire to prevent an escalation of fighting in their regions and their recognition that hostile activities would prompt retaliation that would claim Arab victims. In this way the decision to stand aside turned into actual intelligence collaboration.

People with regional status, mukhtars, and private individuals all were part of this process. The mukhtar of al-Qastel, who sent an emissary to the Jewish workers at the quarry next to his village to warn them of an impending attack, was one example. So was the mukhtar of Fajja, who while proposing an alliance with the Jewish village of Kfar Sirkin reported on the activities of combatants from his village.[28] Sheikh Tawfiq Abu-Kishek did much the same; when asked by Arab forces to provide information that would allow them to sabotage one of the bridges over the Yarkon River, he refused and made sure that news of the plan reached the Shai. Old-timers at Kibbutz Na'an tell of a villager from Na'ana who saved many lives by telling the Jews of a mine that had been laid on a sandy road near the kibbutz. Members of one of the families in the western Samarian village of Qaqun did the same. All of them were interested in keeping the fighting far away from their homes; all were prepared to convey information to the Jews to ensure the tranquility they sought. Presumably most of them did not support the belligerent strategy of the Higher Arab Committee and Arab League. In some cases the informers seem to have acted on the basis of friendship. A young Arab who worked for a Jewish doctor in Zikhron Ya'akov told him about foreigners who had arrived in neighboring villages and their plans to attack Jewish settlements. An old friend of a member of Kibbutz Kfar Glickson provided similar reports, as did veteran Shai informers as well as others who had no previous record of intelligence involvement but had social ties with Jews.[29]

Direct economic interests also motivated the informers. Prime examples were cattle rustlers and food merchants, who continued to do business with Jews while passing on information to them. Arab forces took note of this; the Arab Liberation Army repeatedly arrested suspected smugglers and merchants and sometimes put them on trial.[30] The economic decline during the war pushed more Arabs into serving Jewish intelligence. "I found no work in the Arab sector and my wife and children have no food. There's not even any salt in the house," related a man who once worked for a Jew in Hadera. At the beginning of 1948 he moved to the Tulkarem area and provided the Shai with information from his new location.[31]

The enlistment of new informers and the operating of both new and old informers continued throughout the war. The state of emergency led the Shai's intelligence coordinators to seek to improve the quality of the information. "I considered it my obligation to operate my intelligence network at higher intensity," wrote Moshe Goldenberg, a Shai agent in the Beit She'an Valley, in his memoirs. "I increased payments for reliable information and conducted a kind of contest between the three people who were connected with me in providing intelligence." These efforts, he wrote, produced much important information.[32] Intelligence officer Tzvi Gluzman, stationed in Ben-Shemen, related: "We developed a wide-ranging intelligence network that reached into their commands. It was based, among other things, on local Arabs whose acquaintance we had made previously."[33]

Informers (generally experienced ones) were also prepared to embark on operations behind Arab lines. Just before hostilities commenced, when a training camp for Arab fighters was set up in Qatanna in Syria, a veteran collaborator from the Palestine Labor League was sent there. Soon after training began, the spy was unmasked in the wake of information from Palestine on his contacts with Zionist intelligence. He was expelled from the camp, but not before he acquired information about the number of trainees, their arms, the training program, human relations within the camp, and other such matters. When he returned to Palestine, he submitted a detailed report to his operators.[34]

Veteran collaborators circulated in areas where Arab forces had deployed. Among them were people of high status (especially senior figures in the opposition and supporters of 'Abdallah) who met with officers of the Arab Liberation Army and reported to the Zionists about the army's commanders and order of battle. Farid Irsheid was active in the Jenin area. He traveled to Tubas and reported on the Kurdish-Iraqi force stationed there. He also provided information on a house in Haifa in which attacks on Jewish neighborhoods were being planned. Haganah fighters blew up the house.[35] Hasan Salameh's headquarters south of Sarafand was also blown up in April 1948 thanks to information provided by an Arab informer.[36] Other collaborators visited Arab army camps and reported on the artillery they saw, the size of the forces, and other matters.

Intelligence reports that reached Shai headquarters and later the IDF demonstrate that Arab informers were deployed throughout the country. It is difficult to estimate how extensive this network was. But, given that most intelligence files are still sealed, it is reasonable to assume that it was even broader than described here. In any case, informers provided information not only on events in villages but also from inside the Holy Jihad and Arab Liberation Army. They also penetrated the regular Arab armies prior to their invasion of Palestine.[37] Some were able to put their hands on strategic intelligence as well as tactical information. According to Ze'ev Steinberg, a sergeant in the Mandatory police force who served later as an officer in the Israeli police, the Haganah's intelligence division received the Arab armies' invasion plan through a collaborator who bought land for KKL and had spent time in Syria before the invasion.[38]

The reports indicate that collaborators included Muslims, Christians, and Druze. Some were mukhtars or local notables, others merchants or simple people who were in contact with Jews. Like many who passively opposed the fighting, they were motivated by economic interests, and some belonged to the anti-Husseini opposition and feared a victory by the mufti's forces. Some wanted to save their own lives; others hoped that by supplying information they would keep their own area quiet. They did not believe that the Arabs had the strength to defeat the Jews and reckoned that escalation in the fighting would cause them to be uprooted from their homes. Sayf al-Din Zu'bi was a prime example of this sort of thinking. The Arab Liberation Army suspected him of passing information to Jews. In his memoirs, published at the end of the 1980s after he served as a deputy speaker of the Israeli parliament, Zu'bi did not address these accusations, but he did explain his position on the war. It was clear to him, he wrote, that the Jews would win, so he opposed the mufti's bellicose stance a priori. In his view the partition plan was good for the Arabs in that it acknowledged the power relation between the two sides. His position ensured, he claimed, that the people of the villages inhabited by the Zu'bi clan were able to remain in their homes.[39]

We know a bit more about the intelligence activity of Sheikh Rabbah 'Awad of Ghabsiyya in the Western Galilee. At the beginning of the 1930s, Sheikh Rabbah was involved in land sales to Jews. After the outbreak of the Arab rebellion he "recanted" and organized combat teams that carried out actions against British targets in the Galilee. After a string of successes he declared himself the chief of the rebellion in the Galilee, so a competing local commander sent his men to kill him. He managed to escape, but his friend and patron, Dr. Anwar Shuqayri, was murdered by rebels. At the same time, Rabbah testified, he received orders from headquarters in Syria to kill innocent people. This combination of events led him, he said, to perceive the negative side of the rebellion. He made contact with the British administration and established a peace unit that fought the rebels. In exchange, the British pardoned him for all his past crimes and gave him a large sum of money to buy arms and pay salaries to his men. Toward the end of the rebellion he issued an antirebel placard, and after the outbreak of World War II he enlisted young Arabs from the Western Galilee for the British army.[40]

At the beginning of 1947, 'Awad's name appeared on an al-Husseini hit list. At the end of that year, the Shai received news that 'Awad had reconciled with the Husseinis. Apparently, however, the information was in error. In January 1948 he posted a placard in which he accused the mufti of being the source of Arabs' tribulations, and he asked the Shai's help in distributing the document. At this time 'Awad had close ties to Jewish intelligence figures in his area, and toward the end of January he reported to them about a "gang" that had deployed in Nebi Sabalan in preparation for an attack on Kibbutz Yehiam.[41] At the same time, he tried to get the Arab Liberation Army to name him commander in the Upper Galilee. In this he was no different from others from the peace units who joined up with al-Qawuqji while maintaining their ties to the Jews. But at just that time the army's command in Syria learned that Sheikh Rabbah 'Awad was selling cattle to Jewish butchers in Nahariya in violation of the boycott. His candidacy for the command was rejected. The command seems not to have known about his intelligence work with the Zionists or his weapons smuggling for Jewish settlements.

Two years later, when he led his village's unsuccessful legal battle against the Israeli military government's decision to expel them from Ghabsiyya—as an Israeli citizen and in an entirely different set of circumstances—'Awad submitted the following affidavit to the Supreme Court:

1. During the riots of 47–48 I conducted negotiations with the Jewish forces.

2. I provided intelligence on the movement of Arab gangs to the commanders of the Haganah's Information Service [the Shai]: Mr. Aurbach Haim in Nahariya, Mr. Amnon, formerly mukhtar of Hanita, and Mr. Efrayim, mukhtar of Kibbutz Evron in the Western Galilee and Yosef Fein of Degania, and of course I was in touch with Wonderman from Haifa, today the commander of the Nazareth police, and Mr. Tzvi Sapir of Kibbutz 'Ein ha-Mifratz.

3. About a month before the attack on the Yehiam convoy, Arab gangs calling themselves the Liberation Army invaded our village, Ghabsiyya, with the intent of ambushing convoys to Yehiam.

4. I contacted Mr. Micha, the guard of Kibbutz Evron, despite the risk to my own life and that of my family, and informed him of the danger lying in wait for the convoy, and as a result the convoy did not set out on the day then appointed it.

5. On the day of the attack on the convoy I set out in the morning for Lebanon with the knowledge of the said Haganah men to collect information about the movements of the Arab army, and some 5–6 hours later the attack was carried out. Had I not been absent from the village I would have notified the Haganah about the gangs and the tragedy would not have occurred.

6. Despite the presence of the Liberation Army in Kabri across the Sasa–Nahariya road, a distance of only 2.5 km from our village, I used to walk every two days to Kibbutz Evron to convey intelligence. All members of my family and my supporters among the villages' inhabitants aided me at the time.[42]

'Awad was, then, an informer who was operated intensively and sent on dangerous missions outside his area of residence. His ties with Jews began even before the rebellion and continued at its end (after a hiatus during the uprising's climactic months). It may be presumed that one of his motives was the death sentence the Husseinis issued against him. In the event of an Arab victory, the judgment would be carried out, he reasoned. 'Awad may also have correctly assessed the balance of power in the field and thus expected a Jewish victory.[43] As in many similar cases, his ties with the Jewish settlements around his village were a significant factor in his decision to collaborate.

Special Assignments

Some collaborators were not content merely to provide information. They expressed a desire, or willingness, to go out on missions alongside Jewish forces. Farid Irsheid's initiative to form oppositionist fighting units with Jewish Agency financing did not come to fruition. But people in Wadi 'Ara made a similar proposal on the regional level. It grew out of a local rivalry; a large family from Kufr Qara' found that its status had declined after Iraqi forces entered the village. In summer 1948 the family contacted the Arab affairs advisor to the IDF's Alexandroni Brigade and proposed the establishment of an armed unit of several dozen men from the family, who would take the village from the Iraqis. Their only request, the advisor wrote to the IDF general staff, was that they receive IDF support if they were attacked. The advisor supported the idea. First, he wrote, it was a good opportunity for an offensive operation in cooperation with a local Arab force. Second, he figured, "acting against the 'new [Iraqi] order' would undercut security in the area, encourage defeatism, and serve as an example to others."[44]

As far as is known, no large unit was established. But small squads of Arab informers and scouts (from Kufr Qara', Qanir, and Kufrin) operated in the region at the behest of the IDF's intelligence officers. Some gathered information behind enemy lines. Others engaged in raids and sabotage. During exchanges of gunfire in the region, they fought "shoulder to shoulder" with IDF soldiers.[45]

These collaborators worked under the intelligence officers of the Samaria command and the special operations officers of other units. Two of them went on reconnaissance in Kufr Qara' with the goal of appraising the village's manpower in preparation for a possible offensive. They reported that all the houses in the village were shut up and that there was not a soul there. A week later they returned and set off a large explosion. A few days afterward, a squad composed of Arab collaborators and Jewish scouts made its way into the village of 'Ar'ara and opened fire outside the houses. Their goal was to draw the guards into an ambush and take them prisoner.[46] The chief intelligence officer of IDF Battalion 113, which was deployed in the region, had a team of Arab scouts, refugees from Kufrin. They entered abandoned villages and others held by the Iraqis. One October night in 1948, one of these scouts was captured by Arab forces in 'Ara, but he presented himself as a refugee and managed to get away.[47]

This operational cooperation was fundamentally different from regional peace initiatives in that it was performed by individuals and lacked any element of equality and mutuality. In some cases the men involved were veteran "traitors." A collaborator who went to recover the body of a Jewish soldier killed in Wadi 'Ara had previously sold weapons to the Jews. The same was true of an informer active in the Tulkarem area. Some of the residents of Abu-Ghosh who provided intelligence and secured convoys to Jerusalem had previous contacts with the Zionist underground.[48]

A somewhat organized Arab force that operated under Jewish command was the Heib tribe. The tortuous relations between the tribe and the Jewish settlements around them has been noted in earlier chapters. Al-Heibs now organized to fight alongside the Haganah, and Yitzhak Hankin was appointed their commander. The background to their enlistment was their previous ties to the Jews, the blood feud between them and the Labussiyya tribe in Syria, and the rivalry between Yusuf al-Heib and the Arab national leadership of the Galilee. In May 1948, after the Syrian army invaded, members of the tribe took part in raids on Syrian army camps, explosion of bridges, and other sabotage operations. Al-Heibs also participated in an attack on the Arab village Fir'am in the eastern Galilee when its inhabitants began to return to their homes. They "razed the village and took plunder," the IDF's Yiftah Brigade reported to the command that oversaw the operation.[49] A force composed of al-Heib Bedouin remained active in the months thereafter and, among other operations, was involved in collecting intelligence.[50]

The Heib operation against Fir'am was one kind of mission that seems to have been assigned to collaborators—encouraging Arabs to flee by spreading rumors.[51] Additional evidence directly connecting collaborators to this activity comes from Arab intelligence sources. According to information received by the intelligence officer of Hasan Salameh in Jaffa, the long-standing collaborator 'Ali al-Qasem, together with Tawfiq Abu-Kishek and several of his brothers, spread horror stories about the Jews' strength and their belligerent intentions. By March 1948 such accounts had convinced the Arabs of Sheikh Munis to abandon their homes, just before the grain in their fields ripened. The rumormongers received large sums of money from the Jews. The evacuation was a heavy blow to the Arabs of Jaffa, who were waiting anxiously for the harvest from the village's extensive fields in order to provision themselves with flour. It also constituted a heavy blow to the morale of the Arab forces, because the superiority of the Jewish forces in the region was proved unambiguously. To the best of our knowledge, Arab collaborators performed similar services in the Sharon region and elsewhere.[52]

Raising the White Flag

The removal of Arabs from their homes and settlements was of huge strategic importance. In this, the collaborators were no more than catalysts in what was already under way. They were also involved in another strategic area—turning key points over to Jewish forces and persuading Arabs deployed there to give up. This was especially notable in the Galilee, the area of most of the Arab villages that capitulated during the war. In the eastern Lower Galilee, it was the Zu'bi family's leader who encouraged surrender. In the Western Galilee, veteran Druze collaborators worked with Muslims and Christians from the region. For the most part, the people involved had been in contact with the Zionists for several years.

Surrender negotiations are a classic situation in which opposite concepts of what is treason and what is patriotism come to the fore. In general, during the 1948 war Arab military forces branded as treason villagers' willingness to surrender. But they did not always distinguish between villages that sued for peace only after a battle or because of military inferiority and those that surrendered willingly.[53]

The Zu'biyya villages east of Afula—Nin, Na'ura, Sulam, Tamra, al-Dahi, and Taybe, all within the boundaries of the decreed Jewish state—are prominent examples of those that surrendered of their own volition, consenting to live under Israeli rule. The ruling family in these villages, the Zu'bis, maintained close relations with the Jewish settlements in the region over the course of many years. In the 1930s and 1940s the family's leaders mediated the sale of some of the villages' lands to KKL (over the objections of some of the inhabitants). After the outbreak of hostilities, these villages did not participate in the fighting, and in April 1948 they proposed a peace agreement. That same month the mukhtar of Nin met a Shai representative and presented the position of his village and its neighbors: "We will do all in our power to prevent the entry of the gangs [Arab irregular forces]. And if you [Jews] betray us and kill us, it is better for us to die at your hands than to be killed by the gangs. You at least will not abuse us." He was assured that all efforts were being made to keep his family from harm.[54]

To this point, the story is similar to that seen in many other villages that signed pacts with the Haganah. But the Arab Liberation Army seems to have learned of the agreement between the Zu'bis and the Haganah, and on the eve of the invasion by foreign Arab armies it ordered the inhabitants to evacuate their villages.[55] When it became clear that al-Qawuqji and his forces could not harm them, most of the villagers returned to their homes. Through the mediation of Tzvi Wolf of KKL, who had worked with the Zu'bis on land deals, the villages accepted Israeli rule. Some residents began to work for Israeli intelligence — among them, apparently, Sayf al-Din.[56] In response, a local Arab Liberation Army commander ordered "the arrest of every man from the Zu'biyya because they are traitors and recognized the state of Israel and are serving it."[57]

There were similar cases in the Western Galilee, some involving Muslims and others Druze. A little background on the role of collaborators, especially Druze, in the area will aid an understanding of the snowballing of village surrenders. The prominent Druze who were in contact with Haganah intelligence were sheikhs Labib Abu-Rukun of Daliat al-Karmil, Khneifes of Shefa'amr, and Jaber Dahash Mu'adi of Yarka. These men were dissimilar in character. Sheikh Labib was described by one of his Jewish contacts, Yehoshua Palmon, as "an honest and upright man. He is devoted to the Jews and sees his future and that of his community to be in cooperation with the Jews." Sheikh Saleh Khneifes, in contrast, began to work alongside the Jews after his father was murdered by rebels in 1938. According to Palmon, his major strength lay in "indirect activities." Jaber Dahash Mu'adi of Yarka in the Galilee, whose acquaintance Palmon made through Khneifes, spent time in jail for murder, was active in the rebellion, and was admired by Hajj Amin. Palmon called him "a brave and audacious man."[58]

The first strategic move by the local Druze was to establish a line of contact between the officers of the Arab Liberation Army's Druze battalion and Haganah officers. Their first meeting took place at the height of the battle of Ramat Yohanan (Husha) in mid-April. Shakib Wahhab, the Druze commander, was apparently aware of the meeting but did not attend. The Druze representative was one of his officers, Isma'il Qabalan. The top Jewish representative was Moshe Dayan, whose brother Zurik had been killed the night before in a battle against the Druze. Qabalan proposed that the entire Druze force, numbering 800 men, defect and fight alongside the Haganah. The Haganah's acting chief of staff, Yigael Yadin, turned down the offer, and only Qabalan, along with several dozen other defectors, began to help the Jewish forces.[59]

Even though the "big plan" was not carried out, Wahhab refrained from defending Acre during the battles for the city, despite repeated pleas from the city's residents and the Arab Liberation Army command. Qabalan (then in the Arab Liberation Army, later an officer in the Israeli border guard) entered the city and reported on its defenses. Khneifes advised the Haganah to cut off the city's electricity and water supplies in order to hasten its capitulation. The advice was followed, and on May 17 the city fell to Jewish forces.[60]

The agreement with the Druze and the fall of Acre had an impact on the subsequent campaign in the Galilee. Later in May the Haganah received messages from Shefa'amr that the inhabitants wanted the Jews to conquer the town.[61] The operation was planned by IDF intelligence in cooperation with Khneifes and other Druze and took place in July, after the first truce ended. In accordance with the arrangement they reached, the IDF's 7th Regiment encountered no resistance from the locals; both sides fired some perfunctory shots into the air to create the impression that there had been a battle. After Shefa'amr, the adjacent village of Tamra surrendered; the Druze assisted in its occupation both with advance information and by persuading the village's elders to sign a surrender.[62] Sheikh Saleh Khneifes also acted to conclude a pact with the local Bedouin tribes. Through his agencies, Yehoshua Palmon reported, "we obtained the surrender of the Hjeirat, 'Omariyya, Ka'biyya, and Zbeidat tribes."[63]

Tamra's surrender led to the fall of other villages in the area. The initiative did not always come from the Druze. The mukhtar of Sakhnin, Ibrahim 'Abdallah, was related by marriage to the mukhtar of Tamra,

Jad Mustafa al-Diab; both were Muslim. When the fighting began, 'Abdallah saw to the procurement of weapons for the village and even traveled to Lebanon personally to purchase a machine gun. After Tamra fell, al-Diab sent one of his men to persuade 'Abdallah to surrender, on the grounds that the Jews had taken control of the entire region. 'Abdallah was persuaded, as were many others in his village.[64]

Two years later, when he asked to return to his position as muezzin, one Saleh al-Diab wrote a letter to the Israeli police, in which he described his mission to Sakhnin:

> I am the obedient servant [al-khadem al-muti'] who on the night of 21 July 1948, walked to the villages Sakhnin and 'Arrabet al-Battuf with the army of our government, the government of Israel, when the Arab Liberation Army was stationed in those villages. After I arrived, accompanied by the army, at the village of Mi'ar, I walked to Sakhnin together with Farid Jad Diab [son of the mukhtar of Tamra]. On the morning of 22 July 1948, I met with the village elders and explained to them that our government, the government of Israel, was prepared to reach an understanding with the elders regarding surrender. Their immediate answer was positive. Afterward Sheikh Ibrahim 'Abdallah [mukhtar of Sakhnin] wrote to the villages of 'Arrabet and Dir Hanna to update them on the situation, and all of them accepted the request, in particular Sheikh Fawzi Yasin, who supported it actively.
>
> Then I walked with twelve of Sakhnin's elders to the officer who was at that time in the village Mi'ar . . . and Sahknin was handed over to them together with 'Arrabet and Dir Hanna, and we all returned to Sakhnin and one of the officers received the arms. And on 20 July 1948, I went to the elders of the village of Kabul and it was agreed on handing over their village as Tamra was handed over. . . .
>
> And a death sentence was issued at that time against your faithful servant by the Arab Liberation Army because of his service for the government of Israel, and had I been captured at that time they would have hacked me to pieces.[65]

Apparently the emissary who came to Sakhnin and Kabul was not Saleh al-Diab but a member of his family who was a long-serving Haganah informer.* Still, there is no denying the basic fact that certain inhabitants of Tamra persuaded the villages around them to surrender and hand over their weapons.[66] In a village to the east of Sakhnin, Mghar, the

---

*It was common, after the establishment of Israel, for Arabs to revamp their biographies and boast of their collaboration with the Jewish state. "I have yet to meet a man who applies to the Jewish state who does not claim that he is an old friend of the Jews," Police Minister Bechor Shitrit wrote to an attorney named Hatshuel, 26 October 1951, ISA 3314/3/197.

Druze were again the locals who initiated surrender, simultaneously providing information on the Arab Liberation Army's deployment in neighboring villages.[67] The offensive in the area was delayed when the second cease-fire (18 July–15 October) went into effect. Mghar and the vicinity were taken only at the end of October, at the initiative of a Druze surrender delegation.[68] In the Upper Galilee, Sheikh Rabbah 'Awad of Ghabsiyya acted in the same way, saying: "After these things I and my men nevertheless continued to cooperate with the Haganah and I was able to draw the Druze and the other inhabitants of the villages of Yarka and Tarshiha to the Jewish side, and I brought them and the Haganah together at night. This allowed the Haganah army to conquer the entire Galilee at a later date easily and with small losses."[69]

Inhabitants of Abu-Ghosh in the Jerusalem hills also mediated between the Israeli army and Arab forces in nearby villages, though not in order to let the villagers remain in their homes. "When the Palmach took upon itself to conquer the village of Suba and its environs, one of our men served as a liaison between the Palmach commander and the Arab commander deployed in Suba, and through the agencies of this liaison the entire area was conquered," they wrote.[70]

In these cases, the capitulation was not always complete. Irregular forces continued to fight even though representatives of the inhabitants signed an official surrender.[71] In at least one case fighters killed a person who tried to convince them to give up. Mabruk Hassouna of Lydda, who tried to persuade armed volunteers holed up in the town's police building to cease fighting and turn the city over to the IDF, was shot dead.[72] In general, though, these agreements were of great value to the IDF and saved not only days of combat but also the lives of many soldiers.

Jewish lives were also saved when Arabs turned over strategic points—mostly police stations the British had abandoned—to Jewish forces. Among them was, according to one source, the police station in Abu-Ghosh, which stood above the Tel Aviv–Jerusalem road. Soon before evacuating, inhabitants of the village claimed, its British commander proposed to them that they ready a detachment of men to take control of the station to prevent it from falling into Jewish hands. That same day the villagers notified the residents of next-door Kibbutz Kiryat Anavim, who passed the information on to the Haganah. On the day of the evacuation, dozens of armed men from Abu-Ghosh arrived at the police station, where the British commander officially handed the building over to them. Before the officer left, the Haganah force arrived and joined the Abu-Ghosh detachment.[73]

Before leaving the country with his men, Kamel Hussein ("Kamel Effendi") of the Hula Valley told his friend Binyamin Shapira where to find the key to the police station in Khalsa (the site of today's city of Kiryat Shmonah). Shapira took the key and a Haganah force won control of the building.[74] The Palmach occupied the Rosh Pina police station with the help of the Heib tribe. Al-Qawuqji notified Abu-Yusuf, the tribe's chief, of the approaching British evacuation and asked that the Bedouin take over the building until a detachment of al-Qawuqji's men arrived. Abu-Yusuf notified the Palmach, which quickly seized the police station.[75] The same thing happened at the Wadi 'Ara police station. Local policemen, including some who were acquainted through their jobs with Jewish intelligence agents and those from villages where the mukhtars supported peace initiatives, allowed the Jews to take possession of the police building—a key point on this important road.*

DISCUSSING TREASON IN WARTIME

The fact that Arab collaborators were working alongside Jewish forces was an open secret in Arab Palestinian society. And, as noted, neither did it escape the eyes of Arab soldiers from outside Palestine. Beyond the immediate effect of the acts committed by the collaborators, their very existence had a far-reaching impact on Arab morale. To enlist in a national struggle, a person must believe that he acts in the name of his nation and enjoys its backing. The absence of support from significant sections of the population is liable to make individuals, as nationalistic as their sentiments may be, less willing to risk their lives. The very fact that collaborators were active served as a constant and sharp reminder that many Palestinian Arabs did not accept the nationalist ethos, at least not as it was formulated by the Husseinis. It also implied that there were significant advantages in ceasing to fight and allying themselves with the Jews. Hence the apprehension in nationalist circles that the existence of

---

*The agreement was that the Jewish force would carry out a bogus attack and the Arab policemen, most of whom were from nearby villages and a minority of whom were Iraqis, would withdraw. The object was to prevent combat in the region. The gambit was initiated by Binyamin Vinter of Kibbutz Ma'anit, and it was coordinated by Ze'ev Steinberg, a police sergeant at the station (and later, commander of the facility). The Arab policemen were to receive 500 Palestinian pounds each. The check was written by Ben-Gurion, who was briefed on the operation by Yigael Yadin and Re'uven Zaslani. The station was evacuated according to plan, but the check never reached its Arab beneficiaries because of difficulties in the field. Muhammad 'Aqel, *Al-Mufassal fi Ta'rikh Wadi 'Ara* [A Detailed History of Wadi 'Ara] (Jerusalem, 1999), 209 (in Arabic). For a description of this event, see also ha-Shomer ha-Tsa'ir Archive, Yad Ya'ari, 11-4.95 (6).

collaborators and traitors would legitimize "treason"—as indeed happened with the surrender of villages in the Galilee. The conclusion was that these persons had to be dealt with harshly.

Examples abound. A leaflet distributed in December 1947 claimed that Sheikh Salameh Ibn-Sa'id (chief of the 'Azazmeh tribe) received from the Jews large sums of money in exchange for his commitment to defend the Jewish settlements in the Negev and Hebron areas and to form detachments on the model of the peace units to fight Arab forces.* The leaflet called on its readers to fight Ibn-Sa'id and his allies. But the reason it gave is what interests us: to prevent other people from being influenced to act in the same way.[76] In other words, the traitors had to be fought not only because of the immediate military challenge they presented but also because they offered a tempting alternative to the strategy of the national leadership.

Jerusalem was another battlefield in the fight against traitors. The city's military commander issued a placard stating that all informers and traitors would be tried in a military court and their families expelled from the country. Merchants who did business with Jews were also punished harshly. Two men from the Abu Tor neighborhood were sentenced to death for selling food to the Jews of Mekor Hayyim. Just before his death, 'Abd al-Qader al-Husseini ordered that anyone caught spying for the Jews be executed on the spot, without a trial. The Arab Liberation Army commander in the Galilee handed down death sentences against traitors of various types. The Iraqi forces in Samaria, the Egyptian forces in the south, and local forces all feared collaboration and its consequences and were compelled to devote part of their energies to crushing this phenomenon. This was another way collaborators hurt the Arab nationalist cause.[77]

Reports written by the Arab Liberation Army's intelligence officer in Haifa, Muhammad Yusuf al-Kafi, portray the issue from the point of view of the Arab fighting forces:

> The Jews have enlisted many people in their intelligence service and they are scattered everywhere in Palestine and the Arab countries. . . . It is most

---

*Sheikh Salameh was apparently involved in land sales but did not collaborate during the war and, according to intelligence reports, reported to Egypt about collaborators in his tribe. In contrast, his nephew, Sheikh 'Oda Abu-M'ammar, cooperated with Jewish settlements in the Negev on security, intelligence, and arms procurement. After the establishment of Israel, he was appointed sheikh of the 'Azazmeh tribe in place of his uncle, who left the country. The new sheikh encouraged the men of his tribe to enlist in the IDF. Ya'akov Havakuk, 'Akevot ba-Hol: Gashashim Bedvim Be-Sherut Tsahal [Tracks in the Sand: Bedouin Trackers in the Service of the IDF] (Tel Aviv, 1998), 24–27 (in Hebrew).

unfortunate that there are vile Arabs who collaborate with Jews and supply them with information and provisions. This is known to us with absolute certainty from our activity. We constantly encounter a huge stream of Jewish and Arab spies, refugees and foreigners. In Haifa the enemy has a broad information network. Since the city is of mixed population, it is easier to make contact with Jews and get into their areas. The intelligence service of the Liberation Army fights the enemy's fifth column that tries to penetrate the dangerous triangle [of Samaria]. The [counter]intelligence services in the other cities of Palestine are weak and almost nonexistent.[78]

Another of al-Kafi's reports describes an espionage cell headed by one Sa'id Qabalan. "Sa'id Qabalan spies for the Jews and is dangerous. . . . He is the head of a dangerous group that helps the Jews and their employees, and they are young men of high culture and education who constitute a great danger. Sa'id has helpers in Haifa, Jenin, Tulkarem, Nablus, Nazareth, Samakh, and Balad al-Sheikh. This group is well organized and connected to Jerusalem." Later in the report, al-Kafi notes that the area of Haifa, Sindiana, and Umm al-Zeinat "is full of spies" and sums up: "I admit that there are a lot of collaborators with the Jews."[79]

News or rumors about spies were routine at the time. For example, the common wisdom was that the national committee building in Jaffa was blown up in early January 1948 by "Arab traitors." A later version of the rumor said that three suspects, who also sold arms to Lehi, had been arrested in Tira.[80] A similar story circulated after Etzel operatives lobbed a bomb into a crowd at the Jaffa Gate in Jerusalem, and again subsequent rumors stated that the Arabs involved had been apprehended and had confessed that they committed the crime for money. When a bomb went off in the Semiramis Hotel "minutes" after 'Abd al-Qader al-Husseini left, a whirlwind of rumors implicated his close associates. When the valued commander was killed during the battle of al-Qastel, collaborators were again blamed. The village's mukhtar, 'Adel Imteir, was arrested on suspicion of leading 'Abd al-Qader to his death; the mukhtar's connections with Jews were well known from the time he prevented an Arab attack on nearby quarries.[81] To add to the confusion, Zionist intelligence used collaborators to plant reports about the treason of various people and thus to exacerbate previously existing mistrust and conflicts between different camps.[82]

In the midst of their war against the Jews, the Arab forces were thus compelled to fight domestic enemies. They found it difficult to distinguish between friend and foe and were painfully aware that part of the Palestinian Arab community had serious reservations about fighting. In mid-April, Arab fighters conducted a careful search for informers in the Old City of Jerusalem. Arab sources reported that there were fifteen suspected spies in the lockup at Jerusalem's al-Rawda school.[83] The Arab Liberation Army garrison in Lydda was also forced to track, arrest, and discipline suspected collaborators. In one instance they arrested the occupants of a car after Hebrew documents were found in their bags; in another, Bedouin suspected of selling cattle to Jews; in yet another, two mukhtars from nearby villages and four of their associates, all assumed to have had contacts with Jews.[84]

It was a nationwide phenomenon. On 20 May three men accused of espionage were hanged in Gaza. Three others were arrested by the Egyptian army. An informer from the village of Hoj related the rumor in his village that the number of suspected spies arrested in the area had reached forty. Allegations were leveled against the Murad family in the village of Najd. They were accused of surveillance of the Egyptian army headquarters, housed in the school of al-Breir village, and of Egyptian artillery positions in Majdal. The suspects were nabbed by the Egyptians and identified by soldiers as the people who had been watching them. Also accused was Gaza's mayor, Rushdi al-Shawa. He was said to have received a large sum of money from the Jews, part of which he handed over to an Egyptian artillery officer who promised to sabotage the attack on Kibbutz Yad Mordechai, in which dozens of Egyptian soldiers were killed.[85] This rumor, apparently false, seems to have been based on the Shawa family's record of selling land to Jews. The assumption was that whoever sold land was also likely to be spying and carrying out other such activities. This was not, however, always the case.

In the area of northern Palestine under al-Qawuqji's control, the situation was not much different. An Arab who served as a sergeant in the interrogation department of the British police was executed in Nazareth for espionage after he was caught communicating with Jews by radio from a basement. Less than a month later, just before the city was conquered by Zionist forces, IDF intelligence received information that two Arab commanders in the unit of Abu-Ibrahim and an additional Arab who worked in Afula had been arrested on charges of contact with Jews.[86] Neither were Arab Liberation Army officers immune to suspicion. One source reported that one of al-Qawuqji's officers asked the people of Saffuri to clear away land mines from the dirt road leading to Shefa'amr, ostensibly so that he could attack and conquer the town. In fact, it was claimed, the officer signaled to the Jewish forces that the mines had been cleared, after which the Jews conquered the village.[87]

Such great mistrust had, of course, immediate implications. People who went out without their papers in Jerusalem were arrested, and those suspected of contact with Jews were interrogated and handled brutally. Interrogators checked to see whether the suspects bore Zionist intelligence's "secret mark"—blue dots in the armpit or the inside of the lower lip.[88] An even more serious consequence was the loss of trust—among military forces, between communities and individuals, and between the fighting forces and the civilian population. This was evident in the relationship between Palestinians and the Arab armies. "Iraqi military personnel in general keep their distance from civilians and treat them with suspicion. There are many, many suspected spies. They are placed in detention and scrupulously interrogated. Many are executed. Other suspects are under surveillance," reported an informer after returning from a trip through territory under Iraqi control.[89] One Palestinian, writing about this period, recalled: "[The Palestinians] became scapegoats. Others accused them of betraying their homeland, spying against the Arab armies, selling out Arab officers, leading them into ambushes; they are the ones who handed over their cities and villages."[90]

Dissension grew within Palestinian society. Those who had ties with Jews before the war were suspected of collaboration during the war. In Beisan nationalists refused to cooperate with the local national committee on the grounds that its members had connections with the Jews. It is not hard to imagine how distrust weighed on efforts to unite the town's inhabitants during the months of fighting. In Haifa the situation was reversed; one leader of the local national committee voiced suspicions against an entire population—the Christians. He called them "traitors and pimps for the Jews." Christian community organizations considered walking out of the committee.[91] Intercommunal tension and accusations of treachery adversely affected the city's morale.

It is difficult to determine precisely the extent to which Christians in Haifa tended to collaborate with the Jews more than Muslims did, or the real intentions of the national committee in Beisan, but these accusations testify to the prevalence of suspicions within Palestinian society during the war. After the sabotage of Hasan Salameh's headquarters during the first week of April 1948 (an operation involving, as noted, an Arab collaborator), a rumor spread that Salameh himself had not been hurt because he had been warned about the explosion and left the building earlier. The rumors claimed that Salameh had received a bribe from the Jews and had in exchange reduced the number of guards, and that he had gone off to Ramla to get drunk.[92] I have found no evidence for this unlikely allegation, although Zionist sources state that earlier in his life Salameh had cooperated with and participated in Haganah operations:

In those days, around the time of the disturbances of 1936, he was involved in purchasing arms for the Haganah in order to receive a substantial benefit. Neither did he give up his profits from buying arms as an Arab commander in 1947–1948. When he received large sums of money from villages for the purchase of rifles, he would immediately slip half the money into his own pocket and buy secondhand rifles with the rest.[93]

It is hard to judge the reliability of this information, but there is also Zionist testimony that Salameh helped KKL evacuate tenant farmers from lands near Kibbutz Hulda during the early 1940s.[94] We may assume that such rumors made it difficult for the Holy Jihad to recruit men in the central region, which was under Salameh's command until he was killed in the battle of Qule in June 1948.

One man who was a traitor according to both Palestinian and accepted historiography was the Najjadah commander al-Hawwari, who had extended contact with the Haganah. Fatah operative Abu-Iyyad (Salah Khalaf), who was a Najjadah youth in Jaffa during the war, recalled the effect of al-Hawwari's "treason." "As an unparalleled popular commander, a fervent nationalist with the ability to sweep the masses behind him, al-Hawwari contributed to the decline of morale among many of his sympathizers and admirers when he slid from passivity into collaboration with the enemy."[95]

Mutual suspicion kept Arab settlements from providing assistance to one another, diminishing their defenses against Jewish attack. The events surrounding the Haganah's offensive against Khisas in the Hula Valley in December 1947 are a good example. Some of the village's inhabitants, led by 'Atiyyah Jweid, had in the 1940s been involved in land deals with KKL. When the village was attacked by the Haganah (in a controversial operation), the Hula Valley villagers tried to obtain help from Safed, but because of the dissension between the city and villages around it Safed's residents did not organize a force to lend support to the residents, several of whom were killed. Some Safed Arabs were happy to see the downfall of their Arab adversaries: "The majority were in favor and thought that the people of the Hula deserved this blow from their Jewish friends. . . . [T]hey brought the Jews in and now they deserve this punishment."[96]

Reciprocal assistance faded from outside the battlefield as well. Some refugees from Lifta were unable to find refuge in Jerusalem or nearby villages because of the ties that many in Lifta had had with Jews, their leanings toward the opposition, and their sale of land to Zionists. Suspected collaborators from villages that held out against Jewish forces received similar treatment. When the Haganah attacked the village of Suba west of Jerusalem, the Holy Jihad detachment stationed in the village, commanded by Jaber Abu-Tbeikh, burned down the home of a leading citizen, Yunis 'Abd al-'Aziz. Tbeikh claimed that 'Abd al-'Aziz had known about the impending attack and not passed on the information to the defenders.[97] The arson may have satisfied the Jihadists' urge for revenge and perhaps had some deterrent effect, but it is doubtful that it contributed to the village's resilience or internal unity.

A central problem in the counter-treason campaign was that in many cases top figures in the Arab leadership were themselves suspected of collaboration. Such was the case, as we have seen, with Hasan Salameh, and Abu-Tbeikh was himself a suspect as well. In the 1940s he passed information to the British (and maybe also to the Shai) and helped apprehend rebels from villages in the Jerusalem hills. The Egyptian officers responsible for fighting treason were themselves hardly free of suspicion. An IDF informer caught by the Egyptian army was brought to trial before a military tribunal in Majdal. The army judge, who was responsible for treason trials, took him into the courtroom and closed the door. The defendant got the hint, gave the judge 15 Palestinian pounds, and was acquitted. Other espionage trials ended the same way. An IDF intelligence officer summed up these stories: "Taking bribes is common and acceptable."[98]

Nevertheless, people feared being labeled traitors, in particular during the war's early stages. This meant that the anti-treason campaign had another complex but important effect on Palestinian society. In Haifa, for example, the Jewish leadership sought (sincerely or not) to persuade the city's Arabs not to flee and promised that they would be treated well. Yet most of them nevertheless evacuated the city, according to Bayan al-Hout, because they feared that if they remained under the umbrella of an agreement with the Jews they would be considered traitors.[99] In other words, the fear of being branded traitors caused loss and suffering to the individual Arabs of Haifa and also probably harmed their national interest, since the city became primarily a Jewish one after the war. This is also evidence that an intensive discourse on treason does not necessarily unite a society behind its national demands. It can sometimes alienate part of the public or cause it to panic unnecessarily.

THE PALESTINIANS AT WAR:
WHO BETRAYED WHOM?

Arabs who acted in violation of the Higher Arab Committee, including those who made pacts with Jews or helped them, did not in any way consider themselves traitors. In their view the real treason was Hajj Amin's hopeless war, the dissension he sowed among the Arab population's different components, and his branding of all his opponents as traitors. His actions were aimed at furthering his and not the nation's interests.

Muhammad Nimer al-Hawwari, the Najjadah chief who sent patrols to prevent the Arabs of Jaffa from attacking the Jewish neighborhoods of south Tel Aviv, was called a traitor by the mufti and his associates. In his book *Sirr al-Nakba* (The Secret of the Nakba), published in Israel after he was permitted to return home in 1950, al-Hawwari claimed that he tried to prevent war because he feared that it would lead to the destruction of Arab society in Palestine. That was why he met openly with Jews and wrote articles against the mufti and Arab League under his own name.[100] According to al-Hawwari, the fact that he acted overtly in a cause he saw as manifestly in his people's interest was enough to clear him of treason. In contrast, he wrote, the national leadership acted for the benefit of its members and betrayed its people. His claims were similar to those leveled against the mufti by Muhammad Tawil after the riots in summer 1929. Tawil said then that al-Husseini's militant policies would lead to catastrophe.

I heard a similar claim from Hasan Darwish, the son of 'Abd al-Fattah, head of the Bani-Hasan *nahiya* south of Jerusalem. The elder Darwish belonged to the opposition, was involved in land sales, and prevented the Holy Jihad from operating out of his village, al-Maliha.

> The mufti and his men said that my father was a traitor. But my father tried to prevent the war. He said to the mufti: The war that you are declaring will lead to the loss of Palestine. We need to negotiate. The mufti said *idha takalam al-seif, uskut ya kalam*—when the sword talks, there is no place for talking. They say that my father sold land and that that made him a traitor. He didn't sell. But tell me this, if a man who sold 400 dunams to the Jews is a traitor, what would one say of a man whose policies led to the loss of all of Palestine? Isn't he the biggest of traitors?[101]

Palestinian historiography has not taken kindly to Darwish's claims. When he and others like him receive any attention at all, they are portrayed as turncoats, mainly because of their role in the rebellion of 1936–39. There is even less attention given to treason in the Palestinian historiography of 1948. The crushing defeat in the war, the deaths of thousands of people, the obliteration of hundreds of villages, and the displacement of hundreds of thousands of people have focused narratives and scholarly attention on the common, unifying account rather than on divisive stories. Writings on lost villages seldom mention the collaborators who lived in them during the fighting; the same is true of the extensive historical literature on the Nakba.[102] But Palestinian memory, both personal and collective, has preserved the disagreements of the period preceding 1948 and the war itself, and these disputes receive expression in literature and conversations and in stories that pass from generation to generation.[103]

"Treason" in its different forms, including direct collaboration with the Zionists, continued after the Nakba as well. The devastating defeat destabilized an already divided Palestinian society and dealt a mortal blow to the national movement and its value system. This made it easier for the state of Israel to recruit and operate collaborators. Many of the Shai's informers became refugees in Arab countries, and their operators, now working for IDF intelligence, continued to foster their connections and receive information. Collaborators who remained on their land in the cities and villages of the West Bank also continued, in some cases, to maintain contact with Israeli intelligence. And the same is true of those who remained in Israel and became its citizens. The assistance given by collaborators continued to be an important component of Israel's security strategy. Covert and overt missions by them—and struggle against them—became commonplace in the various Palestinian communities, both in the generation of the Nakba and in those that followed.[104]

CONCLUSION

The study of Palestinian history during the British Mandate generally focuses on the national movement led by the mufti of Jerusalem, Hajj Amin al-Husseini. Arabs who opposed al-Husseini or collaborated with the Zionists are treated as marginal. This is a prejudiced view. It ignores the fact that cooperation and collaboration were prevalent, in a variety of forms, throughout the period and among all classes and sectors. Collaboration was not only common but a central feature of Palestinian society and politics. The actions of many so-called collaborators were not inconsistent with Arab nationalism, yet collaboration was regarded by the mainstream as treason.

The history of the national movement cannot be studied without a thorough examination of collaboration. Zionist institutions shared interests with the Arab rural leadership, with part of the urban elite, and with some members of the public at large. These common concerns and the cooperation that resulted were factors in the defeat of the mainstream nationalists. At the period's two most important historical turning points, Arabs the mainstream labeled as traitors succeeded, with foreign help, in neutralizing the mufti's camp. The Husseinis and other nationalist forces initiated and guided the Arab rebellion of 1936–39. Peace units and local collaborators helped the British and Zionists put down the uprising. To oppose the UN partition plan of 1947, the mufti and the Higher Arab Committee formed the Holy Jihad army and brought the Arab states into war against Israel. "Traitors" refrained from fighting, made alliances with the Jews, in some cases coordinated their moves with King 'Abdallah of Transjordan, and helped frustrate the attempt to establish an independent Arab state in Palestine.

This is not to argue that collaboration with Zionists was the main cause of the Arab defeat. There were many other contributing factors: the Jewish forces' superior military organization; the support the Zionists received from the British during the early Mandatory period and from the international community toward its end; and the mufti's problematic conduct. Nevertheless, it is important to know that central figures in Palestinian society opposed Hajj Amin's bellicosity and consequently joined the Zionists or 'Abdallah. Both sides benefited from this cooperation, even when it was partial. 'Abdallah annexed the West Bank, the Jews enlarged their state beyond the borders set by the partition plan, and "traitors" received posts in the united monarchy's executive branch (e.g., Ragheb Nashashibi and Suliman Tuqan), legislative branch (Farid Irsheid, 'Abd al-Fattah Darwish, Hafez Hamdallah), or religious-judicial branch (Hussam Jarallah). To be sure, some paid a heavy price and became refugees as a result of a war they had sought to avoid. In any case, until the war of 1967, and to a lesser extent until the Intifada of 1987, they and their successors held positions of power in Palestinian society.

When Chaim Weizmann visited Palestine in 1920, the Zionist Executive foresaw that its project would split Palestinian society and undermine its leadership and institutions. The rift among Palestinians in 1948 may be seen as the fulfillment of this prediction. But to understand Palestinians' readiness to cooperate with Jews, one must first picture the Middle East at the beginning of the twentieth century, before nationalism became the focal point of identity and before the borders of the Arab states were drawn. In that period, including the years immediately after World War I, large numbers of Arabs identified themselves first and foremost by their religion, their family, their village, and the region they lived in. Even those who gave priority to their national identity as Arabs were divided on the question of what constituted the Arab nation and what its national territory was. The pan-Arab movement was sometimes stronger and sometimes weaker. Some of its adherents perceived Palestine to be part of an Arab kingdom centered in Damascus, others viewed it as a natural extension of the Transjordan emirate, while still others saw the boundaries of the British Palestine mandate as defining a specific Palestinian Arab identity distinct from other Arab identities. As time passed, the latter became the mainstream, though not the only, view among Palestinian Arabs.

Two opposing forces took form in Palestine's Arab community at the beginning of the Mandatory period. One was the Husseini party, which controlled the national institutions, and the other was the opposition, often identified with a rival Jerusalem family, the Nashashibis, but with many of its leaders from rural and peripheral areas. Both established social and political networks throughout Palestine. Under the new circumstances, old debates turned into ideological debates: how to respond to Zionism; how to relate to 'Abdallah of Transjordan. From the start, the Husseinis took a hostile stance toward both Zionism and the Hashemites. The opposition, in contrast, preferred to seek good relations with the emir and accommodation with the Zionists—not necessarily out of love of the Jews, but rather since they understood that the Zionists could not be defeated by the Arabs. Over the years, senior opposition leaders were in contact with the Zionist movement, and some also sold land to Jews. The Husseini leadership branded them traitors. Their conflict with the mufti led them to prefer the annexation of Arab Palestine to Transjordan, that is, to resist the very core of Palestinian mainstream nationalism as consolidated during the early 1920s.

The opposition did not win the support of a majority of Palestine's Arabs, but the Husseini camp also failed to garner mass support. Part of the reason was an internal contradiction: the Husseinis expected the public to identify itself first and foremost as Palestinian Arabs, just as nationality had become the central component of personal identity in Europe. Such a revolution in self-perception required that other political and family identities become subordinate to the nation. But the Husseini version of Palestinian national identity demanded total allegiance to a specific political camp and, even more so, to a particular leader. In other words, the Husseinis themselves gave priority not always to the interests of the nation, but rather to the interests of the mufti. The unintended result of this contradiction was the strengthening of family and political identities in the opposition. Thus, for many individuals on both sides, as for many who were not affiliated with either, personal and family interests remained paramount and overshadowed national considerations. In the new, post–World War I global order (the "age of nationalism"), this was a political deficiency of the first order. This was even more the case given that the Palestinian national movement's rival was Zionism, whose ideology and political and organizational structure were deeply rooted in the European nationalist tradition.

An important consequence was that those who opposed the Husseinis at the beginning of the British Mandate period largely continued to oppose them thereafter. Then they were joined during those three decades by others who were victims of the rebels during the uprising of 1936–39, or of the aggression and nepotism that characterized the national political leadership of the Husseinis. In other words, the official Palestinian national institutions could not exert their influence on the opposition camp and so block its ties with the Zionists. Regional leaders who in the 1920s joined pro-Zionist organizations or the farmers' parties—such as Muhammad Zeinati of the Beit She'an Valley, members of the Abu-Ghosh family, the Darwish family who led the villages of the southwest Jerusalem mountains, the 'Azzis who headed the villages in the Beit Jibrin area, the Abu-Hantashes of Qaqun, and the Zu'bis of the Lower Galilee—continued throughout these years to act outside, and often against, the Palestinian national organizations. Some of them fought against the rebels in the 1930s, worked with the Jews and British to prepare for a German invasion in the early 1940s, and maintained contact with and often provided intelligence to the Jewish forces in the 1948 war.

The fissure in Palestinian Arab society reflected, in the main, a traditional social and political structure based largely on kinship, with old tensions between landowners and the landless, between religious communities, and between the rural and urban populations. From the beginning, the Zionists were well aware of the strategic and tactical benefits they could reap from these tensions. At first they thought they could use opposition figures to reach a compact with Palestine's Arabs. When that turned out not to be possible, the Zionists took advantage of the divisions to weaken the Palestinian national movement and impede the Palestinian nation-building process. In so doing, they were able to broaden the gaps between the rural and urban leaderships. They slowly strengthened those Druze who opposed the national movement, to the point that Druze forces actually allied with the Jews in 1948. A similar result was achieved with some Bedouin tribes. The Zionists (alongside the British) used the services of collaborators to help suppress the rebellion and obtain vital information. Even more important, this created a cycle of hostility that prevented the Palestinians from uniting. Opposition figures and other collaborators who aided Zionists were hounded by the national movement, but that merely intensified their willingness to work with the Zionists. They extended their collaboration into new areas; political collaborators began to work as land agents, and land agents helped fight nationalist violence. Both provided information to the Haganah's intelligence division, the Shai.

The same process took place on the local level. Shai field operatives identified social fissures or feuds and sought to enlist one of the contending sides into its service. The founder of the Shai's Arab division, Ezra Danin, instructed his agents to use personal and family rivalries in Arab villages to locate and enlist potential collaborators. During the rebellion, additional collaborators came from among Arabs who sought revenge for injuries incurred at the rebels' hands. To get it, they were prepared to aid their enemy's enemy—the Zionists. Other collaborators were motivated by their distaste for the national movement's violent tactics, or because they found it morally repugnant to hurt their Jewish neighbors. Such Arabs provided information on attacks planned against the Jews or continued to do business with them in violation of the boycott declared by the national leadership. At times, of course, their motives were utilitarian, on both the national and the local level.

So, while the Zionists established and reinforced networks of informers, broadened fissures in Arab society, built up their military strength, and expanded their holdings by purchasing land and establishing settlements, Palestinian society was preoccupied with internal battles and was unable to mobilize and unify behind a leadership that all were prepared to accept.

The conduct of Palestinian society might lead to the conclusion that, during the period under discussion and even at its end, Palestinian society's national spirit was not sufficient to the task at hand. According to Benedict Anderson, a national spirit is fraternity that makes it possible for so many millions of people not so much willing to kill as willingly to die for it.[1] This was not the case among Palestinian Arabs, who by and large did not see the nation as the central focus of their loyalties, to use Hans Kohn's definition.[2] This limited willingness to sacrifice their lives (or personal comfort) for the nation can be seen, not only in the low level of mobilization for the decisive war that began in December 1947, but also in their economic activity and involvement in selling land to the Zionists.

Kohn's second component of nationalism is a *shared* tie to a homeland that constitutes a single territorial unit. This, too, was not strong among Palestinian Arabs. Socially and politically, family and factional ties were stronger than national ones, and the same was true when it came to territory. The tie to the land focused on personal holdings or on the lands of a village or region, but not on Palestine as a whole. This, too, was evident during the war. Most of the Palestinian Arabs who took up arms were organized in units that defended their villages and homes, or sometimes a group of villages. Only in extremely rare cases did forces move to distant sectors—a sharp contrast with the high mobility of the Jewish forces. Mobility enabled the Jews to achieve numerical superiority in almost every area where combat took place. Furthermore, in many locations Arabs' links to their villages and community had been disturbed when some villagers sold land or because of individuals' links with Jewish intelligence operatives. This had a negative impact on the villages' resilience and was displayed in internal conflicts during combat.

The lack of a shared view of Palestine as a single entity was expressed in another way as well. An important group among the opposition to Hajj Amin al-Husseini had close ties with Transjordan's ruler, Emir (later King) 'Abdallah. At various points in time these figures supported the annexation of Palestine (or its Arab parts) to 'Abdallah's state. Hajj Amin and his followers considered these people traitors because they rejected his authority. But it is important to stress that their concept of the nation was different not only with regard to the question of who should lead it (a central issue for their rivals, the Husseini party) but also with regard to the definition of the territory in question. They did not see Palestine as a discrete political unit. This is a point of great significance, for land constitutes the territorial and cultural basis of nationalism. The lack of agreement over such a fundamental issue made it difficult to create a common ethos, and difficult for the social unit to function as a nation.*

The lack of such central components of national identity led Zionist spokesmen to claim that no Palestinian Arab nationality existed. Ironically, this same claim was echoed by Palestinian Arab national activists when they sought to unite the public behind them. At times they too sensed that they were not succeeding in turning the national movement into a focal point of identity. To arouse the public, they posted placards warning that the failure to respond to the nation's call would confirm the Zionist claim that the Jews had come to a land without a people.

But things were more complicated than that and cannot be presented as a dichotomy—the presence or absence of a national identity. To better

---

* The Palestinian dispute over the national territory differs from the current Israeli public debate over the status of the West Bank and Gaza Strip. In the latter case there is disagreement about the need for Israel to exercise sovereignty over these lands on its periphery, no matter what their historical, religious, or military importance. At the same time, there is a consensus about the country's sovereignty over the territories within the boundaries demarcated by the cease-fire lines of 1949. In other words, there is a central territory about which there is general agreement. In the Palestinian case, the fact that many preferred the Jordanian option is evidence that they attached no importance to the existence of an independent Palestinian Arab state, and the entire territory of Palestine could, in their view, be a part of the Jordanian kingdom or some other Arab entity. This view negates Palestinian (though not Arab) nationalism.

understand the Palestinian case, it is necessary to deconstruct and dissect the concept of nationalism, to see which components were present and which not, and among whom. It can be stated that national consciousness—that is, the consciousness of belonging to the Arab nation, and specifically to the Palestinian Arab nation, took root among the Arab population of Palestine during the British Mandate. It is almost certain that a large majority of the country's Arab inhabitants, including those who tended to support the Hashemite option, defined themselves as Palestinian Arabs. This identity was produced by several factors, including the establishment of the borders of Mandatory Palestine, the activity of the national movement, and the struggle against Zionism. National sentiment, which as Ernest Gellner has noted is based on resistance to foreign rule, also characterized the Arab population of Palestine.[3] Such sensibility existed at the time of the first waves of Zionist immigration, which created fears that Jews would take control of the country. It grew stronger after the Balfour Declaration and the imposition of the Mandate.

The spread of national consciousness and sentiment is testified to by the terminology used even by those people and groups whom the mainstream termed traitors. Such was the case in the early 1920s with Ibrahim 'Abdin of Ramla, who stressed that he was not a traitor; in his letters to the Zionists he sought to dissuade them from harming the country's Arabs. Similarly, the propagandist Muhammad Tawil, active around 1930, wrote that he opposed the mufti for the sake of the nation. The same was true of peace unit commanders such as Fakhri Nashashibi of Jerusalem, Fakhri 'Abd al-Hadi of 'Arrabet-Jenin, and Rabbah 'Awad of the Western Galilee, who considered the uprising of 1936–39 a "counterfeit rebellion." They called their war against the rebels a rebellion for the nation; local leaders like 'Abd al-Fattah Darwish used the same terminology in 1948.

The Palestinian public thus did not reach identical and unambiguous political inferences from its national sentiments. The national institutions rejected contact with the Zionists. The other, "treasonous" stream maintained that talking and working with the Zionists for the sake of the country's future was patriotic, or at least unavoidable. They added that the Husseinis' militancy was liable to bring catastrophe on Arab society in Palestine. Critics of this latter group said that the claim of patriotism was no more than a fig leaf to cover up their mendacity, whereas at least some of the "traitors" seem to have been sincerely concerned with the public good, and subsequent events in some ways proved their case.

Moreover, on the socioeconomic, as opposed to political and military, level, the public at large did not oppose cooperation on day-to-day matters. Emotional support for Hajj Amin and national sentiment, strong as it was, did not prevent Palestinians from working with and for Jews. The Arabs of Palestine usually distinguished between the private and the political, between daily needs and national sentiments. With the exception of a few specific and isolated points in time, they maintained social ties with Jews and ignored the economic boycott. Some even sold land to Jews. Certainly they did not seek to halt the construction of their nation; rather, their actions sometimes grew out of a conviction, based on a realistic appraisal of their situation, that the Jews had become an integral part of the country's population who could not be uprooted. The political leadership ignored this insight, and that is one of its most colossal failures. Its opponents claimed that personal and party interests blinded the Husseini party. Its proponents said that they could not consent to the expropriation of any part of Palestine.

Palestinian Arabs thus shared a national consciousness and nationalist sentiments but were divided about the practical implications of that nationalism. In the field, this took the form of the very limited willingness to engage in self-sacrifice (the behavior of the leadership was also a factor), the lack of a consensus over what territory constituted the national territory, and the preservation of prenationalist social structures.

Opposition to the national leadership in the first decades of the development of nationalist ideas is a phenomenon well known from other countries. Eugen Weber's comprehensive study of the French peasantry in the decades before World War I depicts much the same picture, perhaps one even more distant from the common image of nationalism. His work shows that, almost one hundred years after the mandatory conscription law of 1789, the rural French still perceived the national army as a hostile force. In many places most young men sought to evade conscription, and the local population made life miserable for army units deployed in their vicinity.[4] The situation Weber described is surprisingly similar to that faced by Arab military units (both Palestinian and those of the Arab countries) deployed in and around Palestinian villages and cities in the rebellion of 1936–39 and war of 1948.

Weber writes that he does not claim that the French were not patriotic. Rather, he shows that at that time patriotism was viewed differently by different French men and women. He concludes that patriotic sentiments on the national, as opposed to local, level are not instinctive. They have to be learned.[5] The same is true of the young countries of the

Middle East. Firsthand testimony of this comes from Faysal I, king of Iraq, speaking of his country in 1933: "In Iraq there is not yet . . . an Iraqi nation, but rather uncounted masses of people, lacking any patriotic ideal."[6] In Palestine there were, in fact, many with patriotic ideals, because of the fear that Jews would take over their country. But they did not necessarily identify with the national leadership, which excommunicated people and factions from the nation. In the end, this prevented the national movement from becoming a significant framework of identity for all Palestine's Arabs. In the war of 1948 the leadership could no longer mobilize the masses, its armed units were crushed, and many Palestinians, from the opposition and others, asked 'Abdallah to "save" Palestine. Ironically, the results of the war led within a few years to the reemergence of the Palestinian national movement and the consolidation of the people around it.

• • •

The Zionist movement's Arabists enjoyed both strategic and tactical successes. It is hardly surprising, then, that the use of political and intelligence collaborators continued to be a fundamental component of Israel's security conception in later years. During the nineteen years in which Jordan ruled the West Bank and Egypt the Gaza Strip, some of the collaborators who had worked with the Zionists during the Mandate period continued to serve Israeli intelligence both within Israel and outside it. When Israel occupied these territories in 1967, it established a well-developed network of collaborators. They were used to help frustrate terrorism, but as in the Mandate period one of the goals was also to frustrate Palestinian nation building. This was the logic behind the establishment of the village leagues at the beginning of the 1980s, and it was also the logic behind planting informers within unarmed political organizations such as trade unions and student organizations.

As during the Mandate, armed Palestinian activists tried and executed many collaborators. Purges took place in the early 1970s in the Gaza Strip and during the first and second Intifadas. But there are two important differences in the way the new Palestinian national movement conducted itself. For one, with the exception of some marginal elements and limited periods, it did not seek to impose an economic boycott on the Jewish economy or to forbid Arabs to work for or with Jews in Israel. In this way it avoided its alienation from the general public. In addition, the central stream of the national movement—Fateh—generally refrained from assassinating its political rivals. The Palestinians learned these two lessons from the fight against "traitors" during the Mandate.

This does not mean that the Palestinian public or its leadership ceased to be concerned about treason and collaboration or to fight them. On the contrary, the issues are very much alive today, and the fields of (and discourse about) collaboration did not change: In the political field the discussion is which compromise with Israel would be legitimate and which should be considered treacherous (a current example is the debate in Israel and Palestine on the Geneva initiative); in the security arena people are preoccupied by Israeli successes in recruiting collaborators even for targeted killing; and the land issue is also of great interest (as was manifested in the discussion of the Greek Orthodox patriarch land deal with a Jewish company in 2005). The hot debates in regard to these issues remind us that the question "What is treason?" is a mirror image of the question "What is patriotism?" and the question "What is unacceptable collaboration?" is another way of asking "What relations should we have with Israel?" and "What does it mean to be 'a good Palestinian'?"

Notes

ABBREVIATIONS

CID   Criminal Investigations Department (of the British police in Palestine)

CZA   Central Zionist Archives (Jerusalem)

HA   Haganah Archives (Tel Aviv)

IDFA   Israel Defense Forces Archives (Ramat Gan)

ISA   Israel State Archives (Jerusalem). ISA holds documents of the Mandatory government in Palestine and what are called "Arab abandoned documents," that is, files of the Higher Arab Committee, the Supreme Muslim Council, and private law firms of Palestinian Arabs, all captured during the 1948 war.

OHD-HU   Oral History Division, Harman Institute of Contemporary Jewry, Hebrew University of Jerusalem. This collection contains hitherto classified interviews (conducted in the late 1960s and early 1970s) with Zionist activists involved in purchasing land from Arabs in the Mandate period.

PRO   Public Record Office (London)

INTRODUCTION

1. See General Ismail Safwat to Jamil Mardam Bey, "A Brief Report on the Situation in Palestine and a Comparison between the Forces . . . ," dated 23 March 1948, in Walid Khalidi, "Selected Documents on the 1948 Palestine War," *Journal of Palestine Studies,* vol. 27, no. 3 (1998): 64–65; Avraham Sela, "Ha-Aravim ha-Falastinim be-Milhemet 1948" [The Palestinian Arabs in the 1948 War], in Moshe Maoz and B. Z. Kedar, eds., *Ha-Tnu'ah ha-Leumit ha-Falastinit: Me-Imut le-Hashlama?* [The Palestinian National Movement: From Conflict to Reconciliation?] (Tel Aviv, 1996), 191 (in Hebrew).

2. See, e.g., René de Chambrun, *Pierre Laval: Traitor or Patriot?* (New York, 1984); Herbert R. Lottman, *Pétain: Hero or Traitor* (New York, 1985); W. O. Maloba, "Collaborator and/or Nationalist?" review of *Koinange-wa-Mabiyu, Mau-Mau Misunderstood Leader* by Jeff Koinange, in *Journal of African His-*

tory, vol. 42 (2001): 527–529; Grant Goodman, "Aurelio Alvero: Traitor or Patriot?" *Journal of Southeast Asian Studies,* vol. 2, no. 1 (1996): 95–103; David Littlejohn, *The Patriotic Traitors* (London, 1972).

3. Ron Dudai and Hillel Cohen, "Triangle of Betrayal: Collaborators and Transitional Justice in the Israeli-Palestinian Conflict," *Journal of Human Rights,* vol. 6, no. 1 (2007): 37–58.

4. Zachary Lockman, *Comrades and Enemies: Arab and Jewish Workers in Palestine, 1906–1948* (Berkeley, 1996), 367.

5. Ted Swedenburg, *Memories of Revolt: The 1936–1939 Rebellion and the Palestinian National Past* (Minneapolis, 1998), chap. 5.

6. Issa Khalaf, *Politics in Palestine: Arab Factionalism and Social Disintegration 1939–1948* (Albany, 1991).

7. Ibid., 247.

1. UTOPIA AND ITS COLLAPSE

1. Undated cable, signed by Hasan Shukri and others, CZA S25/10301. This file contains similar cables from Nazareth, Ramla, Beisan Valley, and villages in the Jerusalem area.

2. [Zionist Executive in Palestine] to the Executive of the World Zionist Organization, budget proposal, 5 May 1920, CZA Z4/2800.

3. The National Committee to Ussishkin, 4 May 1920; Maloul to [Jewish] National Committee, 27 February 1920, CZA L4/999. For a broader discussion, see Yosef Gorni, *Zionism and the Arabs, 1882–1948* (Oxford, 1987), pt. 2; Lockman, *Comrades and Enemies,* 58–62, argues that the denial of the existence of Arab nationalism in Palestine aimed to neutralize the tension between the humanistic and socialist self-image of the Jewish settlers of the second *aliya* (wave of immigration) and their actual activity. On the other side of the Zionist political map stood Ze'ev Jabotinsky, who was among the first Zionists to acknowledge the existence of Arab national sentiments—and the movement—in Palestine.

4. [Kalvarisky to the Zionist Executive, undated], CZA S25/665.

5. The opposition came from both the landowners of the first *aliya*—for national reasons—and David Ben-Gurion and other members of socialist parties, who opposed cooperating with the effendis and believed in the need to ally with fellahin and workers.

6. Yehoshua Porath, *The Emergence of the Palestinian-Arab National Movement: 1918–1929* (London, 1974), 147–158.

7. Al-Mubashir claimed that he convinced the majority of the voters to support participation in the elections, and Shahin reported that the mayor, mufti, and Muslim court judge of Hebron held public meetings in which they announced their opposition to the elections; see al-Mubashir to Maloul, 22 October 1922, Shahin to Maloul, 13 November 1922, CZA J1/291.

8. The continuation of the activity is evident from correspondence between Zionist officials and Shukri, 'Abdin, and others throughout 1924–25; see CZA S25/517, 518, J91/291. In this period there were repeated disagreements about payments.

9. See, e.g., Kisch to Meirovitch, 9 November 1925, CZA S25/665.

10. Kalvarisky to the Farmers' Union, 17 February 1924, CZA S25/10297.

11. Al-Mas'oud to Kalvarisky, 21 January 1925, ibid.; al-Fahoum to Kalvarisky, 18 May 1925, CZA S25/10298.

12. Porath, *Emergence,* 230–240.

13. For the Zionist perspective on the British moves at that time, see Frederick Kisch, *Palestine Diary* (New York, 1974), 208–211.

14. "Report on the Political Work 10 October–10 November 1929," CZA J1/310.

15. Cables from different localities are preserved in CZA J1/310.

16. Mas'oud, Fahoum, and Hajj Dahoud's letters to Zionist Executive, undated, CZA J1/21. It can be assumed that the extent of the support they received was much less than they claimed.

17. Aharon Haim Cohen testimony, July 1953, HA 27.16.

18. Report dated 30 November 1929, CZA J105/21.

19. Tawil to the World Zionist Organization's president, undated, CZA J105/31.

20. For the committee's conclusions, see Yehoshua Porath, *The Palestinian Arab National Movement: 1929–1939, From Riots to Rebellion* (London, 1977), chap. 1.

21. United Bureau to Yosef Rokach, 3 March 1930, CZA J105/8.

22. A. H. Cohen to Shertok, 1 November 1932, CZA S25/3542; "The Meeting at Ajjur," 3 April 1930, and Kalvarisky's report, 28 March 1930, CZA J105/8.

23. Al-Mas'oud to Kalvarisky, 29 March 1930, CZA J105/8; platform of Tawil's Northern Farmers' Party, 7 May 1930, ibid.

24. "On the Establishment of Agricultural Association in Nablus," report dated 30 April 1930, ibid.

25. "For the Organization of Jewish and Arab Villages," undated, CZA J105/15.

26. "Meeting of the Special Committee for Fellahin Affairs," 27 July 1930, CZA J105/8.

27. Other initiatives were those of Akram Tuqan, who worked, according to his own (exaggerated) report "from Ramla to Safed," undated, CZA S25/4122, and of Fahoum, al-Mas'oud, and 'Abd al-Latif Abu-Hantash, who organized a conference in Nazareth with Y. L. Magnes; see report on meeting of Shertok and Fahoum, 23 October 1931, CZA J105/23, and letter from Kinamon to Ben-Zvi, undated, CZA J1/205. For requests of Arabs to meet with Weizmann the same year, see CZA J105/23. On the improvement of Jewish-Arab relations in the Safed area, see 'Abbu to the Joint Bureau, 20 October 1930, CZA J1/205.

28. The platform of the Semitic Union in Nablus, CZA J105/8; on the Jerusalem branch, see report dated 24 April 1930, CZA J105/7, which includes critical comments by the Jewish participants on their Arab interlocutors. On the party in Jaffa, see "Rules of the Workers' Party," 13 August 1930, CZA J105/15, and on the initiative in Hebron, see A. H. Cohen's reports, 21 March 1931, CZA S25/3542, and 28 May 1931, CZA J105/35.

29. For Fahoum's meeting with Shertok, see note 27 above.

30. Reports on meetings with Shibl, January–February 1932, CZA J105/23, S25/3051.

31. Shertok to Arlorsoroff, 17 February 1932, CZA J105/23.

32. "The Congress of the Arab Villages," A. H. Cohen's report, 22 February 1932, CZA S25/3542.

33. "Report on the Political Work" (note 14 above) mentioned a few forgery cases. For disputes on payments, see 'Abdin to Maloul, 17 March 1923, CZA J91/291, and chapter 3 of this volume.

34. Arlorsoroff diary, 26 August 1931, as quoted in Elyakim Rubinstein, "Ha-Tipul ba-She'ela ha-Aravit bi-Shnot ha-Esrim veha-Shloshim" [Dealing with the Arab Question in the 1920s and the 1930s], Ha-Tsiyonut, vol. 12 (1987): 221 (in Hebrew). Eliahu Elyashar, later the head of the Sephardic Committee in Jerusalem, argued that the removal of Oriental Jews from their traditional position as mediators between the Jewish Yishuv and the Arabs of Palestine widened the gap between the communities; see his Li-Hyot im Falastinim [Living with Palestinians] (Jerusalem, 1975) (in Hebrew).

35. Gorni, Zionism and the Arabs, 227.

36. Moshe Shertok's lecture: "Introduction to the Arab Question," Jerusalem, 6 May 1940, CZA S25/22201, pp. 2–4.

37. Ibid., p. 27. This approach is similar to Jabotinsky's concept of the "iron wall," developed in the 1920s. In one of his most famous articles, the Zionist leader described the Arab resistance to Zionism and concluded: "Colonization can therefore continue and develop only under the protection of a force independent of the local population, an iron wall that the native population cannot break through. This is, in toto, our policy toward the Arabs"; Vladimir Jabotinsky, "The Iron Wall," Rassviet (Berlin), 4 November 1923. For elaboration of this concept, see Avi Shlaim, The Iron Wall: Israel and the Arab World (New York, 1999).

38. Kalvarisky to the Zionist Executive [February 1930], CZA J105/11.

39. Kalvarisky to the Zionist Executive, 25 April 1923, CZA S25/10296. For Zionist support for al-Akhbar after Weizmann's visit to Palestine, see Zionist Executive report [1920], CZA Z4/2800I. For attempts to recruit Wadi' Bustani, see Levine Epstein to Ussishkin, 6 February 1920, CZA L4/1001. For early Zionist activity in this field, see Ya'akov Ro'i, "Nisyonotehem shel ha-Mosadot ha-Tsiyoniyim le-Hashpia al ha-Itonut ha-Aravit be-Erets Yisrael, 1908–1914" [Attempts of Zionist Institutions to Influence Arab Press in Palestine, 1908–1914], Tsiyon, vol. 32 (1967): 201–227 (in Hebrew).

40. Al-Shuqayri to Kalvarisky, 15 January 1925, CZA S25/517.

41. "The Work of the Joint Bureau and the Press Department regarding the Arab Press" [undated], CZA J1/308.

42. Tawil, who worked in Nablus, Acre, and Tiberias, had to escape from the country (see pp. 62 and 86).

43. "Propaganda for Peace between Jews and Arabs," news of the Arab bureau [of the Zionist Executive], 5 January 1930, CZA J105/30.

44. Al-Zamr, 16 September 1930 (Acre); see also a summary of the book in CZA S25/3567. The book itself can be found in the Israeli National Library.

45. "Arab Journalists Offer Their Services to the [Joint] Bureau" [25 May 1930], CZA J105/30.

46. Elyashar, *Li-Hyot im Falastinim,* 14.

47. Shalom Reichman, *Mi-Ma'ahaz le-Eretz Moshav* [From an Outpost to a Settled Country] (Jerusalem, 1979), 49–55 (in Hebrew). For details, see in Arye Avneri, *Ha-Hityashvut ha-Yehudit ve-Ta'anat ha-Nishul* [Jewish Settlement and the Claim on Dispossession] (Tel Aviv, 1980), 71–91. For example, Zikhron Ya'akov's land was purchased from the French Consul in Haifa (in 1882), Gdera's land from the French Consul in Jaffa (1891), Menahmiyya's land from the Sursuk family (1902), Binyamina's land from the Baidun family of Acre, Nes Tsiyona (1880) and Migdal (in 1902) from Germans. Vast areas in the eastern Galilee were sold by the heirs of the Algerian Emir 'Abd al-Qader.

48. In the first stage, only 41,000 dunams were bought because of the limited budget; see Avneri, *Ha-Hityashvut ha-Yehudit,* 97.

49. Ibid., 112–114.

50. "The Aliya, the Land and the Question of Settlement," memorandum by Moshe Smilanski, 1930, CZA S25/3542. Other sources argue that as of 1931 Jews had purchased only 994,000 dunams but do not give information on the sellers; see Barouch Kimmerling, *Ha-Ma'avak 'al ha-Karka'ot* [The Struggle over the Land] (Jerusalem, 1974), 48 (in Hebrew). Various churches, and especially the Greek Orthodox Church, also sold land to the Zionists, contributing to the tension between the Greek clergy and the Arab community of believers. On transactions of the Greek Patriarchate in the Jerusalem vicinity, see Aminadav Ashbel, *Hakhsharat ha-Yishuv* [Land Development Company] (Jerusalem, 1976), 21–33 (in Hebrew).

51. Avneri, *Ha-Hityashvut ha-Yehudit,* 148–154. For a detailed list of Arab dignitaries and politicians who sold land to Jews, see Kenneth Stein, *The Land Question in Palestine, 1917–1939* (London, 1984), 228–238.

52. For the survey of land purchased by Jews, see Stein, *Land Question,* 181.

53. Testimony of Moshe Goldenberg, 24 February 1969, OHD-HU 57–3a. On the aid given by the Arab mayor of Beersheva to KKL, see Hiram Danin's testimony, 8 November 1970, OHD-HU 57–6b.

54. Aharon Danin's testimony, 21 December 1970, OHD-HU 57–9b.

55. Aharon Danin's testimony, 23 August 1974, OHD-HU 57–9g.

56. Aharon Danin's testimony, 23 April 1971, OHD-HU 57–9e.

57. Ezra Danin's testimony (with Yehoshua Palmon), 29 May 1971, OHD-HU 57–24c.

58. On Ma'lul, see A. Danin's testimony, OHD-HU 57–9e; *al-Hayat,* 17 December 1930.

59. On the Negev, see Hiram Danin's testimony, OHD-HU 57–6a.

60. Ezra Danin, *Tsiyoni be-Khol Tnay* [A Zionist under Any Condition] (Jerusalem, 1987), 1:119.

61. Tuqan to Kalvarisky, 30 July 1930, CZA J1/308. Sakeb Amin Khawajah of Ni'lin expressed a similar attitude when he offered his land for sale; see A. H. Cohen's report, "Organizing the Neighborliness Relations with the Arab Villagers around Lydda," 18 September 1930, CZA J105/22.

62. Rachel Yana'it and others to the Zionist Commission, 11 Iyar 5678 (Spring 1918), CZA L4/997a.

63. Yoav Gelber, *Shorshey ha-Havatselet* [The Roots of the Lily: The Intelligence in the Yishuv, 1918–1947] (Tel-Aviv, 1992), 11–15 (in Hebrew).

64. Most reports are preserved in CZA L4/734–769.

65. Rivlin to the Zionist Executive, Sivan 5680 (Spring 1920), CZA L18/114c.

66. Shahin to the Zionist Executive, 2 December 1922; Rabbi Slonim to Dr. Maloul, 10 October 1922, CZA J1/290.

67. Gelber, *Shorshey ha-Havatselet,* 32, 46–48.

68. Abu Ali to Maloul, "Wahhabiyya," 1 October 1922, CZA J1/290.

69. A. H. Cohen's testimony, HA 27.16 (Jerusalem, 1953).

70. Ibid.

71. "Information from Ovadiah," various dates 1930–1933, CZA J105/6, S25/3557.

72. Transcriptions of the talks and copies of the documents are in CZA S25/22100, 22103, 22330, 22329, and other files.

73. For Philip Hasoun contacts with Ben-Zvi, see Deborah Bernstein, "Brit Poaley Eretz-Yisrael" [Palestine Labor League], in Ilan Pappe, ed., *Aravim vi-Yhudim Bi-Tkufat ha-Mandat* [Arabs and Jews in the Mandate Period], 150, 156n32 (in Hebrew).

74. For memoirs that mention contacts between Jewish guards *(shomrim)* and Arabs, see Yirmiahu Ravina, *Agudat ha-Shomrim* [The Guards' Association] (Tel Aviv, 1965), 1:197 on Jezreel Valley, 216 on Taybe and Miski, 282 on the Sharon, etc.

75. Gelber, *Shorshey ha-Havatselet,* 103.

76. Ibid., 121–122.

77. CZA S25/3473, 3539.

78. For reports from this period, see CZA S25/22735, 10187, and 3539.

79. The Committee for the Relations with the Arabs to Ussishkin, 4 May 1920, CZA L4/1001.

80. Elie Shaltiel, *Pinhas Rutenberg* (Tel Aviv, 1990), 451 (in Hebrew), based on Rutenberg's archive in Israel Electric Corporation Archives. For a critical approach to the connection of Jaffa to "Zionist" electricity and justified suspicions toward the people involved, see *al-Jazira* (Jaffa), quoted in *Ha'aretz,* 29 May and 10 June 1924.

81. Mizrahi to Col. Kisch, 19 January 1930. Al-Shak'a was involved in land deals with Jews; see Shadmon's testimony, OHD-HU 57-18.

82. Report by A. H. Cohen, 21 March 1931, CZA S25/3542.

83. Muhammad al-Tawil, *Al-Haqa'iq al-Majhula* [Hidden Truths] (Haifa, 1930), 35–44 (in Arabic; not to be confused with a booklet by the same title by Akram Tuqan).

84. See Zachary Lockman and Nader Abbud, and Bernstein in Pappe, *Aravim vi-Yhudim Bitkuufat ha-Mandat,* 73. For a broader discussion, see Lockman, *Comrades and Enemies;* Debora Bernstein, *Constructing Boundaries: Jewish and Arab Workers in Mandatory Palestine* (New York, 2000).

85. Quoted in Lockman, *Comrades and Enemies,* 93–94.

2. WHO IS A TRAITOR?

1. On the strengthening of Palestinian particularistic nationalism *(wataniyya)* at the expense of pan-Arabism in the early 1920s, see Porath, *Emergence*, chap. 2. It is important to bear in mind Doumani's analysis, according to which the formation of Palestinian identity was not simply "an automatic response to foreign encroachment and rule or the uncritical absorption of European definitions. . . . [T]he idea has also regional and local roots," such as local social and economic networks and common cultural practices. Beshara Doumani, "Rediscovering Ottoman Palestine: Writing Palestinians into History," *Journal of Palestine Studies*, vol. 11, no. 2 (1992): 9–10.

2. In the 1880s the Arab political elite—in both Palestine and the neighboring countries—was well aware of Zionism and largely opposed it. See details in Neville Mandel, *The Arabs and Zionism before World War I* (Berkeley, 1976). Khalidi refers to the role of the press in the anti-Zionist campaign in the same period; Rashid Khalidi, *Palestinian Identity: Construction of Modern National Consciousness* (New York, 1997).

3. Here I follow the normative definition of deviation, according to which deviant behavior—including treason—does not exist by itself but rather is socially constructed in a specific time and place and under specific circumstances. As Howard Becker put it, social groups create deviancies by shaping rules whose violation would be considered deviation; see Erich Goode, *Deviant Behavior* (Upper Saddle River, N.J., 1994), 15–16; Howard Becker, "Deviance by Definition," in Lewis Coser and Bernard Rosenberg, eds., *Sociological Theory: A Book of Readings* (New York, 1982), 449ff.

4. Celebrating (real or imagined) consensus while attacking outsiders is a tool in the hands of the attackers to gain legitimacy and prestige. The role of the press in this is important, as argues Graham Murdock, "Political Deviance: The Press Presentation of a Militant Mass Demonstration," in Stanley Cohen and Jack Young, eds., *The Manufacture of News: Deviance, Social Problems and the Mass Media* (London, 1974), 157.

5. Khalidi, *Palestinian Identity*, 119–144; Muhammad Muslih, *The Origins of Palestinian Nationalism* (New York, 1988).

6. *Filastin*, 22 July 1911. It is difficult to ignore the fact that the "prophecy" of Tamr was fulfilled, though not completely.

7. Both in *Filastin*, 7 September 1911.

8. Kimmerling, *Ha-Ma'avak*, 19–20, states that the land was the issue that the elite (with its abstract ideological national concepts) and the peripheral groups (who felt the threat of losing their land) could have consolidated around.

9. *Filastin*, 17 September 1921.

10. Erving Goffman, *Stigma: Notes on the Management of Spoiled Identity* (New York, 1974).

11. *Filastin*, 22 October 1921.

12. Publicizing names of deviants in the press is a common tool of social control. For an early example, see Andy Croll, "Street Disorder, Surveillance and Shame: Regulating Behaviour in the Public Spaces of the Late Victorian British Town," *Social History*, vol. 24, no. 3 (1999): 250–268. The newspapers Croll

refers to faced the accusation that their decision whether to mention names or not was based on personal interest and bribery rather than on the interests of the community. Similar accusations were directed toward Palestinian journalists in the period under discussion.

13. *Al-Yarmuk*, 31 May 1925. Interestingly enough, the fatwa was written in response to a question sent by the editor of the Egyptian newspaper *al-Wataniyya*, not by a Palestinian. Hajj Ibrahim, the editor of *al-Yarmuk*, was a prominent political figure in the Haifa area and close to Sheikh Izz al-Din al-Qassam.

14. The discussion at that time was in rather general terms; see, e.g., a Darwish Miqdadi article that claims that the "sicknesses of the society lead to selling lands," *al-Jami'ah al-'Arabiyyah*, 11 April 1927.

15. *Al-Yarmuk*, 26 October 1929. As we have seen before, *al-Karmil* had the same attitude, especially from 1929 on; see issues dated 4 January 1922, 8 June 1929, 30 October 1929, 21 January 1931, 22 April 1931, 1 May 1931, 6 June 1931.

16. Akram Zu'itar, *Bawakir al-Nidal: Min Mudhakarat Akram Zu'itar* [The Start of the Struggle: From the Memoirs of Akram Zu'itar] (Beirut, 1994), 1:426–427 (in Arabic). The exception was the assassination of Musa Hadeib, discussed below.

17. See *al-Jami'ah al-'Arabiyyah*, 24 May 1934. It seems that newspapers made names public only when the publication converged with economic, family, or social interests of their own.

18. See, e.g., *al-Jami'ah al-'Arabiyyah*, 16 October 1934.

19. Muhammad Izzat Darwaza, *Al-Mallak wal-Simsar* [The Landlord and the Land Shark] (Nablus, 1934, in Arabic).

20. *Diwan Ibrahim, A'mar Sha'er Filastin Ibrahim Tuqan* [Diwan/Collection of Ibrahim's Poems, The Life of Palestine Poet Ibrahim Tuqan] (Beirut, 1975), 75, 156 (in Arabic).

21. See, e.g., *al-Difa'*, 9 November, 26 November, and 5 December 1934; *al-Jami'ah al-'Arabiyyah*, 23 November, 26 November, 3 December, and 29 December 1934. It seems that after a long period of reluctance Hajj Amin decided to openly join the battle against selling land to Jews and to use his position as mufti, to which he was nominated by the British.

22. *al-Jami'ah al-'Arabiyyah*, 24 July 1934.

23. *al-Jami'ah al-'Arabiyyah*, 4 October and 20 November 1934 (Negev). For cases from other areas, see *al-Difa'*, 10 November 1934 (village of Baqa al-Gharbiyya); *Filastin*, 10 November 1934 (Rantis); *Filastin*, 23 December 1934 (Beit Jibrin).

24. The fatwa is quoted in Akram Zu'itar, *Watha'eq al-Haraka al-Wataniyya al-Filastiniyya 1914–1939* [Documents of the Palestinian National Movement, 1914–1939] (Beirut, 1984), 388–391 (in Arabic).

25. *al-Jami'ah al-'Arabiyyah*, 12 February 1935.

26. Muhammad Sa'id Rumman, *Suba: Qarya Maqdasiyya fi al-Dhakira* [Suba: Jerusalemite Village in the Memory] (Jerusalem, 2000), 249 (in Arabic); based on documents of the Supreme Muslim Council.

27. The victim was Saleh Issa Hamdan, but it is not clear whether he was the targeted *simsar*, as Zionist intelligence sources said, or the target was a colleague,

Mustafa Summarin, as mentioned by *al-Jami'ah al-'Arabiyyah,* 14 November 1934.

28. Report dated 12 March 1932, HA 8/30; "Najib" to the Jewish Agency, 26 June 1935, CZA S25/3875; *al-Jami'ah al-Islamiyyah,* 20 December 1932.

29. *Al-Liwaa,* 9 December 1935.

30. Porath, *Emergence,* 189–190 (Jarallah); *Filastin,* 26 November, 10 December, and 14 December 1921 (al-Uri).

31. *Filastin,* 8 and 29 October 1921.

32. Nafe' al-'Abbushi to the Arab Executive, 1921, ISA 65, 984/19.

33. *Filastin,* 16 May 1922.

34. Intelligence report to Jerusalem's governor, 13 April 1922, ISA 165, 834/152; Zionist intelligence report, 17 May 1920, CZA L5/739.

35. *Filastin,* 25 July 1922.

36. These clubs and parties were attacked by both supporters of Hajj Amin and his main opposition; see *Mirat al-Sharq,* 12, 17, and 24 April 1930; report of the United Bureau, 27 April 1930, CZA J105/8; *Filastin,* 8 and 30 October 1930; *al-Jami'ah al-'Arabiyyah,* 16 and 25 October 1930. *Ha'aretz* reported on the meeting of the editors, 10 June 1924, and *al-Karmil* on the contacts of the farmers' parties with the Zionists, in 18 June, 30 July, and 6 August 1924, 28 February 1925, and other issues.

37. Porath, *Emergence,* 101. Ragheb Nashashibi's nephew, Nassir al-Din, portrayed totally different relationships and described Musa Kazem and Ragheb as the best of friends. Nasser Eddin Nashashibi, *Jerusalem's Other Voice: Ragheb Nashashibi and Moderation in Palestinian Politics, 1920–1949* (Exeter, 1990), 62. Indeed, during at least part of this period Musa Kazem was closer to the Nashashibis than to Hajj Amin.

38. Porath, *Emergence,* 225. In his book, Nashashibi portrayed Ragheb's cooperation with the British as part of his struggle against Zionism. Indeed, in the early 1930s Ragheb was considered by the Zionists to be the head of the struggle against them in the Jerusalem area; see Michael Assaf, "Arviyey ha-Arets in 5694" [The Arabs of the Country in 1934], in Asher Barash, ed., *Sefer Hashana shel Eretz Yisrael* [Eretz Yisrael Yearbook] (Tel-Aviv, 1935), 333 (in Hebrew).

39. The Husseinis named Ragheb *mutasahayyen,* i.e., trying to become a Zionist; see Hafez Tuqan to Jamal al-Husseini, undated (1922), ISA 65, 984/19.

40. *al-Jami'ah al-'Arabiyyah,* 24 January 1927.

41. *al-Jami'ah al-'Arabiyyah,* 18 March 1927; for more articles in the same spirit, see 21 and 31 March 1927.

42. *al-Jami'ah al-'Arabiyyah,* 7 April 1927.

43. Elyakim Rubinstein, "Yehudim ve-Aravim be-Iriyot Eretz Yisrael (1926–1933)" [Jews and Arabs in Palestinian Municipalities (1926–1933)], *Kathedra,* vol. 51 (1989): 133 (in Hebrew); see there a photocopy of the leaflet.

44. Ibid., 130–135, discusses the considerations of the Zionist institutions regarding the elections.

45. *al-Jami'ah al-'Arabiyyah,* 9 June and 11 August 1927; see also 4 July and 1 August 1927.

46. Intelligence reports of 17 May and 2 June 1920 to the Zionist Executive, CZA L4/739.

47. See intelligence report of 2 June 1920 mentioned in note 46 above; also, reports dated 27 May, 7 July, 29 August, 5 September, and 19 October 1919, all in CZA L4/765. The Zionist activists felt that the threats changed attitudes toward them in Arab society.

48. Shahin to Maloul, 24 February 1923, CZA S25/518a.

49. Davidesko to Maloul, 11 April 1924, CZA J1/290.

50. Maloul to Col. Kisch, 23 February 1923, CZA J1/290.

51. Shahin to Maloul [January–February 1923], CZA S25/518a.

52. Ibid.

53. Nabhani to Kisch, 1 December 1924, CZA S25/10297.

54. Maloul to Kisch, 23 February 1923, CZA J1/290.

55. Kisch to the government secretary, 21 March 1923, CZA S25/665.

56. Al-Muzaffar's leaflet, 1923, ISA 2, 10/6.

57. Report of 6 December 1921, ISA 165, 834/152; *Filastin*, 9 May 1922. At this stage al-Dajani gave up his aspiration to become a judge through Zionist support; see Dr. Eder report of 24 March 1922, CZA S25/4380.

58. Porath, *Emergence*, 242–243.

59. Ibid., 247–252.

60. Anonymous letter, undated, CZA J105/23.

61. Hebron police to general secretariat, 9 August 1921, ISA 165, 834/152. On Hadeib's involvement in land transactions, see Mustafa Hasan of the village of Battir to the Higher Arab Committee, arguing that Hadeib planned to sell 5,000 dunams to a Jew named Librecht from Petach Tikva, 10 December 1946, ISA 65, 337/1064. Hasan was active in preventing land deals with Jews throughout the Mandate period.

62. Intelligence report, 6 December 1921, ISA 165, 834/152.

63. F. Kisch, "The Palestinian Arabs' Political Development," 6 June 1925, CZA S25/517.

64. Kisch to Jerusalem police commander, Major Saunders, 3 July 1931, CZA J105/23. Actually Hadeib met several times with Dr. David Eder and among other things reported on preparations of Palestinians to riot at the Nebi Musa festival; see Eder's report of 24 March 1922, CZA S25/4380.

65. Porath, *Palestinian Arab National Movement*, chap. 5, describes and analyses the process of radicalization, including the emergence of these armed groups.

66. "Salt"'s report, 12 January 1930, CZA J105/5.

67. "Salt"'s report, 22 January 1930, CZA J105/5.

68. "Secret information," 9 March 1930, CZA J105/5.

69. "Attack on pro-Zionist Arab," report dated 1 May 1930, CZA S25/3567.

70. *Mirat al-Sharq*, 28 May 1930, translation: CZA J105/8.

71. Information of the United Bureau, 18 August 1930, CZA J1/205b. On Tawil, see Alhadif letter to the United Bureau, 7 July 1930, CZA J1/6; see also a report by A. H. Cohen, 4 March 1930, CZA S25/3542. On the aid given by the sheikh of Meroun to Jews, see also Frederick Kisch, *Yoman Eretz-Yisraeli* [Palestine Diary] (Jerusalem, 1939), 311.

72. A. H. Cohen's report, 10 October 1933, CZA S25/3542 (demonstration); "Information from Ovadiah," 3 July 1931, 15 February, 10 March, and

19 December 1932, CZA S25/3557 (opposing joint activities and boycott); "Political Information" by Cohen, 3 February 1930, CZA S25/3542.

73. Cohen's report, 21 March 1931, CZA S25/3542.

74. Na'aman's report, Information of the United Bureau, 5 September 1930, CZA S25/3542.

75. Information of the United Bureau, 29 October 1934, CZA S25/3542; Najib's report, 26 June 1935, CZA S25/3875.

76. "Information Received from Zimroni," 7 March 1933, CZA S25/3558.

77. Sharif Kana'aneh, *Al-Dar Dar Abuna* [It's Our Father's Home] (Jerusalem, 1990), 208 (in Arabic).

78. "Secret Report," Cohen to Shertok, 13 and 15 November 1934, CZA S25/3558; *al-Jami'ah al-'Arabiyyah*, 14 November 1934.

79. See Benedict Anderson, *Imagined Communities: Reflections on the Origins and Spread of Nationalism* (London, 1991), 7.

80. Baruch Kimmerling, *Bein Hevra li-Mdina* [Between Society and State] (Tel Aviv, 1991), 33 (in Hebrew).

81. On this negotiation, see Information of the United Bureau, 8 December 1930, CZA S25/3567.

82. The difference between what the Nashashibis said in closed meetings with Zionist leaders and their declarations to the Arab public was considerable. One can argue that it testifies to the deep enmity toward Zionism in Arab circles. I would argue that it was also a result of lack of ability to lead, that is, to take responsibility for changing attitudes.

83. *Mirat al-Sharq*, 28 April 1927.

84. Mentioned also by Zu'itar, *Bawakir*, 426–427.

85. On the creation of counterculture as a response to social control, see Goode, *Deviant Behavior*, 98–99.

86. Pat Lauderdale and James Inverarity, "Suggestions for the Study of the Political Dimensions of Deviance Definitions," in P. Lauderdale, ed., *A Political Analysis of Deviance* (Minneapolis, 1980), 221–237, suggest an analysis of deviance according to four factors: who the definers are, how they do it, to what extent the definition is accepted, and its influence on changing social status. In our case one can see that the urban elite took on the role of defining deviance (treason), and their main tools were religious preaching and the media. In the next chapters I examine the extent of the acceptance of the definitions and changes of status. It is important to bear in mind these authors' argument that it is difficult to ascertain whether a consensus is accepted willingly (231). I would argue that in cases of "forced consensus" people are more ready to break it, and hence to betray the consensus—in our case, to "collaborate with the enemy."

3. WE, THE COLLABORATORS

1. Sheikhs of Beisan Valley to high commissioner, 22 October 1923, CZA S25/517.

2. *Filastin*, 22 July 1922.

3. Report of Dr. Eder on his meeting with the heads of the associations, 24 March 1922, CZA S25/4380; David Miller of Nablus to Kalvarisky [Decem-

ber 1922], CZA S25/10309 (Tuqan); Hadeib to Kisch, 5 July 1925, CZA S25/517; Abdin to Kisch, 8 May 1927, CZA S25/501. For more requests of this kind, see CZA J1/290, 291.

4. Aharon Danin testimony, 22 April 1971, OHD-HU 57-9; Yosef Shadmon testimony, 29 January 1971, OHD-HU 57-18.

5. "Najib" on al-Qasem, 6 April 1935, CZA S25/3875; Ever Hadani, ed., *Me'ah Shnot Shmira be-Yisrael* [One Hundred Years of Guarding in Israel] (Tel Aviv, 1955), 418-424 (in Hebrew); "Black" to the Shai [intelligence service], 15 October 1942, CZA S25/22645.

6. See Muhammad Izzat Darwaza, *Mudhakkarat Muhammad Izzat Darwaza: Sijill Hafel bi-Masirat al-Haraka al-Arabiyya wal-Qadiyya al-Filastiniyya Khilal Qurn 1887-1984* [Memoirs of M. I. Darwaza: A Full Record of the Advance of the Arab Movement and the Palestinian Problem, 1887-1984] (Beirut, 1993), 3:149 (in Arabic).

7. Aharon Danin testimony, 22 April 1971, OHD-HU 57-9.

8. *Al-Jami'ah al-Islamiyyah,* 28 December 1934; *Filastin,* 29 December 1934, 25 December 1935.

9. Zu'itar, *Bawakir,* 1:427.

10. Aharon Danin testimony, 22 April 1971, OHD-HU 57-9; Yosef Shadmon testimony, 29 January 1971, OHD-HU 57-18.

11. *Al-Yarmuk,* 4 June 1925 (and there also the list of papers that published this simultaneously).

12. Yosef Weitz testimony, 10 January 1969, OHD-HU 57-1.

13. Lawsuit dated 26 June 1930, Jaffa court; ISA 66, 186/14.

14. Aharon Danin testimony, 22 April 1971, OHD-HU 57-9. Sharif Shanti continued to work as a land dealer until his assassination in Tel Aviv in 1961.

15. Yehoshua Palmon and Ezra Danin testimony, 29 May 1971, OHD-HU 57-24.

16. For analysis of this case, see Max Laserson, *On the Mandate: Documents, Statements, Laws* (Tel Aviv, 1937), 190-199.

17. *Filastin,* 29 July 1929.

18. al-Jami'ah al-'Arabiyyah, 27 December 1932.

19. An example of such a play is Burhan al-Din al-Abbushi, *Watan al-Shahid* (Jerusalem, 1947), esp. 45-52; another play is mentioned in "Report on the Visit of H. G. in Jaffa," 12 September 1935, CZA S25/22220.

20. Rabbi Slonim to Maloul, 10 October and 2 December 1922, CZA J1/290.

21. Slonim to Maloul, 14 September 1922, CZA J1/290.

22. Report on an interview with Dr. Eder, 24 March 1922, CZA S25/4380.

23. Report on a meeting between Laniado and Taher al-Husseini, 30 March 1930, CZA S25/3567; meeting between Taher al-Husseini and Ben-Zvi, 2 April 1930, CZA S25/3051. For his meeting with Colonel Kisch, see Tom Segev, *One Palestine, Complete: Jews and Arabs under the British Mandate* (New York, 2000).

24. Personal sheet, HA 105/39.

25. Rosmari Sayigh, *Palestinians: From Peasants to Revolutionaries* (London, 1979).

26. For land transactions in the Negev, see Hiram Danin testimony, 8 November 1971, OHD-HU 57–6; *al-Jami'ah al-'Arabiyyah,* 4 October 1934, 12 February 1935. On the opposition of some Bedouin sheikhs to the national institutions, see *Filastin,* 22 June 1921.

27. Rehavam Ze'evi, "Introduction," in Pesach Bar-Adon, *Be-Ohaley Midbar* [In Desert Tents] (Jerusalem, 1981).

28. "Briefing on the Arabs of Beisan Valley," 4 September 1940, CZA S25/22518. The fact that those tribes were roaming between the east and west banks of the Jordan River might be another reason for their relatively weak attachment to Palestinian nationalism.

29. Sheikhs of Beisan Valley to high commissioner, 22 October 1923, CZA S25/517.

30. Yosef Weitz testimony, 10 January 1969, OHD-HU 57–1.

31. CID, "Intelligence Note," 22 December 1922, ISA 2, 180/6. According to this report, Yusuf al-'Arsan lost his position as sheik because of his land business, and his brother Fadel replaced him. This act was not specifically on nationalistic grounds but rather because his deeds were perceived as harmful to the interests of the tribe. On the other hand, Fadel opposed transferring land to Jews but did not stop the process.

32. Kisch, *Yoman,* 187 (Hebrew version).

33. The agreement is saved in HA Nahmani 80/100/6. The sheiks received money in payment for the obligations they took upon themselves.

34. *Al-Jami'ah al-Islamiyyah,* 22 and 23 December 1934.

35. Moshe Goldenberg testimony, 25 February 1969, OHD-HU 57–3.

36. Ibid.

37. Ibid., and see also Barouchi and Litvak in "Briefing on the Arabs of Beisan Valley," 4 September 1940, CZA S25/22518.

38. Goldenberg's testimony, 25 February 1969, OHD-HU 57–3, and Tahon in "Briefing on the Arabs of Beisan Valley," 4 September 1940, CZA S25/22518.

39. Avira in "Briefing on the Arabs of Beisan Valley," 4 September 1940, CZA S25/22518.

40. On the system of the *nawahi,* see Stewart Macalister and E. W. G. Mastermann, "Occasional Papers on the Modern Inhabitants of Palestine," *PEFQS* (1905): 352–356. On the *nawahi* system in Jerusalem area, see Haim Gerber, *Ottoman Rule in Jerusalem, 1890–1914* (Berlin, 1985).

41. Adel Manna', *A'lam Filastin fi Awakhir al-'Ahd al-Uthmani* [Palestine Dignitaries in the Late Ottoman Period] (Jerusalem, 1986), 24–31 (in Arabic).

42. Yosef Glass, "Rekhishat Karka ve-Shimusheha be-Ezor Abu-Ghosh 1873–1948" [Land Purchase and Use in the Abu-Ghosh Area, 1873–1948], *Kathedra,* vol. 62 (1991): 111 (in Hebrew).

43. Porath, *Emergence,* 81.

44. Intelligence report to the Zionist Executive, 30 May 1920, CZA L4/739, elaborates on the tensions between Sheikh Abu-Ghosh and the Muslim-Christian Associations. For petitions collected by him, see ISA 2, 1/30. For their stand in 1929, see "Abu-Ghosh—briefing by Tuvia Ashkenazi," CZA J105/17.

45. A British CID report from January 1923 spelled out the political attitude of twelve people from Abu-Ghosh. Only two, Sheikh 'Abd al-Hamid and a part-

ner, were defined as pro-Zionist; two were defined as former pro-Zionists, five as anti-Zionists, and the tendency of the final three was not mentioned; ISA 2, 5/151.

46. The relations were dynamic, though. After 'Abd al-Hamid's withdrawal from the Muslim-Christian Associations he was elected to the Arab Executive in the Seventh Congress; see Bayan Nuwayhid al-Hout, *Al-Qiyadat wal-Mu'asasat al-Siyasiyya fi Filastin 1917–1948* [Political Leadership and Institutions in Palestine, 1917–1948] (Acre, 1984), 864 (in Arabic). On his activity with the mufti, see Na'aman's report, 3 February 1930, CZA S25/3542, and February 1930, CZA J105/6.

47. A. H. Cohen's report, 4 March 1930, CZA S25/3542. Cohen attended the event disguised as an Arab.

48. Sari Sakakini (the son of Khalil, the educator) argued that Darwish acted out of greediness; see his report to the U.S. consulate in Jerusalem, "The Husseini-Nashashibi Graph" [1941], CZA S25/9226.

49. On transactions made by Darwish, see Elyashar, *Li-Hyot im Falastinim*, 67; Ashbel, *Hakhsharat ha-Yishuv*, 64.

50. Na'aman's report, 20 January 1932, CZA J105/35; Information on Arab Affairs, 27 January 1935, CZA S25/3539.

51. *Filastin*, 25 July 1922. It is of interest to note that Amin was the person who handed over the guard Mordechai Yigael to the Ottomans during World War I.

52. CID report, January 1923, ISA 2, 5/151.

53. A. H. Cohen, "Neighboring Relations with the Arab Villages around Lydda," 18 September 1930, CZA J105/22.

54. Al-Hout, *Al-Qiyadat*, 860.

55. Porath, *Emergence*, 130.

56. "Details on the Arab Congress in Jerusalem," 27 October 1929, CZA J1/310.

57. CID report, January 1923, ISA 2, 5/151.

58. Aharon Danin testimony, 24 November 1974, OHD-HU 57-9.

59. Ashbel, *Hakhsharat ha-Yishuv*, 64. On the life of Darwish during the revolt, see next chapters. After 1948 he became a refugee in Beit Jala together with most villagers from al-Maliha, strengthened his relations with King 'Abdallah, and became a member of parliament for a few years, representing the refugees of his region. His son Hasan replaced him in parliament after he died.

60. Yehoshua Palmon and Ezra Danin testimony, 29 May 1971, OHD-HU 57-24; al-'Azzi was a unique family among the landlords since they were "newcomers," having arrived from Egypt during the late nineteenth century and established themselves as shepherds and farmworkers. They managed to register vast plots of land under their name by paying the taxes of fellahin from the area; see David Grossman, *Ha-Kfar ha-Arvi u-Vnotav* [Expansion and Desertion: The Arab Village and Its Offshoots in Ottoman Palestine] (Jerusalem, 1994), 202 (in Hebrew).

61. A. H. Cohen, "Neighboring Relations with the Arab Villages around Lydda," 18 September 1930, CZA J105/22.

62. Al-Hout, *Al-Qiyadat*, 179–180; see also David Hacohen, *Et le-Saper*

[Time to Tell] (Tel Avv, 1974), 94 (in Hebrew). There are other versions of his dismissal, but all agree that it related to his pro-Zionist attitude.

63. Shukri to Shertok, February 1937, CZA S25/4127.

64. Hacohen, *Et le-Saper*, 94.

65. Al-Hout, *Al-Qiyadat*, 181, 304–305.

66. "Memorandum," Daniel Oster, 24 June 1935, CZA S25/3051.

67. *Ha'aretz*, 16 December 1929 (quoting his testimony before the inquiry committee).

68. Muhammad al-Tawil, *Tariq al-Hayah* [Way of Life] (Haifa, 1930) (in Arabic).

69. Tawil's booklet [January 1931], CZA J1/309.

70. Fragments from Tawil's booklet, CZA S25/3567.

71. Alhadif to Shabtai Levi, 30 April 1930, CZA J105/4.

72. Tawil to the chairman and members of the Jewish National Council, 25 June 1930, CZA J1/308.

73. Tawil to Ben-Zvi [January 1931], CZA J1/205b.

74. Ben-Zvi to Tawil, 29 January 1931, CZA J1/205b.

75. Tawil to Ben-Zvi, CZA J1/205.

76. Moshe Goldenberg testimony, 25 February 1969, OHD-HU 57–3.

77. Moshe Smilanski, *Nes Tsiyona* (Nes Tsiyona, 1953), 88–90 (in Hebrew), tells that Shukri was a nationalist leader and member of the Sixth and Seventh Arab Exectives and sold land to Jews.

78. 'Abdin speech, 15 December 1922, CZA J1/291.

79. 'Abdin to Maloul, 22 September 1926, CZA J1/291: "We do not betray our national homeland [*watanana*] but rather work for its development and future."

80. Letters of 'Abdin, various dates, CZA S25/518; Dizengoff to Kalvarisky regarding 'Abdin's debts and commitment not to ask for more money, 19 June 1925, CZA S25/501. For a while the Zionist Executive stopped subsidizing 'Abdin; see his letter to Maloul, 17 March 1923, CZA J1/291.

81. Yosef Trumpeldor, *Me-Hayey Yosef Trumpeldor* [Extracts from the Diary of Yosef Trumpeldor] (Tel Aviv, 1922), entries for 6, 7, 25 January and 9 February 1920 (in Hebrew).

82. Hadani, *Me'ah Shnot Shmira*, 292.

83. Ravina, *Agudat ha-Shomrim*, 1:125–126.

84. Al-Heib's testimony, HA 68/6, taken in the early 1950s. Interestingly enough, in 1920 his men participated in the attack on the kibbutz of Ayelet ha-Shahar, but in 1929 friendship took priority.

85. A. H. Cohen's report, 4 March 1930, CZA S25/3542.

86. Yehoshua Palmon and Ezra Danin testimony, 24 May 1971, OHD-HU 57–24.

87. Ulya al-Khatib, *Arab al-Turkeman* (Amman, 1987), 71–72 (in Arabic).

88. A. H. Cohen to the Arab bureau of the Jewish Agency, "The Return of Jews to Hebron," CZA J105/35.

89. Ibid.

90. This is consistent with the declaration of Ibn Sa'ud's advisor during the disturbances, according to which Ibn Sa'ud sees Palestine as holy for the three

religions and "wholeheartedly desires Christians, Jews, and Muslims to live together in friendship"; quoted in Michael Kahanov, "Emdato shel Ibn-Saud Klapei Sikhsukh Eretz Yisrael bein Shtei Milhamot Olam" [Ibn Sa'ud's Position toward the Palestine Conflict during the Intra-war Period] (M.A. thesis, Tel Aviv University, 1980), 15 (in Hebrew).

4. OLD COLLABORATORS, NEW TRAITORS

1. Porath, *Palestinian Arab National Movement*, 162–163.

2. On the outset of the general strike, see ibid., 163–164; on the violent activity, see 178ff.

3. In many cases it is impossible to determine whether a murder took place on political grounds.

4. The announcement of the establishment of the Higher Arab Committee, as published in *al-Liwaa*, 26 April 1936.

5. See leaflets in CZA J1/6181 and S25/3441.

6. Report by E[liahu] S[asson], 1 May 1936, CZA S25/3441.

7. HA 8/41. See also a statement signed by Arab law students in *al-Difa'*, 15 May 1936, which mentions "the British, the Jews and their tails [i.e., collaborators]" as the enemies to be fought against.

8. *Al-Liwaa*, 6 May 1936.

9. *Al-Liwaa*, 3 May 1936 (al-Ramla villages), 6 May ('ulama of Acre), 11 May (Beit Jibrin), 12 May (*nahiya* Bani-Hasan), 15 May 1936 (villages of al-Wadiyeh).

10. *Al-Liwaa*, 26 April 1936.

11. *Al-Liwaa*, 23 April 1936.

12. Intelligence report, 7 July 1936, HA 8/39.

13. "Report on the Start of the Arab Revolt," 2 February 1941, CZA S25/22318.

14. *Al-Liwaa*, 26 and 27 April 1936.

15. *Al-Liwaa*, 3 May 1936 (Nablus); "Information on Arab Affairs," 12 July 1936, CZA S25/3252 (Jerusalem); Tsadok Eshel, *Ma'arkhot ha-Hagana be-Haifa* [The Haganah Battles in Haifa] (Tel Aviv, 1978), 135 (in Hebrew).

16. *Al-Liwaa*, 26 April 1936 (Acre); for other examples see this newspaper and *Filastin* and *al-Difa'* throughout the months of the general strike. See also Brakha Habas, *Sefer Me'ora'ot Tartsav* [The Book of 1936 Riots] (Tel Aviv, 1937), 108, 116 (in Hebrew).

17. Habas, *Sefer Me'ora'ot*, 107–108.

18. *Al-Liwaa*, 15 May 1936.

19. *Al-Liwaa*, 7 May, 12 May, and 15 May 1936.

20. *Al-Liwaa*, 17 June 1936. This punishment was common in the ancient East.

21. See pp. 40 and 62. Similar methods were adopted by the fighters for "Hebrew work" in the Jewish Yishuv; see Dan Horowitz and Moshe Lissak, *Origins of the Israeli Polity: Palestine under the Mandate* (Chicago, 1978), 29–30.

22. *Al-Liwaa*, 5 May 1936.

23. "Information on Arab Affairs," 13 May 1936, CZA S25/3252. The sus-

pect was released a few days later because of lack of evidence against him. See also the official announcement of the Mandate government in the Arab and Jewish newspapers of the day.

24. Habas, *Sefer Me'ora'ot*, 85; *al-Liwaa*, 16 May 1936.

25. Report from Haifa, 11 July 1936, HA 8/39. The religious-legal arguments were not published in the leaflet, but it seems that the basis for this jurisdiction was the same that led to the fatwa against land dealers, that is, that they help the enemies of Islam to control Islamic land and people.

26. Habas, *Sefer Me'ora'ot*, 153.

27. Ibid., 98, 254.

28. Report no. 117, 2 July 1936, HA 8/39; for similar cases see Darwaza, *Mudhakkarat*, 2:213.

29. *Al-Liwaa*, 7 and 12 May 1936.

30. *Al-Liwaa*, 2 May 1936.

31. Undated report by Gershon Ritov and Yitzhak Avira, HA 8/66.

32. Nahmani to Ben-Zvi, 26 June 1936, HA Nahmani 80/100/1.

33. *Do'ar ha-Yom*, 8 July 1936; report of 6 July 1936, HA 8/39; see also Darwaza, *Mudhakkarat*, 2:94, who argues that the victims supplied the Zionists with information.

34. Mukhtars were formally responsible for maintaining order in their villages; many of them were considered collaborators with the British, sometimes with Jews as well.

35. On the resignation of mukhtars, see examples in *al-Liwaa*, 21 June and 26 June 1936; *Filastin*, 17 June 1937; *al-Difa'*, 17 June 1936.

36. "The Situation in Nablus Area," 3 July 1936, HA 8/30.

37. *Al-Liwaa*, 12 and 19 May 1936.

38. Habas, *Sefer Me'ora'ot*, 90, 96, 122. Local policemen in the service of the colonial powers were targets for killing in other rebellions, such as Algiers, where new recruiters to the FLN were assigned to kill policemen.

39. Reports from Haifa, 24 July and 2 August 1936, HA 8/39.

40. *Jabha Sha'biyya*, 14 August 1936; reports of 2–3 August 1936, HA 8/38; report of 4 August 1936, HA 8/40; *Ha'aretz*, 3 August 1936.

41. Darwaza, *Mudhakkarat*, 2:94.

42. Salman himself managed to sustain good contacts with the rebel commander in the region, Yusuf Abu Durra, with the British, and with the Jews. Together with his close friend Hafez Nijem he was involved, according to a Zionist source, in selling land to Jews; see undated report on al-Tira, HA 8/66.

43. Report from Haifa, 24 August 1936, HA 8/40.

44. Report dated 12 August 1936, HA 8/40.

45. On 'Abdallah's attempts to mediate, see Porath, *Palestinian Arab National Movement*, 202–214; on criticism of the opposition in this matter, see Darwaza, *Mudhakkarat*, 2:128–129.

46. Cohen's report, 9 July 1936, HA 8/39. It took the rivals of 'Abdallah fifteen years, since he was not assassinated until 1951.

47. Porath, *Palestinian Arab National Movement*, 207.

48. *Filastin*, 15 August 1936 (Hebron); report of 14 August 1936, CZA S25/3875 (first attempt, al-'Isa); Habas, *Sefer Me'ora'ot*, 215 (bomb).

49. "Information on Arab Affairs," 21 September 1936, CZA S25/3252.

50. Shai reports, 27 and 28 September 1936, HA 8/41; Habas, *Sefer Me'ora'ot*, 186, 223–224; see also May Seikaly, *Haifa: Transformation of a Palestinian Arab Society, 1918–1939* (London, 1995), 260n29, where she mentions that Taha was considered a person inclined toward the opposition and had good contacts with Jews. On Taha, see also Yosef Washitz, "Tmurot Hevratiot ba-Yishuv ha-Arvi shel Haifa bi-Tkufat ha-Mandat ha-Briti" [Social Changes in Haifa's Arab Community during the Mandate] (Ph.D. dissertation, Hebrew University of Jerusalem, 1993), 167 (in Hebrew).

51. *Filastin*, 18 August 1936.

52. Moshe Sharett [Shertok], *Yoman Medini* [Political Diary] (Tel Aviv, 1976), 1:270 (in Hebrew).

53. Darwaza, *Mudhakkarat*, 2:94.

54. Porath, *Palestinian Arab National Movement*, 191–192.

55. Report of 24 June 1936, HA 8/38.

56. *Ha'aretz*, 22 June 1936; Shai report from Haifa, 4 July 1936, HA 8/39; report of 18 August 1936, HA 8/40.

57. Habas, *Sefer Me'ora'ot*, 142, 160.

58. For similar cases in Algiers, Cyprus, Ireland, and Malaya, see Adam B. Schesch, "Popular Mobilization during Revolutionary and Resistance Wars" (Ph.D. dissertation, University of Wisconsin, Madison, 1994), 557–560.

59. Eshel, *Ma'arkhot ha-Hagana*, 133.

60. "Information on Arab Affairs," 12 July 1936, CZA S25/3252. On a transaction he took part in, see Aharon Malkov testimony, 8 January 1973, OHD-HU 57-35, in which he argues that the death of al-Dajani was not natural and that he was poisoned by nationalist activists because of the transaction.

61. *Al-Liwaa*, 1 May 1936.

62. "Information on Arab Affairs," 30 November 1936, CZA S25/3252.

63. *Filastin*, 25 July 1936.

64. Report on the talk in the mosque, 1 June 1936, HA 8/38; on the leaflet, see report dated 11 July 1936, HA 8/39.

65. *Filastin*, 13 July 1936.

66. Darwaza, *Mudhakkarat*, 2:94.

67. *Al-Liwaa*, 5 May 1936.

68. On the murder of a father and son who were suspected of being informers, see *Do'ar ha-Yom*, 11 October 1936. In later stages of the revolt murders became more frequent, as discussed in chapter 5.

69. *Al-Liwaa*, 12 May 1936.

70. Cohen's report, 20 November 1936, CZA S25/3051; 'Abd al-Qader al-Husseini's personal sheet, HA 8/43.

71. *Al-Liwaa*, 13 May 1936 (Lydda); 15 May 1936 (Abu Dis). The land sold to Jews in the 1930s in Abu Dis is partially inside the municipal borders of Jerusalem, and now the settlers' organization Ateret Kohanim and the municipality are planning a new Jewish neighborhood here.

72. Ashkenazi's report on the Arab families and villages in and around Jerusalem, December 1930 (p. 45), CZA J105/17.

73. "Qaryat al-'Enab (Abu-Ghosh)," 1 September 1940, CZA S25/22518 (probably by Ya'akov Lisser).

74. Rabbah 'Awad's personal sheet, HA 105/416. A photocopy of his agreement with the government is in HA 8/2.

75. E. Eilath, "The Activity of the Arab Gangs in Palestine," 1 November 1936, CZA S25/3441. As in many other cases, it is difficult to assess the reliability of this information.

76. A. H. Cohen, "Vandalism and Robbery by the Terrorist Gangs," 6 November 1938, CZA S25/10615. This report was written in the second phase of the revolt and includes historical background.

77. Report dated 24 July 1936, HA 8/39.

78. David Hacohen to Moshe [Shertok] on his visit in Beirut and talk with Qaraman, 22 October 1936, CZA S25/9783.

79. Shahin to Ben-Zvi, 22 July 1936, CZA S25/10200.

80. Palestine Labor League, *Kashf al-Qina'* [Removal of the Mask] (Haifa, 1937) (in Arabic). On the League during the revolt, see also Lockman, *Comrades and Enemies*, 248–251.

81. Report dated 1 June 1936, HA 8/38.

82. Shaltiel, *Pinhas Rutenberg*, 451.

83. Cohen to Shertok and Ben-Zvi, 3 and 4 May 1936, and A[lfiyye] to Shertok, 26 June 1936, both in CZA S25/9783. Shanti was also an informer; see report of 28 October 1937, CZA S25/3539. *Al-Liwaa*, 3 May and 12 July 1936, wrote about failed attempts to break the strike by the Zionists, such as hiring "dissolute" Arab women to buy in Jewish shops.

84. 'Azar to Shlush, 16 May 1936, CZA S25/9783. Reports by him, see, e.g., CZA S25/22518, various dates.

85. Communications between Shertok and Shukri, January–February 1937, CZA S25/4127.

86. Report of 6 June 1936, CZA S25/9173, and other reports from 1937 in CZA S25/3539; see also report of 22 April 1937, CZA S25/3571.

87. Sharett, *Yoman Medini*, 1:238–239.

88. Ibid. A search of the house at which the camels arrived uncovered nothing suspicious.

89. Finestein to Shertok, 11 August 1936, on Abu-'Oda's information about a plan to attack Jewish transportation, CZA S25/3252.

90. Ravina, *Agudat ha-Shomrim*, 2:468.

91. Ibid., 2:587–588.

92. Dan Even, who became a major general in the Israel Defense Forces, wrote in his autobiography *Shnot Sherut* [Years of Service] (Tel Aviv, 1973), 10–19 (in Hebrew), about Arab friends who supplied him and his colleagues with information about planned attacks.

93. Reports dated 17 and 19 August 1936, HA 8/40.

94. "A Letter from Hadera" by Ezra Danin, 2 June 1938, CZA S25/3541.

95. Porath, *Palestinian Arab National Movement*, 214–219.

5. UNITY ENDS

1. Basta, who had survived an attempt on his life in October 1936, was the only one of these four people who was actually killed by the rebels in spring

1937; see Slutski, *Sefer Toldot,* 2:657, 715. On attempts to assassinate Shukri, see his letters to Shertok, January–February 1937, CZA S25/4127. On Na'aman, see report dated 22 April 1937; CZA S25/3571.

2. Plans to assassinate traitors including land dealers were also reported to the Jewish Agency; "Information on Arab Affairs," 9 April 1937, CZA S25/4127.

3. Report from Nablus, CZA S25/3575

4. Report dated 30 June 1937, CZA S25/3539.

5. "Information on Arab Affairs," 7 June 1937, CZA S25/4127.

6. Darwaza, *Mudhakkarat,* 2:415–417; *Filastin,* 6 July 1936; HA 77/1.

7. *Davar,* 4 July 1937.

8. Darwaza, *Mudhakkarat,* 2:415–417; for the decision of the Defense Party and the response of the Higher Arab Committee, see al-Hout, *Al-Qiyadat,* 760–761.

9. Great Britain, Colonial Office, *Palestine Royal Commission Report* (London, July 1937), 380–382.

10. Porath, *Palestinian Arab National Movement,* 229–230.

11. *Al-Liwaa,* 9 and 12 July 1937; *al-Difa',* 11 July 1937.

12. For analyses of Arab support of the partition plan, see Yoram Nimrod, "Hakdama la-Sefer ha-Lavan" [Introduction to the White Paper], *Ha-Tsiyonut,* vol. 10 (1985): 201 (in Hebrew); for a British report on Arab supporters of the partition, see CZA S25/3292; for Zionist reports, see Hirschfeld to Zaslani, 2 and 8 August 1937, CZA S25/22449.

13. Hirschfeld to Zaslani, 17 July 1937, CZA S25/22449; "Information on Arab Affairs," 15 July and 25 August 1937, CZA S25/4127.

14. Report dated 20 July 1937, CZA S25/3292; *Filastin,* 21 July 1937; HA 77/1.

15. Darwaza, *Mudhakkarat,* 2:488.

16. Porath, *Palestinian Arab National Movement,* 231–232.

17. Higher Arab Committee, finance report of 8 September 1937, ISA 65, 402/3528.

18. *Davar,* 21 November 1938. Darwaza argued that Barqawi was murdered because of a political dispute at the local level, and that the opposition tried to use the murder to sully the mufti; see *Mudhakkarat,* 3:21. Barqawi positioned himself in the opposition as early as 1921; see Abushi to the Arab Executive [unreadable date], 1921, ISA 65, 984/19. Barqawi also supported the planned elections to the legislative council in 1923, as reported in *Lisan al-Hal,* 30 March 1923.

19. Report from 25 September 1937, CZA S25/3292.

20. Davidesko's report, 3 August 1937, CZA S25/3292. The irony is that Davidesko, one of the first Zionists to operate collaborators, was killed by Lehi members in 1945 after being charged for collaboration with the British.

21. David Hacohen to Moshe Shertok, 16 September 1937, CZA S25/4144.

22. Sheikh Farhan was handed over by an informer and hung in November 1937.

23. Sheikh 'Atiyyah was the commander of the attack on the kibbutz of Tirat Tsvi in the Beisan Valley in February 1938; he was killed with dozens of his men in the battle of Yamoun in March 1938.

24. Hacohen to Shertok, 16 September 1937, CZA S25/4144.

25. On the measures taken by the British, see Yigal Eyal, *Ha-Intifada ha-Rishona* [The First Intifada: The Suppression of the Arab Revolt by the British Army in Palestine] (Tel-Aviv, 1998), 310–317 (in Hebrew).

26. Porath, *Palestinian Arab National Movement*, 236–237.

27. Sharett, *Yoman Medini*, 2:373, 386.

28. "Letter from Hebron" [December] 1937, CZA S25/3539. On attempts to assassinate Tahboub, see letter from Hebron dated 23 December 1937, CZA S25/3541. On the mukhtar of Tirat-Haifa, see report dated 5 November 1937, CZA S25/3292.

29. Darwaza, *Mudhakkarat*, 3:129.

30. A. H. Cohen's report, 15 December 1937, CZA S25/3539.

31. "Political Information," 26 December 1937, and "A Letter from Nablus," 24 December 1937, CZA S25/3541.

32. "A Letter from Nablus," 19 December 1937, ibid.

33. *Al-Liwaa*, 1 January 1938; "News from the Arab Press," 2 January 1938, CZA S25/22301.

34. "Information on Arab Affairs" [6 October 1937], CZA S25/3539.

35. A. Hushi to Zaslani, 15 May 1938, HA Hushi 8/6; "Political Information," 29 April 1938, CZA S25/3541; review dated 26 May, including a report of 16 May 1938, CZA S25/22253. Tuqan and al-Shak'a were just back in the country. They left for Lebanon in February, as testified by Ihsan al-Nimer, who advised them to leave; see his *Ta'arikh Jabl Nablus wal-Balqaa* [The History of Mt. Nablus and al-Balqaa] (Nablus, 1975), 3:14 (in Arabic).

36. "Political Information," 23 May 1938, CZA S25/10098.

37. "The Terror in Jerusalem Area," 14 July 1938, CZA S25/3541. Two months later the head of the family, Ibrahim 'Abd al-Razeq, was killed by rebels, an event that "shocked all villagers north to Jerusalem," according to "Political Information," 15 September 1938, ibid.

38. "Political Information," 6 July 1938 (p. 10), CZA S25/10098.

39. Testimonies in al-Ghazzalah's trial, quoted in *Davar*, 2 January 1940, and *ha-Boker*, 7 January 1940.

40. "Political Information," CZA S25/10098.

41. Porath, *Emergence*, 190.

42. Darwaza, *Mudhakkarat*, 3:527.

43. 'Aref 'Abd al-Razeq to the members of the Supreme Muslim Council, 4 November 1938, CZA S25/22510; Cohen, "Political Information," 14 November 1938, CZA S25/10098.

44. A. H. Cohen to Dr. L. Cohen, 21 November 1938, CZA S25/3541.

45. Dov Hoz to Shertok, "Summary of Conversation with H. S. Dajani," 1 November 1933, CZA S25/3051.

46. "The Reasons behind Killing Dajani," 16 October 1938, CZA S25/10098; the description of al-Dajani's last day is identical. 'Abd al-Razeq's son claimed that his father had nothing to do with the murder, and that it is possible that the British, Zionists, or Nashashibis were behind it; see Faysal Aref 'Abd al-Razeq, *Amjad Thawriyya Filastiniyya wa-Hayat Batal min Abtaliha* [Praises of the Revolt and the Life of One of Its Heros] (Taybe, 1995), 91–92 (in Arabic).

47. A. H. Cohen to Shertok, 9 November 1938, CZA S25/3541.

48. High commissioner to the minister of colonial secretary, 27 January 1939, PRO CO-932/21. Khaled al-Fahoum, the nephew of Rafe' and former chairman of the Palestinian National Council (of the PLO), related in his memoirs that his uncle had supported the revolt and supplied the rebels with information and arms. He claims that Rafe' was killed after the British leaked false information, according to which he was collaborating with them—this in order to undermine the revolt. "Khaled al-Fahoum Yatadhakkar," *al-Quds*, vol. 2 (September 1998).

49. A. H. Cohen to Shertok, 18 December 1938, CZA S25/3541. These examples reveal the social aspect of the revolt, the schism between city dwellers and villagers, and the antagonism of the latter toward the urban elite, who exploited them financially through exorbitant interests on loans.

50. On four people he killed just after his return, see CID 60/38, "Armed Gangs," 5 December 1938, copied in CZA S25/22732.

51. A. H. Cohen, "'Abd al-Qader's Affairs in the Vicinity of Jerusalem," 29 November 1938, CZA S25/22732; the information was published in the Histadrut's newspaper in Arabic, *Haqiqat al-Amr*, 7 December 1938. According to Haganah records, al-Khatib was killed in 18 March 1939; see HA 77/1.

52. "Political Information," 20 September 1938, CZA S25/22732.

53. On the assassination of Mustafa, see report of 16 October 1938, HA 8/2, and undated report in CZA S25/22424, which identify the assassin.

54. Shaltiel, *Pinhas Rutenberg*, 516. Shaltiel quoted minutes of the Jewish Agency Executive from January and February 1939 that testify that Rutenberg was criticized for his independent activities.

55. Porath, *Palestinian Arab National Movement*, 281–287.

56. Ibid., 290–294.

57. Al-Nimer, *Ta'arikh Jabl Nablus*, 3:10–11, 11n1.

58. Darwaza, *Mudhakkarat*, 3:359. This apologetic stance aimed to blame the opposition for the internal killings rather than the mufti and leaders of the revolt.

59. The regulations were published in 11 November 1937. Sharett, *Yoman Medini*, 2:405–406, mentions his meeting with the acting high commissioner on the previous day on this matter.

60. *Al-Jami'ah al-Islamiyyah*, 18 January 1938; Darwaza, *Mudhakkarat*, 3:133, 166. *Filastin*, 1 December 1937, as quoted in "news from the Arab press" of that date, CZA S25/22301.

61. Darwaza, *Mudhakkarat*, 3:52, 54, 94.

62. Ibid., 3:107, 146; see also the Egyptian paper *al-Shabab*, 22 December 1937, quoted in Muhsin Muhammad al-Saleh, *Al-Quwwat al-'Askariyya wal-Shurta fi Filastin 1917–1939* [Army and Police Forces in Palestine, 1917–1939] (Amman, 1996), 542 (in Arabic).

63. "Information from Jaffa," 22 December 1937, CZA S25/3541.

64. "Political Information," 26 December 1937, ibid.

65. Darwaza, *Mudhakkarat*, 3:216–218. The leaflet is quoted in a report from Haifa, 21 December 1937, CZA S25/3292.

66. Darwaza, *Mudhakkarat*, 3:111, claims that the Abbushis were responsible for turning Sa'adi over to the British, whereas Porath, *Palestinian Arab National Movement*, 257, writes that it was the Irsheid family.

67. Porath, *Palestinian Arab National Movement*, 237; Yuval Arnon-Ohana, *Falahim ba-Mered ha-Arvi 1936–1939* [Fellahin in the Arab Revolt in Palestine, 1936–1939] (Tel Aviv, 1978), 83–85 (in Hebrew).

68. A letter from Hadera [Ezra Danin], 24 April 1938, CZA S25/22533.

69. Darwaza, *Mudhakkarat*, 3:353.

70. Ibid., 3:353, 370, 373–374, 389, 399, 404.

71. A. H. Cohen, reports of 2 and 4 May 1938, CZA S25/22273; report from Haifa, May 1938, CZA S25/22253.

72. *Filastin*, 19 December 1937, referred to the harsh situation in the villages after the beginning of the second stage of the revolt: "The government tortures them for any small suspicion, while the rebels persecute them when they try to assist the helpless government to save their lives."

73. The collection of money by the rebels was criticized sometimes not only by public opinion but also by the revolt's headquarters in Damascus; see letters from the headquarters quoted in Ezra Danin, *Te'udot u-Dmuyot me-Ginzey ha-Knufiyot ha-Arviyot 1936–1939* [Documents and Characters from the Archives of the Arab Gangs in 1936–1939 Riots] (Jerusalem, 1984), 13–15 (in Hebrew).

74. A. Garbadian, who went without *kufiyya*, was sentenced by the rebels; CZA S25/22437. Yusuf Abu Durra distributed a leaflet prohibiting carrying identity cards; CZA S25/22269. Bans on wearing shorts and renting flats to Jews are mentioned in reports of 2 and 7 September 1938, CZA S25/4405. *Al-Akhbar*, 1 September 1938, refers to the endorsement of these rules in various areas. The attempt of the fellahin to compel the wearing of traditional clothes—with their symbolic meaning—is discussed in Swedenburg, *Memories of Revolt*, 32–35. This has been a common feature in peasant insurgencies, as we see in Eric Hobsbawm, "History from Below—Some Reflections," in Frederick Krantz, ed., *History from Below: Studies in Popular Protest and Popular Ideology in Honour of George Rude* (Montreal, 1985), 71–72.

75. 'Abd al-Razeq, *Amjad Thawriyya*, 207–210, quotes leaflets on the killings of an opposition member and an informer by a purge unit.

76. "Political Information," 6 July 1938, CZA S25/10098; 'Abd al-Razeq, *Amjad Thawriyya*, 203.

77. See, e.g., "The Security Situation in Jaffa and Its Surroundings," 5 September 1938, CZA S25/5341.

78. A. H. Cohen to B[ernard] Joseph, 25 December 1938, CZA S25/5341.

79. Report of 27 December 1938, CZA S25/4144.

80. Abba Hushi, "The PLL Today," 17 August 1938, HA Hushi 8/6.

81. The leaflet is in CZA S25/22312 [undated]; for correspondence regarding Sufan, see Cohen to Assaf, 11 June 1939, CZA S25/22209. The articles were published in *Haqiqat al-Amr*, 21 and 28 June, 1938.

82. Report dated 11 June 1939, HA 8/2; CZA S25/22269.

83. On the Jerusalem contingent, see "Emergency Information for Action," 14 September 1938, CZA S25/3541.

84. "What Is Done and Heard in Jaffa," 3 October 1938, CZA S25/3541; see also a detailed report by Cohen, "The Brutality of the Terrorist Gangs among the Arab Population," 6 November 1938, which refers to attacks on Christians on p. 7, ISA 65, 366/2288. Actually, a cruel, contemptuous approach was not limited to Christian informers and policemen; see al-Saleh, *Al-Quwwat al-*

'Askariyya, 541. The fatwa mentioned in chapter 2 contained a similar approach to land dealers, regardless of their religion.

85. Hacohen to Shertok, 7 November 1938, CZA S25/10098.

86. Darwaza's memoirs contain invaluable information on kidnapping and assassination at that time.

87. *Al-Jami'ah al-Islamiyyah*, 15 December 1937. *Filastin*, 17 December 1937, also urged a stop to the political assassinations. Both papers published this article after the failed attempt to assassinate Nablus mayor Suliman Tuqan. Both were close to the opposition circles, and the editor of *Filastin*, 'Isa al-'Isa, had also experienced an assassination attempt in August 1936.

88. Ahmad Shuqayri, *Arba'un 'Aman fi al-Hayat al-Arabiyya wal-Dawliyya* [Forty Years in the Arab and International Life] (Beirut, 1969), 187–189 (in Arabic).

89. Al-Hout, *Al-Qiyadat*, 403.

90. 'Ala al-Din's evidence in CID, 21 November 1941, ISA 65, 365/2277.

91. Ya'akov Shimoni, "Ha-Hit'argenut ha-Politit shel Arviyey Erets Yisrael" [The Political Organization of the Palestinian Arabs], in *Ha-Mandat ve-ha-Bayit ha-Le'umi* [The Mandate and the National Home], vol. 9 of Yehoshua Porath and Ya'akov Shavit, eds., *Ha-Historia shel Erets Yisrael* [The History of the Land of Israel] (Jerusalem, 1982), 284 (in Hebrew).

92. Arnon-Ohana, *Falahim*, 140.

93. *Ha'aretz*, 8 September 1977.

94. Fakhri Nashashibi, *Sawt Min Qubur Filastin al-Arabiyya* [A Call from the Graves of Arab Palestine] ([Jerusalem], 1938), 36, 44. This is a collection of his letters and articles. In a conference he held in Yatta (south Hebron region) in November 1938, he stated that 292 of his supporters were killed by the mufti's men. Though there were other people killed without connection to him, the number did not reach "thousands." Maurice Pearlman's *Mufty of Jerusalem* (London, 1947) is by no means supportive of the mufti or an attemmpt to reduce the number of killings, but it also quotes (27) the lower figures mentioned by Nashashibi.

95. Nashashibi, *Sawt Min Qubur*, 52. Walid Khalidi, *From Haven to Conquest* (Washington, D.C., 1987), 846–849, cites the British figures and argues that one should add 20 percent to reach the actual number, but still this does not change the picture as a whole.

96. Ya'akov Shimoni, "Ha-aravim Likrat Milhemet Yisrael-Arav 1945–1948" [The Arabs toward the Israeli-Arab War, 1945–1948], *Ha-Mizrah he-Hadash*, vol. 12 (1962): 192n3 (in Hebrew).

97. High commissioner to the governors, report on casualties for 1938, appendix to a letter, 16 January 1939, PRO CO-933/21.

98. *Davar*, 2 January 1939. The same figures are found in the daily reports of the Haganah, HA 77/1 (1 September 1938–15 August 1939).

99. *Davar*, 4 July 1939.

100. Even if we add 20 percent, as suggested by Khalidi, we reach no more than 1,100 people. The only contemporary source that published higher figures during the revolt itself was the Histadrut's organ, *Haqiqat al-Amr* (e.g., in 22 June 1938 and 25 January 1939, in which the monthly and weekly figures are significantly higher than those in other sources). If one does not give this paper more credit than intelligence sources, there are two options: publication was

either part of the Zionist psychological warfare or was not professional enough and used unreliable sources.

6. THE "TRAITORS" COUNTERATTACK

1. Elyashar, *Li-Hyot*, 67–70.
2. Haim Ben Menachem's testimony, HA 196/57.
3. Report of Ben-Zvi, 20 December 1936, CZA S25/3051.
4. According to David Ben-Gurion's memories, quoted in Porath, *Palestinian Arab National Movement*, 251.
5. Franko to Shertok, 18 March 1938, CZA S25/3051.
6. As mentioned on pp. 53–55, the "treacherousness" of the Nashashibis before the revolt was an image disseminated by the Husseinis, who claimed that the Nashashibis supported the Zionists. The decision of the Zionist leadership not to support the Nashashibis in Jerusalem's municipal elections of 1933 is an indication that Zionist-Nashashibi relations did not yield results prior to the revolt.
7. For the details of the joint plan, see Sasson to Shertok, 20 March 1938, CZA S25/4550, and his letters from 10 and 19 March for background. Darwaza, in *Mudhakkarat*, 3:179, mentions earlier contacts between these parties. According to Reuven Erlich, *Bisvakh ha-Levanon 1918–1958* [In the Lebanese Tangle, 1918–1958] (Tel Aviv, 2000), 89–91 (in Hebrew), al-Ahdab was on the payroll of the Jewish Agency when he was a journalist. Gelber, *Shorshey ha-Havatselet*, 241, mentions the allocation of "Zionist" money to Nashashibi.
8. The Histadrut's newspaper was among those that published his activity at length; see, e.g., issues of 7 and 21 December 1938 and 1 January 1939.
9. *Yorkshire Post*, 24 October 1938; Nashashibi, *Sawt Min Qubur*. Blaming 'Abd al-Razeq and others for selling land to Jews aimed not only at discrediting them but also at strengthening Nashashibi's image as a national leader. In his *Amjad Thawriyya*, Faysal 'Aref 'Abd al-Razeq denied this charge.
10. *Times*, 1 December 1938; appendix to CID report 90/38, 21 December 1938, copy at CZA S25/22732.
11. CID report 90/38, 21 December 1938, copy at CZA S25/22732. *Al-Difa'*, quoted in CID report 86/38, 7 December 1938, claimed that Fakhri received Jewish money for hiring people from various villages to announce their support of him; copy in CZA S25/22732. On an anti-Nashashibi demonstration held in Beirut with a similar claim, see report of 1 September 1939, CZA S25/22424.
12. CID report 86/38 quotes letters sent to the headquarters in Syria by local commanders, who described the battle in which 'Abd al-Qader was injured for the second time.
13. Sasson to B. Joseph, 28 December 1938, CZA S25/10098.
14. Cohen to B. Joseph, 25 December 1938, CZA S25/3541.
15. Members of the Abu-Ghosh family lived in al-Qubab, al-Ramla district.
16. "The Meeting in Sarafand, 31 December 1938," CZA S25/22269; Cohen to Joseph, 25 December 1938, CZA S25/3541.
17. "The Meeting of the Army Officers with Sheikh Nimer Abu-Ghosh in Emwas, 22 January 1939," CZA S25/22269.

18. Residents of Abu-Ghosh to the speaker of the Knesset [1950], ISA 79, 260/2; I did not find other documentation of this activity or even its date.

19. The village of Qatanna is 3 km north of Abu-Ghosh; on the "uprising" of its inhabitants, see Cohen to Shertok, 18 December 1938, CZA S25/3541.

20. Darwaza, *Mudhakkarat*, 3:179. For earlier plans to contact 'Abd al-Hadi, see Gelber, *Shorshey ha-Havatselet*, 237.

21. Darwaza, *Mudhakkarat*, 3:179, 392–393.

22. R. Newton to assistant district commissioner, Samaria, 17 December 1938, copy at CZA S25/22793; "Political Information," 2 January 1939, CZA S25/3541.

23. Reports dated 17 November 1938, 5 and 13 December 1938, CZA S25/4405; report by the revolt's headquarters, quoted in Danin, *Te'udot*, 24. Four people were killed in the attack in 'Arrabet, HA 77/1. See also the leaflet of 30 November 1938, attached to CID report 90/38, 21 December 1938, copy at CZA S25/22732.

24. Leaflet no. 71, dated 17 Shawwal 1357 [10 December 1938], CZA S25/22510.

25. "Announcement of the *Mujahidin* to the Noble Arab Nation" [May 1938], CZA S25/10098, which tells of a robber caught in a village who carried a police pistol and cards of the British forces. For other leaflets with similar claims, see Abd al-Wahhab Kayyali, *Watha'iq al-Muqawama al-Filastiniyya al-Arabiyya* [Documents of the Palestinian-Arab Resistance] (Beirut, 1968), 613–616.

26. A. H. Cohen, "The State of Security," 26 November 1938, CZA S25/3541.

27. Report by Zvi Woolf, 8 January 1939, CZA S25/2614.

28. Report dated 8 January 1939, HA 8/2.

29. Darwaza, *Mudhakkarat*, 3:388, claims that the reason for the murder is unclear since the Irsheids were not disloyal to the nation.

30. Hajj Muhammad was criticized even by his men for killing the Irsheids; see Danin, *Te'udot*, 30–34. For a sympathetic oral history–based account of this commander, see Nimer Sirhan and Mustafa Kabaha, *Abd al-Rahim Hajj Muhammad: Al-Qa'id al-'am li-thawrat 1936–1939* ['Abd al-Rahim al-Hajj Muhammad: General Commander of the 1936–1939 revolt] (Ramallah, 2000).

31. On the reservations of the British concerning these peace units, see Porath, *Palestinian Arab National Movement*, 255–256.

32. According to undated intelligence report of the Nazareth police headquarters titled "Nazareth Town," the Fahoums were unpopular among the fellahin for their involvement in land deals with Jews and exploitation of the fellahin; they joined the antirebellion initiative after the murder of Rafe' al-Fahoum. The report adds that they sent Fa'iz al-Fahoum to infiltrate a rebel unit and aid British intelligence. He did a good job until he was exposed and killed in July 1939; ISA 17, 4212/8. For Khaled al-Fahoum's version of the events, see "Khaled al-Fahoum Yatadhakkar," *al-Quds*, 2 September 1998.

33. Fakhri's contacts with personalities throughout the country can be traced through the summaries of his telephone talks, made by Jewish Agency agents who tapped his lines; CZA S25/22837.

34. "A Briefing on the Security Situation in the Upper Galilee, Safed District," 17 November 1938, CZA S25/10615. The revolt's headquarters was aware of the

collaboration of Kamel Effendi and was ready to pardon him on condition that he repent. However, they advised him to leave the area, since they knew that the rebels wanted to take revenge on him; Darwaza, *Mudhakkarat*, 3:400.

35. Landsman to Zaslani, 20 February and 3 August 1939, CZA S25/22413.

36. Ibid. For al-Heib's relations with the Jews, see also Sheikh Yusuf al-Heib's testimony, HA 68.6.

37. "Report on My Visit to Jenin and Arrabe," 8 August 1939, HA Hushi 8/6.

38. Ibid. On his self-definition as a nationalist, see the leaflet he distributed in January 1939, published in *al-Jihad*, 7 January 1939; translation in HA 8/2 (general files).

39. A. H. Cohen, "Report on a Talk with Yosef Yakobson," 30 November 1937, CZA S25/3539. An earlier report on the phenomenon is from Haifa: "The Arab policemen and officers mislead the few informers still active and fight against them" [November 1937], CZA S25/3292.

40. Reports of 13 and 27 July 1937, CZA S25/3292; "A Letter from Hadera," 3 June 1938, CZA S25/3541; report of 12 September 1938, CZA S25/4405.

41. Nadav Baskind's testimony, HA 41/81; he added that this Arab remained in Israel after 1948 and the good relations continued as well.

42. Danin, *Tsiyoni*, 149. The methods used at the political level and the local level are similar—basically, using internal disputes and allying with one side.

43. Ibid., 130.

44. Ibid., 130–131.

45. Hushi's report, 26 February 1937, HA Hushi 8/6. As mentioned on pp. 138–39, some of Hushi's informers were kidnapped, tortured, or executed.

46. Hushi's report, 28 February 1939, HA Hushi 8/6.

47. Ibid.

48. Report dated 31 March 1939, HA Hushi 8/6.

49. Feitelson to Zaslani, 29 November 1938, CZA S25/10615.

50. Feitelson to Zaslani, 12 December and 16 December 1938, CZA S25/4960.

51. Zikhron Ya'akov local committee to the Jewish Agency, 18 January 1939, CZA S25/4960.

52. [Danin to the Jewish Agency], 27 January 1939, HA 8/2.

53. Report of 12 February 1939, HA 8/2; M. to Zaslani, 30 May 1939, CZA S25/22424.

54. Danin to Zaslani, 15 October 1939, CZA S25/10098; Danin suggested not trusting them too much since he had received information that they had had a reconciliation ceremony with Sabri Hamed.

55. An interesting case is mentioned in Swedenburg, *Memories of Revolt,* 155–156; the al-Zaban family from Bidia, central Samaria, helped the British forces. The mukhtar of the family told Swedenburg that the revolt was not an all-Palestinian, national one but an initiative of the lower class, so they didn't identify with it. Moreover, since the rebels hurt the family, they had to be revenged, and the aim of their cooperation with the British was to use the British, not to be used by them, so there was nothing wrong with it.

56. *Haqiaqt al-Amr,* 25 January 1939.

57. Nathan Fisch's testimony, HA 179/12.

58. The dates of these events were not mentioned in their memoirs, but these methods were established during the revolt.

59. Ravina, *Agudat ha-Shomrim,* 1:104.

60. Ibid., 1:113–117.

61. Ibid., 2:79; Ben-Ami, *Arayot Sho'agim,* 55.

62. Ravina, *Agudat ha-Shomrim,* 1:428–429.

63. Raziel Mamat and Avi Blier, *Me-Nikrot Tsurim* [From the Clefts of Rocks: The Amazing Story of Ya'akov Barazani] (Tel Aviv, 1979), 159–163, 209 (in Hebrew).

64. Ibid., 145, 196–197; Ravina, *Agudat ha-Shomrim,* 1:454–456.

65. Ravina, *Agudat ha-Shomrim,* 1:177–180. This phenomenon is also mentioned in contemporary documents, such as the case of one Issa Hajj Ahmad, who killed a Jewish laborer and on another occasion warned a Jewish friend who faced an assassination attempt; see Danin to Shiloah, 4 August 1940, CZA S25/22518.

66. On the debate in the Druze community regarding the nationalist question, see A. H. Cohen, "Report on a Visit to the Druze in the Northern Areas," 20 October 1932, CZA S25/3542.

67. Kais Firro, *A History of the Druzes* (Leiden, 1992), 329.

68. Ibid., 330–331.

69. Gelber, *Shorshey ha-Havatselet,* 144.

70. David Hacohen to Ben-Gurion and others, 4 January 1937, CZA S25/3441.

71. Darwaza, *Mudhakkarat,* 3:153, diary entry of 26 December 1937.

72. Report of A[bba] H[ushi], 12 April 1938, CZA S25/3541; [A. Hushi], "PLL Today," 18 August 1938, HA Hushi 8/6.

73. Khneifes was killed as he left the moshav of Yavne'el in January 1939 (Firro, *History,* 340). His son Saleh was at the time in the Druze religious college in Bayyada, Lebanon, and returned home to take revenge. Two decades later he served as a Knesset member, after aiding the Jewish forces in the 1948 war (see pp. 246–47).

74. Tuvia Umani's testimony, 18 February 1971, HA 95/23.

75. Report from Haifa, 2 April 1939, CZA S25/8151.

76. Leaflet from Haifa, 20 April 1939, CZA S25/8151 (translated into Hebrew); Firro dated it to 1936, but the date on the translation is 1939 and it is filed with documents from this period. The original leaflet was not found.

77. Porath, *Palestinian Arab National Movement,* 319.

78. Ibid., 320.

79. Report of A. H. Cohen, "The Security Situation," 28 October 1938, CZA S25/10098.

80. A. H. Cohen, 2 December 1937, CZA S25/3539.

81. See the Shai report on the village of al-Reine in the Galilee, which notes that the mukhtar of the Christians supplied the government with information, "as Christians used to do everywhere"; al-Reine sheet, HA 105/178.

7. WORLD WAR, LOCAL CALM

1. Report, 20 June 1939, HA 8/2; Letter from Beirut, 19 July, ibid.; A. H. Cohen's report, 7 September 1939, CZA S25/3541.

2. *Palestine Post*, 20 February 1940 (the policemen); *Ha'aretz*, 17 January 1941 (Sadeq)—both reported from the sentences of the suspects. Darwaza wrote on the brothers al-Karami: "Mahmoud al-Karami in Beirut, like his brother 'Abd al-Ghani in Damascus, conducts a propaganda campaign against the revolt and the holy warriors together with persons from the opposition and the British intelligence. . . . 'Abd al-Ghani is a bit lighthearted while Mahmoud is more serious"; *Mudhakkarat*, 3:788. 'Abd al-Ghani later became closer to Emir 'Abdallah and one of the men of his court. He maintained his contacts with Zionist officials during the 1950s.

3. A. H. Cohen, "Conversation with the Mufti of Hebron," 13 July 1939, CZA S25/3051; Cohen reported on the decision to execute Tahboub in his 6 July 1938 report, CZA S25/10098; attempts on his life are mentioned in chapter 5.

4. E. Sasson to B. Joseph, 20 December 1939, CZA S25/3140. As mentioned earlier, the Fahoums had close contact with Fakhri Nashashibi.

5. Malhi to Danin, 28 September 1940, CZA S25/22619.

6. The 'Azzi's were attacked by the peace units after they joined the revolt; see "Directing and Financing [the Revolt]," undated, CZA S25/22518; Danin's "A Tour in Gaza and Beit Jibrin," July 1940, CZA S25/22597 (report of his meeting with the family).

7. Letter to the Shai headquarters in Tel Aviv, 5 October 1940, CZA S25/22597.

8. Report of 12 June 1940, CZA S25/22596.

9. Slutski, *Sefer Toldot*, 3:106.

10. S. Somekh to E. Sasson, 8 September 1940, and D. Neishtadt to Shertok, 15 September 1940, CZA S25/22518.

11. Yitzhak Avira's report, November 1940, CZA S25/22525.

12. *Davar*, 22 January and 21 May 1940.

13. Yerushalmi to Yitzhak, 23 September 1940, CZA S25/22525.

14. *Haboker*, 8 May 1940.

15. E. Sasson to B. Joseph, "A Talk with Hamdi Kan'an," 28 February 1940, and "Second Talk with Hamdi Kan'an," 10 March 1940, CZA S25/3051. Sasson determined that Kan'an was sent by Mayor Suliman Tuqan, who demanded 7,000 Palestine pounds to consent to the connection—5,000 for himself and the rest for other town dignitaries.

16. Report on the tour in CZA S25/22525. Half a year later, when tension was higher, "Eiloni" reported that the Bedouin of al-'Aramshe (led by Qasem Mamluk of Idmit) prepared a huge meal for the members of the kibbutz and promised to protect them in case of attack; report of 1 May 1941, CZA S25/22341.

17. Report of 16 September 1940, CZA S25/22559; *ha-Tsofe* reported (25 September 1940) that in a Jewish-Arab meeting in Sheikh Mu'nis one of the Arab speakers suggested publicly condemning the bombings at Tel Aviv and Haifa.

18. G[eorge] 'A[zar]'s report, 30 September 1940, and report of an informer from Sajd, 7 September 1940, who maintained that Arab popular opinion around Hebron and Jerusalem was to wait for the British defeat in the war; both CZA S25/22518.

19. Report by A. S., 4 April 1941, HA 105/197.

20. G[eorge] 'A[zar] to E[liahu] S[asson], 18 November 1940, CZA S25/22525. *Davar,* 8 August 1939, reported on a Palestinian who informed his Jewish neighbors of Kibbutz Kfar Menachem about a mine put by the road leading to their homes, saying: "We are already three years in this business. We are fed up."

21. "A Talk with Muhammad al-As'ad from 'Attil," 12 October 1941, HA 105/197.

22. Reports to the Shai, 27 March and 1 April 1941, HA 105/78.

23. In spring 1941 when the Kilani revolt in Baghdad seemed (for a few weeks) to be successful, Arabs in Palestine severed their open ties with Jews and propaganda against the opposition intensified; see reports by Yariv, 7 May 1941, Mifratsi, 28 April 1941, Yakhini, 7 May 1941, Lot, 9 May 1941, all in CZA S25/22341.

24. "On Events among Palestinian Arabs," 15 April 1941, CZA S25/22341; Amitai to Shai, 4 April 1943, CZA S25/22342; "A Meeting with a Commander of a Gang," 25 June 1945, HA 105/87. There were also rebels who established partnerships with Jews, such as Mahmoud 'Ala al-Din, who was close to Darwaza and when he returned to Palestine in September 1941 became a subcontractor for Jews who received projects from the British army; see CID headquarters, 21 November 1941, ISA 65, 365/2267.

25. "Agent 127" to Shai, 22 November 1940, CZA S25/22534.

26. Ezra Danin to Sh[aul] M[eirov] (head of the Shai), 15 September 1940, CZA S25/22518. It should be noticed that this was written before the establishment of the extermination camps, though five years after the publication of the race laws.

27. "A Meeting in Tel Aviv," 12 January 1941, CZA S25/22318.

28. E. Sasson, "Work Plan for the Arab Department for 1943," 23 August 1942, CZA S25/22155; Sasson, memorandum of 6 December 1942, CZA S25/22154; R. Shiloah, "A Visit to Organize Relations in the Karkur Region," 5 September 1940, CZA S25/22534.

29. Anita Shapira, *Land and Power: The Zionist Resort to Force, 1881–1948* (New York, 1992); Uri Ben-Eliezer, *The Making of Israeli Militarism* (New York, 1992).

30. *Ha-Boker,* 7 June 1940; *Ha'aretz,* 19 July 1940; *Palestine Post,* 4 July 1940.

31. Danin to Shiloah, after talking with intelligence officer Hacket, 4 August 1940, CZA S25/22518; E. Sasson's report on his discussion with Irsheid, in which the latter suggested three-way cooperation (opposition, Jews, and Emir 'Abdallah) against the Husseinis, cited in Moshe Gabbay, *Falastinim al Falastin* [Palestinians on Palestine: Documents and Testimonies] (Tel Aviv, 1988), Document no. 69 (in Hebrew).

32. Zeinati's note in a report of 3 August 1940, CZA S25/413, that some par-

ticipants had not known about the agreement with the Jewish Agency testifies to the existence of such a secret agreement.

33. Danin to Shiloah, 4 August 1940, CZA S25/22518. The coordination lasted in the following months; see report of 21 February 1941 on a meeting in Tiberias, CZA S25/22318.

34. On the failure of the opposition to recruit Arabs to the British army, see "A Talk with the Watchman," 2 October 1940, CZA S25/22518, in which he stated that he succeeded in recruiting only nine people. On British confiscation of arms from the peace units, see G[eorge] 'A[zar], 27 November 1939, and Y[a'akov] C[ohen], 17 December 1939, CZA S25/10098.

35. "A Talk with the Watchman," 2 November 1940, HA 105/197.

36. "A Talk with the Gardener," 27 May 1941, CZA S25/22340.

37. Danin, *Tsiyoni,* 157–158. See also Haviv Kena'an, *200 Yemei Harada* [200 Days of Dread] (Tel Aviv, 1974), 227–233 (in Hebrew).

38. Sasson to Shertok, 24 July 1940, CZA S25/3140I; Danin to Shiloah, 4 August 1940, CZA S25/22518; see also "A Meeting with the Watchman," 31 January 1941 and 11 April 1941, HA 105/197.

39. Danin to Zaslani, 15 October 1939, CZA S25/10098; "Information," 1 January 1940, CZA S25/22596; "A Meeting with the Watchman," 30 October 1940 and 23 November 1940, CZA S25/22525. On a rare case in which peace units were permitted to chase rebels, see report by "Meretz" (Danin), 27 November 1940, CZA S25/22525.

40. G[ershon] R[itov], 13 October 1940, CZA S25/22317.

41. Danin's letter, 9 November 1940, and "The Case of Hafez Hamdallah [the Watchman]," 19 September 1941, HA 105/197.

42. Danin to Shiloah, 4 August 1940, and "Information from Nablus Area," 17 September 1940, CZA S25/22518.

43. "A Meeting with S[uliman] T[uqan], 12 September 1941, CZA S25/8970. In this period the Jewish Agency strengthened its contacts with Tuqan, and reports on meetings with him are preserved mainly in CZA S25/22349; see also "A Meeting with the Watchman," 2 November 1940, HA 105/197.

44. "Conversation with the Watchman," 8 September 1940, CZA S25/22518.

45. Gelber, *Shorshey ha-Havatselet,* 521.

46. E. Sasson to Shertok, "A Talk with T[aher] A[araman]," 6 May 1941, CZA S25/3140I.

47. Noah's report, 12 September 1941, CZA S25/22349.

48. Ibid.

49. Danin, "A Meeting with the Cantor," 15 September 1941, ibid. Danin revealed his doubts regarding the sincerity of "the Cantor."

50. Sasson to Shertok, "A Talk with al-Muzaffar," 24 February 1941, CZA S25/22318.

51. Letter to Shimoni, 13 July 1945, CZA S25/22159.

52. Report of 13 November 1937, CZA S25/3539.

53. Report of G[eorge] 'A[zar], 6 October 1940, CZA S25/22518; report of 23 March 1941, CZA S25/3140.

54. Reports of 23 March and 25 May 1941, CZA S25/3140.

55. "Arab Information," 2 July and 27 July 1940, CZA S25/22615.

56. *Omer,* 4 March 1940.

57. "A Meeting with Shehori," 4 June 1941, CZA S25/22349.

58. Danin to Shiloah, 4 August 1940, CZA S25/22518; report of 14 September 1941, CZA S25/22349. Danin recalls in his memoirs that the information arrived, indirectly, from his acquaintance Abdalla al-Saba', who helped him in his first investigation after a murder in Nahalal; see his *Tsiyoni,* 120.

59. Report of 15 May 1941, CZA S25/22340. I did not determine if he went there.

60. Reports, different dates, 1941, all in CZA S25/22336; report of R. A. G. on a rumor regarding A. Q. al-Husseini's return, 2 November 1942, CZA S25/22645.

61. Reports of 28 April and 17 November 1941, CZA S25/22349; report of 18 March 1941, HA 105/197; "Information on the Murder," 29 December 1940, CZA S25/22317.

62. "On Events among the Arabs," 1 April 1942, CZA S25/22339; and see chapter 8 for additional cases.

63. Undated report, 1941, CZA S25/22341.

64. A. H. Cohen received information in August 1941 on the travels of the mufti from Teheran to Rome. But the mufti left for Rome only on September 19.

65. The surveys are preserved in different files in CZA S25, HA, and the Shai files. On this project, see in depth Shimri Salomon, "Sherut ha-Yedi'ot shel ha-Hagana u-Proyekt Skirot ha-yishuvim ha-Aravim be-erets Yisrael 1940–1948" [The Haganah's Arab Intelligence Service and the Project of Surveying the Arab Settlements in Palestine, 1940–1948] in *Daf me-ha-Slik* [A Sheet from the Cache: The Haganah Archive Quarterly), vols. 9–10 (December 2001): 1–29 (in Hebrew).

66. Yosef Weitz, *Hitnahlutenu bi-Tkufat ha-Sa'ar* [Our Settlement in Stormy Days] (Jerusalem, 1947), 11–14 (in Hebrew). He notes that KKL purchased more land during the four years of the revolt than in the previous four years (94,000 and 73,000 dunams, respectively), but the private sector failed to "fulfill this assignment."

67. Kimmerling, *Ha-Ma'avak,* 31.

68. Meeting with G. A., 9 February 1940, CZA S25/4144.

69. Weitz, *Hitnahlutenu,* 15.

70. Kimmerling, *Ha-Ma'avak,* 29.

71. Sasson to B. Joseph, 26 February 1940, CZA S25/22597. According to this report, Emir 'Abdallah praised the members of the delegation for preserving good relations with their Jewish neighbors.

72. Weitz, *Hitnahlutenu,* 15.

73. Ibid.

74. Avraham Gissin's testimony, 26 January 1971, OHD-HU 57–13. The involvement of this family in *samsara* was preserved in the collective memory of the people of the region; see, e.g., a reference to it during an interview conducted in the late 1980s in Swedenburg, *Memories of Revolt,* 24.

75. Gissin testimony, 26 January 1971, OHD-HU 57–13 (on al-'Azzi and Irsheid). Ze'ev Levanon mentioned in his testimony, February 1974, OHD-HU 57–39, transactions of land made by al-'Azzi in the early 1930s.

76. E. Danin and Palmon's testimony, 29 May 1971, OHD-HU 57–24b.

77. Hamdallah to Shertok, April–June 1941, CZA S25/3033.

78. Sharon's testimony, 11 January 1971, OHD-HU 57–15.

79. Gissin's testimony, 26 January 1971, OHD-HU 57–13.

80. S. B. Sasson to Police Minister Shitrit, 6 June 1949, ISA 119, 3314/3/131. That year al-Mustaqim asked permission to return to Jaffa on the grounds of his good relations with Jews but was refused because he was allegedly involved in criminal activity.

81. Svardlov's testimony, 16 June 1971, OHD-HU 57–27. In many other cases the British police removed the tenants through legal processes.

82. Assistant to the chief of police to the government's chief secretary, 13 April 1943; committee report of 17 May 1943; memorandum by Gaza governor, 9 April 1943—all in ISA 2, SF 215/40.

83. The Dajani family has been one of the prominent aristocratic families in Jerusalem, called also Dahudi because of its role as custodian of the King David tomb at Mt. Zion; Malkov's testimony, OHD-HU 57–35.

84. See Judge Yehuda Treibush's testimony, 21 January 1971, OHD-HU 57–11.

85. Hiram Danin's testimony, 23 December 1970, OHD-HU 57–6d.

86. Report to the Higher Arab Committee regarding Dahudi [al-Dajani] involvement in selling land in Qatanna through public auction [1945?], ISA 65, 413/3875; Sa'id al-Din to the Higher Arab Committee, ISA 65, 392/3142. For a list of the plots of land he bought, see Galilee governor to the chief secretary, 29 May 1946, ISA 2, SF 215/40, and in the same file the complaint of the head of Sunduq al-Umma (the Arab "Nation's Fund"), Ahmad Hilmi Pasha, to the Mandate government, dated 10 October 1946.

87. Malkov's testimony, OHD-HU 57–35.

88. Sheikh Shehade al-Faghuri, the owner, sold the land to al-Dajani, who sold it to Tenebaum; the agreements are preserved in ISA 66, 249/23.

89. Hiram Danin's testimony, OHD-HU 57–6d.

90. "From Hertzelia Area," 28 December 1941, CZA S25/22345.

91. Affidavit dated 16 July 1946 in 'Abd al-'Aziz Abu-Ghosh and others' lawsuit against Ahmad Rashid (the mukhtar of Abu-Ghosh) and Ali al-Qasem, Hankin, and others, ISA 66, 215/12 (later, the sides reached an agreement outside the court); Shehade 'Azzuni to the Higher Arab Committee [summer 1947], ISA 65, 385/2864 (south); Yarkoni [to Shai], 25 March 1946, HA 105/265.

92. Slutski, *Sefer Toldot*, 1:86, 687n. In the 1948 war most of them left the country, but they were invited back by KKL and were settled in a neighborhood in Ramla that received their name—Jawarish (which became known in the 1990s as a center for drug dealing and other criminal activities).

93. Hiram Danin's testimony, OHD-HU 57–6a.

94. E. Danin and Palmon's testimony, 24 May 1971, OHD-HU 57–24a. His partnership with Jews in land transactions was exposed by Sunduq al-Umma, which complained to the high commissioner in a letter dated 26 August 1945, ISA 2, SF 215/40.

95. E. Danin and Palmon's testimony, 24 May 1971, OHD-HU 57–24a.

96. Shmuel Soforik, HA 19/45, recalled that in the early 1930s the Haganah

purchased arms from fellahin in the Hebron mountains; and Moshe Roten Roteshtein said that the Jews of Rosh Pina bought weapons from Arabs as well (including the tribe of al-Heib), HA 151/13 and 151/14.

97. Arab merchants began selling weapons to the Haganah instead of Etzel in mid-1947 because of the latter's economic difficulties; report to "Delphi" titled "Arms Business," 30 May 1947, HA 112/1175.

98. Yitzhak Hasson, *Ha-Zaken va-Ani* [The Old Man and Me: The Personal Account of Lehi's Head of Intelligence] (Tel Aviv, 1993) (in Hebrew). Yisrael Eldad, *Ma'aser Rishon* [First Tenth] (Tel Aviv, 1960), 322; "Yousef Mahmoud Abu-Ghosh, Personal Sheet, June 1947," a copy from CID files preserved in HA 47/27—personal.

99. Negbi to Bina, 7 September 1945, HA 112/1175; this file contains reports of the Haganah surveillance of Etzel and Lehi arms deals (mainly with Arabs).

100. Ibid., reports of 14 June 1946 and 15 April 1947. According to information received in September 1947 (ibid.), the nationalist circles in Jaffa decided to kill Abu-Yasin.

101. J. Fforde, assistant inspector-general, CID, to the chief secretary, 12 November 1947, ISA [2], GN 92/185, referred to two cases of bombs thrown at the house of Rafiq al-Tamimi, the deputy head of the Higher Arab Committee, in September 1947. Fforde mentioned that a suspect admitted that he was involved in other bombings in the service of Jews, but there are doubts about the reliability of the confession.

102. The suspects were two Egyptian workers who were consequently dismissed from their jobs; the Shai revealed that they had contacts with Jews, probably Etzel's supporters; see "King David's Workers," 12 August 1946, HA 112/1175.

103. Reports of 8 and 10 July 1947, ibid.

104. Reports of 21 October and 5 November 1946, 6 and 23 January, and 28 October 1947, ibid. Rechtman and al-Dajani's son was in the 1990s a member of the Likud.

105. Aharon Danin's testimony, 23 April 1971, OHD-HU 57-9e.

106. Shakhevitz's testimony, 11 March 1971, OHD-HU 57-29.

107. Shalom Svardlov's testimony, 16 June 1971, OHD-HU 57-27.

108. Aharon Danin's testimony, 23 April 1971, OHD-HU 57-9e.

109. Aharon Danin's testimony, 24 November 1971, OHD-HU, 57-9h.

8. PRELUDE TO WAR

1. "In the Country and the Neighboring Countries," 18 November 1941, CZA S25/4131; report no. 235 by an informer, 12 November 1941, CZA S25/22336; Akram Zu'itar, *Bawakir*, 97–98. On previous attempts on Nashashibi's life, see report of 22 October 1940, HA 105/197. See also Nashashibi, *Jerusalem's Other Voice*, 81.

2. "In the Country and the Neighboring Countries," 18 November 1941, CZA S25/4131.

3. "The Arab Morale after Fakhri's Assassination," 28 November 1941, CZA S25/4131. "News from Nablus," 13 November 1941; Bin Nun's report, 20 November 1941 (Tiberias area); report by Shahor, 21 November 1941 (the Sharon); "From Beit She'an Area," 14 November 1941—all in CZA S25/8972.

4. "From Beit She'an Area," 14 November 1941, CZA S25/8972.

5. Report on the murder, 9 October 1940, CZA S25/22595; letter to "Sharoni," 18 October 1940, CZA S25/22311; report of 1 November 1940, CZA S25/22525.

6. "From the Watchman," 18 August 1941, CZA S25/8970 (preserved also in HA 105/197).

7. Y[a'akov] L[isser], "A Collection of Rumors and Impressions," 20 June 1940, CZA S25/22597; report of 22 October 1940, HA 105/197.

8. "News from Nablus," 7 January 1941, CZA S25/22318; "From Y[a'akov] C[ohen]," 18 November 1941, and "News from Nablus," 25 January 1941, both in CZA S25/22349.

9. On the maltreatment of Arabs because of their contact with Jews, see report of 9 July 1940, CZA S25/22311 (Jaffa); reports of 8 August and 25 August 1940, CZA S25/22581, and Eliahu Eitan to Danin, 22 October 1940, CZA S25/22619 (Lower Galilee); "Summary of Information from the North," 1 October 1942, CZA S25/22843; report of 17 January 1943, CZA S25/22342 (Jezreel Valley); "Taking Revenge of Arab Teacher," report of 7 October 1941, HA 105/197 (Qalansawa).

10. "Information" (Jezreel Valley), 26 December 1939, and report of 18 September 1941 (Galilee), both in CZA S25/22312; Landsman to Danin, 8 September 1940, CZA S25/22354 (Hula Valley); information dated 18 and 28 April 1943, CZA S25/22348 (Wadi 'Ara).

11. On threatening collaborators with revenge after Nazi victory, see report from Kfar Menachem, August 1940, CZA S25/22597; from the Sharon, 21 September 1940, CZA S25/22518; from "Mifratzi" (Western Galilee), 29 October 1940, CZA S25/22525; leaflet against collaboration, 6 June 1940 (Shweikeh), and "News from Nablus," 4 August 1940, both CZA S25/22311; leaflet against collaborators, Britons, and Zionists, 2 May 1941, received from Hamdallah, HA 105/197, and in HA 105/78 see leaflet from Jerusalem in the same spirit. See also "News from Nablus," 7 February 1942, CZA S25/22843; "News from Nablus," 14 June 1942, CZA S25/22339; "From A. A.," 6 August 1942, CZA S25/4131; leaflet dated 15 December 1940, CZA S25/22317.

12. Al-Hout, *Al-Qiyadat*, 469. These people were involved in attempts to revive formal Arab leadership in Palestine.

13. On political activity of the period, see ibid., 470–477.

14. Ibid.; see also Ya'akov Shimoni, *Arviyey Eretz Yisrael* [The Palestinian Arabs] (Tel Aviv, 1947), 347–348; Gelber, *Shorshey ha-Havatselet*, 665–667.

15. Muhammad Izzat Darwaza, *Hawla al-Haraka al-Arabiyya al-Haditha* [On the Modern Arab Movement] (Sidon, 1955), 4:38–39.

16. The fatwa is preserved in CZA S25/2991 (undated).

17. Leaflet of 22 February 1946, Haifa, and resolutions of a conference in that regard, both in ISA 65, 987/127.

18. Leaflet of 16 May 1946, Jerusalem, HA 105/63.

19. Leaflet of the economic committee of the Higher Arab Committee, 14 August 1946, Jerusalem, HA 105/63.

20. See, e.g., al-Difaʻ, 9 June 1946, 2 January 1947; Filastin, 16 August 1946.

21. Report of 7 July 1947, HA 105/358; al-Husseini to the chambers of commerce, 16 July 1947, ISA 65, 402/3510.

22. Arab Department to Komei, 15 May 1946, and "Arab News" of 25 June 1946, CZA S25/22381, which also reported on Arab neglect of the boycott and a decision to strengthen the surveillance. On the Legion's involvement, see HA 37/40/1 (a soldier who killed an Arab woman who went to a Jewish doctor), and report from 13 March 1946, HA 105/63.

23. Report of 22 August 1946, HA 105/63.

24. For copies of the warnings, see the Higher Arab Committee files, ISA 65, 402/3510.

25. The chief inspector in Jerusalem [to Jamal al-Husseini], 10 December 1946, ibid.

26. "List of Assassinations—Boycott 1946," HA 37/40/1.

27. Al-Khadra's notebook, July–August 1947, ISA 65, 330/827.

28. Al-Huriyya leaflets, translated into Hebrew, HA 105/263.

29. Ibid.

30. Leaflet no. 5, al-Huriyya, 29 July 1947, ISA 65, 392/3142.

31. In Jaffa there were also a few attacks on violators of the boycott, but such actions were sporadic.

32. Gideon Mark-Amir argues that the competition among groups that aimed to enforce the boycott contributed to its failure; see his "Ha-Maʻavak ha-Kalkali shel Arviyei Eretz Yisrael ba-Yishuv ha-Yehudi" [The Economic Struggle of the Palestinian Arabs against the Jewish Yishuv] (M.A. thesis, University of Jerusalem, 1985), 112–123.

33. Al-Wahda, 5 September 1947.

34. See such evaluation in a Shai report, 6 January 1947, HA 105/154.

35. Letters from Daliat al-Karmil to the Higher Arab Committee, ISA 65, 392/3142.

36. For details, see Rachelle Taqqu, "Peasants into Workmen: Internal Labor Migration and the Arab Village Community under the Mandate," in Joel S. Migdal, ed., Palestinian Society and Politics (Princeton, 1980), 261–285.

37. Al-Hout, Al-Qiyadat, 486–488. For a contemporary Zionist analysis, see Aharon Cohen, Tnuʻat ha-Poalim ha-Arvit [Arab Workers' Movement] (Haifa, 1947), 58–62 (in Hebrew).

38. Cohen, Tnuʻat, 69. Estimates of the number of organized workers were between 10,000 (Cohen) and 50,000 (Sami Taha).

39. "Briefing on the Activity of the Arab Department February–May [1944]," CZA S25/22124; report for May 1943–May 1944, ibid.

40. For photocopies of entries from the diary and their translation, see Yosef Washitz, "Jewish-Arab Relations in Haifa 1940–1948," in Ha-Aravim Mul ha-Tnuʻah ha-Tziyonit veha-Yishuv ha-Yehudi 1946–1950 [The Arabs versus the Zionist Movement and the Jewish Yishuv, 1946–1950] (Kiryat Tivon, 1987), 34–37 (in Hebrew).

41. Cohen, *Tnu'at*, 61–62, 69; al-Hout, *Al-Qiyadat*, 525–528.

42. Hacohen, *Et le-Saper*, 66–67, 305.

43. *Filastin*, 10 March 1945; *al-Difa'*, 10 March 1945; Department of Arab Affairs, "Quotes from Newspapers," 15 May 1946, CZA S25/22381. Placard from this period, 6 May 1945, HA 105/266; report of an informer on the play in al-Maliha, 11 May 1945, CZA S25/22555.

44. Bulletin of the Arab Department [Jewish Agency], 25 June 1946 (Muslim Brotherhood); bulletin of 14 June 1946 (Bludan); fund-raising for the Nation's Fund and reports on its activity, HA 105/266, 8/4, 8/4a, 8/5c.

45. Bulletin of the Arab Department, 15 May 1946, CZA S25/22381.

46. Bulletin of the Arab Department, 14 and 25 June 1946, ibid.

47. Tzur Co. to KKL, 29 April 1947, ISA 69.04, 928/7 (files of Ya'akov Solomon); Yosef Stromza's testimony, 26 March 1969, OHD-HU 57–5c.

48. Mustafa Hasan was a bitter rival of the mukhtar Na'aman of Battir, who had maintained contacts with Zionist intelligence services since the late 1920s, as mentioned in chapter 3.

49. Hasan to Higher Arab Committee, 13 December 1946, ISA 65, 337/1064.

50. For Zionist sources on his activity, see Malkov's testimony, 26 February 1974, OHD-HU 57–35h; Gissin's testimony, 26 January 1971, OHD-HU 57–13. The British authorities were also aware of his activity; see Gaza governor to the chief secretary, 20 March 1943, ISA 2, SF-215/40.

51. 'Ali Zu'bi to Higher Arab Committee, 21 July 1947, ISA 65, 323/522; A. Danin's testimony, 21 December 1970, OHD-HU 57–9b. A prominent figure of this family, Shafiq Qa'war, survived an assassination attempt during the revolt; see Nazareth police headquarters, "Nazareth Town" [1940s], ISA 17, 4212/8.

52. Letter from 'Isfiya to Higher Arab Committee, 10 September 1947, ISA 65, 392/3142; Shakhevitz's testimony, 10 March 1971, OHD-HU 57–20.

53. Anonymous letter to Higher Arab Committee, undated, ISA 65, 392/3142; Malkov's testimony, 15 January 1974, OHD-HU 57–35.

54. Dibbeh Fallah to Higher Arab Committee, 21 February 1947, ISA 65, 327/714. Muhammad al-Khatib to Higher Arab Committee, 22 May 1947 (southern districts), ISA 65, 325/595; Gissin's testimony, 26 January 1971, OHD-HU 57–13.

55. Al-Tamimi divided the sellers into three groups: those who had debts, those who needed money to cultivate their land, and the greedy. The first type should receive aid, the second should lease their land to the nation, and the third should be reeducated; memorandum of 1 July 1947, ISA 65, 413/3888. See other suggestions in ISA 65, 377/2618, and al-Khatib's in his letter to Higher Arab Committee, 22 May 1947, ISA 65, 325/595.

56. Shai report, 10 July 1947, HA 105/78, quotes an article against traitors that was censored—probably not the only one.

57. Undated fatwa, ISA 65, 413/3875.

58. Shai report, 7 July 1947, HA 105/358.

59. Ibid.

60. "Additional Details from the Youth Conference in Jaffa," 4 July 1947, HA 105/358.

61. Summary of a conversation between B. Joseph and the chief secretary, 26 March 1945, ISA 2, SF 215/40.

62. Shai report, 20 August 1945, HA 105/39; reports of 1 and 22 October 1945, HA 8/7.

63. According to an interview conducted by al-Hout; see *Al-Qiyadat*, 403.

64. On his contacts with the left-wing party ha-Shomer ha-Tsa'ir, see Ya'akov Hazan's speech, 26 December 1946, HA 105/54.

65. It is difficult to determine the exact number of assassinations for land selling because of lack of information about the real motivations of a few of them. Yosef Weitz in his *Hitnahlutenu* (164–165) mentions eight cases; Shai reports mentioned nine ("Summary of Land-Related Terror, 1946," HA 37/40/1); and I have found two additional cases.

66. Bulletin of the Arab Department, 20 May 1945, HA 105/266; "On the Murder of Taleb Subh," 25 February 1946, HA 105/265. The possibility that he was killed because of criminal activity or women affairs was also discussed; see reports of 20 February and 13 May 1946, HA 105/266.

67. Avraham's report, 11 March 1946, HA 105/266. On Salim's position in the Nation's Bank, see *Filastin*, 24 April 1947.

68. Translation of the placard, HA 105/265; "Internal Arab Terror January 1946–March 1947," 28 March 1947, CZA S25/2968.

69. "Events in Nazareth" [11 April 1946], CZA S25/2968.

70. "Internal Arab Terror January 1946–March 1947," 28 March 1947, CZA S25/2968.

71. As'ad Taha, who assisted Shakhevitz of the Shai and KKL, was described by the latter as a "proud, colorful and wild character. He liked to go out to the restaurants and cafés of Acre, to have a drink and talk freely." See Mordechai Shakhevitz, *Le-Pa'atey Mizrah u-ba-Levav Pnima* [To the Far East and Inside the Heart] (Kiryat Bialik, 1992), 232 (in Hebrew). For activity against *samasirah*, see Bulletin of the Arab Department, 25 June 1946, CZA S25/22381; see also a letter from the organization in Dir al-Ghusun to Higher Arab Committee, ISA 65, 392/3142; "Directing the Arab Terror in the Villages," 9 February 1947, HA 105/195.

72. Mandelman's testimony, 27 December 1972, OHD-HU 57–34; Feiglin's testimony, 27 December 1972, OHD-HU 57–21a.

73. On al-Tayyeb, see Feiglin's testimony (part e), 27 December 1972, OHD-HU 57–21a. Report on the murder in 'Anabta, October 1946, HA 105/265; personal sheet of the murderer, Abed Srur, HA 105/113; for other cases, see "Summary of Land-Related Terror," HA 37/40/1.

74. The police officer who investigated the first attempt on 'Abd al-Ra'ouf's life wrote that his land business with Jews may have been the reason, but he also suspected that he shot himself to receive a license for a gun; investigation reports of 18 January and 14 May 1946, ISA 17, 4215/274.

75. Barouchi's testimony, 22 January 1971, OHD-HU 57–10.

76. For different stages of the planning and implementation of this project, see Aharon Yafe, "The Redemption of the Ghazawiyya Land and the Relocation of the Tribe in Trans-Jordan," *Mehkarim be-Geografia shel Eretz Yisrael* [Studies in the Geography of Eretz Yisrael], vol. 13 (1993): 23–29 (in Hebrew).

77. Reports of 29 January and 3 April 1947, HA 105/263.

78. Bulletin of the Arab Department, 8 May 1947, ibid.

79. "Neron" in his report to Shai, 23 June 1947, ibid., suggested that the murder was done by another family member as a result of a dispute over the commission of the land deals. In his testimony (29 August 1974, OHD-HU 57–35k), Malkov argued that the killers were sent by nationalists.

80. I do not present all assassination attempts but illustrate the campaign against the *samasirah* by referring to the important cases. For additional attempts, see reports of 6 and 20 April 1947, HA 105/380, and 15 April 1947, HA 105/19. Kamel Hussein of the Hula Valley was one of the targets, but he survived the attempts until 1949, when he was killed by Syrian intelligence agents.

81. Odeh to Higher Arab Committee, 17 October 1946, ISA 65, 402/3510; report of 9 February 1947, HA 105/95.

82. Information received on 25 March 1946, HA 105/265; "From the Mouth of a Merchant," 2 October 1946, and "Briefing on the Situation in Jerusalem," 21 November 1946, both in HA 105/63; complaint to Higher Arab Committee, 22 January 1947, and Bandak to Higher Arab Committee, 28 January 1947, both in ISA 65, 402/3510.

83. Abbushi to Higher Arab Committee, 11 December 1946, and anonymous to Higher Arab Committee, 28 January 1947, both in ISA 65, 326/623. Without judging the accuracy of these pieces of information, we can nevertheless tell about the state of mind within various groups.

84. Sheikhs' letter [to Higher Arab Committee, undated], ISA 65, 413/3888.

85. Information received 22 October, 30 November 1945, and 31 December 1946, HA 8/7.

86. Report of 15 July 1947 ("Hayogev"), HA 105/358. Al-Hawwari himself was at the time in contact with Jewish Agency officials.

87. Gelber, *Shorshey ha-Havatselet*, 666.

88. Palmon's testimony, 24 May 1971, OHD-HU 57–24.

89. Gelber, *Shorshey ha-Havatselet*, 533.

90. A. Danin's testimony, 23 April 1971, OHD-HU 57–9e.

91. Gissin's testimony, 26 January 1971, OHD-HU 57–13.

92. For a complaint about the involvement of Arab national activists in land transactions with Jews, see letter from 'Isfiya to Higher Arab Committee, 10 September 1947, ISA 65, 392/3142.

93. Y. Shimoni to B. Joseph, "Our Contacts with the Druze," 20 March 1946, CZA S25/22159; "Warning the Druze," February 1946; "Abu Yusuf Reports," 3 May 1946; and "Threat Letters to Druze Sheikhs," 2 February 1947, all in HA 105/195.

94. Shem-Tov to Delphi [Shai], 6 April 1947, HA 105/325. According to this source, the attempt took place in the village of Safria (near Jaffa), and as a result al-Hawwari left Jaffa for a while.

95. Bulletin of the Arab Department, 20 May 1945, HA 105/266.

96. "Tsiklag" to Shai, 9 January 1947, HA 105/54; report of 15 April 1947, HA 105/19.

97. Yosef Weitz, ed., *Yosef Nahmani: Ish ha-Galil* [Yosef Nahmani: The Man of the Galilee] (Ramat Gan, 1969), 244 (in Hebrew); on contacts with Hussein,

see 186, 190, 218, where he is characterized as volatile but useful. On intelligence he provided to the Zionists, see Gelber, *Shorshey ha-Havatselet,* 692–693.

98. There was a previous attempt on the life of Fakhr al-Din, in July 1946; see his complaint to the police, 2 August 1946, ISA 17, 4215/275.

99. Police report of 27 March 1947, ISA 17, 4215/287; *Filastin,* 18 June 1947.

100. "An Attempt to Assassinate Jamal [al-Husseini]," report of 26 March 1947 and monthly reports of March and April, HA 105/263.

101. Danin, *Tsiyoni,* 174–175.

102. *Al-Ittihad,* 5 January, 16 February, and 14 April 1947, and also Rushdi Shahin to Higher Arab Committee, 2 August 1947, ISA 65, 326/652.

103. Summary of the Arab press, July 1947, HA 105/263. Even the meeting between the opposition leaders and the mufti held in Lebanon in October was not a sign of real unity, as we learn from the behavior of both parties in the following months. See Avraham Sela, "She'elat Erets Yisrael ba-Ma'arekhet ha-Bein-Arvit 1945–1948" [The Palestine Question in the Inter-Arab System . . . 1945–1948] (Ph.D. dissertation, Hebrew University, 1986), 394 (in Hebrew).

9. TREASON AND DEFEAT: THE 1948 WAR

1. Abdullah ['Abdallah], King of Jordan, *My Memoirs Completed: Al-Takmilah* (Washington, American Council of Learned Studies, 1954), accused the Arab states of leaving Jordan alone on the battlefield. At the same time he accused the Higher Arab Committee of being irresponsible and forcing its view on the Palestinians. The Jordanian officer, 'Abdallah al-Tal, described the Arab League's withdrawal from al-Ramla and Lydda as betrayal, he labeled the Jordanian premier, Tawfiq Abu-al-Huda, "traitor," and he argued that the disarmament of the Holy Jihad militia by 'Abdallah was also an act of treason; see his *Karithat Filastin: Mudhakkarat Abddullah al-Tal* [Palestine's Tragedy: The Memoirs of 'Abdallah al-Tal] (Acre, 1968), 261, 203, 359–360 (in Arabic). The commander of the Holy Jihad in the Jerusalem area, 'Abd al-Qader al-Husseini, is quoted as attacking the military committee in Damascus just before he was killed in al-Qastal: "You are criminals; you are traitors. It will be written in history that you have caused the loss of Palestine." These sentences were quoted in a leaflet distributed by the Orient House (the PLO headquarters in East Jerusalem) on the fiftieth anniversary of the battle of al-Qastal from the memoirs of one of al-Husseini's lieutenants, Bahjat Abu Gharbiyya, in his *Fi Khidm al-Nidal al-Arabi al-Filastini* [Within the Turbulence of the Palestinian Arab Struggle] (Beirut, 1993), 206–207.

2. Zvi Alpeleg, *Mi-Nekudat Mabato shel ha-Mufti* [From the Mufti's Point of View] (Tel Aviv, 1995), 51 (in Hebrew).

3. Higher Arab Committee decision, 30 November 1947, ISA 65, 366/2308.

4. See Gen. Ismail Safwat to Jamil Mardam Bey, "A Brief Report on the Situation in Palestine and a Comparison between the Forces . . . ," dated 23 March 1948, in Khalidi, "Selected Documents," 64–65.

5. Avraham Sela explained the low participation of the Palestinians in the fighting by the severe socioeconomic fissures that existed in Palestinian society;

the ideological, political, and institutional weakness of the national leadership; and the tendency to rely on the Arab countries. Another reason for the passivity was the absence of most of the Higher Arab Committee members from Palestine. See Avraham Sela, "Ha-Aravim ha-Falastinim," 191. For analysis of the weakness of the Higher Arab Committee, see also Khalaf, *Politics in Palestine,* 155–158.

6. All reports dated December 1947–February 1948 in HA 105/72. On Lydda, see report of 27 March 1948, and "Disagreement between Lydda's Commander and the Population," 30 March 1948, both in IDFA 7633/49/17. "Tsefa" intelligence report, "The Situation in the Lower Galilee," 17 March 1948, IDFA 7249/49/86.

7. For reports on agreements from various localities, including Deir Yasin, see HA 105/72. The mukhtar of Deir Yasin reported on 2 February 1948 that 'Abd al-Qader al-Husseini asked the villagers to volunteer to his militia but was refused. An unconfirmed Arab source reported a day before the attack on Deir Yasin that the people of the village and of 'Ayn Karem were asked to host *mujahidin* (Arab fighters). The latter agreed, but the former refused and "argued that they are in a peaceful relationship with their Jewish neighbors and the presence of foreigners would disturb it"; "'Ayn Karem," 7 April 1948, IDFA 6400/1949/66.

8. HA 105/72; for additional contacts in Wadi 'Ara, see IDFA 6400/1949/66.

9. "Lion" [Hawwari], "The Situation in Jaffa," 11 December 1947, CZA S25/4011, and see Muhammad Nimer al-Hawwari, *Sirr al-Nakba* [The Secret of the Nakba] (Nazareth, 1955), 41ff (in Arabic). For other local peace initiatives from the same time, see HA 105/54a.

10. All reports dated December 1947–February 1948 in HA 105/72; on Subbarin and its neighboring villages, see also Tene reports, 9 May 1948, IDFA 922/75/1061.

11. "Arab News," 21 March 1948, IDFA 2644/49/353; on Kababir, see report of 24 February 1948, IDFA 7249/49/131. According to the mukhtar of Ma'lul, the Arab Liberation Army's soldiers in the village killed sheep and cattle and shot a few people, so the rest ran away; testimony dated 3 August 1948, IDFA 922/52/1267. An example from the Jerusalem vicinity: "Activists' Delegation Approached Abu-Ghosh and Qatanna," 22 January 1948, IDFA 5254/49/104. For the Lower Galilee, see "Dammuni Reports," 22 February 1948, HA 105/54.

12. Report on a meeting dated 22 October 1947, CZA S25/3300.

13. Ibid.

14. This was the assessment of the heads of the 'Azzi family from the Beit Jibrin area; see "Meeting with Hajj Muhammad al-'Azzi," 16 January 1948, HA 105/72. Hasan Muhanna, an influential leader from Masmiyya, had a similar view; "Meeting with Hasan A. Aziz Muhanna of Masmiyya," 4 February 1948, ibid. 'Abd al-Ra'uf 'Abd al-Razeq, the brother of 'Aref, commander in the revolt, also supported the annexation of the Arab parts of Palestine to Transjordan, according to a report of a meeting conducted with him on 13 January 1948, HA 105/215. Mustafa [Abu] Hantash of Qaqun told his Jewish neighbors news about the situation and promised to work together with 'Abdallah to control the

mufti and his men; "Meeting with Mustafa Hantash in Gan ha-Shomron," 6 February 1948, ibid.

15. "In the Arab Camp," 4 January 1948, HA 105/142. Sela, "Ha-Aravim ha-Falastinim," 141, 146.

16. "A Talk in the Evening after the Fast," 2 September 1947, HA 105/54. The source was probably a villager from Tira.

17. Khalaf, *Politics in Palestine*, 157.

18. 'Aref al-'Aref, *Nakbat Bayt al-Maqdis wal-Firdus al-Mafqud* [The Catastrophe of the Holy City and the Lost Paradise] (Saida, 1956), 1:30 (in Arabic). See also Avi Shlaim, *The Politics of Partition: King Abdullah, the Zionists and Palestine, 1921–1951* (Oxford, 1990), 104; Joseph Nevo, *Abdallah and Palestine* (London, 1996), 55–58, 122–123.

19. "The Position of the Fellahin in the Gaza Region," Tene report, 15 February 1948 (the source is defined as serious), HA 105/72.

20. Undated Haganah report titled "Arabs Who Tend to Cooperate with Jews," HA 105/54. For a detailed analysis of the political contacts during the war in Haifa, see Washitz, "Jewish-Arab Relations," 21–37. The tendency to reach agreements with Jews was based, according to Washitz, on the interests of the civil society as opposed to political interests.

21. Reports on the continuation of commercial contacts—and attempts to enforce the boycott—are preserved in HA 105/66. For different Zionist opinions in regard to the reliance on the opposition, see Nimrod, *War or Peace*, 69–74.

22. Dammuni's reports, 22 February 1948, HA 105/54; "Beit Makhsir," 13 May 1948, IDFA 5545/49/114; Tsori to Tene, "Meeting with Representative of the Villages of Ulam, Hadtha and Sirin," 9 May 1948, HA 105/54.

23. Report on a meeting with an informer, 28 January 1948, HA 105/72. "Ha-Yogev" shared this view. After the arrival of the Iraqi volunteers in Jaffa, he said, "You should forcefully strike the Arab army who just came. . . . [I]f not—their number might increase"; "Extracts from Conversations with ha-Yogev," 11 February 1948, HA 105/215.

24. "Ha-Yogev" report, 5 January 1948, CZA S25/9051. This is a surprising report since al-Husseini had many supporters in Surif, and one of his lieutenants, Ibrahim Abu Dayye, was from this village. Thus the Shai was not sure of its reliability. An informer from the Sharon area analyzed the weakness of al-Husseini in this region by referring to his cruelty and the fact that he continued the "gangs' methods"; "The Situation in the Sharon," 18 February 1948, HA 105/215.

25. There were Muslims who argued that Christians did not take part in the national struggle and ignored the boycott of the Jews. Sometimes it was true. On the other hand, the centrality of Islam in the Palestinian Arab national movement was among the reasons for this alienation. For reports on interreligion tensions in Shfa'amer, see 3 February 1948 (Jerusalem), 9 February 1948 (Haifa), 11 February 1948, HA 105/195. In at least one case—the village of Bassa in the Galilee—it is argued that the Christians' relations with Jews were better than the Muslims'; see David Koren, *Ha-Galil ha-Ma'aravi be-Milhemet ha-Atsma'ut* [Western Galilee in the War of Independence] (Tel Aviv, 1988), 62 (in Hebrew).

26. Arab Liberation Army files, in IDFA 1/57/158. Most Arab Liberation Army files in the IDFA are still classified, but the titles of many documents appear

in a special catalogue edited in 1962; see Israel Defense Forces Archives, *Tsva ha-Hatsala bi-Tkufat Milhemet ha-Atsma'ut* [The ALA during the War of Independence) (in Hebrew). See also report of 18 January 1948, HA 105/195.

27. On the contacts with these two people in 1948, see ISA Ministry of Foreign Affairs 3749/1 and 3749/2. For al-Dajani's support for partition, see Shimoni to G. Meirson, 27 June 1947, CZA S25/3300. 'Abdallah al-Tal criticized King 'Abdallah for appointing al-Karami to negotiate with the Jews, since he was married to a Jewish woman, his brother was killed for collaboration, and he himself was a supporter of the Jews; see *Karithat Filastin*, 344.

28. Report of 12 March 1948, HA 105/54.

29. Tiroshi to Tene, "Arab Plan to Explode the Yarkon Bridge," 12 February 1948, HA 105/72. Kibbutz Na'an, *Adama Na'aneit* [Land Replies] [Na'an, 1981], 98 (in Hebrew). "Explanation of the List of Objects in the Photo of Qaqun," IDFA 6400/49/66.

30. See the catalogue of the Arab Liberation Army documents (see note 26, above). See also anonymous letter to the Arab Liberation Army with names of smugglers of cows to Jews, 26 March 1948, HA 105/66.

31. Intelligence officer, Front B, "Report on Interrogation of an Arab [POW]," 2 January 1949, IDFA 1041/49/26. This person had been imprisoned in Tulkarem for collaboration with Jews and was captured near the border when he returned.

32. Musa Goldenberg, *Ve-Hakeren Odena Kayemet* [And the Fund Still Exists] (Merhavia, 1965), 199-201 (in Hebrew).

33. Quoted in Alter Walner, *Hamushim lifnei ha-Mahane* [Armed in Front of the Camp] (Tel Aviv, 1984), 233 (in Hebrew); see also 176-177, 235, on the information supplied by those informers, some of them probably cattle merchants.

34. "Report from a Person Trained . . . in Qatanna," [December 1947], HA 105/358.

35. Ha-Ganan (the "Gardener") reports of 23, 29 January and 10 February 1948, HA 105/215. On the explosion at Haita's house, see "Events among the Arabs of Haifa," January 1948, IDFA 7249/49/152.

36. On this operation, see Slutski, *Sefer Toldot*, 3:1561-1562; on the source of the information, see Avraham Eilon, *Hativat Giva'ti be-Milhemet ha-Komemiut* [Givati Brigade in the War of Independence] (Tel Aviv, 1959), 392 (in Hebrew).

37. Reports delivered by informers from Hebron and the Jerusalem area, including members of the Holy Jihad, are preserved in IDFA 5254/49/104 (December 1947 onward) and 2384/50/16 (summer 1948). Reports from Nablus and Samaria villages, IDFA 2384/50/10 and 7249/49/172. Reports of informers from Jenin and the Triangle, IDFA 1041/49/26. Reports on Arab League units that entered Palestine from summer 1948 onward, IDFA 1261/49/10. These are only some of the available examples—most intelligence files of 1948 in IDFA are still classified.

38. Z. Steinberg to the Israeli police—Northern District, "The Military Government in the Central Areas" [1952], ISA 79, 2293/11.

39. Sayf al-Din Zu'bi, *Shahed Ayan: Mudhakkarat* [Eyewitness: Memoirs] (Shfa'amer, 1987), 10-11 (in Arabic).

40. Copy of the agreement signed in July 21, 1939, HA 8/2 (general files). Rabbah 'Awad's statement against the revolt was published in *Davar*, 13 August 1939. An intelligence file about the sheikh is in HA 105/416. For an interview with him that contains both information and interesting analysis, see Swedenburg, *Memories of Revolt*, 157–164.

41. Report of 26 January 1948, HA 105/215.

42. Supreme Court plea 19/50, also in IDFA 721/72/844.

43. Shai officer Amnon Yanai assumed that most Arabs who collaborated with the Jewish intelligence did so because they were persecuted by Arab nationalists; see Koren, *Ha-Galil ha-Ma'aravi*, 62. There were, however, Arabs who evaluated the situation more clearly than the national leadership, which was outside Palestine for years, and did not believe that the Arabs could defeat the Jews.

44. Advisor for Arab Affairs—Alexandroni Brigade to IDF general staff, 9 July 1948, IDFA 6400/49/66.

45. "Report of Sapir on the Operation of 16.9," IDFA 2384/50/8.

46. "Patrol by the Two Arabs in Kufr Qara'," 18 September 1948, IDFA 2384/50/8. Headquarters of the Northern Front, daily report of 26 September 1948, and "'Ar'ara," 27 September 1948, both in IDFA 1041/49/26.

47. "Report on Patrol," 13 October 1948, IDFA 7249/49/178.

48. "Acquisition of Weapons from Arabs by Lehi-Binyamina," report to Tene, 25 December 1947, HA 112/1175; Tiroshi to Tene, "Arrests of Arabs," 29 April 1948, HA 105/254; Front B, intelligence, "Report of Interrogation of an Arab," 2 January 1949, IDFA 1041/49/26; report to Tene, "Mahmoud Rashid," 1 January 1948, HA 112/1175; Yeruham to Tene, "Yusuf of Abu-Ghosh," 16 May 1948, HA 112/1175; Kiryat Anavim to the Jewish Agency, 29 April 1948, CZA S25/9194.

49. Yiftah Brigade to the council [general staff], 23 and 28 May 1948, IDFA 922/75/1216; Slutski, *Sefer Toldot*, 1596.

50. Ministry of Minorities Affairs, Safed, report of 22 September 1948, ISA 79, 306/109.

51. Morris, *Birth*, 120, 122–124.

52. Reports "top secret, urgent" and "'Ali al-Qasem," ISA 65, 336/2292, sent by the intelligence officer of the Arab forces in Jaffa.

53. See, e.g., Wasfi al-Tal of the Arab Liberation Army [later the Jordanian premier], as quoted in Mas'ud Ghana'im, *Sakhnin* (Sakhnin, 2000), 19 (in Arabic).

54. Tsori to Tene, "Information about the Zu'bis," 27 April 1948, HA 105/54.

55. IDF intelligence service, "Emigration of Palestinian Arabs 1 June 1947– 1 June 1948," quoted in Morris, *Birth*, 67.

56. Sayf al-Din survived two attempts on his life in 1947; see British police reports, ISA 17, 359/47. During the war the Arab Liberation Army issued an order to arrest him; Yarmuk Brigade to Lebanese Battalion, August 1948, IDFA Arab Liberation Army 1/57/279.

57. Tsori to Tene, "Events in Nazareth and the Region," 4 July 1948, HA 105/154; "On the Problem of the Arab Refugees" (conversation of Ezra Danin with Hussein Zu'bi), 8 October 1948, IDFA 121/50/178.

58. Yehoshua Felman [Palmon], "Our Activities among the Druze," 5 August 1948, ISA MFA 2565/8. Those who led the cooperation with the Jews became members of the Israeli parliament, including Jaber Dahash Mu'adi, who was sentenced to prison by the British for murder. Years later, in 1981, the sons of Mu'adi murdered Bedouin sheikh Hamad Abu Rbei'ah, who competed with him for a seat in the Knesset.

59. Giora Zeid, who was involved in the event, described it to Ben-Ami, *Arayot Sho'agim*, 74–76. Lila Parsons wrote that Wahhab was not in contact with the Jewish forces until May 10; see her "The Palestinian Druze in the 1947–1949 Arab-Israeli War," *Israel Studies*, vol. 2, no. 1 (1997): 79.

60. Ben-Ami, *Arayot Sho'agim*, 76–77.

61. Karmeli Brigade—information, 24 May 1948, IDFA 128/51/71.

62. Yehoshua Felman [Palmon], "Our Activities among the Druze," 5 August 1948, ISA MFA 2565/8; letter of al-Diab to the Israeli Chief of Staff and the Inspector General of the Israeli police [1953?], ISA 79, 2179/19.

63. Felman, "Our Activities among the Druze," 5 August 1948, ISA MFA 2565/8. For a detailed description of the events in the Lower Galilee and Bedouin-Druze relations, see Rohn Eloul, "Culture Change in Bedouin Tribe: An Ethnographic History of the 'Arab Al-Hjerat, Lower Galilee, Israel, 1790–1977" (Ph.D. dissertation, University of Michigan, 1982), 143–152.

64. Ghan'im, *Sakhnin*, 17–24; earlier that year the IDF had occupied the village but withdrew from it for lack of manpower.

65. Saleh al-Diab to Haifa police, 18 June 1950, ISA 79, 139/30.

66. Zevulon police—investigation bureau to the station inspector, 31 July 1950, ibid. Saleh, according to this report, was involved in killing Jews and sent the letter in order to deceive the authorities and get a job as a muezzin.

67. "Uri" to "Ger," 23 July 1948, IDFA 128/51/71.

68. Information from the intelligence officer of the Northern Front, 30 October 1948, IDFA 715/49/16.

69. 'Awad's affidavit to the Supreme Court, Plea 19/50, also in IDFA 721/72/844.

70. Representatives of Abu-Ghosh to the Knesset's speaker [July 1950], ISA 79, 260/2.

71. This seems to be the case in Eilaboun, where the Christian residents raised a white flag while the Arab Liberation Army continued the fight.

72. Israeli police, Ramla special branch, 3 November 1960, ISA 79, 351/15.

73. Abu-Ghosh to Israeli minister of foreign affairs Moshe Sharett, 9 July 1950, ISA MFA 2564/22. The general picture is confirmed by a letter from Kibbutz Kiryat Anavim, 29 April 1948, in which they ask the Jewish Agency to assist their neighbors of Abu-Ghosh, CZA S25/9194.

74. Moshe Elyovitz's testimony, 27 April 1972, OHD-HU 57–30.

75. Ben-Ami, *Arayot Sho'agim*, 82, quoting Hankin, the commander of the Minorities Unit.

76. Leaflet, December 1947, HA 105/54; undated letter, HA 105/154.

77. Leaflet of 29 February 1948, HA 105/358; report of 24 March 1948, HA 105/66; Yavne to Tene, "Confirmed Information," dated 6 April 1948, HA 105/154.

78. Haifa headquarters—intelligence, report [February 1948], translated by the Haganah intelligence service on 12 May 1948, HA 105/45.

79. Al-Kafi's report, translated on 31 March 1948, HA 105/154; undated report on the execution of Qabalan, ibid.

80. "Tene's Information," 9 January 1948, IDFA 922/75/1205. "News from Jaffa," 13 January 1948, HA 112/1175. Another suspected of collaboration with Lehi, who was not captured, was married, according to the rumors, "to a [Jewish] Yemenite woman," lived in Tel Aviv, and spoke Hebrew and Yiddish; "Tene" news, 21 January 1948, HA 105/32.

81. "Rumors among the Arabs," 21 January 1948, HA 112/1175; al-'Aref, *Nakbat Bayt*, 81. "Reliable News," 13 April 1948, IDFA 500/48/59. Years later a collaborator from the nearby village of Qalunia who converted in the 1960s to Judaism claimed to be the person behind the al-Husseini killing; Dani Rubinstein, "Why Did Abd al-Qadir Talk in English?" *Ha'aretz*, 6 November 1998.

82. The Arab newspaper *al-Sarih* wrote about a collaborator who participated in the psychological warfare and was caught by Arab forces; see translation from 31 March 1948 in HA 105/154. The case is also mentioned in al-'Aref, *Nakbat Bayt*, 247. In his testimony (HA 168/14), Palmon mentioned this kind of activity.

83. "Arab Prisoners," 14 April 1948, HA 105/154. See also Hawwari, *Sirr al-Nakba*, 6.

84. National committee in Lydda to the commander of the local garrison, 2 April 1948; summons of suspects, 20 April 1948; national committee in Lydda to the commander of the local garrison, demand to investigate suspects, 9 June 1948, all in ISA 65, 342/1278.

85. Reports of 5, 9, 20 May and 26 June 1948, HA 105/154; "Reports of Informers," June 1948, ibid.

86. Reports of June 1948 and 7 July 1948, ibid.

87. Hawwari, *Sirr al-Nakba*, 194–195.

88. Report of 24 March 1948, HA 105/66; Tiroshi to Tene, "Arrests of Arabs," 29 April 1948, HA 105/254 (also in IDFA 6400/49/66); "The Situation in Nazareth according to an Arab Driver of the Municipality," 17 June 1948, HA 105/154. The origin of the myth of the "secret mark" is not known.

89. Appendix no. 1 to the daily intelligence report of 28 October 1948, IDFA 2384/50/6.

90. Anis al-Qasim, *Min al-Tiya ila al-Quds* [From the Desert to al-Quds] (Tripoli, 1965), quoted in Yehoshafat Harkavi, *Ha-Falastinim mi-Tardema le-Hit'orerut* [The Palestinians: From Quiescence to Awakening] (Jerusalem, 1979), 10 (in Hebrew).

91. The youth of Beisan to Higher Arab Committee, 25 December 1947, ISA 65, 346/1489; "Report on Events in Haifa," 11 February 1948, IDFA 7249/49/152.

92. Tene report, 7 April 1948, IDFA 7633/49/17.

93. Yosef Olitski, *Mi-Me'ora'ot le-Hagana* [From Riots to Defense: Chapters in the History of the Haganah in Tel Aviv, November 1947–15 May 1948] (Tel Aviv, 1949), 41 (in Hebrew).

94. Malkov's testimony, 24 February 1972, OHD-HU 57–35g.

95. Abu Iyyad, *Le-Lo Moledet* [Without a Homeland: Conversations with Eric Rouleau] (Tel Aviv, 1983), 32–33 (in Hebrew).

96. Report of 28 December 1947, HA 105/358; Slutski, *Sefer Toldot,* 3:1415.

97. Tene from "a reliable Jewish source," 21 February 1948, HA 105/215. The mukhtar of Lifta, Muhammad Issa, was detained by the Holy Jihad a bit later; "Suba," 22 April 1948, IDFA 5545/49/114.

98. Report by "Khalil," June 1948, HA 105/154. On bribing an Iraqi judge to release an Arab agent of the IDF, see a document of the Israeli police in regard to this person, who built his house without a permit, 18 April 1957, ISA 79, 77/7.

99. Al-Hout, *Al-Qiyadat,* 630.

100. Hawwari, *Sirr al-Nakba,* 4–12, and see there his definitions of treason.

101. My interview with Hasan 'Abd al-Fattah Darwish, July 1992. One should not necessarily conclude that Darwish publicly advocated negotiation with the Jews at the time, but his deeds testify to his negative attitude to the war.

102. Two exceptions are al-'Aref, who was close to the Palestinian mainstream camp, and al-Hawwari, who opposed the formal leadership.

103. Salient examples are Imil Habibi [Emile Habiby], *The Secret Life of Sa'id: The Pessopsimist* (London, 1985), and Elias Khury, *Gates of the Sun* (New York, 2006).

104. Hillel Cohen, *Aravim Tovim* [Good Arabs: The Israeli Intelligence and the Israeli Arabs] (Jerusalem, 2006).

CONCLUSION

1. Anderson, *Imagined Communities,* 7.

2. Hans Kohn, *Nationalism: Its Meaning and History* (Princeton, 1955), 9.

3. Ernest Gellner, *Nation and Nationalism: New Perspectives on the Past* (Malden, Mass., 2006), 1.

4. Eugen Weber, *Peasants into Frenchmen: The Modernization of Rural France, 1870–1914* (Stanford, Calif.,1976), 292–299.

5. Ibid., 114.

6. Quoted in Malcolm Yapp, *The Near East since the First World War* (London, 1996), 69–70.

Bibliography

HEBREW SOURCES

Newspapers

ha-Boker
Davar
Do'ar ha-Yom
Ha'aretz
Omer
ha-Tsofe

Books and Articles

Abu Iyyad. *Le-Lo Moledet* [Without a Homeland: Conversations with Eric Rouleau]. Trans. Nurit Peled. Jerusalem: Mifras, 1983.

Alpeleg, Zvi. *Mi-Nekudat Mabato shel ha-Mufti* [From the Mufti's Point of View]. Tel Aviv: Tel Aviv University, 1995.

Arnon-Ohana, Yuval. *Falahim ba-Mered ha-Arvi 1936–1939* [Fellahin in the Arab Revolt in Palestine]. Tel Aviv: Student Union of Tel Aviv University, 1978.

Ashbel, Aminadav. *Hakhsharat ha-Yishuv* [Land Development Company]. Jerusalem: LDC, 1976.

Assaf, Michael. "Arviyey ha-Arets in 5694" [The Arabs of the Country in 1934]. In *Sefer Hashana shel Eretz Yisrael* [Eretz Yisrael yearbook]. Edited by Asher Barash. Tel-Aviv: Shem, 1935.

Avneri, Arye. *Ha-Hityashvut ha-Yehudit ve-Ta'anat ha-Nishul* [Jewish Settlement and the Claim on Dispossession]. Tel Aviv: Ha-Kibbutz ha-Me'uhad, 1980.

Bar-Adon, Pesach. *Be-Ohaley Midbar* [In Desert Tents]. Jerusalem: Kiryat Sefer, 1981.

Ben-Ami, Uriel. *Arayot Sho'agim Bimtula* [Lions Roar in Metula]. Tel Aviv: Ministry of Defense Press, 1990.

Ben-Natan, Yigal. *Talja Arsan.* Tel Aviv: Poalim, 1981.

Bernstein, Deborah. "Brit Poaley Eretz-Yisrael" [Palestine Labor League]. In *Aravim vi-Yhudim bi-Tkufat ha-Mandat* [Arabs and Jews in the Mandate

Period]. Edited by Ilan Pappe. Givat Haviva: Institute for Peace Research, 1995.

Cohen, Aharon. *Tnu'at ha-Poalim ha-Arvit* [Arab Workers' Movement]. Haifa: ha-Histadrut, 1947.

Danin, Ezra. *Te'udot u-Dmuyot me-Ginzey ha-Knufiyot ha-Arviyot 1936–1939* [Documents and Characters from the Archives of the Arab Gangs in the 1936–1939 Riots]. Jerusalem: Magnes, 1984.

———. *Tsiyoni be-Khol Tnay* [A Zionist under Any Condition]. Jerusalem: Kidum, 1987.

Eilon, Avraham. *Hativat Giva'ti be-Milhemet ha-Komemiut* [Givati Brigade in the War of Independence]. Tel Aviv: Ma'arakhot, 1959.

Eldad, Yisrael. *Ma'aser Rishon* [First Tenth]. Tel Aviv: Lehi Veterans, 1960.

Elyashar, Eliahu. *Li-Hyot im Falastinim* [To Live with Palestinians]. Jerusalem: Sephardic Community Committee, 1975.

Erlich, Reuven. *Bisvakh ha-Levanon 1918–1958* [In the Lebanese Tangle, 1918–1958]. Tel Aviv: Ministry of Defense Press, 2000.

Eshel, Tsadok. *Ma'arkhot ha-Hagana be-Haifa* [The Haganah Battles in Haifa]. Tel Aviv: Ministry of Defense Press, 1978.

Even, Dan. *Shnot Sherut* [Years of Service]. Tel Aviv: Milo, 1973.

Eyal, Yigal. *Ha-Intifada ha-Rishona* [The First Intifada: The Suppression of the Arab Revolt by the British Army in Palestine]. Tel-Aviv: Ma'arakhot, 1998.

Gabbay, Moshe. *Falastinim al Falastin* [Palestinians on Palestine: Documents and Testimonies]. Tel Aviv: Seminar ha-Kibutzim, 1988.

Gelber, Yoav. *Shorshey ha-Havatselet* [The Roots of the Lily: The Intelligence in the Yishuv, 1918–1947]. Tel-Aviv: Ministry of Defense Press, 1992.

Glass, Yosef. "Rekhishat Karka ve-Shimusheha be-Ezor Abu Ghosh 1873–1948" [Land Purchase and Use in the Abu-Ghosh Area, 1873–1948]. *Kathedra*, vol. 62 (1991): 107–122.

Goldenberg, Musa. *Ve-Hakeren Odena Kayemet* [And the Fund Still Exists]. [Merhavia: ha-Kibutz ha-Artsi, 1965].

Grossman, David. *Ha-Kfar ha-Arvi u-Vnotav* [Expansion and Desertion: The Arab Village and Its Offshoots in Ottoman Palestine]. Jerusalem: Yad Ben Tsvi, 1994.

Habas, Brakha. *Sefer Me'ora'ot Tartsav* [The Book of 1936 Riots]. Tel Aviv: Davar, 1937.

Hacohen, David. *Et le-Saper* [Time to Tell]. Tel Aviv: Am Oved, 1974.

Hadani, Ever. *Me'ah Shnot Shmira be-Yisrael* [One Hundred Years of Guarding in Israel]. Tel Aviv: Chechik, 1955.

Harel, Issar. *Bitahon ve-Demokratya* [Defense and Democracy]. Tel Aviv: Idanim, 1989.

Harizman, Mordechai A. *Nahshonei ha-Hula* [The Pioneers of the Hula]. Jerusalem and Yesod ha-Ma'alah: Merkaz, 1958.

Harkavi, Yehoshafat. *Ha-Falastinim mi-Tardema le-Hit'orerut* [The Palestinians: From Quiescence to Awakening]. Jerusalem: Magnes, 1979.

Hasson, Yitzhak. *Ha-Zaken va-Ani* [The Old Man and Me: The Personal Account of Lehi's Head of Intelligence]. Tel Aviv: Brerot, 1993.

Havakuk, Ya'akov. *'Akevot ba-Hol: Gashashim Bedvim be-Sherut Tsahal*

[Tracks in the Sand: Bedouin Trackers in the Service of the IDF]. Tel Aviv: Ministry of Defense Press, 1998.

Israel Defense Forces Archives. *Tsva ha-Hatsala bi-Tkufat Milhemet ha-Atsma'ut: Katalog Te'udot* [The ALA during the War of Independence: A Catalogue of Documents]. Tel Aviv: IDFA, 1962.

Kahanov, Michael. "Emdato shel Ibn-Saud Klapei Sikhsukh Eretz Yisrael bein Shtei Milhamot Olam" [Ibn Sa'ud's Position toward the Palestine Conflict during the Intra-war Period]. M.A. thesis, Tel Aviv University, 1980.

Kena'an, Haviv. *200 Yemei Harada* [200 Days of Dread]. Tel Aviv: Mul-Art, 1974.

Kibbutz Na'an. *Adama Na'aneit* [Land Replies]. Na'an, 1981.

Kimmerling, Barouch. *Bein Hevra li-Mdina* [Between Society and State]. Tel Aviv: Open University, 1991.

———. *Ha-Ma'avak 'al ha-Karka'ot* [The Struggle over the Land]. Jerusalem: Hebrew University Press, 1974.

Kisch, Frederick. *Yoman Eretz-Yisraeli* [Palestine Diary]. Jerusalem: Ahiasaf, 1939.

Koren, David. *Ha-Galil ha-Ma'aravi be-Milhemet ha-Atsma'ut* [Western Galilee in the War of Independence]. Tel Aviv: Ministry of Defense Press, 1988.

Layish, Aharon. "Ha-Mimsad ha-Dati ba-Gada ha-Ma'aravit" [The Religious Establishment in the West Bank.] In *Eser Shnot Shilton Yisraeli bi-Yehuda ve-Shomron* [Ten Years of Israeli Rule in Judea and Samaria, 1967–1977]. Edited by Rafi Yisraeli. Jerusalem: Magnes, 1981.

Lockman, Zachary. " 'We Opened the Arabs' Brains': Zionist Socialist Discourse and the Rail Workers of Palestine, 1919–1929" (in Hebrew). In *Aravim vi-Yhudim bi-Tkufat ha-Mandat* [Arabs and Jews in the Mandate Period]. Edited by Ilan Pappe. Givat Haviva: Institute for Peace Research, 1995.

Mamat, Raziel, and Avi Bleir. *Me-Nikrot Tsurim* [From the Clefts of Rocks: The Amazing Story of Ya'akov Barazani]. Tel Aviv: Ministry of Defense Press, 1979.

Mark-Amir, Gideon. "Ha-Ma'avak ha-Kalkali shel Arviyei Eretz Yisrael ba-Yishuv ha-Yehudi" [The Economic Struggle of the Palestinian Arabs against the Jewish Yishuv]. M.A. thesis, Hebrew University of Jerusalem, 1985.

Nimrod, Yoram. *Brerat ha-Shalom ve-Derekh ha-Milhama* [War or Peace: Formation of Patterns in Israeli-Arab Relations, 1947–1950]. Givat Haviva: Institute for Peace Research, 2000.

Olitski, Yosef. *Mi-Me'ora'ot le-Hagana* [From Riots to Defense: Chapters in the History of the Haganah in Tel Aviv, November 1947–15 May 1948]. Tel Aviv: ha-Hagana, 1949.

Ravina, Yirmiahu. *Agudat ha-Shomrim* [The Guards' Association]. Tel Aviv: ha-Shomer be-Yisrael, 1965.

Reichman, Shalom. *Mi-Ma'achaz le-Eretz Moshav* [From an Outpost to a Settled Land]. Jerusalem: Yad Ben Tsvi, 1979.

Ro'i, Ya'akov. "Nisyonotehem shel ha-Mosadot ha-Tsiyoniyim le-Hashpia al ha-Itonut ha-Aravit be-Erets Yisrael, 1908–1914" [Attempts of Zionist Institutions to Influence the Arab Press in Palestine, 1908–1914]. *Tsiyon*, vol. 32 (1967): 201–227.

Rubinstein, Dani. "Why Did Abd al-Qadir Talk in English?" *Ha'aretz,* 6 November 1998.

Rubinstein, Elyakim. "Ha-Tipul ba-She'ela ha-Aravit bi-Shnot ha-Esrim veha-Shloshim" [Dealing with the Arab Question in the 1920s and the 1930s]. *Ha-Tsiyonut,* vol. 12 (1987): 209–242.

———. "Yehudim ve-Aravim be-Iriyot Erets Yisrael (1926–1933)" [Jews and Arabs in Palestinian Municipalities (1926–1933)]. *Kathedra,* vol. 51 (1989): 122–147.

Salomon, Shimri. "Sherut ha-Yedi'ot shel ha-Hagana u-Proyekt Skirot ha-yishuvim ha-Aravim be-erets Yisrael 1940–1948" [The Haganah's Arab Intelligence Service and the Project of Surveying the Arab Settlements in Palestine, 1940–1948]. *Daf me-ha-Slik* [A Sheet from the Cache: The Haganah Archive Quarterly], vols. 9–10 (December 2001): 1–29.

Sela, Avraham. "Ha-Aravim ha-Falastinim be-Milhemet 1948" [The Palestinian Arabs in the 1948 War]. In *Ha-Tnu'ah ha-Leumit ha-Falastinit: Me-imut le-Hashlama?* [The Palestinian National Movement: From Conflict to Reconciliation?]. Edited by Moshe Maoz and B. Z. Kedar. Tel Aviv: Ministry of Defense Press, 1996.

———. "She'elat Erets Yisrael ba-Ma'arekhet ha-Bein-Arvit 1945–1948" [The Palestine Question in the Inter-Arab System . . . 1945–1948]. Ph.D. dissertation, Hebrew University, 1986.

Shakhevitz, Mordechai. *Le-Pa'atey Mizrah u-ba-Levav Pnima* [To the Far East and Inside the Heart]. Kiryat Bialik: Gderot, 1992.

Shaltiel, Elie. *Pinhas Rutenberg.* Tel Aviv: Am Oved, 1990.

Sharett, Moshe. *Yoman Medini* [Political Diary]. Tel Aviv, 1976.

Shimoni, Ya'akov. *Arviyey Eretz Yisrael* [The Palestinian Arabs]. Tel Aviv: Am Oved, 1947.

———. "Ha-aravim Likrat Milhemet Yisrael-Arav 1945–1948" [The Arabs toward the Israeli-Arab War, 1945–1948]. *Ha-Mizrah he-Hadash,* vol. 12 (1962): 189–211.

———. "Ha-Hit'argenut ha-Politit shel Arviyey Erets Yisrael" [The Political Organization of the Palestinian Arabs]. In *Ha-Mandat ve-ha-Bayit ha-Le'umi* [The Mandate and the National Home], vol. 9 of *Ha-Historia shel Erets Yisrael* [The History of the Land of Israel]. Edited by Yehoshua Porath and Ya'akov Shavit. Jerusalem: Keter, 1982.

Slutski, Yehuda, et al. *Sefer Toldot ha-Hagana* [The History Book of the Haganah]. 3 vols. Tel Aviv: Zionist Library, 1954–72.

Smilanski, Moshe. *Nes Tsiyona.* Nes Tsiyona: Local Council, 1953.

Trumpeldor, Yosef. *Me-Hayey Yosef Trumpeldor* [Extracts from the Diary of Yosef Trumpeldor]. Tel Aviv: ha-Histadrut, 1922.

Walner, Alter. *Hamushim lifnei ha-Mahane* [Armed in Front of the Camp]. Tel Aviv: Ministry of Defense Press, 1984.

Washitz, Yosef. "Jewish-Arab Relations in Haifa 1940–1948." In *Ha-Aravim Mul ha-Tnu'ah ha-Tziyonit veha-Yishuv ha-Yehudi 1946–1950* [The Arabs versus the Zionist Movement and the Jewish Yishuv, 1946–1950]. Edited by Yosef Nevo and Yoram Nimrod. Kiryat Tivon: Seminar ha-Kibutsim, 1987.

———. "Tmurot Hevratiot ba-Yishuv ha-Arvi shel Haifa bi-Tkufat ha-Mandat ha-Briti" [Social Changes in Haifa's Arab Community during the Mandate]. Ph.D. dissertation, Hebrew University of Jerusalem, 1993.

Weitz, Yosef. *Hitnahlutenu bi-Tkufat ha-Sa'ar* [Our Settlement in Stormy Days]. Jerusalem and Merhavia: ha-Kibutz ha-Artsi, 1947.

————, editor. *Yosef Nahmani: Ish ha-Galil* [Yosef Nahmani: The Man of the Galilee]. Ramat Gan: Masada, 1969.

Yafe, Aharon. "The Redemption of the Ghazawiyya Land and the Relocation of the Tribe in Trans-Jordan." *Mehkarim be-Geografia shel Eretz Yisrael* [Studies in the Geography of Eretz Yisrael], vol. 13 (1993): 23–29.

Ze'evi, Rehavam. "Introduction." In Pesach Bar Adon, *Be-Ohaley Midbar* [In Desert Tents]. Jerusalem: Kiriat sefer, 1981.

ENGLISH SOURCES

Anderson, Benedict. *Imagined Communities: Reflections on the Origins and Spread of Nationalism.* London: Verso, 1991.

Becker, Howard. "Deviance by Definition." In *Sociological Theory: A Book of Readings.* Edited by Lewis Coser and Bernard Rosenberg. New York: Macmillan, 1982.

Ben Eliezer, Uri. *The Making of Israeli Militarism.* Bloomington: Indiana University Press, 1998.

Bernstein, Deborah. *Constructing Boundaries: Jewish and Arab Workers in Mandatory Palestine.* Albany, N.Y.: SUNY Press, 2000.

Chambrun, René de. *Pierre Laval: Traitor or Patriot?* Trans. Elly Stein. New York: Scribner, 1984.

Croll, Andy. "Street Disorder, Surveillance and Shame: Regulating Behaviour in the Public Spaces of the Late Victorian British Town." *Social History*, vol. 24, no. 3 (1999): 250–268.

Doumani, Beshara. "Rediscovering Ottoman Palestine: Writing Palestinians into History." *Journal of Palestine Studies*, vol. 11, no. 2 (1992): 5–28.

Dudai, Ron, and Hillel Cohen. "Triangle of Betrayal: Collaborators and Transitional Justice in the Israeli-Palestinian Conflict." *Journal of Human Rights*, vol. 6, no. 1 (2007): 37–58.

Eloul, Rohn. "Culture Change in Bedouin Tribe: An Ethnographic History of the 'Arab Al-Hjerat, Lower Galilee, Israel, 1790–1977." Ph.D. dissertation, University of Michigan, 1982.

Firro, Kais. *A History of the Druzes.* Leiden: E.J. Brill, 1992.

Gellner, Ernest. *Nation and Nationalism: New Perspectives on the Past.* Malden, Mass.: Blackwell, 2006.

Gerber, Haim. *Ottoman Rule in Jerusalem, 1890–1914.* Berlin: Klaus Schwarz Verlag, 1985.

Goffman, Erving. *Stigma: Notes on the Management of Spoiled Identity.* New York: Jason Aronson, 1974.

Goode, Erich. *Deviant Behavior.* Upper Saddle River, N.J.: Prentice Hall, 1994.

Goodman, Grant. "Aurelio Alvero: Traitor or Patriot?" *Journal of Southeast Asian Studies*, vol. 27, no. 1 (1996): 95–103.

Gorni, Yosef. *Zionism and the Arabs, 1882–1948*. Oxford: Oxford University Press, 1987.

Great Britain, Colonial Office. *Palestine Royal Commission Report*. London, July 1937.

Habibi, Imil [Emile Habiby]. *The Secret Life of Sa'id: The Pessopsimist*. London: Zed Books, 1985.

Hobsbawm, Eric. "History from Below—Some Reflections." In *History from Below: Studies in Popular Protest and Popular Ideology in Honour of George Rude*. Edited by Frederick Krantz. Montreal: Concordia University, 1985.

Horowitz, Dan, and Moshe Lissak. *Origins of the Israeli Polity: Palestine under the Mandate*. Chicago: University of Chicago Press, 1978.

Khalaf, Issa. *Politics in Palestine: Arab Factionalism and Social Disintegration, 1939–1948*. Albany, N.Y.: SUNY Press, 1991.

Khalidi, Rashid. *Palestinian Identity: Construction of Modern National Consciousness*. New York: Columbia University Press, 1997.

Khalidi, Walid. *From Haven to Conquest*. Washington, D.C.: Institution for Palestine Studies, 1987.

———. "Selected Documents on the 1948 Palestine War." *Journal of Palestine Studies*, vol. 27, no. 3 (1998): 60–105

Khury, Elias. *Gates of the Sun*. Trans. Humphrey Davies. New York: Archipelago Books, 2006.

Kisch, Frederick. *Palestine Diary*. New York: AMS Press, 1974.

Kohn, Hans. *Nationalism: Its Meaning and History*. Princeton: Van Nostrand, 1955.

Laserson, Max. *On the Mandate: Documents, Statements, Laws*. Tel Aviv: Igereth, 1937.

Lauderdale, Pat, and James Inverarity. "Suggestions for the Study of the Political Dimensions of Deviance Definitions." In *A Political Analysis of Deviance*. Edited by P. Lauderdale. Minneapolis: University of Minnesota Press, 1980.

Littlejohn, David. *The Patriotic Traitors*. London: Heinemann, 1972.

Lockman, Zachary. *Comrades and Enemies: Arab and Jewish Workers in Palestine, 1906–1948*. Berkeley: University of California Press, 1996.

Lottman, Herbert. *Petain: Hero or Traitor*. New York: Morrow, 1985.

Macalister, Stewart, and E. W. G. Mastermann. "Occasional Papers on the Modern Inhabitants of Palestine." *PEFQS* (1905): 352–356.

Maloba, W. O. "Collaborator and/or Nationalist?" Review of *Koinange-wa-Mabiyu, Mau-Mau Misunderstood Leader,* by Jeff Koinange. *Journal of African History,* vol. 42 (2001): 527–529.

Mandel, Neville. *The Arabs and Zionism before World War I*. Berkeley: University of California Press, 1976.

Morris, Benny. *The Birth of the Palestinian Refugee Problem, 1947–1949*. Cambridge: Cambridge University Press, 1987.

Murdock, Graham. "Political Deviance: The Press Presentation of a Militant Mass Demonstration." In *The Manufacture of News: Deviance, Social Problems and the Mass Media*. Edited by Stanley Cohen and Jack Young. London: Constable, 1974.

Muslih, Muhammad. *The Origins of Palestinian Nationalism.* New York: Columbia University Press, 1988.

Nashashibi, Nasser Eddin. *Jerusalem's Other Voice: Ragheb Nashashibi and Moderation in Palestinian Politics, 1920–1949.* Exeter: Ithaca, 1990.

Nevo, Joseph. *Abdallah and Palestine.* London: Macmillan, 1996.

Parsons, Lila. "The Palestinian Druze in the 1947–1949 Arab-Israeli War." *Israel Studies,* vol. 2, no. 1 (1997): 72–93.

Pearlman, Maurice. *Mufty of Jerusalem.* London: Gollancz, 1947.

Porath, Yehoshua. *The Emergence of the Palestinian-Arab National Movement: 1918–1929.* London: F. Cass, 1974.

———. *The Palestinian Arab National Movement: 1929–1939, from Riots to Rebellion.* London: F. Cass, 1977.

Sayigh, Rosmari. *Palestinians: From Peasants to Revolutionaries.* London: Zed Books, 1979.

Schesch, Adam B. "Popular Mobilization during Revolutionary and Resistance Wars." Ph.D. dissertation, University of Wisconsin, Madison, 1994.

Segev, Tom. *One Palestine, Complete: Jews and Arabs under the British Mandate.* New York: Metropolitan, 2000.

Seikaly, May. *Haifa: Transformation of a Palestinian Arab Society, 1918–1939.* London: Tauris, 1995.

Shapira, Anita. *Land and Power: The Zionist Resort to Force, 1881–1948.* Trans. William Templer. New York: Oxford University Press, 1992.

Shlaim, Avi. *The Iron Wall: Israel and the Arab World.* New York: Norton, 1999.

———. *The Politics of Partition: King Abdullah, the Zionists and Palestine, 1921–1951.* Oxford: Oxford University Press, 1990.

Stein, Kenneth. *The Land Question in Palestine, 1917–1939.* Chapel Hill: University of North Carolina Press, 1984.

Swedenburg, Ted. *Memories of Revolt: The 1936–1939 Rebellion and the Palestinian National Past.* Minneapolis: University of Minnesota Press, 1998.

Taqqu, Rachelle. "Peasants into Workmen: Internal Labor Migration and the Arab Village Community under the Mandate." In *Palestinian Society and Politics.* Edited by Joel S. Migdal. Princeton: Princeton University Press, 1980.

Weber, Eugen. *Peasants into Frenchmen: The Modernization of Rural France, 1870–1914.* Stanford, Calif.: Stanford University Press, 1976.

Yapp, Malcolm. *The Near East since the First World War.* London: Longman, 1996.

ARABIC SOURCES

Newspapers

al-Akhbar
al-Difa'
Filastin
Haqiqat al-Amr

al-Hayat
al-Ittihad
Jabha Sha'biyya
al-Jami'ah al-'Arabiyyah
al-Jami'ah al-Islamiyyah
al-Karmil
Lisan al-Hal
al-Liwaa
Mirat al-Sharq
al-Wahda
al-Yarmuk
al-Zamr

Books and Articles

al-Abbushi, Burhan al-Din. *Watan al-Shahid.* Jerusalem: al-Matba'a al-Iqtisadiyya, 1947.

'Abd al-Razeq, Faysal Aref. *Amjad Thawriyya Filastiniyya wa-Hayat Batal min Abtaliha* [Praises of the Revolt and the Life of One of Its Heroes]. Taybe: author, 1995.

Abdullah, King of Jordan. *My Memoirs Completed: Al-Takmilah.* Washington, D.C.: American Council of Learned Studies, 1954.

Abu Gharbiyya, Bahjat. *Fi Khidm al-Nidal al-Arabi al-Filastini* [Within the Turbulence of the Palestinian Arab Struggle]. Beirut: Mu'asasat al-Dirasat al-Filistiniyya, 1993.

'Aqel, Muhammad. *Al-Mufassal fo Ta'rikh Wadi Ara* [A Detailed History of Wadi 'Ara]. Jerusalem: al-Amal, 1999.

al-'Aref, 'Aref. *Nakbat Bayt al-Maqdis wal-Firdus al-Mafqud* [The Catastrophe of the Holy City and the Lost Paradise]. Beirut-Sidon: al-Maktaba al-Asriyya, 1956.

Darwaza, Muhammad Izzat. *Al-Mallak wal-Simsar* [The Landlord and the Land Shark]. Nablus, 1934.

———. *Hawla al-Haraka al-Arabiyya al-Haditha* [On the Modern Arab Movement]. Sidon: al-Maktaba al-Asriyya, 1955.

———. *Mudhakkarat Muhammad Izzat Darwaza: Sijill Hafel bi-Masirat al-Haraka al-Arabiyya wal-Qadiyya al-Filastiniyya Khilal Qurn 1887–1984* [Memoirs of M. I. Darwaza: A Full Record of the Advance of the Arab Movement and the Palestinian Problem, 1887–1984]. Beirut: Dar al-Gharb al-Islami, 1993.

Diwan Ibrahim: A'mar Sha'er Filastin Ibrahim Tuqan [Collection of Ibrahim's Poems: The Life of Palestine Poet Ibrahim Tuqan]. Beirut: Dar al-Quds, 1975.

al-Fahoum Khaled, "Khaled al-Fahoum Yatadhakkar." *Al-Quds,* 2 September 1998.

Ghana'im, Mas'ud. *Sakhnin.* Sakhnin: Islamic Movement, 2000.

Hawwari, Muhammad Nimer. *Sirr al-Nakba* [The Secret of the Nakba]. Nazareth: al-Hakim, 1955.

al-Hout, Bayan Nuwayhid. *Al-Qiyadat wal-Mu'asasat al-Siyasiyya fi Filastin*

1917–1948 [The Political Leadership and Institutions in Palestine, 1917–1948]. Acre: al-Aswar, 1984.

Kana'aneh, Sharif. *Al-Dar Dar Abuna* [It's Our Father's Home]. Jerusalem: Markaz al-Quds al-'alimi lil-Dirasat al-Filistiniyya, 1990.

Kayyali, Abd al-Wahhab. *Watha'iq al-Muqawama al-Filastiniyya al-Arabiyya* [Documents of the Palestinian-Arab Resistance]. Beirut: Mu'asasat al-Dirasat al-Filistiniyya, 1968.

al-Khatib, Ulya. *Arab al-Turkeman.* Amman: Dar al-Jalil, 1987.

Manna', Adel. *A'lam Filastin fi Awakhir al-'Ahd al-Uthmani* [Palestine Dignitaries in the Late Ottoman Period]. Jerusalem: Jam'iyyat al-Dirasat al-Arabiyya, 1986.

Nashashibi, Fakhri. *Sawt Min Qubur Filastin al-Arabiyya* [A Call from the Graves of Arab Palestine]. [Jerusalem], 1938.

al-Nimer, Ihsan. *Ta'arikh Jabl Nablus wal-Balqaa* [The History of Mt. Nablus and al-Balqaa]. Nablus: Jam'iyyut Ummal al-Matabi', 1975.

Palestine Labor League. *Kashf al-Qina'* [Removal of the Mask]. Haifa: Palestine Labor League, 1937.

Rumman, Muhammad Sa'id. *Suba: Qarya Maqdasiyya fi al-Dhakira* [Suba: Jerusalemite Village in the Memory]. Jerusalem: Matba'at Ayn Rafa, 2000.

al-Saleh, Muhsin Muhammad. *Al-Quwwat al-'Askariyya wal-Shurta fi Filastin 1917–1939* [Army and Police Forces in Palestine, 1917–1939]. Amman: Dar al-Nafa'is, 1996.

Shuqayri, Ahmad. *Arba'un 'Aman fi al-Hayat al-Arabiyya wal-Dawliyya* [Forty Years in the Arab and International Life]. Beirut: al-Nahar, 1969.

Sirhan, Nimer, and Mustafa Kabaha. *Abd al-Rahim Hajj Muhammad: Al-Qa'id al-'am li-Thawrat 1936–1939* ['Abd al-Rahim al-Hajj Muhammad: General Commander of the 1936–1939 Revolt]. Ramallah: al-Qastal, 2000.

Tafsir Muqatil bin Suliman. Cairo: al-Hay'ah al-Masriyyah lil-Kitab, 1979–89.

al-Tal, Abdallah. *Karithat Filastin: Mudhakkarat Abddullah al-Tall* [Palestine's Tragedy: The Memoirs of Abdallah al-Tal]. Acre: Dar al-Jalil, 1968.

al-Tawil, Muhammad. *Al-Haqa'iq al-Majhula* [Hidden Truths]. Jerusalem: Mallul, 1930.

———. *Tariq al-Hayah* [Way of Life]. Haifa: Warhaftig, 1930.

Zu'bi, Sayf al-Din. *Shahed Ayan: Mudhakkarat* [Eyewitness: Memoirs]. Shfa'amer: Dar al-Mashraq, 1987.

Zu'itar, Akram. *Bawakir al-Nidal: Min Mudhakarat Akram Zu'itar* [The Start of the Struggle: From the Memoirs of Akram Zu'itar]. Beirut: al-Mu'asasa al-Arabiyya lil-Dirasat wal-Nashr, 1994.

———. *Watha'eq al-Haraka al-Wataniyya al-Filastiniyya 1914–1939* [Documents of the Palestinian National Movement, 1914–1939]. Beirut: Mu'asasat al-Dirasat al-Filistiniyya, 1984.

Index